The Family and Descendants
of St Thomas More

To those who have paved the way, and especially to my dear wife Teresa, without whose patience and support over many years of research and sporadic writing this work would never have seen the light of day.

The Family and Descendants of St Thomas More

Martin Wood

GRACEWING

First published in 2008

Gracewing
2 Southern Ave, Leominster
Herefordshire HR6 0QF

All rights reserved. No part of this publication may be reproduced, stored in a retrieval system, or transmitted in any form, or by any means, electronic, mechanical, photocopying, recording or otherwise, without the written permission of the publisher.

© Martin Wood 2008

The right of Martin Wood to be identified as the author of this work has been asserted in accordance with the Copyright, Designs and Patents Act 1988.

Cover picture of Cresacre More (1572–1649), circle of
William Larkin.
Reproduced by kind permission of Mark Weiss, Weiss Gallery, Jermyn Street, London.

ISBN 978 0 85244 681 2

Typesetting by Action Publishing Technology Ltd,
Gloucester, GL1 5SR
Printed in England by
Biddles Ltd, King's Lynn PE30 4LS

Contents

	Introduction	1
1.	An Extended Family: John More to John Donne	12
2.	Sir Thomas More and his Family	43
3.	The Family of John More II	90
4.	Thomas More II and his Family	112
5.	Cresacre More and his Family	151
6.	The Family of Thomas More V	183
7.	Basil More and his Family	209
8.	The Family of Christopher Cresacre More	234
9.	Thomas More VIII and his Family	246
	Notes	266
	Bibliography	285

Introduction

Although it is over four hundred and seventy years since he died, the name of Sir Thomas More, one-time Chancellor of England under King Henry VIII, still lives on. In Europe, and particularly America, there is a huge demand for information on his life and works. There are books, papers, films and websites on both Sir and Saint Thomas More; there are St Thomas More Churches and Thomas More Schools and Colleges; there are university-based centres for the studies of Thomas More, and Thomas More Societies and Associations.

In England, period plays on television and programmes like those regularly shown on the History Channels feed a continuous interest in our past. Tudor times in particular – with Henry VIII and his wives, the power struggle between Church and State, and the emergence and establishment of the new 'Protestant' Church in England – appear to offer a particular fascination. The reasons for this are not immediately obvious, but perhaps it has something to do with the fact that, in Europe at least, we live in a period of considerable religious indifference, a world where so many statesmen and politicians are, unlike Thomas More, prepared to put the party line before the dictates of their consciences. It may also have something to do with the fact that we live in a world where religious intolerance is once again on the increase, and the hope that we might, perhaps, learn something from the mistakes that have been made in handling this in the past.

The story of Thomas More is likely to be well known to most of my readers and it is not my intention to repeat it in any great detail in this book. My story is different, and I have been moved to tell it because of two things. The first, is the fact of my own descent, on my mother's side, from Sir Thomas More – he was my fourteen times great-grandfather – and the pride that all the families in 'our' line have always had in that descent, both before and after his beatification and canonization. It was a great honour when one of my relatives was invited to represent our line in a special area reserved for descendants during the canonization ceremony by Pope Pius XI in St Peter's, Rome, on 17 May 1935. Because of our pride in that descent a family tree has been handed down from generation to generation showing a line of descent via his only son John, but with only basic dates and details until the time of my great-great-grandmother in the early 1800s when fuller records began to be kept. The second thing that moved me to write my story was a simple question on the message board of a Thomas More website that I found one day, which asked 'Can anybody tell me what happened to his descendants?' It was while researching and expanding the former that I found I had a fascinating answer to the latter.

The author of the Book of Genesis tells of God promising Abraham that his descendants will be as numerous as the stars in the sky. Of course it doesn't require a divine intelligence to know that or, given enough time, any divine action to bring it about! In Thomas More's case, while his descendants may not yet be as numerous as the stars in the sky, they must certainly be numbered in the hundreds of thousands and, according to the mathematics of genealogy, probably much more – though how many are living today is anyone's guess. Of these it is likely that most do not know of their descent. My claim to descent is therefore nothing special, but my knowledge of it is.

Thomas More himself made no claim to sanctity, indeed, he sometimes pointed out that all the saints had also been sinners. In his personal life he was as devoted to the Sacrament of Reconciliation as he was to the Mass and the Blessed Sacrament and, even those who know little else about his life, know of his commitment to the Catholic Church. Having said that, he was well aware that the Church of his day needed reformation. In theology he had no time for those who engaged in 'scholastic subtleties and trifling'. As we will see, he could dispute with a friar who was preaching that the recital of the rosary every day could guarantee a place in heaven, and he could poke fun at other superstitious beliefs and practices. He venerated the saints, but had no time for the far-fetched miracles sometimes attributed to them – though he advised that all the miracles in the Bible should be believed. He had the greatest respect for the monks he knew personally and for the monastic life that he had, at one time, considered for himself, but this did not stop him being scathing in his comments about hypocrisy and immorality in the cloister and about contemplative monks who spent 'good hours reading bad books, and even more time on slanderous gossip'.

For Thomas More there could be only one Catholic Church, and the Pope, the successor of St Peter, was its head. However, in his day, the Pope was not only the head of the Church but also a secular prince who commanded an army. It is not surprising that reports of Pope Julius II leading his victorious army in a triumphal procession into Bologna in 1506 – dressed and behaving more like Caesar than the humble Messiah entering Jerusalem – should further fuel the mixed feelings that he, and many others, had about the nature and extent of papal power and authority.[1]

Henry VIII was opposed to the Protestant Reformation initiated by Martin Luther that was tearing Europe apart. In 1520–21, while Henry was writing what turned out to be a best-selling book in defence of the seven sacraments, Thomas More advised him to tone down his lavish praise of the Pope (Leo X) on the grounds that kings and popes often fell out and that there was always the possibility that he might be embarrassed by what he had written at some later date. How right Thomas More was – though when the fall out came ten years later, it was not Henry who was embarrassed but the Pope, then Clement VII, whose predecessor had granted him the title of Defender of the Faith.

Henry's need to produce a male heir to continue and strengthen the Tudor dynasty soon brought him into conflict with the Pope. In 1509 he had been granted permission to marry Catherine of Aragon, his brother's widow, and when she could not produce a son, he seems rather to have expected the granting of a similar favour – the annulment of that marriage so that he could marry Anne Boleyn. The Pope's refusal brought an immediate change in Henry's attitude towards the papacy. In 1532 he appointed Thomas Cranmer Archbishop of Canterbury who declared Henry's marriage to Catherine to have been illegal, thus leaving the way open for him to marry Anne. Henry then passed an Act declaring that England was an empire in which he, the King, held the whole and entire authority over the realm, and he followed this in 1534 with the Act of Supremacy that declared him to be the Supreme Head of the Church of England.

For Thomas More there was no way that Henry, a secular prince, could usurp the spiritual power and authority of the papacy – a power and authority that had been given to St Peter, the first Pope, by Jesus himself. There was, therefore, no way that he could with a good conscience submit to the Act of Supremacy. He was, as he said, the King's good servant, and God's first – and for refusing to change that position he paid with his life.

Thomas More's execution was immediately recognized in Catholic Europe as 'effectively' a martyrdom. Cardinal Pole, Henry VIII's cousin (later Papal Legate and Archbishop of Canterbury under Queen Mary), even referred to it as 'the blood drinking of wild beasts', thereby likening it to the martyrdom of Christians in Roman times. In England, however, no such view could be openly expressed. Even before Thomas's execution, Henry had confiscated and destroyed most of the family's documents and, for their own protection, the family destroyed others. It wasn't long, however, before a network of members of the family and their friends, both in England and on the Continent, established what amounted to an underground movement to make sure that his name and fame – and his martyrdom and his sanctity – should not be forgotten. Their work involved gathering eyewitness accounts and memories that people had of him and his family, as well as other documentary evidence, and recording it on manuscripts that were treasured by the family and secretly passed around within the Catholic community.

The earliest complete life of Sir Thomas More, begun around fifteen years after his death, was written by his nephew William Rastell. It only ever existed in manuscript form and, sadly, only a few fragmentary notes from it have come down to us. The next manuscript life, mostly written during Queen Mary's reign (1553–1558), was by William Roper, Thomas More's son-in-law, who had lived in the More household for many years. Notes supplied by him were used by his friend Nicholas Harpsfield, Archdeacon of Canterbury, when he wrote *The Life and Death of Sir Thomas More* sometime around 1557. Although not a 'Life', Ellis Heywood's *Il Moro, A Dialogue in Memory of Thomas More*, his great-uncle, (written in Italian and dedicated to Cardinal Pole) was published at Florence in 1556. Another manuscript life, attributed only to 'Ro:Ba:' – possibly the result of cooperation between the Roper and Bassett families – was written around 1599.

Various copies of these manuscript lives were made as they were passed around. However, after the accession of Elizabeth to the throne it was not safe to print them in England, and the first one to be published abroad was by Thomas Stapleton. He was a friend of the members of the 'More Circle' who had chosen exile on the Continent at the beginning of the reign of Queen Elizabeth. His *Life and Illustrious martyrdom of Sir Thomas More*, written in Latin, was first published at Douai in 1588. Roper's life was eventually printed at Paris in 1626. Stapleton's 'Life' was not translated into English and published until 1928 and Harpsfield's manuscripts were not edited and published until 1932.

The only life written by a direct descendant of Thomas More was by his great-grandson, Cresacre More. This is particularly interesting because of the information it gives us about Thomas's grandchildren. Cresacre's *Life*, to my mind the most poignant of all the lives, was started around 1616 and published at Douai in 1631. As time went on, and it became increasingly clear that England was not likely to return to the Catholic faith, this and the other works kept the memory of Thomas More alive and acted as an inspiration to the members of the More family, and to the wider Catholic community, as they struggled to maintain the faith of their fathers in the face persecution.[2]

In addition to the lives of Sir Thomas More, his descendants also carefully preserved and handed down a number of 'relics' of their illustrious ancestor. The most notable of these was his parboiled head (later buried with Margaret Roper), a tooth, and his hairshirt, but also, among others, his cap, a gold cross, a silver seal die with his arms and crest on it, a cameo, and a pouncet or perfume box.[3]

In 1583 Pope Gregory XIII allowed a series of frescoes to be painted in the Church of the English College in Rome. These depicted those who were recognized as having given their lives for their faith during the reigns of Henry, Edward and Elizabeth. The Pope also sanctioned the use of their relics at the consecration of altars when relics of the ancient martyrs could not be obtained. Although not an official declaration of sanctity, these acts amounted to a tacit acceptance of their status as martyrs and must have been sources of great pride to the More family and especially, perhaps, to Thomas More, a great-grandson of Sir Thomas who was, at that time, studying for the priesthood at the College. We know that the memory of Thomas More was kept alive at the English College, and that by 1612, a 'Tragedy' named after him was regularly performed there during carnival time.[4] The author of this work is said to have been a Jesuit and it may be that yet another Thomas More, a great-grandson of Sir Thomas, who studied at the English College before becoming a Jesuit in 1611, may have contributed to its writing.

The story of Thomas More's immediate family, and his descendants, can only be told against the background their refusal to recognize the King's supremacy over the Church of England and the religious changes that followed it in subsequent reigns as each generation came and went.

As a lawyer Thomas More knew well the consequences of the path he had chosen to take. He sought to distance himself as much as he could from his immediate family and tried to make arrangements for his various properties to be put beyond the King's grasp. Not surprisingly, the King could not be thwarted and, in due course, both Lady Alice More (his widow) and Lady Alice More (his father's widow) were thrown out of their homes. Over the next ten years all of Thomas More's children and their immediate and extended families were 'watched' carefully, and were in constant fear for their lives. John More (Thomas's only son and heir) and William Daunce (who had married Elizabeth More) narrowly escaped the scaffold, but Giles Heron (who had married Cecily More) paid with his life at Tyburn in 1540 on trumped up charges of treason.

For the great majority of ordinary Catholics, Henry's declaration that he was Supreme Head of the Church of England made little difference. He didn't alter the Creed, abolish the seven sacraments, or change the liturgy and, at the local level, parish life remained largely unchanged. In practice, most priests remained in office, and Sunday Mass and other church celebrations went on much as they had always done. This was a confusing time for Catholics generally, a period during which, as we will see, the members of the More family and others like them 'muddled through' not knowing quite what to do.

It wasn't until the reign of Edward VI (1547–1553) that Protestant doctrines, imported from the Continent, really began to be imposed and the familiar decor of churches to be changed by the removal, mutilation or whitewashing of images and the suppression of chantries and shrines. Edward's reign, however, was short, and it was followed by the restoration of Catholicism from 1553–1558 when Mary succeeded to the throne.

Queen Mary's reign gave Catholics a bit of a breathing space. However, her marriage to King Philip of Spain and her persecution of Protestants – the latter said to have been opposed in Parliament by Thomas More's grandson – did nothing to endear

Introduction

her to the people of England. In the circumstances it is not surprising that when a Protestant Queen returned to the throne again in 1558, in the person of Elizabeth I, Catholics should fear a backlash and be very concerned about what was going to happen to them in the future.

In April 1559 a new Act of Supremacy was passed declaring the Queen to be the Supreme Governor of the Church of England, and clergy who refused to swear the Oath of Supremacy were deprived of their livings. The Act of Uniformity, passed in 1559, ordered the use of a 'Book of Common Prayer' in all churches and imposed a fine of one shilling (more than a week's wages for most people) on anyone who failed to attend services in their local parish church on Sundays. This was followed in 1563 by the publication of the Thirty-Nine Articles, summarizing the dogmas of the Church of England. These included declarations that the Bishop of Rome had no jurisdiction in England and that Masses offered for the souls of the living and dead were 'blasphemous fables and dangerous deceits'.

At this stage, the descendants of Sir Thomas More were, like most Catholics, still unsure about their relationship to the new State church. Elizabeth said that all she wanted was external conformity and that she was not interested in people's personal beliefs – implying perhaps that she thought they should take the required oaths, as it were, with their fingers crossed behind their backs! It didn't help that the advice they got from their spiritual advisers about taking oaths and attending Protestant services was contradictory – some said it was permissible if done solely in obedience to the Queen, while others said it was a grave sin. The result was that many Catholics reached a practical compromise, continuing as best they could to practise their old faith in private, but also attending their local parish church on Sundays, thereby avoiding the penalties for non-attendance. Such Catholics were often referred to as 'church papists'.

The excommunication of Elizabeth by Pope Pius V in January 1570 made explicit a conflict of loyalty to the Church of Rome and to the State that put an end to any hope that Catholics might have had about the possibility of reaching some form of compromise. In his Bull of Excommunication entitled *Regnans in Excelsis* Pius described Elizabeth as the 'Servant of Wickedness' and declared her to be 'deprived of her pretended Title' of Queen. It went on to absolve all her subjects from any allegiance to her, commanding them not to obey her or her laws.

Pius V's actions made the position of Catholics in England even worse. It forced Elizabeth to see all Catholics as a threat to her own personal safety as well as to the safety and security of the nation as a whole. As a result, in the rest of her reign, and in the reigns of successive monarchs, there followed a wide range of legislation that made it a criminal offence – known as 'recusancy' – for English Catholics, or 'Papists' as they were usually called, to practise their faith. We will come across the effects of these Acts on Thomas More's descendants as our story unfolds, but the names of a few of them gives an indication of their scope and intent: the 'Act against recusants' (Elizabeth I in 1593), the 'Act for the better discovering and repressing of Popish Recusants' (James I in 1606), the 'Act for preventing dangers which may happen from Popish recusants' (Charles II in 1674 – tightened up under William and Mary in 1689 and 1698, and under Queen Anne 1715). At various times these and other Acts and Ordinances made saying and hearing Mass illegal, limited the movements of Catholics from their family homes, made it illegal to send their children to be educated abroad, barred them from obtaining degrees at university, from being called to the Bar, from entering many professions, and from public office, as well as affecting their purchase and inheritance of land and other property. This was the world in which Thomas More's grandson and his later descendants lived.

The identification of priests and Catholic laypeople was often put into the hands of professional pursuers, or 'pursuivants', who sent out spies and offered inducements to help them collect information that could be used as evidence to obtain their conviction as recusants in court. The network of spies extended to the Continent where many Catholics took refuge from persecution, and even as far as Rome where they infiltrated the Catholic community so successfully that they could report back on supposedly secret meetings at the English College in Rome.

In practice, the extent to which Catholics were reported, or 'presented' for recusancy, and fines collected from them often varied from place to place. The local churchwardens whose job it was to do the presenting sometimes had a Catholic wife or family, or were the friends and neighbours to those they were supposed to report. As we will see, Catholic landowners, including the members of the More family and their relatives, became adept at spreading ownership of their property among different members of the family and even passing it temporarily to relations or sympathetic friends. They also became quite skilled at absenting themselves from their homes at times when they knew lists of recusants were due to be drawn up.

Although knighted by Henry VIII, Thomas More was not a member of the nobility. His male descendants could, however, take pride in the title 'Gentleman' (often abbreviated to 'Gent.') or 'Esquire' and, as we will see most of the families into which their daughters married were recusant Catholic families of a similar standing. The Mores were not large landowners but, at various periods they owned estates in Hertfordshire, Yorkshire and Herefordshire that, had they remained intact, would have been of sufficient size to provide them with an income that would mark them out today as being relatively rich and privileged.

Much has been written about anti-Catholic legislation and the effect of the recusancy laws in general, but no one has, to the best of my knowledge, ever written the story of the effects these had on one family from the time of Henry VIII to the Catholic Emancipation Act of 1829 during the reign of George IV when, once again, Catholics were accepted back into mainstream society, allowed to hold public office and to sit in Parliament. That is what makes my story different. It is both a genealogy and a real life family history. In many ways it is the story of ordinary laymen and women and, in every generation, of priests and nuns, all of whom had a deep faith and an extraordinary courage, and all of whom were inspired by the example of their illustrious forbear. Although not the story of any More martyrs it is, as we will see, the story of the members of a family who, at various times and in various places, had their houses searched and their property confiscated, who spent periods in prison, and who were hauled before the courts and regularly fined for refusing to attend Protestant services in their local parish church – though still required by law to have their marriages and the baptisms of their children registered there. This, to my mind, makes them worthy of being listed among the 'Confessors' of the faith – minor confessors, may be, but confessors nonetheless. In these days of so much religious indifference and lack of religious commitment by so many who still call themselves Christians of one denomination or another, they provide an example to us all.

My information about the descendants of Thomas More has come from a wide range of sources. The earliest 'pedigree' of the More family – what today we more usually call a 'family tree' – comes from the 'Visitation' of Yorkshire in 1563–4. Visitations of other counties, and documents based on them, have also provided information about the families into which they married. The 'Visitations' took place between 1530 and 1688 when 'Heralds' were sent out at various times to all the counties of England. In each county the Sheriff was required to make a list of knights, esquires and gentlemen so that they could be summoned to appear before the Heralds to show proof of their arms, pedigrees and other title deeds and documents relating to their family. Kept for centuries in manuscript form in places like the College of Arms, the details collected during the Visitations began to be published in the late 1800s and early 1900s in response, presumably, to an increased interest in family origins. While these pedigrees are invaluable in tracing ancestors and descendants up to the time they were recorded there is inevitably an element of memory in them – so that they are not by any means infallible – and as they go back in time so the number of datable events tends to become fewer. Also, in line with the custom of the time, they concentrate on what I call the 'mainline' members of a family – the male heirs who inherited the largest portion of money and property belonging to the family by reason of their position as eldest sons, or eldest surviving sons. While the names of the 'lesser' members of the family – the younger sons and the daughters – are usually recorded, few, if any, details are given of descent from them. In the case of daughters, the main exception to this is when they became heiresses in their own right due to the failure of the male line.

As most of the members of More family were recusants their names appeared quite regularly in the records of Ecclesiastical and other associated Assize and Quarter Sessions Courts in the areas where they lived. These give details of their offences – more often than not their refusal to present themselves at their local Anglican church – and the fines imposed on them. For information about these I have relied heavily on studies of recusancy made by various Catholic historians, especially in the 1960s and 1970s. Other information, including records of births, baptisms, etc., has come from local studies sections of various libraries, and in County Archives and Record Offices. I also have copies of some documents that have been handed down in the More family itself.

For most of the period covered in this book dates were usually recorded to include two years – for example 1531–2. This is because from the late twelfth century until 1752, the beginning of the ecclesiastical and civil year in England (and most of Europe) was 25 March – Lady Day, the Feast of the Annunciation. Dates between 1 January and 24 March were therefore at the end of the year rather than at the beginning. From my point of view the old style of dating is cumbersome and I have followed the example of most modern authors by adapting the old dates to fit in with what is sometimes called the 'new style', that is, the way we use them today with the new year beginning on 1 January. If any reader should find slight differences between my dates and the ones they have come across, I can only say that I have tried my best to be accurate.

In addition to modernizing dates, I have tried to give some idea of the present day value of 'old' money. Such comparisons are very difficult to make, depending as they do on the interpretation of a number of sociological and economic factors. My figures should, therefore, only be regarded as a rough guide. Even so, they provide some idea of the sums of money involved in fines for recusancy and in the value of pensions (equivalent to our modern salary), and legacies.

My story of the family of Thomas More begins properly with his father and mother, and his brothers and sisters and the families into which they married. After that each chapter follows the lives of a new generation, headed by the son who succeeded to the family estates. Rather than provide an index at the end of the book I have, at the end of each chapter, provided a 'Genealogical Summary' that will enable readers to see at a glance the various people that have been mentioned and the way they fit in to what can, at times, be a complicated pattern of relationships.

My story concludes around the middle of the nineteenth century when, after the death in 1795 of Fr Thomas More, SJ, the last mainline male heir of the family, what remained of the family's estates passed to his sister Bridget and to her heirs. By this time the Catholic Relief Act of 1778 had already begun to reduce the burdens that had, for so long, been placed on the backs of Catholics, a process that was completed by the passing of the Catholic Emancipation Act in 1829 when Catholics were, once again, allowed to hold public office and sit in Parliament. It is at this time that my story comes full circle and my telling of it ends. It is the story of a faith held as 'a pearl of great price' – and the price paid for it by the members of the More family who inherited it during a period of over 350 years.

Chapter One

An Extended Family: John More to John Donne

No record of the birth John More, Sir Thomas More's father, has survived, but from the evidence available it can be said to have taken place during or around the year 1451. At one time he was believed to have been the son of John More who was admitted to membership of Lincoln's Inn in 1470 as a reward for his services as a butler and steward.[1] However, it is now known that he was, in fact, the son of William More a citizen of London and a wealthy baker, and Johanna the daughter and heir of John Joye, also a citizen of London, and a prosperous brewer. Both families were well known and respected in the City, and at Court. It was in the light of this parentage that Thomas More described himself on the epitaph he wished to be placed on his tomb as 'a Londoner born, of no noble family, but of an honest stock'.

In addition to John, William and Johanna More (née Joye) had three other sons: Abel, who became a Doctor of Laws at Exeter, William and Nicholas, and two daughters, Katherine and Alice.[2] William More (senior) made his will on 1 August 1467 and died sometime between then and 9 September of the same year when his will was proved. He was buried in St Dunstan's in the West, London. Johanna died in 1470.

John More was a young lawyer recently admitted to Lincoln's Inn when he married Agnes Graunger at St Giles without Cripplegate, London, on 24 April 1474. A study of the quartering of the Arms of Sir Thomas More has identified Agnes' father as Thomas Graunger who, with his two brothers Alleyn and John, was granted Arms by John Wrexworth, Guienne Kinge of Armes, sometime around 1460. Thomas was probably born in the 1430s and, at the granting of arms, was described as being 'a discreet and notable man of worshipful disposition'. In his will of 12 January 1510 (proved 5 December 1510) he describes himself as

'Alderman of London and M'chaunt of the Stapell att Caleys'.³

Agnes was the mother of all John More's children. She died in 1499 and was buried with her brother-in-law Abel More (who had died in 1486) in the Church of St Michael Bassishaw in Basinghall Street, London. The church, and the monument to Agnes and Abel, was destroyed in the Fire of London and, although the church was rebuilt afterwards, it was finally demolished in 1900. Fortunately, the Latin text on the tomb was recorded by John Weaver in 1631 and it has been translated as follows:

> Come hither, wayfarer, and measure with thine eyes
> How small an urn holds two persons enclosed.
> What thou art today, this man once was, and so was this woman
> Now each of them is part of this icy soil.
> His name was Abel, More his surname, and at Exeter
> City he was a Doctor of Civil Law.
> Agnes was the other's name, and she was the wife of John More,
> once the brother of this Abel here.
> As thou wishest, then, the living should do to thee after thy demise,
> so thyself, now, whoever thou art, utter this short prayer:
> May this Abel in the first place and this Agnes relieved
> by the Lamb who previously washed his sheep in his blood.
> Abel died 1486, Agnes 1499.
> May their souls through the mercy of God rest in peace.⁴

After Agnes's death John More married again three times. There are differing opinions as to names and the order in which he married his other wives, but he appears to have married for the last time when he was around seventy, and his last wife was Alice Clark, the widow of John Clark, a Citizen and Draper of London, but by birth the daughter of John More of Loseley in Surrey.

By the time John More began his career in law he had already begun to build up his own business interests in the City. After finishing his law studies and being called to the Bar he was, in November 1503, appointed a Sergeant-at-Law, a position only given to a small number of the best law scholars in the land. Over the next few years he progressed to become successively a judge in the Court of Common Pleas and a Judge in the Court of the King's Bench. His service was recognized by King Henry VIII by the granting of a knighthood in 1518.

As an important person in the City of London Sir John maintained a home in Milk Street, in the Ward of Cripplegate (now

WC2). According to John Stow, the London chronicler, the street was 'so called of milk sold there'. He added that, in the street, 'there be many fair houses for wealthy merchants and others'.[5] In addition to this house, Sir John had inherited a manor in the parish of North Mymms, Hertfordshire.[6] This provided an ideal retreat for the family when they wanted to get a breath of fresh air away from the hustle and bustle of the city or to avoid diseases that could spread rapidly in the heat of the summer. The manor owned by the Mores was, over the years, known by various names – More Place, Gubbins and, more properly, as Gobions. The manor of Gobions took its name from Sir Richard Gobion who, in a pedigree of his family, is described as 'Lord of the Manor of Gobion, in the parish of Stapleford, Herts, temp. Stephen' that is, in the time of King Stephen (1135–1154). The manor was inherited by Sir Richard's son Sir Anselm Gobion, from whom it passed down through three generations to Hawise Gobion who inherited it when her father Richard Gobion died in 1300. It passed into the possession of the Staffordshire Boteler family when Hawise married Sir Ralph Boteler of Norbury.[7] The More family is first recorded as having an interest in Gobions during the reign of King Richard II (1377–1400) and it was, in due course, inherited by Sir John. In addition to Gobions, he also held lands in Hatfield and St Albans.[8]

Sir John made his will in 1526 and left Gobions to his son Thomas with the provision that his widow, Lady Alice, should live there for the rest of her life. As a landowner of considerable means in the North Mymms/Hatfield area – and in accordance with a religious custom of the times – he stipulated in his will that 'for his soul and the souls of all Christians' £40 (equivalent to around £15,000 today) should be given by his executors for repairing the highway between Potters Bar and the Bell Bar on the road (now the A1000) leading from Barnet towards Hatfield.[9]

Sir John died in November 1530 and was buried in the Lady Chapel of the Church of St Lawrence Jewry. Following the execution of Sir Thomas More in 1535 Lady Alice More was evicted from Gobions and went to live at Northaw, a village few miles away. She died in 1545 and was buried in the church there.

John and Agnes More had six children: Joan (Latin = Johanna or Joanna), Thomas, Agatha, Edward and Elizabeth. There was also a stillborn child, probably born between Joan and Thomas. The birth dates of all the children were discovered in the late 1860s written on two blank pages of a Latin manuscript in the library of Trinity College, Cambridge.

An Extended Family: John More to John Donne

Other than the dates of their birth I have not been able to discover anything else about Agatha, 'born between seven and eight o'clock on the morning of 31 January 1479', and Edward, 'born between two and three on the morning of 3 September 1480'. It has been suggested that they died young, probably of the 'sweating sickness' that swept through London in 1485.[10]

Joan, the eldest child, was 'born between one and two on the afternoon of 11 March 1475'. She married Richard Staverton of London, the second son of Richard Staverton of Bray in Berkshire, a Master of the Bench at Lincoln's Inn and, according to the *Visitations of Berkshire, 1623*, a descendant of the Staverton family of Staverton Manor at Warfield in Berkshire.[11] Richard was one of the Prenotaries of the Sheriffs' Court of London before being admitted to Lincoln's Inn on 24 June 1520 at the request of Thomas More, his brother-in-law. Richard and Joan had a number of children including a son Richard (who married Lettice the daughter of Richard Paten), and a daughter Frances. Richard (the elder) died in 1538 and Joan four years later.

Thomas (who became Sir Thomas), born 'between two and three in the morning' of 7 February 1478, will be the subject of the next chapter.[12]

John More, 'born between ten and eleven o'clock on the morning of 6 June 1479', became a Scrivener, or Scribe, and was for some time his brother Thomas's secretary. I have not been able to find any record of his marriage and he is believed to have succumbed to an illness and died early in 1512 when he was in his early thirties.

Elizabeth More, the youngest child, was 'born between four and five o'clock on the morning of 22 September 1482'. She married John Rastell sometime around 1500. The full story of John Rastell, Thomas More's brother-in-law, and his descendants, the Heywood and the Donne families could fill a book on its own and this chapter would not be complete without some account of it.[13] For the sake of clarity I will put each line of descent under a separate heading. The genealogical table at the end of the chapter will show them all together.

The Rastell Family

John Rastell was born in Coventry in 1475. His grandfather, Thomas Rastell, was Warden of Coventry, and his father, also

Thomas, a member of the Guild of Corpus Christi in the city and a Justice of the Peace for Warwickshire. Given their positions, both were heavily involved in the business and legal affairs of the city that was in those days regarded as the capital of the Midlands. John was a law student when he met and married Elizabeth More. He later qualified and was admitted to the Bar as an utter barrister at the Middle Temple. After their marriage the couple lived in Coventry where John succeeded his father as Coroner in 1505 and where he presided over the Court of Statute Merchant and acted as Clerk of Recognizances of Debts. Records exist of his involvement in various Chancery suits and with the affairs of the wealthy wool and cloth merchants of the city, Members of the Staple of Calais.[14] In addition to his property in Coventry he was in 1508 granted a share in a crown estate of 600 acres in Warwickshire.

We know that Thomas More visited his sister and brother-in-law at Coventry a number of times, travelling by horse. The image of Thomas on horseback is not one that comes readily to mind, but it reminds us that anyone wanting to travel any distance in those days had to use this mode of transport. In one of his letters he refers to an occasion (not on the way to Coventry) when he was drenched by soaking rain, his horse often stumbling and putting him in danger of being thrown off, and regularly getting bogged down in mud.

An amusing story tells how, on one visit to his sister in Coventry, he had scarcely had time to dismount from his horse when some of the residents of the city tried to involve him in a controversy about the teaching of a local friar to the effect that no one who recited the rosary every day would be eternally damned. Ever the lawyer, Thomas refused to answer the question directly – much to the annoyance of the friar and his followers. In his own way, however, he made quite clear his own belief that a person's place in heaven depended on the life he led rather than on the prayers he said.

John Rastell was a man of many talents – a lawyer, as we have seen, but also an author and playwright, a printer, and a designer of grand pageants. He was interested in cosmography and mathematics, and his knowledge of these played a major part in helping him to design sets for the colourful festivities and pageants for which Coventry was famous. These were staged on special occasions during the year and when important people or royalty visited.

It was probably a combination of his legal and printing interests, his organizing abilities, and his links to the More family, that led to John's resignation as Coroner of Coventry in 1508 and to his move to London. By 1512 he was well established there as a translator, editor and printer of law and other books. Later he became the first person to produce type for printing music scores. His first premises were at 'the Abbott of Winchcombe's place', near the Fleet Bridge. His success there led him to open a shop on the south side of the churchyard at St Paul's Gate. Over time, some sixty works were produced on his various presses.

In addition to supervising his printing press, John also undertook some work from 1512–14 as an assistant to Sir Edward Belknap, a Privy Councillor to both Henry VII and VIII. This included overseeing the unloading of heavy cannon at Tower Wharf on their return from Henry's war in France and re-siting them within the Tower of London. He is recorded as having been paid twelve pence a day for this work and as being assisted by an officer and a number of carpenters and labourers.

At the beginning of 1515 John took out a lease on a country house at Monken Hadley near High Barnet, not far from his father-in-law's manor at North Mymms. He was obviously doing well for himself for a few months later he took out another lease on 'Lydgraves', a manor nearby. Monken Hadley would appear to have become the family home where he spent much of his time. Here he used his design skills again, enlarging the property considerably, adding a 'fair-hall', a parlour and chambers with glazed bay windows and, outside, clearing the grounds to set out a new garden. He entertained on a large scale, creating his own shooting, running and other games to entertain his many guests.

In my view, the most fascinating period of John Rastell's life began in the year 1517 when, inspired perhaps by his brother-in-law's book *Utopia* which had recently been published, and armed with letters of recommendation from the King, he chartered a ship to join a small fleet sailing out of Greenwich on a voyage of discovery to the 'New Found Lands' – the coast of North America, now Canada. He used his own money and an advance from the Royal Treasury for which John More his father-in-law, Thomas More his brother-in-law, and two of his friends stood surety. He also made arrangements with his father-in-law for the upkeep of Elizabeth and their servants for the three years he expected to be away.

The master of the *Barbara* was John Richards, and to sail with them John Rastell employed John Ravyn as purser. He was an experienced and well-known sailor and the owner of the *Mary Barking*, one of the other ships in the fleet. Among those sailing with them on the *Barbara* were John Rastell's partner, Richard Spicer, a London Merchant, four servants – including a 'factor' or business manager, and a printer – thirty or forty soldiers, and the Prior of Truro. John Rastell had to buy provisions for the journey, and these included beef, bacon, beer, biscuit, flour, salt and tallow. Also in the cargo were packs of hides and furs, chests of fabrics and clothes, including fur coats, as well as household items such as feather beds and pots and pans. There were also tools for masons and carpenters and 'other ingynes' – possibly printing equipment – 'that he had preparyd for the new lands'.

Although the expedition had the King's blessing, Thomas Howard, the Lord Admiral, was not too happy about it. He wanted as many ships as possible to be available for use against the French if the need should arise. In the event, the expedition appears to have been doomed to failure from the start, and it seems likely that the mutiny of the Master and Purser that brought the expedition to an end was pre-planned and had at least the tacit approval of the Admiral.

In the case of the *Barbara*, Richards and Ravyn, the master and the purser, employed delaying tactic after delaying tactic. When the other ships sailed, the *Barbara* had to wait for Ravyn to arrive on board at Gravesend. Ravyn had to stop at Dartmouth to buy some things he should have provided before they started. The ship sprung a leak – said to have been caused deliberately by Ravyn using 'naylys spykys and other thyngs' – in Plymouth Haven. Both Richards and Ravyn went ashore for seven or eight days in Falmouth, apparently to arrange to buy tin to sell at Bordeaux – a port in the opposite direction to the one they were meant to be taking. Eventually the *Barbara* set sail towards Ireland where it now needed to pick up more provisions in Waterford. Here Richards and Ravyn told John Rastell that they would sail no further for him. They suggested that he could make more money if he would 'fall to robbing upon the sea' – something he flatly refused to do. Finally, they abandoned him to his own devices and set off, as they had threatened to do, to sell the cargo in Bordeaux. John later recorded his feelings about this episode in his 'Play of the Four Seasons':

> But they that were the venturers
> Have cause to curse their mariners
> False of promys and dissemblers
> That falsly them betrayed.

As the failed voyage came to an end in Ireland by or before the end of the summer of 1517 and John didn't return to England until the summer of 1519, he spent almost two years in that country. How he supported himself while there we do not know, but from the way he set about printing new works immediately on his return he must have spent some considerable time writing. He was there long enough to get to know the people and their character well, and from hints that he drops he seems to have liked them though not, it seems, the way some of them – 'the kernys and the galowglashes' – treated their womenfolk.

In October 1519 John printed his own translation of the *Abbreviation of the Statutes*, a law dictionary. This was an important book and was protected from competition or piracy by the granting of a special royal privilege.

In November 1519 John took legal proceedings against Ravyn in the Court of Requests. Sixteen charges were set out, and Ravyn denied them all. Rastell's business manager was the chief witness for the prosecution, and various members of the crew who were called to testify supported his testimony. For his part Ravyn appears to have been unable to produce anyone who was willing to speak in his defence, and he lost the case.

In 1520 John rented other premises for printing. These were known as the 'Mermaid', and were in a house belonging to the Masters of the Bridge House at St Paul's Gate, next to Cheapside. Among the works published at 'the sygne of the meremayd at Powlysgate' were *A dyaloge of Syr Thomas More* (1529).

From around 1520 there are signs that John began to experience financial difficulties arising out of the need to repay the Royal Treasury monies he had borrowed for his ill-fated voyage. He also found himself in court as a result of claims that he had failed to honour other agreements he had entered into after the King had granted him the wardship of Margaret and Mary Hunne (see below).

Also in 1520, after an urgent request to Cardinal Wolsey for his services, John went to France to assist Sir Edward Belknap and Sir Nicholas Vaux who had been given responsibility for erecting the Great Hall at Guisnes for the Field of Cloth of Gold. Three thousand workmen were employed on this task, and his special skills were called on for the construction and decoration of the roofs of the Banqueting Hall.

In spite of his apparent financial difficulties in 1524, John was still in a position to be able to take out a lease on a one and three-quarter acre plot of land in 'Fynnesbury Felds' (Finsbury Fields) with a frontage on Old Street, on which he built a house. He laid out a garden in which he built a stage where he could present his plays. Here we have a brief glimpse of Elizabeth Rastell's involvement in his work – assisting a tailor to make garments for the players.[15]

In 1527 John was called upon to put on a pageant at Greenwich to entertain ambassadors who had come from France to arrange a marriage with Princess Mary, the daughter of the King and Catherine of Aragon. He called the pageant 'Father of Heaven' – a reference, not to the Christian God, but to Jupiter! It was staged in one of two halls specially built for the occasion – the other hall being for the associated banquet. Hans Holbein painted a picture, 'The Taking of Tourenne', which was placed on an arch separating the two halls. In addition to writing the dialogue for the pageant, John's special skills were used, as they had been at the Field of Cloth of Gold, in the design of the roof of the hall in which the pageant was to be staged. This was filled with large representations of the earth surrounded by sea, by the twelve signs of the zodiac, and the seven planetary gods. Preparations for the pageant took nearly two months to complete and, in addition to a carpenter (the same one as he had employed to build his own stage), he also employed the King's painter and ten other workmen. For all of this work he charged the sum of £26 11s. 3d. (equivalent to around £8,000 today).

The later years of John's life see him continuing his writing and publishing work but becoming increasingly engaged in legal affairs, first as a Chancery lawyer under Chancellor Wolsey, then under his brother-in-law Sir Thomas More. However, from around 1529 when his favour at Court and wide circle of influential friends enabled him to be elected a Member of Parliament for the Cornish Borough of Dunheved for the series of Parliaments which began in the autumn of that year, a change occurred which was to lead to his estrangement from the More family and their associates.

A staunch Catholic up till now, the publication in 1530 of one of John's last works *A Newe Boke of Purgatorie* – a defence of the

Catholic doctrine of Purgatory using 'natural reason and good philosophy' rather than recourse to Scripture – drew him into a dispute with John Frith, a young priest, and one of the leading scholars of England fired with a passion for the reform of the Church along Protestant lines. Contrary to what might have been expected, the effect of Frith's teachings on John was to bring about his conversion to the Protestant cause and to draw him into the service of Thomas Cromwell, Earl of Essex, who was responsible for drafting the legislation to make the Church of England independent of Rome. It was this service that was to lead to his downfall.

No doubt with an eye to some printing work for himself, John suggested to Cromwell that a book of approved sermons should be printed and sent to all clergy with an order that they should be read, or form the basis of other sermons, on Sundays. He also proposed a book designed to prove that priests should be allowed to marry, that images should not be worshipped or have offerings made to them, and that prayers for those who have died are of no use to them. Cromwell may well have passed on these suggestions to Thomas Cranmer who became Archbishop of Canterbury in 1533 and who helped to shape the doctrines of the Church of England under Henry and Edward. One of the tasks Cromwell gave to John was to search the Charterhouse (the home of the Carthusian Monks in London) for suspect books written by their founder, St Bruno. He also visited the Charterhouse over several days in an attempt to convert the monks to the new religion.

Working for Cromwell seems to have taken up most of John's time but it obviously didn't pay well. Writing to Cromwell he complained that others who did less earned more than he did, and that he didn't now earn as much as he used to do through his printing and legal work. Not wanting to overdo it, and in those times of religious fervour thinking perhaps of the parable of the rich man, he protested that he regarded 'ryches' only as much as he did 'chyppes' and that all he wanted was 'to have a lyffyng out of det'. In view of this plea of poverty it is interesting to note that on 22 November 1533 John and nine other men, including Thomas Cromwell, were granted a twenty-one-year lease on all the lead mines in Dartmoor Forest at the rent of one tenth of all the metal found. The grant was made by Sir John Heron and John Hales, Surveyors of the Crown, on the orders of the King.

Unfortunately for John it was his over-enthusiasm for religious reform that was his undoing. Opposition to the payment of mortuary fees, tithes, and other offerings to the clergy had been a matter of heated debate ever since he had been a young man in Coventry and it seems that, although the King had settled the matter in favour of the clergy by Royal Proclamation in 1535, John continued to openly oppose the practice which, to use the language of today, he regarded as a 'rip-off'. As a result he was called to appear before the Archbishop's Court where he was charged with opposing it and, being found guilty, was committed to prison.

On 25 April 1536 John drew up his will, appointing Sir Francis Bigot as executor. The will indicates that he may have been experiencing considerable pangs of conscience as it begins with an unusually long preamble in which he acknowledges that he has lived in sin and throws himself on the merciful goodness of God, begging forgiveness for anything harmful that he has said, written or done. After that he bequeaths his house in St Martin's and his goods and chattels to Elizabeth – who he refers to as 'my poor wife' – and make small bequests for his three children.[16]

Soon after making his will John wrote again to Cromwell pointing out how much time he had spent upholding the King's cause and opposing the Pope, with the resultant loss of both his printing business and his legal practice. He protested at the great wrong that he believed had been done to him, telling Cromwell of his extreme misery at finding himself forsaken by his kinsmen, destitute of friends and without comfort and succor. He died on 25 June 1536 and his will was proved on 3 July – a sad end to what otherwise might be regarded as a brilliant career. After her husband's death Elizabeth Rastell appears to have gone to live with the Heywoods, her daughter and son-in-law (of whom see below), but she died later the same year.

John and Elizabeth Rastell had three children, John, William, and Joan – Sir Thomas More's nephews and niece. On the recommendation of Sir Edward Belknap the King had also granted John the wardship of Margaret and Mary Hunne, after the murder of their father at the end of 1514. Apparently John intended them to become wives for his two young sons though, in the event, this did not happen as the financial arrangements made as part of the settlement – regarding the disposition of their father's lands and the payment to the Crown of the value of the girls' dowries – led to litigation and the loss of their wardship in 1523.

We do not know the exact date of birth or very much about the life of John and Elizabeth's eldest son, known as John Rastell junior. Born in Coventry sometime around 1506, he became a member of one of the Inns of Court in London and there is evidence of him pleading in a number of Chancery Court cases. In 1531 he was nominated by Cromwell as Member of Parliament for Tavistock, Devon. The practise of law does not seem to have fulfilled John junior's ambitions and, having perhaps inherited some of his father's spirit of adventure, he joined a voyage of exploration to Labrador in 1536, the year of his father's death. Although the ship did, this time, reach its destination, the expedition can hardly be described as successful. It may be that the members of the expedition were ill-informed about the conditions they might find in Labrador, or that the ship was not adequately provisioned for the voyage and an extended stay once they reached their destination. Either way, once on land they soon faced starvation and, to supplement the herbs and roots they managed to gather, the crew resorted to killing a number of their fellow sailors one by one and to broiling pieces of their flesh – until the practice was discovered by the officers on board. The arrival of a French ship, said to have been a sign of God's mercy in answer to their prayers, saved the situation from deteriorating any further and enabled them to re-provision and return to England during 1538 or 1539.

John and Elizabeth's second son, William Rastell, was born in Coventry in 1508. From around the age of sixteen he started to work with his father in his printing business and in his legal practice in London. He was sent to Oxford in 1525 where he studied logic and philosophy but for some reason didn't sit for a degree. In 1527 his father employed him again during the design of the pageant at Greenwich in 1527 when he was paid 8d. a day for forty-four days work. He continued to work for his father who had now begun to print some of his brother-in-law's books against Lutheranism and heresy.

By 1529 William had set up his own printing business with premises at a house belonging to his father in St Bride's churchyard, Fleet Street. Here, furnished with new typefaces, he set about printing his own works – beginning with his translation of Caesar's Commentaries and Cicero's *De Amicitia* – as well as some of the works of his uncle and close friend Thomas More, now Chancellor to Henry VIII.

In 1532 William decided to become properly qualified in law and was admitted to Lincoln's Inn in September, most probably on Thomas More's recommendation. For a while he continued his printing business working, especially during 1533, on his uncle's answers to the arguments of the Protestant reformers Tyndale and Frith, and on his own *Natura Brevium*, a collection of legal textbooks for law students. However, his close association with Sir Thomas, especially after his recent resignation as Chancellor, increasingly brought him under suspicion and he finally sold his business to Thomas Gibson, another London printer, in 1534.

William completed his law studies and was called to the Bar in May 1539. His practice was obviously successful and according to the *Black Books*, the records of Lincoln's Inn, he soon had a number of clerks working for him. In 1542 he was doing well enough to purchase Hawkeshall, an estate of over two hundred acres not far from Gobions (the manor belonging to the More family but at that time sequestered), and also a number of properties and land in Tottenham. Through his marriage to Winifred Clement in 1544 he forged even closer ties with the extended family of Sir Thomas More. Winifred, born in 1526, was the daughter of Dr John Clement who had been Thomas More's personal assistant as well as a tutor to his children, and had become his son-in-law through marriage to his adopted daughter Margaret Giggs.

Appointed a Pensioner of Lincoln's Inn in 1545, William began to rise progressively through the hierarchy of that establishment becoming an Autumn Reader, or Lecturer, and then a Bencher in 1546. In April 1547 his increasing prosperity enabled him, in partnership with William Roper, to take over the lease of Crosby Place and a number of surrounding properties from Antonio Bonvisi, an Italian merchant – properties they sublet three months later. He also bought a lease on a large property called Skales Inn, in Whittington College, and two other properties in Maiden Lane, off the Strand.

In 1549 William was appointed Treasurer of Lincoln's Inn, but then, on 1 December, faced with the increasing repression of Catholics during the reign of Edward VI, he fled with all his family to Louvain in Flanders where they came under the protection the Emperor Charles. The price they had to pay for 'deceitfully and rebelliously taking flight' without the permission of the King was the sequestration of their 'goods and chattels'. An Inquisition regarding this, held at the Guildhall in February 1551, shows that William Rastell owned a total of eight properties in the City. His property in Hertfordshire does not appear to have been sequestered.

While in Louvain, William began to write the life of his uncle,

Sir Thomas More, of which, as we have seen, only a few fragments have survived. He also spent his time collecting together and editing his uncle's English works fearing that they would otherwise be lost to posterity. He prepared these and some legal works for publication when, he hoped, the religious situation in England would improve sufficiently to allow him to return. On 17 July 1553 Winifred Rastell died of the fever. Aged only twenty-seven, she had been married to William for just nine years, and they had no children. Winifred was buried on the right-hand side of the altar of the Blessed Virgin Mary in the Church of St Peter, Louvain.

After Mary came to the throne in 1553 William and his wife's parents returned to England where, by a special order of Queen Mary dated 24 September, anyone who held their former lands or goods were commanded to hand them back. William was appointed one of the Chief Justices of the Queen's Bench and took up residence at Lincoln's Inn where, once again, he became Treasurer. In 1554 he contributed towards a painting of the taking down of Christ from the Cross that was hung over the altar and the provision of rich altar cloths. In return for this the Governors agreed that he and his widow and their 'parents, kinfolk and friends' would be remembered during every Mass in the chapel. In addition to his legal work he completed the preparation of the *Works of Thomas More* that were published in one volume of over 14,000 pages in 1557.

After the accession to the throne of Elizabeth I in 1558 William continued in his post as one of the Chief Justices and in February 1559 he was appointed 'Justice of Itinerant and of Assize in the Counties of Durham and Sedbergh' while the See of Durham was vacant.[17] However, increasing anti-Catholic legislation caused him, and his wife's parents, to realize that they could have no safe future in England and, on 3 January 1562, they fled back to Louvain. Again his goods – including his books, maps, gowns and furniture from Lincoln's Inn – were assessed for value and forfeited to the Crown.

William made his will on 8 August 1564 and lodged a copy of it with the Registrar of Antwerp. He appointed his nephew Ellis Haywood (of whom see later) and his father and mother-in-law John and Margaret Clement his executors.[18] He appointed Ellis Heywood his heir, leaving him his property in North Mymms. He left gifts of jewellery and/or money to all his close relatives and friends as well as to the exiled English nuns of the Order of Sion and the nuns of the monasteries of St Ursula and St Clare in Louvain. He died of the fever in Louvain on 27 August 1565 and was buried next to his wife in St Peter's church. Probate was granted to his will on 5 October 1565. The agreement with Lincoln's Inn about the remembering of himself and his family at Mass was eventually abolished as 'an abomination and superstition' at a meeting of the Governors held on 16 August 1581.

The Heywood Family

John and Elizabeth Rastell's only daughter, Joan, was born in Coventry in 1504. She married John Heywood, probably in 1523, the year in which, at the request of the King, he was granted the Freedom of the City of London.[19] Like the Rastells, the Heywoods also hailed from Coventry where John's father, originally from Stock in Essex, appears to have been associated with the same legal practice as John Rastell. Through his extended family he also had connections with Lincoln's Inn and the legal practice of Sir John More.

John Heywood, born in 1497, had three brothers. Thomas, the youngest of the three, became an Augustinian canon at St Osyth's in Essex. At the dissolution of the monastery in 1539 he received a pension of £6 13s. 4d. a year from the King (equivalent to around £2,300 today). He was arrested on Palm Sunday 1574 after being caught celebrating Mass in the house of Lady Browne (a More relation) and, after conviction, was executed on 14 June.

The claim made by John's biographers that, by or before his teens, he became a Royal Chorister may well be incorrect.[20] However, after studying at Broadgates Hall, Oxford (now Pembroke College) – and probably on the recommendation of Thomas More he did enter Court service at the age of twenty-two in 1519. In the King's Book of Payments for the end of Michaelmas (dated 29 September) of that year he is recorded as having been paid a first quarterly wage of 100 shillings (approx £1,800 today).[21] In the following years he also received various other annuities at the King's pleasure, 'in consideration of his good and faithful service'.[22] Although he received some payment as a singer, his main role at Court appears to have been that of 'a player of the virginals', an early form of spinet, a role in which he would have been much in demand during Court revels and banquets.

It was not however as a Court musician that John achieved his greatest fame but as one of the first English dramatists to move away from the old medieval-style miracle, morality and folk plays to form a new genre known as 'Interludes' – short, comic dialogues or plays. He also became famous as an epigrammatist or writer of short, witty sayings. For both of these, and for his 'mad merry wit', he came to be referred to as 'merry John Heywood' by his biographers. One of his earliest interludes, probably written in 1519, is 'The Mery Play between the Pardoner and the Frere, the Curate and Neybour Pratte' a satire on the subject of the sale of relics and indulgences.[23] Later interludes include titles such as 'A Play of Love' and 'The Play of the Wether', both printed in the 1530s by his brother-in-law William Rastell.

As we have already seen John was, at the King's request, granted the freedom of the City of London in 1523 which means that he must by then have been a householder in the City, probably in St Bride's parish. In 1525 the cost of the King's war with France necessitated a reduction in the number of those employed in the Royal service. Even so, John was not discharged until 8 November 1528 at which time he was awarded an 'annuell pencion' of £10 a year for life (equivalent to around £3,000 today).[24] In 1529 he was described as a 'citizen and Stacyoner of London' when he was received into the Mercers Company as a 'Comen measurer or meter of lynnen Clothes'.

Although no longer holding an official position at Court John's discharge from royal service did not end his relationship with Henry VIII. In January 1533 the King gave him a New Year's Gift of a gold cup with a cover, weighing thirty-three ounces and, as we will see, the King also gave him various grants of land. Records of payments made to him indicate that he continued to be a regular entertainer in the royal household throughout the reigns of Henry, Edward and Mary.

After the death of Thomas Cromwell John became involved in a Catholic plot – The Plot of the Prebendaries – to remove Cranmer from his position as Archbishop of Canterbury on grounds of spreading heresy. Unfortunately for him and the other 'conspirators' – including young John More II, William Roper and William Daunce – it was in the King's own interests to keep Cranmer in office, rather than send him to the stake as a heretic and, in March 1544, they were convicted of treason and sentenced to death and the forfeiture of their property. At first John

Heywood refused to submit, but on Sunday 6 July he gave in and was pardoned after being forced to dress in a white gown and make a grovelling public recantation at St Paul's Cross. In his recantation he acknowledged

> the great and inestimable clemency and mercifulness of our most soveraign and redoubted Prince the Kings Majesty, to which his highness hath most graciously used to me a wretch, most justly and worthily condemned to dye for my manifold and outraigous offences, haynously and traitorously committed against his Majesty and his Laws.

He went on to declare that the King's Supremacy is 'surely and certainly grounded, and established on the very Word of God' and confessed that

> For lack of grace I have most willfully and obstinately suffered myself to fall to such blindness, that I have not onely thought that the Bishop of Rome hath been and aught to be taken the chief and Supream Head of the Universal Church of Christ here on earth, but also, like no true Subject, concealed and favoured such as I have known or thought to be of that opinion. For the which most detestable Treasons and untruths, I here and most humbly and with all my heart ... ask the Kings Majesty forgiveness ...

He continued his confession,

> I do utterly and with all my heart recant and revoke all mine aforesaid erroneous and traitorous opinions. And (as my Conscience now doth force) I protest that even with my heart I firmly think and undoubtedly believe, that the Bishop of Rome neither now hath, nor at any time hath had, or can have by any Law of God or Man, any more Authority, without the precinct of his own Country about him, than any other Bishop hath within his Diocese. Whereby I assuredly take the abolishing of the pretended and usurped Power or Authority of the Bishop of Rome out of this Realm, to be justly and truly by the Law of God. And also I take our Soveraign Lord the Kings Highness to be Supreme Head, immediately next under Christ, of the Church of England and Ireland, and all other his Graces Dominions, both of the Spirituality and Temporality ...[25]

John's fall from grace did not last long and he did not suffer any lasting financial penalty. His recantation appears to have been a formality officially required of one who had offended the King but, apart from that, of no great significance. Certainly his adherence to the Catholic faith was never called into question.

Henry VIII died in 1547 and he was succeeded by Edward VI who was crowned on 20 February. He was only nine years old at the time and real power was exercised first by the Duke of Somerset as Lord Protector and then, from 1550, by the Earl of Warwick as Lord President of the Council. The Duke of Somerset was leader of the Protestant faction in the Privy Council and under him new religious reforms were pushed through – a *Book of Homilies* or specimen sermons was issued to all the clergy, chantries were abolished, images removed from places of worship and Cranmer's Book of Common Prayer imposed. Faced with these changes, and fearing for their lives should they oppose them, a number of prominent Catholics – including, as we have seen, William and Winifred Rastell and Winifred's parents – sought refuge on the Continent. John however took a calculated risk and hung on, probably hoping that his popularity at Court would see him through – which it did. He held on to the honorary title of Sewer of the Chamber and in 1552, his pension was increased to £40 a year (approx. £7,000 today). He retained his title under Queen Mary whose personal friend he had been since she was a teenage princess, and who was proclaimed Queen on 20 July 1553 after the nine-day rule of Jane Grey came to an end. The chronicler Stow records that during Mary's coronation parade in September 1553 'In Paul's Churchyard against the Schoole, one Master Heywood sate in a pageant under a vine, and made to her an Oration in Latine and English'.[26] He also wrote a ballard to celebrate her marriage to Philip II of Spain in July that year. His favour at court and his influential friends, especially Sir Robert Rochester, Chancellor of the Duchy of Lancaster, and Bishop Gardiner, led to his return as Member of Parliament for Lancaster in the Parliament of April 1554 and for Hindon in that of November 1554.[27]

During Mary's reign John's 'witty works' became favourites at Court and by a patent dated 5 April 1555 he was rewarded with a final increase in his pension to £50 per year (equivalent to around £8,800 today). In 1556 he completed his longest allegory 'The Spider and the Flie' in which the spider represents Protestants and the fly Catholics. It is said that he personally amused Mary with his pleasantries on her deathbed.

Over the years John clearly became a man of some considerable wealth, his income coming from royal pensions, from rents gained by subletting property and from land that he bought himself or that was given to him by royal favour. He was Lord of the Manor of Broke Hall at Tolleshunt Knights near Tiptree in Essex, a property he leased from the monastery at St Osyth where his brother was a monk.[28] In November 1540 he purchased the leases of two properties called 'Butlers' and 'Iveries' in North Mymms from the Lord of the Manor there. The agreement made specified that these were to be held for the lives of himself and his son Ellis and for seventy years after. In 1545 he is listed as being one of the owners of an estate in Whitechurch parish, Dorset, property that had once belonged to Mylton monastery, and in 1546 a grant in fee was made to him of Kirby Bellars Priory near Melton Mowbray in Leicestershire.[29] In the 1550s he appears to have been living on an estate at Hinxwell (now Hinxhill) near Ashford in Kent, and, in December 1554, a royal patent of Philip and Mary granted him a forty-year lease (his estimated life expectancy at that time) of over 200 acres of land in the Romney Marsh. Finally on 12 November 1558, a few days before her death, Mary granted him a forty-year lease on the manor of Bulmer and other lands, in Yorkshire.[30]

The accession of Elizabeth I to the throne on 17 November 1558 soon faced John with a dilemma that he knew, this time, would not go away. In April 1559 a new Act of Supremacy declared the Queen to be Supreme Governor of the Church of England and a new Oath of Supremacy could now be demanded of people who held public or church positions. A first offence against the Act of Supremacy could mean loss of all goods and movable possessions. A new Act of Uniformity, also passed in April 1559, introduced heavy penalties for those who refused to conform to the Church of England. Failure to attend the new Sunday service in a local church was punishable by a fine of one shilling, and attending a Catholic Mass by a fine of 100 marks (approx. £13,000 today). Similar punishments were threatened against anyone who criticised the Book of Common Prayer. Once again John bided his time; he had known Elizabeth for a long time and initially he was obviously still welcomed as an entertainer at Court. In August 1559 he is recorded as having been involved in entertaining the Queen at 'Non-shyche' during a great banquet that went on 'tyll iij in the mornyng'.[31] Away from Court he worked on a new edition of his Proverbs that was published in 1561, and his six hundred or so epigrams and proverbs, written throughout his life, were printed as a collection in 1562 under the title *John Heywoodes Woorkes*.

By 1564 John must have found the pressure on him to conform to the Church of England too great. He was now sixty-seven years old and probably felt that most of his life's work was now completed so, after making arrangements for his daughter and son-in-law to collect the rents on his properties, he went into exile on 20 July 1564 and settled in Malines in the Spanish Netherlands. He must have been well aware of the price that he would have to pay when the authorities caught up with him and, in due course, at a Commission charged with inquiring into his properties both he and his son Ellis were charged with having 'contemptuously departed and fled, without licence, into parts across the sea in Flanders and Brabant, under the obedience of Philip of Spain, and that, in spite of a proclamation calling upon them to return, they refused to do so'. No mention is made of his wife and it has been assumed that she was already dead.

Away from England John became homesick and, in 1574, he approached his friend and fellow author Dr Thomas Wilson who was at that time the Queen's ambassador to Antwerp regarding the possibility of getting permission to return to England. Wilson indicated that Elizabeth would look favourably on him should he make such a request – providing that he did not engage in any rebellious practices.[32] In the event, failing health, and poverty, seem to have prevented his return. On 18 April 1575 he sent a pleading letter to Lord Burleigh and his wife saying that he had been robbed of what little he had by a group of Spanish and German soldiers, and asking them to use their good offices at the Exchequer to arrange for his daughter to send him the arrears of rents she had collected on his properties – something which she had, for some years, been afraid to do. Noting his age to be seventy-eight, and believing himself to be almost at the end of his life, he says: 'I will live as a poor, honest, quiet old man, and spend my time in prayer and looking to my last end.'[33] The request for funds was, it seems, successful.

John's son, Ellis, who had been on the staff of the Jesuit College in Antwerp since 1573, visited his father frequently in Malines. However, as this interfered with his official duties, the Father General, Head of the Jesuits, offered John his own separate accommodation in the College in 1576 so that they could be near each other. His hopes that, perhaps, he might end his days in peace there were shattered when trouble broke out in 1578 between Catholics and Protestants in Antwerp and he, in the company of some of the older priests from the College, was sent to Cologne. Unfortunately, when they arrived at the gates of the city they were arrested and sent back to Antwerp. The College was sacked in April and the Jesuit priests, and John, were sent to Malines where, on arrival, they found that the gates of the city had been closed against them. Fortunately for them Archduke Matthias, having heard that the Duke of Orange had plans to have them put to death outside the walls of the town, arranged for a detachment of troops to be sent to protect them. The escort arrived just in time to save them and they were able to proceed to the Catholic stronghold of Louvain where they arrived on 26 May 1578.[34] Not surprisingly the old man, now in his eighties, was severely traumatized by this experience and, although the exact date of his death is not known, it is thought likely that he died a few months later. It is said that the priest who attended at his deathbed kept repeating the phrase 'the flesh is weak, the flesh is weak' to which John, in his last words, replied 'But you shouldn't blame the Almighty for making me a fish!' – so he made a fitting end to a life of jests and merrymaking. Almost a decade later, in 1587, Thomas Newton, issuing a new edition of John's Epigrams wrote a few lines that, it seems to me, make a fitting epitaph:

> This author Heywood dead and gone, and shrinde in tombe of clay,
> Before his death by penned workes did carefully assay
> To build himself a lasting tombe, not made of stone and lyme,
> But better farre and richer too triumphing over Tyme.[35]

John and Joan Heywood had two sons, Ellis and Jasper (whose names have already been mentioned in passing) and three daughters, two of whom were called Elizabeth. Ellis Heywood was born in London in 1530 and, after a period of studies with private tutors at home, he was sent to study at Oxford where he matriculated in his early teens. In 1548 he was elected a Fellow of All Souls College and began his law studies that culminated in the award of a Bachelor of Civil Law degree on 18 July 1552.

After the completion of his law studies Ellis travelled to Europe where he became a private secretary to Cardinal Reginald Pole in Rome. After the accession of Queen Mary, however, Cardinal Pole returned to England where he became Archbishop of Canterbury charged with the task of restoring England to the Catholic faith. Ellis would appear to have returned at around the same time and may even have continued to work for the Cardinal. In 1554, he was appointed Prebend of Eccleshall, near Stafford, in the Diocese of Lichfield. Whether Ellis had by this time been ordained a priest or whether this was an honorary position – a means of providing him with an income – we do not know.

As we have seen, Ellis's *Il Moro* was published in Florence in 1556, but why he wrote it in Italian, why it was published in Florence and whether he went there to oversee its publication remains a mystery. The full title is *Il Moro d'Heliseo Heivodo Inglese*, or *The More, by Ellis Heywood, Englishman*. This, his only known work, was dedicated to Reginald Cardinal Pole and contained a series of fictitious conversations between Sir Thomas More, his great-uncle, and some of the learned men of his time.

What Ellis did between this time and his departure from England – probably with his father – in 1664 is not known. He was an ardent Catholic and it seems unlikely that he could have held on to his prebendship under Elizabeth. The next recorded event in his life was in 1566 when he joined the Society of Jesus, or Jesuits, at their house in Dillengen, Bavaria, where his brother Jasper (of whom more later) was on the staff.[36] Ellis spoke many languages and was therefore especially valuable in promoting the international work of the Jesuits. In pursuit of his duties he made a number of visits to England and it was from here that he was sent to Antwerp on business in 1573 by the Father General of the Order. While there he was appointed the Spiritual Director to the house of the professed religious (i.e. those who had taken their religious vows of poverty, chastity, obedience and obedience to the Pope) and so stayed on in Antwerp. When the Jesuits were expelled from the city in 1578 he was amongst those, including his father, who found refuge in Louvain. Also traumatized by the experience he died a few months after his father on 2 October 1578. In his will, dated November 1568, he left the property he had inherited from his uncle (William Rastell) to the Jesuits to further their educational work. A codicil added in 1572 passed some of the income gained from this for the benefit of the Jesuit students at Louvain.[37]

Jasper Heywood was born in London in 1535, the year of his grand uncle's execution. As a boy he was one of the pages of honour to Princess Elizabeth but at the age of twelve he was sent to study at Oxford where his brother was already a student. He obtained his BA degree in July 1553. In 1554 he was elected a probationary fellow of Merton College where it is said 'he bare away the bell in disputations at home and in the public schools'.

Jasper and his brother are both said to have been 'for a time very wild, to the great grief of their father'.[38] This may account for Jasper's falling foul of the College authorities and for his decision to resign from the fellowship on 4 April 1558 rather than face expulsion after three warnings for misbehaviour. Notwithstanding this, he gained his MA in July 1558 and in November of the same year he was elected a fellow of All Souls' College. While at Oxford he wrote a number of poems, drew up a Compendium of Hebrew Grammar, and translated three of Seneca's Tragedies into English verse. The dedications of these latter works – to Queen Elizabeth, to Sir John Mason a Privy Councilor and to William Herbert, Earl of Pembroke – give some indication of the people with whom Jasper was familiar.[39]

Jasper's high-profile position meant that he, like his surviving More, Rastell and Heywood relations, soon came under suspicion when Elizabeth I began her reign. There was a special determination to push religious reforms through at Oxford and Cambridge, the two great seats of learning, and it was not long before he had to resign his fellowship at All Soul's because, as a Catholic, he refused to conform.

The exact order of events around this time is not clear. At some stage Jasper was ordained priest, probably on the recommendation of his friend Cardinal Pole, but whether this was in England or in Italy we do not know. What we do know is that he was already a priest when he joined the Jesuits in Rome where he began his novitiate on 21 May 1562. After teaching philosophy and theology for two years in the Roman College he was sent to Dillengen in Bavaria where he was professor of moral theology and controversy for seventeen years. In the mean time he continued his own higher studies and gained his Doctorate in Divinity on 25 July 1570.

In 1581, at the request of Pope Gregory XIII, Jasper was sent to England to replace Fr Persons as superior of the Jesuit Mission that was working under cover in England. In addition to organizing the mission he spent some time preaching in Staffordshire where it is said he made a notable number of converts. Perhaps inevitably he became involved in the controversy between Marian priests (those who had studied and been ordained in England during Mary's reign) and Seminary priests (those who had studied and been ordained in seminaries abroad) – the former feeling that they were being 'taken over' by the latter. It appears that the Marian priests took exception to Jasper's opposition to the severe fasting laws observed by Catholics in England –

though, in fact, he had only proposed the adoption of the fasting laws laid down for the whole Church at the Council of Trent in 1545. The situation in England was difficult and dangerous enough without being exacerbated by conflict between different groups of priests and, probably in the interests of prudence, Jasper was withdrawn from England by his superiors.[40]

While sailing for Dieppe, Jasper's ship was blown back onto the English coast where, on landing, he was arrested as a suspected priest and sent in chains to London where he was imprisoned in the Clink on 9 December 1583. He was examined several times by the Privy Council and strongly urged to conform, but neither bribes – it is said he was offered a bishopric – nor threats, could persuade him to give up his Catholic faith. On 5 Feb 1584 he was brought to trial at Westminster Hall with five other priests. A letter written at the time reports:

> Mr. Heywood and five other priests were brought to the Kingsbench barre, indited of high treason for conspiring at Rhemes and Rome ... They all pleaded not guilty and so were conveyed to the Tower. Fr. Heywood was in Jesuit's weed, so grave a man as ever I sett my eyes upon ... The 9 of February the five priests were brought againe to the barre, and arrained upon the former endightment: they pleaded and protested innocency ... The Jury found them out of hand Guilty, and the Judge gave sentence of death. Whereupon the priests sung *Te Deum* and such like godly verses.[41]

While the five other priests were condemned to death and executed, Jasper was taken away before the trial ended and imprisoned in the Tower for seventeen months. He was very ill in prison and his sister Elizabeth Donne (of whom see later) was, unusually, given permission to visit him and offer him some nursing care. It may well be that the leniency shown to Jasper was the result of the intervention of the Queen who had fond memories of him as her page, and also of his father.

In November 1584 Parliament considered an Act making it high treason for any Jesuit or seminary priest to be found in England and, although the Act had not yet been finally passed, the authorities thought it better to exile Jasper and twenty other priests before it came into force. On 21 January 1585 they were taken down to a ship moored at Tower stairs. From there they were transported to the French coast where, after being told they would face death if they returned to England, they were forcibly put ashore at Boulogne-sur-Mer. In Boulogne the authorities looked favourably on them and gave them safe conduct to Abbeville from where Jasper made his way to the Jesuit College at Dôle in Burgundy. In 1589 he was called to Rome by the Father General of the Jesuits who some time later sent him 'as an example of holiness' to the Jesuit College in Salerno and, finally, to the house of the professed Jesuits at Naples, where, worn out by the sufferings and hardships he had undergone, he died in 1598 at the age of sixty-three.[42]

We know very little about Joan and the Elizabeth, the older daughters of John and Joan Heywood, but they are thought to have been born between 1531 and 1539. In the will of William Rastell (1564) they are referred to under their married names – Stubbes and Marvin. Joan's husband, Christopher Stubbes, was a member of Lincoln's Inn. From an investigation into the property that had been owned by her father and her brother Ellis we know that Elizabeth Marvin's husband – whose first name has not come down to us – had died before 1571 as she is at that time referred to as a widow. The same investigation also revealed that Ellis had given her a farm called 'Hawkshead' which, at her death, was to be passed on to her daughter, Anne. For some time Elizabeth lived in St Bartholomew's Close in a house rented from St Bartholomew's Hospital, but on 9 March 1577 she was deprived of the lease for subletting it contrary to the conditions of the lease. We do not know when she died.[43]

The Donne Family

Elizabeth Heywood, the second daughter with that name in the family, and the youngest child of John and Joan Heywood, was born in the early 1540s. We know nothing about her early life except that she married John Donne, most probably in March or April 1563 and that she received £300 (approx. £44,500 today) from the sale of her father's land in Romney Marsh as her dowry. John was also a Catholic, a citizen of London, a prosperous ironmonger, and a prominent member of the Ironmongers' Company. He owned property in Catte Street, Oxford, and leased the family home next to the Mitre Tavern and opposite the parish church of St Nicholas Olave in Bread Street, London, from the Ironmongers Company.[44] It was here that all their children were born. John was descended from the ancient Welsh family of Dwn from Kidwelly in Carmarthenshire who traced their line back to

'Meirick King of Dyvet' who legend has it was one of the sword-bearers at the coronation of King Arthur. One of his more recent ancestors had been Sir John Donne, knighted by Edward IV after the battle of Tewksbury. He died in 1503 and is buried in St Georges Chapel at Windsor. He was also related to the Herberts, Earls of Pembroke.[45]

John Donne senior became ill, made his will on 6 January 1575 and died about a year later in January or early February 1576. As was the custom of the time he left one-third of his property to his wife, one-third to his children, and one-third for the payment of debts and legacies. There was a proviso that should his wife or any of his children die before the will was proved, their share should be divided among the survivors. The total value of his assets was in the region of £3,500 (approx. £512,500 today) so he was, by any account, a wealthy man.

As a widow with a young family to support Elizabeth Donne's first need was to find another husband and she married John Syminges a few months later. He was a widower in his fifties with three grown-up children and they were probably well known to each other before they married. A prominent London doctor, John had qualifications from Oxford and the University of Bologna in Italy and was twice elected President of the Royal College of Physicians. There were no children from this marriage and it came to an end after twelve years when John died on 7 July 1588.

Elizabeth married her third and last husband, Richard Rainsford, in 1590 or early 1591. Richard was also a staunch Catholic. He had a home in Southwark, which is where they may have lived after their marriage until 1595 when, in order to be able to practise their religion without hindrance, they went to live in Antwerp. Elizabeth had brought into the marriage a 'statute staple', a bond of £2,000 (equivalent to around £295,000 today) that had been raised from the sale of John Syminges' manors in Monmouthshire, but this was forfeited to the Crown when they 'wente beyond Seas and remayned there without licence'.[46] The bond was restored by James VI in May 1606 when, probably at the instigation her son, they returned to England. Back home, and living in the parish of St Bartholomew the Great, Richard found himself in trouble again in 1611 when he refused to take the Oath of Allegiance and was committed to Newgate prison until February 1613.[47] We do not know the date of Richard's death but Elizabeth survived him and lived on into her nineties. She spent the last few years of her life living with her son John who, as we will see below, had become Dean of St Paul's Cathedral. In spite of this she never gave up her Catholic faith. She died at the beginning of 1631 and was buried on 28 January 1631 in the parish church at Barking.

John and Elizabeth Donne had six children – Elizabeth, Anne, John, Henry, Mary and Catherine – born most probably in that order. We do not know the actual date of birth of any of the daughters but three of them died early – Elizabeth in 1577 when she would have been approaching her teens, Mary and Katherine, both young children, in November 1581. Anne, born probably in 1565 or 1566, married her first husband, Avery Copley, in 1585. When he died in 1591 leaving her with a young child to support he had squandered her marriage portion of £500 (approx. £73,800 today) and a loan of £600 from her mother and was heavily in debt. Anne's second husband, William Lyly, died of the plague in 1603 while on a visit to London to seek employment under James VI. We know nothing else about Anne except that she probably died in 1616.[48]

John and Elizabeth Donne's eldest son, John was born in the first half of 1572. He and his younger brother Henry, born 1574, were educated by tutors at home before being sent to Hart Hall at Oxford University, a favourite College for Catholics as it did not have a chapel of its own, making it more difficult for their non-attendance at Protestant divine service on Sundays to be detected. John and Henry both matriculated on 23 October 1584 at the ages of eleven and ten respectively, but they did not go on to take degrees as this would have required them to take the Oath of Allegiance. John and Henry both went to Thravies Inn, an Inn of Chancery, to start their higher studies. Unfortunately, while they were there, a Catholic priest, John Harrington, was discovered in Henry's chambers and he was sent to the Clink and then to Newgate Prison where, soon after his admission, he died of the plague. Fr Harrington was hanged, drawn and quartered on 18 February 1594.

John continued his studies and was admitted to Lincoln's Inn on 6 May 1592.[49] The Inns of Court acted rather like finishing schools where the curriculum included the study of sacred and secular literature as well as singing, dancing, and games. While there John gained the reputation as a bit of a playboy – 'a great visiter of Ladies, a great Frequenter of Playes ... and a great writer of conceited verses'.[50] We do not know whether John initially intended to complete the full seven-year course of study, but he was never called to the Bar.

John was deeply affected by the death of his brother and it brought to a head a range of issues that had been troubling him – his Catholicism, his loyalty to the Crown and, last but not least, his future career. He wrote a number of satires around this time in which he expressed some of the skepticism he felt about society in general and about the types of people he came across – fat-cat lawyers, and religious hypocrites of various religious persuasions. In order to face up to these issues he devoted a good deal of time over the next few years to the study of both Catholic and Protestant theology a course of study which, sometime before the end of the 1590s, led to his rejection of the Catholic faith of his ancestors and the embracing of the Church of England.

It is not my place here to tell the fascinating story of the rest of John's life – that can be read elsewhere.[51] Suffice it to say that John came into contact with many of the most influential men and women of his day. His experiences at sea, on land, in England and in Europe, influenced much of the poetry for which he became famous. After many attempts to gain employment at Court he was eventually told by his friends, and by the King (James I), that he could not expect any preferment unless he took Holy Orders. After much resistance he finally agreed, and he was ordained by the Bishop of London in the chapel of his Palace next to St Paul's on 23 January 1615. After this, the preferment he had been promised began to materialize. He was appointed Chaplain-in-Ordinary to the King, and granted various benefices as well as the Degree of Doctor of Divinity. In 1616 he preached the first of many sermons at Court and, after his appointment as Divinity Reader at Lincoln's Inn, was required to preach there every Sunday afternoon. All this led, ultimately, to his appointment, by royal command, to the position of Dean of St Paul's Cathedral on 22 November 1620, a post which he held until his death on 31 March 1631.

In 1598 John had been employed as a private secretary in the home of Sir Thomas Egerton and, while there he met and fell in love with Anne, the daughter of Sir George Moore of Loseley. They married secretly on 5 December 1501; when Sir George found out he had John thrown into the Marshalsea Prison for a while on the grounds that the marriage was against both Canon and Common Law, and retracted his promise of a dowry of £800 for Anne. Writing to tell Anne of his predicament John used the now famous phrase 'John Donne – Anne Donne – undone'. Although the marriage was declared to be valid in April 1602 after John appealed to the Court of Audience at Canterbury, Sir George did not relent until 1608 when he finally paid Anne her dowry, equivalent today to around £82,000.[52]

John and Anne had twelve children between the years 1602 and 1617. Two of the children were stillborn, one of which was their last daughter. Anne died five days after her birth and they were buried together on 16 August 1617. John was devastated by Anne's death and he wrote the moving sonnet which begins 'Since she whom I lov'd hath paid her last debt'. The names of their children are listed in the Genealogical Summary at the end of this chapter. John was survived by six of his children. His eldest son John was responsible to gathering all his father's works together and for arranging their printing.

Genealogical Summary

John More to John Donne

John More (c.1453–1530) m. Agnes Graunger (1st wife)
Children:
1. Joan (1475–1542): m. Richard Staverton (d.1538)
2. Thomas (1478–1525): m. (1) Jane Colt (2) Alice Middleton
3. Agatha (b.1479): ? died an infant.
4. John (1480–c.1512): unmarried.
5. Edward (1481): ? died in infancy.
6. Elizabeth (1482–1536): m. (c.1500) John Rastell (1475–1536)
   Children:
   i. John: Born c.1506.
   ii. William (1508–1565): m. Winifred Clement (1527–1553)
   iii. Joan (1504–c.1564): m. (1523) John Heywood (1497–1578)
      Children:
      i. Ellis (1530–1578): became a Jesuit
      ii. Jasper (1535–1598): became a Jesuit
      iii. Joan: m. Christopher Stubbs
      iv. Elizabeth: m. ... Marvin
      v. Elizabeth (1540–1631): m. (1) John Donne, an ironmonger (d.1576)
         Children:
         1. Elizabeth (?d.1577)
         2. Anne (1565/6–1616): m. (1) Avery Copley (d.1591) m. (2) Wm. Lyly (c.1550–1603)
         3. Mary (d. Nov. 1581)
         4. Katherine (d. Nov.1581)
         5. Henry (1574–1593)
         6. John (1572–1631): the poet. Dean of St Paul's
            m. Anne More (1584–1617)
            Children:
            1. Constance (b.1603): m. (1) 1623, Edward Alleyn (1566–1626), probably the most famous actor of his time. Edward's 2nd wife. No children. m. (2) 1630, Samuel Harvey. Three children by 1634.
            2. John (1604–1662): m. Mary Staples. No children.
            3. George (b.1605): Names of wife and their daughter not known. George died on his way to Virginia in 1639.

4. Francis (1607–1614)
5. Lucy (1608–1627): unmarried
6. Bridget (b.1609): m. (1633) Thomas Gardiner Esq., of Peckham (son of Sir Thomas Gardiner of Camberwell). Three or four children. Thomas died in 1641.
7. Mary (1611–1614)
8. Stillborn child: buried 1612
9. Nicholas (b.1613): died before 1617
10. Margaret (1615–1679): m. 1633, Sir William Bowles (d.1681) of Clerkenwell. Three sons and five daughters.
11. Elizabeth (b.1616): m. 1637, Dr Cornelius Laurence
12. Stillborn daughter
    Anne Donne died five days after the birth.
    Mother and child buried together on 16 August 1617.

Chapter Two

Sir Thomas More and his Family

As we saw in the last chapter, Thomas More was born between two and three o'clock on the morning of 7 February 1478. The family home in Milk Street, Cheapside, was in the parish of St Lawrence Jury and this is most probably where he would have been baptized a few days later. Educated from the age of seven at St Anthony's School in Threadneedle Street – one of the best Latin Grammar Schools in London – he entered the household of John Morton, Archbishop of Canterbury and Chancellor of England, at the start of his teens. In the Archbishop's great house at Lambeth he continued his religious and social training until 1492 when Morton, newly appointed a cardinal, sent him on a scholarship to Canterbury College, Oxford.

At Oxford Thomas proved himself to be a brilliant student and he soon became the friend of many of the most notable men of letters of his day. Fearing that his son was getting too involved in the new Renaissance learning, and determined that he would follow in his own footsteps as a lawyer, his father ordered him back to London after only two years and sent him to study law, first at New Inn and then, from 12 February 1496, at Lincoln's Inn. Here he was called to the Outer Bar around 1501.

When Thomas chose Jane/Joan Colt to be his wife in the autumn of 1504 his rise to fame had already begun.[1] He had been a lecturer at Furnival's Inn for three years, had given a series of public lectures in the Church of St Lawrence Jewry and, in the Parliament of 1504, had been returned as a Member, probably for the constituency of Gatton in Surrey for which his father had sat in 1492.

Nether Hall, the home of the Colt family at Roydon in Essex was only about fifteen miles from the country home of the More family at North Mymms in Hertfordshire and it is quite likely that the families had known each other for some time. Writing about his father-in-law, William Roper says that Jane's father 'one Master Colt, a gentleman of Essex' had often invited Thomas to visit their home, hoping that he would 'set his affection' on one of his three daughters. When he did finally accept the invitation 'His mind most served him to the second daughter, for that he thought her the fairest and best favoured – yet when he considered that it would be both great grief and some shame also to the eldest to see her younger sister in marriage preferred before her, he then of a certain pity framed his fancy to her, and soon after married her.'[2] Whether this story is true or not no one knows, but it does follow a pattern of rather unkind 'put-downs' or stories which circulated within the family circle.

The English branch of the Colt family appears to have descended from the Colts of Gartsherrie in Scotland and to have moved down to Roydon in Essex via Carlisle in Cumberland (now Cumbria).[3] Jane's grandparents were Thomas Colt of Carlisle and Johanna, the daughter of John Tresbutt of Runcton Holme in Norfolk. Thomas had served as Administrator of the estates of Richard Duke of York, as Keeper of the Rolls of Chancery in Ireland, and as a Privy Councillor to Edward IV. Thomas bought the manor of Nether Hall – so called because of its low-lying position near the place where the rivers Lea and Stort converge. Thomas died on 22 August 1471 and he and his wife are buried in the parish church at Roydon. Thomas Colt's son and heir John – Jane's father – was still a minor when his father died and the king appointed Sir John Elrington as his guardian, but when he was twenty-one the king (then Henry VII) granted him his father's estates. During his life he acquired the manor of Downhall and other lands in Essex, as well as Grey's Hall (later called Colt Hall) at Cavendish in Suffolk.[4] Jane's mother (his first wife) was Elizabeth, the daughter of Sir John Elrington of Hackney, Middlesex, one-time Treasurer of the Household of Edward IV.[5] After Elizabeth's death John Colt married Mary, the daughter of Sir John DeLisle. John and both his wives are buried in the Colt chapel at St Peter's church in Roydon. Beneath his first wife there are four sons and eight daughters, and beneath his second wife there are three sons and three daughters. I have only been able to discover the names of two of Jane's full brothers – the eldest of her brothers, George (b.1491), and a younger brother Thomas – and five of her sisters – Alice, Mary, Bridget, Edyn and Elizabeth. As Jane died when she was only twenty-three she may not have known any more than these.

Jane Colt was only seventeen and Thomas More not quite twenty-seven when they married in January 1505. Based on a story told by Erasmus, Thomas's biographers have depicted Jane as an uneducated country girl who needed to be taught the proper decorum and manners that she would need as the wife of an up-and-coming city lawyer. They tell of Thomas instructing her 'in learning and all kinde of musicke' and making her repeat the main theme of sermons they had heard, so as to fashion her 'according to his owne minde'.[6] Bored by the repetition expected of her in her lessons and frustrated by the way she was being treated it is said that she would cry and, sometimes, throw herself down and bang her head on the floor – behaviour that caused Thomas to take her to her father for a good talking to. Fortunately he did not take his father-in-law's advice that he should beat her!

After their marriage the couple moved into a large house that Thomas leased from the Order of Hospitallers at St Thomas of Acon in Cheapside. He had been made a freeman of the Mercers Company in March 1509 and they had their headquarters on a plot of land adjoining the Hospitaller's church. On the south side of Bucklersbury opposite the Church of St Stephen Walbrook,[7] and known as the 'Old Barge', the house was one of a number that stood in gardens that had, before it was covered over, extended along the banks of the Walbrook, a small river that flowed through the area into the Thames. Nothing now remains of the house, but when Thomas moved to his Great House at Chelsea he transferred the lease to John and Margaret Clement. As we will see, they fled to Flanders in 1549 but, before they went, they made an inventory of the contents in the various rooms and from this we can get a good idea of what the house was like.[8] The house is described as 'a gret mansion' and the inventory shows that it had a great hall with a gallery around it, and that adjoining the gallery there was a 'Chamber' (bedroom) and a 'Maydes Chamber'. There was another, larger chamber, the 'Gret Chamber', that gave access to a further 'Lytle Chamber'. Downstairs there was a 'Gret Studye' as well as a 'Closet beside the gret studye', a 'Somer Parlor', and a 'Chapell'. The domestic quarters included a 'Kytchen', a larder, and a cellar, as well as a stable with a chamber next to it. The gardens must have been quite sizeable as 'Three fair herberes' (herb gardens) and 'a gret cage for birds' are mentioned. The gardens probably included the area where a Temple of Mithras was uncovered during building work in 1954.

In the autumn of 1505, probably in October, Jane gave birth to their first child, Margaret, known affectionately within the family as Meg; Elizabeth followed in 1506, Cecily, known as Cecy, in 1507 and John, their only son, known in the family as Jack, in 1509. The exact dates of their births or baptisms are not known as any records relating to them have either been lost or destroyed. However, we do know that two of them were baptized by Fr John Bouge, a Carthusian monk, who was vicar of St Stephen Walbrook. The children were not to know their mother for long as she died in 1511, most probably giving birth to a child that also did not survive the trauma. Jane was buried at St Stephen Walbrook, the funeral service being conducted by Fr Bouge.[9] Her body was later moved to Chelsea Old Church after the family chapel had been built onto it. In the epitaph Thomas later wrote for his tomb he touchingly refers to Jane as his 'dear little wife', who had been united to him in his youthful days and had given him a boy and three girls to call him father.

After Jane's death, Thomas's immediate need was to find someone to care for his young family. He was now a busy lawyer, a Reader at Lincoln's Inn, and one of the Under-Sheriffs of London. Much to the surprise of some of his friends he had, within a month, obtained a dispensation from Cuthbert Tunstall, Bishop of London, to marry again without the need to call the banns, and had asked Fr Bouge to perform the ceremony. The lady he chose was Alice Middleton, and they were married at St Stephen Walbrook in the autumn of 1511.

As with Jane, so also Alice has been 'put down' by many of Thomas's biographers. Nicholas Harpsfield, one of the earliest, called her 'aged, blunt and rude' and says that Thomas thought her vain because of the time she spent binding up her hair 'to make her a faire, large forehead' and using painful bracing 'to make her middle small'. For her part, Alice thought that Thomas had a tendency to personal untidiness that did not befit his position. Thomas is reputed to have referred to Alice as 'neither a pearl nor a girl' and, as with Jane, he is again said to have 'fashioned' her to his ways and to have had her instructed in how to play and sing at the lute and the virginals. Harpsfield also informs us that Thomas married Alice rather 'for the ruling and governing of his children, house and family, than for any bodily pleasure' and attributes his ability to cherish her 'no lesse lovingly and tenderly than if she had beene his first yonge wife' to his own piety and godliness.[10] However that may (or may not) have been the case, it is obvious from what we know of Alice that she was no pushover, and that she gave back as good as she got! Alice was certainly not an ignorant old maid. Born about 1475, she was only about three years older than Thomas who was thirty-three when they married. She had been a widow for two years, having previously been married to John Middleton, a wealthy citizen of London, a dealer in fine silks and textiles, and a Merchant of the Staple of Calais. Given their connection with the Mercer's Company and the City of London, and the fact that they owned property close to each other in Hertfordshire, it is likely that the two families were well acquainted and that Thomas and Alice knew each other long before they married. The Middletons hailed originally from Yorkshire where they owned Stockeld Park near Wetherby in North Yorkshire. Alice was, by birth, the daughter of Elizabeth Ardern and her second husband Sir Richard Harpur; Her grandparents were Sir Peter Ardern of Markhall in Essex and Katherine Bohun. Through the marriage of her cousin, Mary Bohun, Alice was related to Henry VIII.[11] Alice was an heiress in her own right and inherited property from both the Ardern and Middleton families.

After Thomas's marriage to Alice, her eleven-year-old daughter, also called Alice (Middleton), came to live at Bucklersbury for four years until her marriage in 1516 to Thomas Elrington, a cousin of Jane Colt, and wealthy landowner with properties in Kent, Middlesex, Yorkshire and Hertfordshire. Their main home, furnished by Sir Thomas, was at Hitchin in Hertfordshire and they had three children: Mary, born 1520, Thomas junior, born 1522, and John, born 1523.

Thomas More's love of his children is recognized by all his biographers, and from his letters we know that he expressed this love through physical contact – by sitting them on his knee, talking to them, and by hugging them and kissing them. However, mindful perhaps of the biblical advice that to spare the rod was to spoil the child, he also believed in strict discipline. In one of his letters to his children he refers to whipping them, but only occasionally – though, as if to say that this hurt him as much as it hurt them – he reminds them that he only used a peacock's tail so that 'sorry welts might not disfigure their tender seats'![12]

As soon as his children were old enough, Thomas made arrangements for them to be educated in the family home, and he carefully selected the tutors he engaged to educate them in the subjects he thought most important – divinity, Latin, Greek, mathematics, philosophy, logic, astronomy, geometry and music. Lady Alice also assisted with their education, as did Thomas himself when the opportunity presented itself. He obviously had a great love of nature and is said to have taught them the names of flowers and plants in the garden as well as the weeds that grew in the hedgerows around his estate, and the various medicinal and other uses to which they could be put. He also taught them how to care for animals, insisting that they would not be allowed to keep their pets – dogs, rabbits, foxes, ferrets, mice, weasels, and a monkey – unless they looked after them properly. He helped them to understand animal behaviour and, using the example of the behaviour of their monkey, the moral lessons that humans could learn from it! When he was away from home he expected the children to write daily letters to him in Latin, telling him about what they had been doing in their lessons, and his replies to these letters give us a glimpse of the emotional pressure he put them under to encourage them to learn – making it clear that this was a major way in which they could please him, and earn even more of his love.[13]

Some biographers say that, once established, the 'school' soon expanded to include Anne Cresacre, Margaret Giggs, Giles Heron, Joan and William Rastell and Frances Staverton (Thomas's nieces and nephew). However, in his letters Thomas only refers to the education of his own children and Margaret Giggs, and I have not seen any evidence that Thomas's sisters and their families either lived in the More family home or sent their children to be educated there. As we saw in the last chapter, the Rastells had their own home at Monken Hadley, and the only time I can think of when their children might have gone to stay with Thomas and his family was while their father was away from home during and after his ill-fated voyage of discovery. Giles Heron joined the family in 1523 when he was nineteen, and Anne Cresacre in 1524. Given the marriage dates of Thomas's children and the birth dates of their children, there must also be some doubt about the statement that eleven of Thomas's grandchildren were educated in the family school.[14]

By the time they were adults all of Thomas's daughters had earned a public reputation for their learning – a reputation that had much to do with the fact that he took every opportunity to tell people of importance how intelligent they were! From an early age, however, Margaret had shown herself to be the most intelligent. It was this that seems to have made her his favourite daughter and to have been the source of the particularly deep affection that he showed towards her.

Thomas's biographers have universally held up the classical and literary education he gave to his daughters as a shining example of enlightenment in an age when most women were, apart from their knowledge of domestic matters, thought capable only of idle chatter or the discussion of feminine trifles. It has to be said, however, that though he wanted educated daughters, he was no promoter of equality for women. His polemical writings, in particular, show that he remained firmly committed to the male-centered view of the mediaeval Catholic Church that women – images of Eve – were both inferior, and natural born temptresses.[15] While his daughter Margaret was expecting her first child he wrote to her:

> We pray most earnestly that all may go happily and successfully with you. May God and our Blessed Lady grant you happily and safely to increase your family by a little one like to his mother in everything except sex. Yet let it by all means be a girl, if only she will make up for the inferiority of her sex by her zeal to imitate her mother's virtue and learning.[16]

In addition to his stepdaughter Alice Middleton, Thomas also took a number of other young people into his home forming an extended family group. There seems little doubt that he saw those he accepted as possible future marriage partners for his own children.

The statement by some of Thomas's biographers that Anne Cresacre was one of the earliest additions to the family after his second marriage, and that she was about three years old at the time, cannot be true. Anne is not mentioned in any of Thomas's letters to the young members of his extended family, nor is she mentioned by Erasmus when describing the family in a letter he wrote in the autumn of 1521. More importantly, the case of Rokeby v. Constable recorded in the Yorkshire Star Chamber Proceedings for the year 1524 shows clearly that she was still living in Yorkshire at that time – when she was about fourteen years old.[17]

Margaret Giggs (or Gyggs) was, after Alice Middleton, the first to join the family. Almost nothing is known about her origins, but a pedigree of the Clement family (she married John Clement) refers to her as 'the daughter of a gentleman of Norfolk'. Thomas's biographers describe Margaret variously as an unofficial ward, as an adopted daughter, as a foster-sister for Margaret More, and also as the daughter of a relative. In my view, however, the most likely explanation that has been put forward is that the Giggs family rented the tenement attached to the Old Barge – a Thomas Gyggs is described in one document as having been a tenant there – and that while nursing her own infant, born in 1505 or 1506, Margaret Giggs's mother acted as wet-nurse to Margaret More, the two Margarets being brought up together.

After Margaret Giggs, the next to join the extended family was William Roper. The Roper family was of Norman origin, probably taking its name from Rupierre near Caen in Normandy, from where William de Rupierre had come to England with William the Conqueror. Settling first in Derbyshire where they were Lords of the manor of Turnditch (near Belper) and where they also held other estates, the family branched out into Norfolk and Kent in the east, and into Flintshire in Wales to the west. The *Visitations of Kent* trace the family back as far as Edwin Roper in the 1300s.[18]

William, born between 25 February and 15 May 1498, was the first son and heir of John Roper of Well Hall, Eltham, and of St Dunstan's, Canterbury, Kent. In addition to being Attorney to King Henry VIII. John was Sheriff of Kent in 1521 and sat on various commissions in that county. William's mother was Jane, the daughter of Sir John Fineux of Faversham and Herne in Kent, a Chief Justice of the King's Bench.[19] William had two younger brothers, Christopher and Edward, and six sisters. Christopher married Elizabeth Blore whose family came from Rainham in Kent. From them the Lords Teynham (Roper Curzon) and the Trevor-Roper lines are descended.

Having received his early education at one of the universities, probably Oxford, William was admitted to Lincoln's Inn on Christmas Day 1518, and it was around this time that he was 'adopted' into the More family. The Mores and Ropers had been associated through their law practices for years and the arrangement enabled William to pursue his studies away from home while continuing to experience family life and the watchful supervision that went with it. Although propriety was demanded at all times in the More household it was natural, given the circumstances, that William's thoughts would eventually turn towards marrying into the family. An amusing story tells us that when, early one morning, he plucked up courage to ask if he could marry one of his daughters, Thomas took him upstairs to a room where two of them were asleep in their 'truckle-bed'. At the bedside he pulled off the sheet thus exposing them lying on their backs 'with their smocks up as high as their armpits' When this woke them up they 'turned on their bellies' causing William to exclaim, 'I have seen both sides'. With that he made his choice, patting Margaret on the buttock and saying, 'Thou art mine'.[20] That, he later said, was all the wooing he did! Although attributed to William himself this story probably owes more to the customs of 'Utopia' whose citizens were recommended – in the presence of suitable chaperones – to see each other naked before they married. It may also owe something to the practice of inspecting future brides to make sure they had no supernumerary nipples, as these were believed to be the mark of a witch.[21]

Mindful perhaps of the New Testament saying that it is easier for a camel to pass through the eye of a needle than for a rich man to enter the Kingdom of Heaven, some biographers have tended to play down Thomas' wealth. There is, however, no doubt that the years from 1518 to 1530 were the most prosperous years for the More family. Financially, apart from any fees he earned from his public Court duties and his own legal work on behalf of various Merchant Companies of the City of London, Henry VIII had, in gratitude for services rendered, granted Thomas an annuity of £100 for life in 1518 (approx. £36,000 today). He also received a pension from the King of France. Then, in 1520, after accompanying the King to the Field of Cloth of Gold and negotiating over trade disputes on his behalf with the Hanseatic League in Bruges he was appointed Under-Treasurer of the Exchequer, and knighted, early in May 1521. In June 1524 he was appointed High Steward of Oxford University, in July 1525 Chancellor of the Duchy of Lancaster, and in September 1525 High Steward of Cambridge University. All these positions paid appropriate fees and additional allowances and incidental expenses. There were also other positions he held that offered small 'honoraria' – such as Steward of the Priory of St Mary, Clerkenwell, for which he received 53 shillings and 4 pence per year. During these years Sir Thomas's income also steadily increased from rents and leases. He was one of the co-owners of the manor of Mardites in Essex and later bought farms in Battersea and Chelsea. In May 1522 he was granted the manor of South, near Tunbridge Wells in Kent after it had been confiscated from the Duke of Buckingham, and in January 1525, following the death of Sir Thomas Lovell, he was granted the manors of Doglington and Fringford in Oxfordshire and Barley Park in Hertfordshire. Doglington, now called

Ducklington, is near Witney, about fifteen miles from Oxford, and Fringford is near Bicester; Barley is a few miles from Royston. These grants were followed in October 1526 by the grant of the manor of Dourehouse in the parish of Roydon in Essex. This manor was a freehold manor belonging to the Abbey of the Holy Cross at Waltham, whose Abbot had leased it to the Colt family in 1459. It later passed to Richard Redman, the Bishop of Ely, whose executors transferred the remainder of a ninety-nine-year lease on it to Sir Thomas.[22]

Further advancement in the service of the King followed in the second half of this decade. In 1526 he was appointed a member of the King's Chamber, being one of the Counsellors who was required to attend the King twice each day in his own private offices. Then, between March 1527 and July 1529 the King appointed him a member of a number of commissions negotiating peace between the various factions in Europe. Finally, in late October 1529, he was appointed Lord Chancellor. This brought Sir Thomas to the pinnacle of his power – and to the highest level of remuneration that went with it. Thomas also received gifts ' in kind', and an interesting entry in the Records of the City of London for 1529 reads 'The Lord Chancellor of England to have a tun of good wine of red and claret.' A 'tun' was equivalent to 252 gallons or 1,144 litres – a nice gift of 1,525 of our modern 75cl bottles of wine! This was no doubt the City's way of using the occasion to show its appreciation of the work he had done on its behalf. Another 'tun' was given to him at Christmas 1530. The City had also regularly rewarded his father in a similar way – but only with a 'hogshead', or large cask, of wine.[23]

While the 1520s were busy and financially rewarding years for Sir Thomas, they were also years of family celebrations and further family expansion. On 2 July 1521 by a licence issued by the Bishop of London, Margaret More described as 'of St. Stephen's Walbrook' married William Roper 'of St. Andrew's Holborn.'[24] She was sixteen and he seven years older. As part of the marriage settlement Thomas transferred some of the land he had recently bought in Chelsea to William. Harpsfield tells us that around the time of their marriage William, attracted by the teachings of Luther, became so zealous a Protestant that he was charged with heresy before Cardinal Wolsey. Fortunately for him, because of his father-in-law's friendship with Wolsey, he was let off with a friendly warning whereas some of his co-religionists, charged at the same time, had to make a public recantation at Paul's Cross.[25]

As tolerance of heretics was, as we know, not one of Thomas's strong points (he described Luther (in Latin) as an ape, an arse, a shit-devil, a drunkard, a lousy little friar, a piece of scurf, a pestilential buffoon and a dishonest liar!) life in the More household must have been, to say the least, very difficult for a while – until William 'turned again' to the Catholic faith, allegedly as a result of the prayers of his father-in-law.[26]

After their marriage William and Margaret continued to live at the Old Barge with the rest of the More family. Here Margaret could complete her education under the supervision of her father, and William could continue his legal work as Clerk of the Pleas or Protonotary of the Court of the King's Bench, a position he held jointly with his father.

The next person to join the growing family was Giles Heron. He arrived in 1523 after Thomas was granted his wardship following the death of his father, Sir John Heron of Hackney, Middlesex, on 15 June 1522.[27] Giles was born in 1504 and educated at Cambridge. He was the oldest of Sir John's five children by his second wife, Margaret, the daughter of Griffith Rees of Wales. Their other children were Edmund, Henry, Christopher, John (called 'the younger' in his mother's will) and Ursula. Margaret survived her husband by nine years. She died sometime between 27 September 1532 when she made her will, and 23 October 1532 when it was proved in the Prerogative Court of Canterbury.

The Heron family can be traced back to the border country of Northumberland in the time of King Henry III (1216–1272) who granted them arms. Giles's great-grandfather, Sir John Heron, was Sheriff of Northumberland in 1444, and had his seat at Chipchase Castle. His grandfather, William Heron (Sir John's youngest son), was based at Ford Castle.[28] Giles's father, Sir John Heron, had been a Privy Counsellor to Henry VII and held a number of positions under Henry VIII – Master of the Jewel House, Treasurer of the King's Chamber, Receiver General of the lands of minors (1509–1518), Collector of the Petty Customs in the Port of London, and one of the general surveyors of Crown Lands. Sir John's first wife was Elizabeth, the daughter of John Roper of Kent. They had three children, John, Margaret and Joan.

The last person to join the More family was fifteen-year-old Anne Cresacre. Anne's father, Edward Cresacre of Barnburgh in Yorkshire, had died in 1511 when she was only about six months old and, since then, she had been a Ward of Court. However, as we will see in the next chapter, her wardship was disputed and the matter was not finally settled until 1524, after which it was purchased by Sir Thomas.

With a growing family Thomas now needed to move to a larger house and in 1520 he began to buy land (including an arable farm with farmhouse) in Chelsea, a pleasant rural village with a population of not many more than a hundred adults and children. Then, in early in June 1523, he bought the lease of Crosby Place, a City merchant's palace in Bishopgate Street. This comprised Crosby Hall – a great hall with spacious rooms and galleries set out around courtyards and overlooking gardens – and a number of surrounding tenements.[29] Why he bought this property remains a mystery. He may have felt that he didn't yet have enough land in Chelsea to meet his needs and was anxious to get his family settled, or he may have changed his mind about having his own house built. Whatever the reason may have been, there is no evidence that he took up residence at Crosby Place and, in fact, before the end of January 1524 he had sold the lease at a profit to his friend Antonio Bonvisi, an Italian wool merchant. A few months later he bought another twenty-seven acres of land in Chelsea (as well as land in Kensington and on the other side of the Thames in Battersea) and, having negotiated a loan of £700 (approx. £256,000 today) from the King, work started on what became known as his 'Great House'. Whether this was started from scratch or arose out of modifications to, or enlargement of, an already existing building is not clear. It is not now possible to determine the exact size of the whole estate, but it is believed to have occupied an area bounded now by King's Road and Cheyne Walk to the north and south and by Milman's Street and Old Church Street to the west and east.

Before the Great House was finished a double marriage took place when, on 29 September 1525, Elizabeth More married William Daunce and Cecily More married Giles Heron. The marriage agreement between Sir John and Sir Thomas had only been drawn up on 16 September. The ceremony was carried out under licence from the Bishop of London and was conducted in the private chapel of the Elrington family at Willesden in Middlesex.[30]

William Daunce, born around 1500, was the eldest son of Sir John Daunce (1484–1545) and his first wife Lady Alice, the daughter of Thomas Latton of Berkshire. Sir John was a goldsmith, and a member of the Company of Goldsmiths in London. He was appointed a Teller of the Exchequer in 1505 and throughout the reign of Henry VIII worked to improve the coinage. He became Receiver General of wardship lands in 1509, Paymaster of War in 1514 and Chief Butler of England in 1515, and it seems certain that he had known Sir Thomas for some time, at least since his (Sir Thomas's) appointment as Under-Treasurer of the Exchequer in May 1521 at which time he held the position of Surveyor General to King Henry VIII. Sir John had a house in Mark Lane, London, but the family came from Thame, in Oxfordshire, and also held lands in Buckinghamshire. Lady Alice Daunce died in 1527 and was buried in the parish church of Blewbury (then in Berkshire but now in Oxfordshire), where a brass was placed depicting her with Sir John and their five sons and two daughters. Sir John married a second time to Elizabeth Peche, the widow of Sir John Skeffington of London who had died in 1525. No children are recorded of this marriage, but Sir John had an illegitimate son, Edward, by a lady called Agnes Maryott. Edward was still a minor when Sir John died on 7 December 1545.[31]

Early in 1526 Sir Thomas's adopted daughter, Margaret Giggs, married John Clement who had been one of the family's tutors for three or four years before being appointed a reader in Greek at Cardinal Wolsey's new college at Oxford. In 1520 he went to study medicine at Padua and qualified as a Doctor of Medicine at Siena in 1525. On his return to England he was granted the title of 'Sewer of the Chamber' in the Royal Household' and shortly after became one of the Court physicians. He was admitted to the Royal College of Physicians in 1528, and was a member of its Council for many years. He was President of the College in 1544. Margaret had herself become a Greek scholar and is said to have helped her husband when translating difficult Greek idioms. She was also well read in the science of medicine.[32]

The Great House, a two-storey mansion built in what we now call Tudor redbrick, was completed early in 1526 and the family were able to move in. As we saw earlier, the lease of the Old Barge was transferred to the Clements. The Great House faced South across the river Thames on the banks of which it had its own private landing stage.[33] From here, rowed in his great barge by liveried watermen, Thomas could commute the two and a half miles it took to get to the Palace at Westminster and to the City. Surrounded by gardens and orchards and approached via two large gated courts, the house had a frontage of around 50m. There was a Great Hall 22m long in the west wing, and a 'Long Gallery' facing north and extending 26m across more than half of the back of the first floor.[34] Ellis Heywood, one of Sir Thomas's cousins (see chapter one) described it in spring as a place of marvellous beauty with gardens full of flowers and blossoming fruit trees, with green meadows and wooded hills on every side. He tells how, after dinner, Thomas would take his guests 'about two stones throws' into the garden where, walking across a lawn and up a green hillock, they would pause to look round them to see from one side almost all of the City of London, and from the other the Thames, surrounded with green fields and wooded hills.[35]

Such a large house provided ample accommodation for family, guests and both residential and day staff. A census carried out in 1528 after an epidemic of plague and a disastrous harvest recorded that there were 100 people in the house on a daily basis. One of Thomas's biographers estimates that in addition to the adult family members, the grandchildren, John Harris (Thomas's personal secretary), Dorothy Colly (Margaret More's personal maid), and around a dozen other chamber servants who attended to the family's personal needs, there were some fifty domestic staff in the kitchens, laundry, stables and gardens as well as eight waterman who maintained and rowed the barge.[36]

In spite of its size Sir Thomas seems to have found the Great House a busy and noisy place to live, and it wasn't long before he had what he called the 'New Building' erected nearby to the east of the main building from which it was approached via a raised (and probably covered) terrace. This building comprised a chapel (though there was a chapel in the Great House), a library, a gallery, and probably a bedchamber. Here Thomas could find peace and quiet when he wanted to study or write.

Shortly after their move to the Great House in 1526, Hans Holbein the Younger – introduced to Sir Thomas by his friend Erasmus – came to make the first pen and ink sketch for his famous group portrait of the More family. This sketch is now preserved in the Kuntsmuseum in Basel. We know that Holbein modified his sketch, altering some of the figures and the background before starting on the final work. These alterations were most probably made at the request of Sir Thomas and Lady Alice who, as the artist's patrons, must have been able to have a say in how their family was to be presented. For his medium Holbein chose water-based distemper on cloth, and the picture was painted in one of the rooms of the Great House before being hung in the Long Gallery. The whole work must have been completed by or before August 1528 when Holbein returned to Basel.

Unfortunately, Holbein's original painting has not survived. Some time after Sir Thomas's execution and the subsequent sequestration of his properties it was removed from the house and, after passing through a number of hands – including, as we will see, some other members of the More family – it found its way onto the Continent in the 1600s where, in 1673, it came to its final resting place at the summer palace of the Bishop of Olmütz. There it was destroyed during a fire in 1752.[37] Fortunately for us a number of copies were made of the Holbein painting before it was destroyed. Some of these have been adversely affected by over-painting and other restoration work, but the one on display in the Lower Hall at Nostell Priory near Wakefield in Yorkshire is said to be the oldest, most like the original, and the best.[38]

The completion of Holbein's great picture was followed in November 1528 by the completion of the family chapel in the parish church at Chelsea. In their own different ways both events must have been a source of great pride to the family – a pride further increased when Sir Thomas received the Great Seal of England and took the Oath as Lord Chancellor on 25–26 October 1529.

The happy family events of the 1520s were brought to a fitting end with the marriage of John More and Anne Cresacre in December 1529. The exact date and place of the wedding has not come down to us. John (known to family historians as John II) and Anne, and their family, will be the subject of the next chapter.

The last years of Thomas's life are well documented by his various biographers and it is not my intention to give more than a brief overview here. Suffice it to say that during the opening years of the 1530s he managed to remain in the Royal favour by not getting too involved in the King's attempts to establish his supremacy over the Church in England and in the associated 'great matter' of the annulment of his marriage to Catherine of Aragon to clear the way for his marriage to Anne Boleyn. He was, however, a prominent public figure and the King was not to let him 'sit on the fence' for long. On 15 May 1532 the clergy accepted Henry as Supreme Head of the Church in England – 'so far as the Law of God allows' – and, under increasing pressure to declare himself in favour of the King's actions – and in conscience unable to do so – he offered his resignation as Lord Chancellor on the following day, giving ill-health as the reason. He had, in fact, suffered from 'chest problems' since around the time of his father's death in November 1530 and no doubt his overall health was adversely affected by increasing stress. Now, with time on his hands, he devoted himself to writing on matters close to his heart – the defence of the teaching of the Catholic Church and the 'confutation' of heretics. The resulting works were published by his nephew William Rastell at his printing press in St Bride's churchyard.

Just as some of Thomas's biographers have tended to minimize his riches, so they have also tended to maximize the poverty to which the family was reduced after his resignation as Chancellor. William Roper, writing some twenty-five years after the event, tells us that the resultant loss of income necessitated a reduction in the number of servants at the Great House and that his father-in-law gave his boat and boatmen to Sir Thomas Audley, his successor as Chancellor, and made arrangements for some other servants to be well-placed with various noblemen and bishops. He also tells us of a family meeting in which Thomas warned them all that they were going to have to tighten their belts and, maybe, even contribute something towards the household expenses.[39] The news was apparently received with shocked silence or silent disbelief but, either way, it didn't seem to elicit any offers of assistance! In the light of this, Harpsfield's story that Thomas 'was inforced and compelled, for lacke of other fuell, every night before he went to bedd, to cause a great burden of ferne to be brought into his owne chamber, and with the blase thereof to warme himself, his wife and his children, and so without any other fyres to goe to their beddes' would, to say the least, appear to have been a bit of an exaggeration.[40]

After his resignation Thomas knew that he would not be allowed to enjoy peace and quiet for long and, as if to be prepared for the worst, he composed the epitaph that he wished to be placed on his tomb. He also knew that when action was taken against him the consequences for his family could be severe and he sought to minimize their involvement by physically distancing himself from them. According to Stapleton, 'He settled his children, all now married and blessed with children of their own, in various places, keeping only Margaret and her husband with him in the same village of Chelsea, though no longer under the same roof.'[41] This statement seems to imply that all of the children had continued to live in the family home even after they were married, and that they stayed there right up to this time. If, as tradition has it, this is true, then it would have been very much contrary to the common practice. Thomas's stepdaughter Alice left home when she married Thomas Elrington, and Giles Heron and John More the younger (through Anne Cresacre), had both inherited family estates.[42] For his part, William Daunce had by this time been granted estates in his own right. There is therefore no reason why the children, after their marriages, should not have gone to live with their husbands in their own homes – even if, for business or other reasons, they continued to spend a good deal of their time at the Great House. In the case of the Ropers, however, there is, as we have seen, ample evidence that they continued to live for most of the time at the Great House. Perhaps foreseeing, or expecting, that Margaret would want to remain near to him and Lady Alice in the difficult times ahead he placed her and William in a house nearby, probably in the original farmhouse that he had bought with the land on which he had built the Great House.[43]

While Thomas was in retirement events at Court began to overtake him. The King took matters into his own hands and secretly married Anne Boleyn on or around 25 January 1533.[44] On 23 May 1533 Archbishop Cranmer officially declared Henry's marriage to Catherine invalid and, five days later, declared his marriage to Anne Boleyn valid. Already six months pregnant, she was crowned Queen in Westminster Abbey on 1 June 1533. Pope Clement VII's belated declaration in March 1534 that Henry's marriage to Catherine could not be annulled and that therefore his marriage to Ann was invalid was by that time an irrelevance.

On 23 March 1534 the Act of Succession received its third reading in parliament. It included a provision that would make all adults liable to have to swear an oath to the effect that the King's union with Catherine of Aragon had not been a lawful marriage, that his union with Anne Boleyn was a true marriage, and that their offspring would be legitimate heirs to the throne regardless of the objections of any foreign authority, prince or potentate. Thomas knew well that he would soon be called to take the Oath and that, if he refused, any action taken against him would include imprisonment and the sequestration of his properties. So, on the following day (25 March 1534), in a further attempt to protect his family's interests, he drew up a deed conveying his Chelsea property to twelve 'feoffees' (trustees), including his son John More, John Clement, Richard Heywood and William Rastell. Two days later he drew up another deed conveying a separate part of the property to his daughter Margaret and her husband. Roper tells us a bit more about this:

Then made he a conveyance for the disposition of his lands, reserving for himself an estate thereof only for the term of his life, and after his decease assuring some part of the same to his wife, some to his son's wife for a consideration that she was an inheritrix in possession of more that an hundred pounds land by the year, and some to me and my wife in recompense of our marriage money with divers remainders over ...[45]

Events now moved swiftly. The first Act of Succession was passed on 30 March 1534, and on 13 April Thomas was called to appear before the Royal Commissioners at Lambeth to take the Oath. He declared himself willing to accept the royal succession, but not the validity of the King's marriage; he gave no reason and would not condemn anyone who was prepared to take the Oath. After twice refusing to swear the Oath he was committed to the custody of the Abbot of Westminster, one of the commissioners before whom he had appeared. While in the Abbot's custody Archbishop Cranmer and Thomas Cromwell suggested offering him a way out by proposing that he be allowed to swear to a form of oath that he felt comfortable with, but the contents of which would be kept secret. The King, however, would have none of it and, after again refusing the Oath, he was committed to the Tower on 17 April 1534.

While certainly not a home from home, life in the Tower was not, at first, too uncomfortable. The Lieutenant of the Tower was his friend Sir Edmund Walsingham who allocated him a special 'chamber' for his accommodation. Lady Alice was able to visit him and he was allowed to have his personal servant John à Wood to wait on him. He was free to write and send and receive mail, though this would have been carefully scrutinized. His chamber door was not locked during the day, and he was able to attend Mass every morning and to walk in the gardens. Unlike today, Lady Alice had to pay for his board and lodging while he was in the Tower – fifteen shillings a week for Thomas and five shillings for his servant (a total of approx. £320 per week today).[46] As we have seen Lady Alice was a rich woman in her own right, and the story that she had to sell off some of her gowns to help pay for this must surely be an invention.

In November 1534 the Act of Supremacy was passed by parliament. This officially added 'Supreme Head of the Church of England' to the King's titles, and it became treason to maliciously deny him any of his royal titles. The Act did not contain the previous get-out clause 'so far as the law of Christ allows'. For a while

Thomas was left alone to contemplate his fate, perhaps in the hope that he would change his mind. During this period his health began to deteriorate rapidly and Lady Alice, Margaret Roper and Lady Alice Allington – all of whom had asked him to swear the Oath – petitioned the King for his pardon and release, but to no avail.

In February 1535 an Act of Treasons came into effect, and a special Act of Attainder was passed against Thomas. This latter Act declared him guilty of 'misprision of treason' for refusing to take the Oath. The lands he had been granted in Oxfordshire and Kent began to be withdrawn and assigned to others. A Private Act of the King annulled the Deed of Feoffment he had made the previous March regarding his Chelsea property on the (dubious) grounds that it had been made fraudently.

From 30 April until the middle of June 1535 Thomas was subjected to a number of interrogations by members of the Council and by Richard Rich the Solicitor General. During this period he was kept in close confinement in the Tower and, deprived of his books, he is said to have withdrawn into darkness, ordering the windows of his cell to be covered up.[47]

Thomas was formally indicted and his trial begun, and ended, before eighteen judges at Westminster Hall on 1 July 1535. On the way back to the Tower his daughter Margaret, his son John, and Margaret Clement (née Giggs), pushed themselves through the crowd, kissed him and said goodbye to him.[48]

Early in the morning of 6 July his friend Sir Thomas Pope brought him the news that he was to die before nine o'clock that morning. The 'good' news was that the King had commuted his sentence from one of hanging, drawing and quartering to one of execution by beheading. Margaret Giggs was the only member of the family to witness the sentence carried out. After his execution his headless body was returned to the Tower where it was buried in the chapel of St Peter ad Vincula (St Peter in Chains). Lady Alice, Margaret Roper, her maid Dorothy Colly, and Margaret Clement were present. Thomas's head, after being partly boiled was placed on a pole over Tower Bridge where it remained for about a month until retrieved by Margaret Roper.[49]

Little or nothing now remains of the original monument to Sir Thomas in Chelsea church. It suffered badly from the effects of time and, about 1644, Sir John Lawrence of Chelsea is said to have erected a new inscription in marble. The whole monument was again remade in 1833.[50] The church was badly damaged during a

German air raid on London on the night of 16–17 April 1941 and the inscription was broken. After the war the church was rebuilt on its original foundations.

The Aftermath

A delay in the ratification of the Act of Attainder that provided for the sequestration of Thomas's personal properties meant that it did not come into force until 1536, and Lady Alice was therefore able to continue to live in the Great House. As we have seen she was an heiress in her own right, but before the Act came into force she raised some ready capital by selling a farm and some farm stock belonging to the manor of Sutton Court which had been bought by Sir Thomas. From 1536 Sir William Paulet, Comptroller of the King's Household, and later the first Marquis of Winchester, was given custody of the lands formerly belonging to Thomas but he does not seem to have taken up residence at the Great House until later. The King appears to have dealt quite leniently with Lady Alice, perhaps because she was related to him. In 1537 he granted her an annuity of £20 (approx. £7,000 today), and allowed her to continue to receive the benefit of lands in Hertfordshire that she jointly owned with the other Lady Alice, the widow of Sir John More. She was also allowed to keep the farmland in Battersea that had been granted to Sir Thomas by the Abbot of Westminster in 1529. For some reason William Roper – not apparently the most sensitive of men – tried to obtain the lease of the latter for himself, but Lady Alice fought him through the Courts and he wasn't able to get hold of it until around 1543 when Lady Alice may have transferred the lease to him. It is quite possible that Lady Alice did not have to leave the Great House until around 1544 when she was given the lease to another property in the village of Chelsea – probably the rectory that had formerly belonged to Sir Thomas. Lady Alice died in 1551.[51]

The deed by which Thomas had conveyed some of his land and the farmhouse at Chelsea to the Ropers was not called into question and they are believed to have continued to live there for some time. The property was still in the possession of their descendants in the early 1600s.

Nothing remains of the original 'Great House'. Sir William Paulet conveyed the estate to his son, the second Marquis, and it then passed then through various hands, including those of the

Cecil family who, in 1595, had plans drawn up for alterations and extensions to the house. In 1599 it passed from Sir Robert Cecil to Henry the second Earl of Lincoln whose son-in-law, Sir Arthur Gorges, inherited it in 1615. He built Gorges House in the grounds. Sometime around 1620 Lionel Cranfield the Earl of Middlesex bought the estate. He pulled down the north wing and made other modifications to the house before having to surrender it to Charles I after he incurred the royal displeasure. The King granted it to the first Duke of Buckingham in 1627 but the Parliamentary Commissioners occupied it during the period of the Commonwealth, before it was returned to the second Duke of Buckingham who had to dispose of it to pay off his debts. In 1674 the trustees of the Earl of Bristol held the house until his wife sold it to Henry, Marquess of Worcester in 1682. After becoming Duke of Beaufort he renamed the house 'Beaufort House', and it remained in the possession of his family until 1720. The house seems to have been unoccupied after this and, having become derelict, it was finally pulled down after Hans Sloane had purchased it 1737.[52]

The Ropers and their Descendants

As we have seen, Margaret More and William Roper were married on 2 July 1521. Their first child, probably Elizabeth, was born in 1523. Two sons and three daughters followed in due course. All of the children married into Catholic families and all remained loyal to their Catholic faith in spite of the financial penalties incurred as a result of the penal laws.

When William's father died in 1524 the Roper family could not agree over the provisions he had made in his will. The disagreement was so strong that the matter eventually had to go before Parliament which settled it finally in 1529. The end result was that William inherited the family's main estate at Well Hall in Eltham, Kent (now the Royal Borough of Greenwich, SE9) and the estate at St Dunstan's in Canterbury. The rest of the estate went to his brothers Christopher and Edward.[53]

The estate at Well Hall in Eltham had its own moated mansion, but it was eight miles from London and it seems that William and Margaret continued to spend most of their time at the Great House in Chelsea especially as, after his father's death, William held alone the position of Protonotary, or Clerk of the Pleas of the King's Bench.[54]

Even before his father-in-law's execution William had completed his legal studies. Entries in the *Black Books* of Lincoln's Inn note that he was called to the Bar at the next 'Moot' after Ascension Day in 1525.[55] He was a member for Bamber in the Parliament which began in 1529 and which eventually passed the Acts to which his father-in-law could not assent. However, he appears in Cromwell's lists as one of the members who were opposed to some of the measures put before the House.

Margaret was briefly imprisoned in the Tower, but she and William both took the Oath and so avoided the further wrath of the King. In spite of this, both maintained their allegiance to the Catholic Church. William continued his legal work from chambers in Lincoln's Inn and held on to his post as Protonotary of the King's Bench. An entry in the *Black Books* for 24 June 1534 notes: 'he shall be an Assistant of the Bench, and may have a clerk at the yeoman's commons for 14d a week, and a bower to his chamber when in commons as Outer Barristers have.' An entry for Hilary Term 1535 records his calling to the Bench. It was no doubt due to his legal standing that he was appointed to sit on various Commissions for the Peace in both his home county of Kent and in Middlesex.[56]

William was well known for his generosity towards fellow Catholics who were suffering for their faith and in 1543 he was briefly imprisoned in the Tower and fined £100 (approx. £29,000 today) 'for relieving by his almes a notable learned man, Master Beckenshawe'. It seems that Beckenshawe was involved in the 'Plot of the Prebendaries' to have Archbishop Cranmer charged with heresy.[57] This brief brush with the authorities does not seem to have harmed his career.

Margaret Roper died on Christmas Day, 25 December 1544. I have not been able to discover whether she and William ever moved to live permanently at Well Hall, though there is a local tradition that they did, and that Margaret carefully tended the gardens that she had set out there. It is also known that Holbein's painting of the family was moved to Well Hall.

William Roper was deeply affected by his wife's death and never remarried. Exactly where he lived, and who helped him to look after his young children after Margaret's death, we do not know. Some eighteen years later, in 1562 – when his children would have been grown up – he is described as 'of Lincoln's Inn'. That he actually lived there would appear to be confirmed by an entry in the *Black Books* which indicates that he ceased to reside there in 1574.[58]

William was elected as a member of parliament for Rochester in 1545, and again in 1547 for the first parliament of Edward VI. On the accession of Queen Mary in 1553 he was appointed a governor of Lincoln's Inn (a post he kept until the reign of Elizabeth I), and was Sheriff of Kent in 1553 and 1554. He represented Winchelsea in the parliament of 1553 and Rochester in the parliaments of 1554 and 1555.

It was around this time that William began to write his *Lyfe of Sir Thomas More, knighte*. Had it not been for the accession of Elizabeth I in 1558 there seems little doubt that this would have been printed in England but, in the event, it had to be circulated among family and friends in manuscript form and it was not printed until 1626, and then at Paris.

William was well known in Canterbury where, as we have seen, he had inherited St Dunstan's (outside the West gate of the City) from his father after his death in 1524. He also owned other property in Kent, including an estate at Chevening which he bought in 1540. In September 1555 he was admitted with William Rastell (his father-in-law's nephew) as a freeman of the City of Canterbury, a city he subsequently represented in the parliaments of October 1555 and January 1557–8.[59]

With the changing religious scene after the accession of Elizabeth I to the throne in 1558 William, almost immediately, came under suspicion. He had previously sat as a Justice of the Peace on the Bench for Canterbury and for Middlesex but, one after the other, he was removed from both of these offices. He did, however, continue his legal work and retain his position as Protonotary of the Queen's Bench. His sons were now lawyers in their own right and an entry in the *Black Books* of Lincoln's Inn for 1 July 1565 notes:

> William Rooper, a Bencher, obtained admission to his own Chamber for his sons, Thomas and Anthony, Fellows of this House, and afterwards for William Dawtrey, his daughter's son ...[60]

This is just another example of how close family ties remained.

William obviously trod a careful path, and he managed to avoid further trouble until 8 July 1568 when he was summoned before the Privy Council for having given financial assistance to 'certain persons' who had fled the country and who had printed books against the Queen's government. He submitted, and promised 'from henceforth to obey all the laws and ordinances set forth by Her Majesty's authority, in all matters of religion and orders ecclesiastical'. He also promised to appear before the Council again when summoned. It maybe that around this time William moved to live on his estate at Well Hall where he rebuilt the mansion.

When the Commissioners went down to Kent in 1569 to present the Oath to all justices and former justices William pleaded old age (he was seventy-two) and 'great infirmities and diseases' and asked that, with the Queen's permission, he might be allowed to follow his conscience. His plea succeeded and instead of having to sign a subscription to the Act of Uniformity he was bound over for the sum of 200 marks (approx. £21,700 today) to be of good behaviour to the Queen and her people. He made his will on 10 January 1577 and, in it, asked to be buried 'in the vault with the body of my dearly beloved wife (whose soul our lord pardon) where my father-in-law Sir Thomas More (whose soul Jesus bless) did mind to be buried'. In that year he also resigned as Protonotary of the Queen's Bench, a position he had held for fifty-four years. He died on 4 January 1578.[61]

As with the body of Sir Thomas, so there has been controversy about the place where Margaret and William were buried. Over the years it has been said that Margaret was buried at Chelsea (with her father's head in her arms), and that she is still there. It has also been claimed that her body was later removed to the vault in the Roper Chapel (the chapel of St Nicholas) in St Dunstan's, Canterbury. It has similarly been said that William was buried at Chelsea and then transferred to St Dunstan's. It is recorded, however, that there used to be a monumental inscription from 1578 (the year William died) in the church of St Dunstan's that, translated from the Latin read: 'Here lie ... William Roper and Margaret his wife.' When the Roper vault was opened (for the fourth time) in 1978 a proper archaeological survey was carried out during which the remains of a human skull were found in a leaden casket in a niche behind an iron grating in the north wall. This is believed to be the head of Sir Thomas that may well have been removed from Margaret's tomb and placed in the niche when Thomas Roper, grandson of Sir Thomas, enlarged the vault. On the evidence available it seem fair to say that the bodies of William and Margaret both now rest in St Dunstan's.[62]

William is known to have been a generous benefactor of St Dunstan's church, Canterbury where his great-grandfather had founded a chantry. Estimates of how much a year he gave away vary from £500 to £1,000 or more – considerable sums by today's standards. We know that he helped to support people like Beckinshawe, and others who fled to the Continent during the reign of Elizabeth, and maybe this included some of his own extended family. In 1569 he is recorded as having offered a freehold estate in Candlewick Street and number of tenements on Bermondsey Street to the Merchant Taylors Company on condition that they gave twenty shillings a year to buy bread and coal for the poor prisoners in Newgate, Ludgate, the King's Bench and the Marshalsea and, when they turned the offer down – apparently because they were in a very poor condition – he offered them, and an additional property in Candlewick Street, to the Worshipful Company of Parish Clerks. They, being much less well endowed, were happy to accept the gift.[63]

William and Margaret Roper had five children. We know from a letter of Erasmus to Margaret that their first child was born in 1523, and that may well have been Elizabeth. The other daughters were Margaret and Mary. A legal document indicates that Thomas was born in 1533, and this is confirmed by the monument erected in his memory by his eldest son. As elder son and heir, he inherited the family's main estates.[64] Anthony was born in 1544, the year of his mother's death. I will deal with the daughters first.

Elizabeth Roper was married twice, first to John Stephenson and then to Sir Edward Bray the younger, the son of Sir Edward Bray of Vachery Park in Surrey and his second wife Beatrix, the widow of Edward Elrington of London and Udimore, but by birth the daughter of Sir Ralph Shirley of Wiston, Sussex. Sir Edward Bray the younger had previously been married to Mary the daughter of Thomas and Alice Elrington, the granddaughter of Lady Alice More. Sir Edward and Elizabeth lived at Baynards Park, one of the Bray family mansions near Cranleigh in Surrey. Their son and heir, Reginald, was baptized on 1 May 1555. Sir Edward's life seems to be have been marred by mounting debts and by the selling of the family estates to pay them off. After the death of Elizabeth on 24 April 1560 he married twice more. He died on 7 or 8 May 1581 and was buried at Shere. He was succeeded by Reginald who married Elizabeth, the daughter of Richard Covert of Hascombe, Surrey.[65]

Margaret Roper, born around 1526, married William Dawtrey Esq. of Chichester in 1547. William was the first son of Sir John Dawtrey of More House at Petworth in Sussex, and his second wife Joan, the widow of Richard Ashby (or Assheby), but by birth the daughter of William Scardeville and his wife Anne. The Dawtrey name was an Anglicized form of de Hauterive, William de Hauterive having been granted lands in Sussex when he came to England with William the Conqueror. William's grandfather, Sir John Dawtrey, had been Comptroller of Customs at Southampton and had been involved with the building of the *Mary Rose*, the flagship of Henry VIII's fleet.

William Dawtrey was probably a merchant of the Staple of Calais. He and Margaret lived in Chichester, Sussex. He was described by the Bishop of Chichester, as a 'misliker of religion and godly proceedings' and as 'very superstitious' – which means he was a Catholic! He was a Justice of the Peace for Sussex from 1559 until 1565 when, because he refused to conform to the Church of England, he was deprived of the position. It was, however, restored to him in 1568 although, as a matter of conscience, he still refused to sign the Oath of Supremacy. He was a Member of Parliament for Sussex in 1563 and Sheriff of Surrey and Sussex during the years 1566-7. He was presented for not receiving Communion in his parish church in 1573, examined for 'Popery' in 1576, and reported for being long absent from Communion in 1580. Margaret died sometime around 1578, and on 27 November 1581 William then married Mary, the daughter of Edward Stoughton of Singleton in Sussex. William appears to have conformed to the Church of England after his second marriage and to have become a regular communicant at the parish church in Petworth. He made his will and died on 13 June 1591; his will was proved on 23 November.

William and Margaret had four sons: William, John, Charles and Anthony, and one daughter, Jane – the great-grandchildren of Sir Thomas More. Their eldest son, William II, born about 1547, was admitted to Lincoln's Inn during 1565. He became a Justice of the Peace in Sussex, a position he lost due to his persistent recusancy in 1587. He married Dorothy, the daughter and co-heir of Richard Stoneley of London, a Teller of the Exchequer. William II died before his father and so his son Henry – who became Sir Henry – inherited the family estates. The main Dawtrey line died out when William Dawtrey of More House, Petworth and Doddinghurst Hall, Essex – the last male heir – died without issue in 1758 leaving his estates to his nephew, Richard Luther Esq. of Myles's in Essex.[66]

Mary Roper, born sometime between 1527 and 1532, was married first to Stephen Clarke and then, after his death, to James

Bassett of Umberleigh, the third son of Sir John Bassett of Umberleigh in Devon by his second wife, Honor, the daughter of Sir Thomas Grenville of Stowe in Kirkhampton, Cornwall. James, born in 1523, had started his education at Reading Abbey in 1534 before being sent to Calvy College in Paris, in 1535. He was mistreated by his 'master' at the college and, in August 1536, being very unhappy, was taken away by his stepfather (his father having died, his mother had married Arthur Plantagenet, Viscount Lisle, Deputy of Calais, in 1529). He went briefly to a private tutor in St Omer before returning to Paris in December 1536. Said to have learned to dance, sing and write by August 1537, he was sent to the College of Navarre in Paris to complete his Latin studies. He complained about his treatment at this college as well and, although his stepfather didn't believe him, his mother is said to have worried about him, so he was allowed to leave and return to England in August 1538. Back home, no doubt through the influence of his parents, he took up the position of 'Gentleman of the Household' to Stephen Gardiner, Bishop of Winchester. Although Gardiner had supported Henry's declaration of supremacy he remained faithful to the old religion and, as a result, he was imprisoned in the Tower and deprived of his bishopric in 1550, during the reign of Edward VI. James, however, remained faithful to him after his imprisonment and helped him to conduct his defence at his trial in 1551. As a result, he came under suspicion himself and was briefly imprisoned in October 1551. On his release he felt it prudent to flee to Flanders. Like other More family relations he returned to England after the accession of Mary in 1553 when Gardiner, now restored to his bishopric and newly created Lord Chancellor, received him back into his service and helped him to be returned as Member of Parliament for Taunton and Downton both of which were episcopal boroughs. Later in 1553 he was appointed a gentleman of Queen Mary's Privy Chamber and, after her marriage to King Philip of Spain (son of the Emperor Charles V) in July 1554, he was also appointed a gentleman of the King's Privy Chamber. The Queen chose James to carry confidential dispatches to King Philip in Brussels informing him of the progress of her pregnancy – a pregnancy which didn't develop and which is now thought to have been a tumour. In gratitude, Philip awarded him a pension of 1300 crowns.[67]

The exact date of Mary Roper's marriage to James Bassett is not known, but as her first husband died during 1554 it was probably in 1555. King Philip gave them presents to mark the occasion. Mary had been employed as a lady-in-waiting to Princess Mary during the reign of Edward VI, a position she retained when Mary became queen. It seems certain therefore that it was at Court that the couple became acquainted.

Mary was well-educated and, while she was married to Stephen Clark, she translated the *Ecclesiastical History of Eusebius* from Greek into English. Later, as Mary Bassett, she also translated her grandfather Sir Thomas More's *Treatise on the Passion* from Latin into English, dedicating it to 'Lady Mary' the future queen. She is reputed to have contributed most of the money required for the publication by William Rastell of Sir Thomas More's works in 1557.[68]

James's loyal service to the Queen was rewarded with grants of land, beginning in May 1555 with the granting of the lease of some of the lands which had been confiscated from Sir Peter Carew when he fell out of favour through his opposition to the Queen's marriage to Philip. The manor house at Chelsea also came into his possession. A few months later he was granted the manor of Torrington in Devon. His increasing prosperity is shown by his ability to pay in the region of £1,000 (approx. £188,000 today) for further property in Devon in 1558, and by his election as Knight of the Shire for Devon in the last three Parliaments of Mary's reign.

Mary and James's marriage was, sadly, short-lived, and they had only two children: Philip and Charles. Philip was named after the king who gave him a present at his christening. Mary was pregnant with Charles when James made his will on 6 September 1558, appointing his father-in-law William Roper and his friend Ralph Cholmley (Recorder of London and fellow Member of Parliament) as his executors.[69] To his wife he left half his goods, his house in Chelsea, and a life interest in his other lands – property that would eventually pass to his elder son and heir Philip. To his unborn son Charles he left the lease of his house near the Savoy in London. He died two months later on 21 November, probably before the birth of his second son. He was buried at Blackfriars, Smithfield, on 26 November 1558. Mary did not marry again and devoted herself to raising their two children at their home in Chelsea. She died on 20 March 1572. In her will she appointed her father, William Roper, and his chaplain, as the executors of her will, charging them with the ordering of her two sons until they came of age.[70] Presumably because Philip had been sufficiently well provided for in his father's will she left all her lands, tenements and hereditaments in Sandwich, Kent – property that had probably formed part of her marriage settlement – and the right and title to her lands in Devonshire, to Charles. She left her son Philip a ring that had belonged to her grandfather Thomas More, the wedding ring that James had given her, and a ring given to her by King Philip. She stipulated that her legacies to her sons should become void if they became heretics.

Little is known about Philip Bassett. According to the *Visitation of Devon* in 1620 he married a lady with the surname 'Verney' and had two daughters. The lady in question may have been a daughter of Sir Edmund Verney (1535–1599) of Pendley Manor, Tring, in Hertfordshire, but who also owned property in Chelsea and was related to the Bray family into which Elizabeth Roper had married. Philip probably lived at the family home in Chelsea and, if so, it was there in 1581 that he was being carefully watched by the authorities who suspected him of harbouring Jesuits.[71] There is some indication that he spent time in prison and that he may have sought exile on the Continent.[72]

Charles Bassett became involved with the Jesuit mission to England and helped both Fr Campion and Fr Persons. In July 1581 he was seized in St Paul's churchyard and sent to the Marshalsea after falling into a trap that had been set by the authorities as part of a plan to catch Fr Persons. Fortunately he was able to obtain his release – though how is not known – and no doubt deeming it now too dangerous to remain in England, he fled to France from where Fr Persons sent him with a letter of recommendation to the English College in Rome. Charles became a student at the College on 8 October 1581 and, at around the same time, joined the Society of Jesus. Unfortunately his studies for the priesthood were disrupted by ill-health in April 1583. The college authorities thought he would make a better recovery in France and he was sent to the English College in Rheims in the company of George Gilbert who had also fled to France and become a student at the English College in Rome on the same day. They travelled via Rouen where they stayed with some nuns, before passing on to Douai where they arrived sometime around the second week in June 1583. It seems that Charles's health recovered during the next year, and he revisited Rouen in September and spent some time with Fr Persons in Paris in October 1584 before returning to Rheims where he died, seemingly unexpectedly, towards the end of November. During his short life he had given considerable sums of money to support the Jesuit Mission in England and later to support the work of the English College in Rome and the nuns in Rouen; when he died he left all his temporal goods to the college at Rheims.[73]

Coming now to William and Margaret Roper's sons: Anthony, their younger son, born 1544, followed his father into the legal profession and, as we have seen, came to share Chambers with him at Lincoln's Inn 1565. On his father's death he inherited the family estates in London (including the lease on Crosby Place), as well as lands in Middlesex and Oxfordshire. He married Anne Cotton, the daughter of Sir John Cotton of Landwade and his wife Isabel, the daughter of Sir William Spencer of Wormleighton and Althorpe – the thirteen times great-grandfather of the late Diana, Princess of Wales.

Anthony and Anne lived at Farningham in Kent and had two sons, Anthony (who became Sir Anthony Roper), John, and Henry, and two daughters, Isabel and Jane. Isabel married Sir Thomas Wiseman of Rivenhall, Essex (born 1570), by whom she had ten children. Isabel died in 1622. Jane would not appear to have married.

Anthony died in 1597 and an inscription on the wall of Farningham parish church reads:

> Here lieth the bodies of Anthony Rooper Esq younger sonne of Will'm Rooper of Eltham Esq. He lived 53 years and died 23 July AD 1597. And of Anne Rooper his wife, daughter of Sir John Cotton, Knight. By whom he had sonnes viz Anthony John Henry and two daughters viz Isabell married to Thomas Wiseman Esq and Jane.

Thomas Roper, Anthony's older brother, was born in 1533. He studied at Lincoln's Inn and was admitted to his father's Chambers at the same time as his younger brother. He sat as a member of North Shoreham, one of the Duke of Norfolk's boroughs, in the first parliament of Queen Mary's reign and for Newport juxta Launceston in the parliament of 1558. He succeeded to the position of Protonotary of the Queen's bench on his father's resignation in 1577 and inherited the family estates at Well Hall and Eltham on his father's death. In 1577 he was listed with his father and one of his brothers as one of the recusants at Lincoln's Inn and, in 1578, was ordered to conform or to lose his chambers. He chose not to conform.

Thomas married Lucy, the youngest daughter of Sir Anthony Browne of Battle Abbey (near Hastings) and Cowdray Park (near Eastbourne), in Sussex, and his wife Alice Gage, the daughter of Sir John Gage of Firle, Sussex, and his wife Philippa, the daughter of Sir Richard Guldeford. Sir Anthony Browne was Master of the Horse to Henry VIII. His son Anthony – Lucy's brother – was created first Viscount Montague at the coronation of Queen Mary. Later, in spite of their firm adherence to the Catholic faith, their opposition to both the Act and the Oath of Supremacy, and the fact that they maintained their own priests and gave refuge to missionary priests in their houses at Battle and Cowdray, the Browns managed to retain their position as trusted public servants throughout the reign of Queen Elizabeth who added further honours to Viscount Montague by knighting him in 1591 while she was on a visit to Cowdray Park.

In spite of their family connections, Thomas and Lucy did not fare quite so well. Their house at Eltham was searched by the authorities in 1581 and equipment for saying Mass was discovered. As a result Thomas was imprisoned in the Fleet prison for a month and only released after he gave assurances that he would attend the Anglican church in Orpington, Kent. This, of course, did not mean that he renounced his Catholic faith.

Thomas made provision for his children before he died in 1598 and did not make a will. The enquiry after his death showed that, in addition to his manor at Eltham and a house in Canterbury, he also held a manor at Redbrook in Kent, and lands (over 1,500 acres) in Whitstable, and in Staffordshire. The memorial put up in his memory by his eldest son William (see below) in St Dunstan's church, Canterbury, sums up better than anything the feelings that lay at the heart of this family. The original inscription in Latin may be translated as follows:

> Stay, you who pass by and read these few words that you may gain the power of learning to live better and to die better. You are unconcerned? Behold, in a short time, perhaps while still unconcerned, you also will be an example of our mortal condition! In pious dedication to his parents, Thomas Roper, armiger, grandson to Thomas More through his daughter Margaret (a cause of special honour to this family) inheritor also of his virtues, and following his father William of whom in that function, he could be seen as a partner rather than a successor. In the court or on the King's Bench, the highest court in the whole realm, he acted as First Secretary for twenty-four years or more, as much by his own great deserts as by

wit of his high standing among all men, in firm and public display of good faith, never accustomed to pronounce judgement deceitfully or to sell it at an inordinate price either to litigants or defendents. As his wife unparalleled as such, he had Lucy, daughter of Anthony Browne, sprung from the illustrious family of Montague, Knight Commander of the Horse to King Henry VIII (1509–47) and also one of his Councilors. By her he begot twelve children, six of each sex. On both sides was there wonderful and perfect love, great harmony and mutual esteem. Thus, (both publicly in the court and privately at home) everywhere passing his life in holiness and modesty, when he had come to a quiet old age, like one who falls asleep he rested in Christ in the 65th year of his life, on the 21st day of January in the year 1598. William Roper as a most dutiful son to a most loving parent.[74]

As we have just seen, Thomas and Lucy Roper had twelve children, six of each sex. Accounts of their names differ, and in some they are clearly muddled with the children of other branches of the family. The times in which they lived were dangerous for Catholics and, in the circumstances, it is not surprising that little or nothing has been recorded about them – with the exception of Catherine and William, Thomas and Lucy's eldest son and heir.

Catherine Roper, born around 1564, married Edward Bentley, Gent., probably in 1582. About Edward's ancestry we know nothing, but we do know he owned the lease of a property in the hamlet of Hungry Bentley in the parish of Longford, about eight miles due west of Derby, and this is where the family lived. Their first child, Frederick, was born on 25 April 1583. He was educated at St Omers and Douai before being sent to the English College in Rome in 1603 when he stated that he had four brothers and six sisters. He had not at that time decided to become a priest, and he must have left soon after. One of Frederick's brothers, Edward, born in London in 1588, also went to St Omers before going to the English College in Rome in 1606.

The Bentley family was staunchly Catholic and, in March 1588 Edward and Catherine were presented for having been recusants at Longford since September 1586. They also harboured priests at their house. Edward was convicted of having participated in the Babbington Plot to free Mary Queen of Scots and was imprisoned and condemned to death in 1587. However, his denial of any implication in the plot led to further investigations by the Privy Council and the Queen's Attorney – with permission to put witnesses to 'the torture of the Rack' if necessary – and to his subsequent release. Sometime after this, with the help of the Spanish Ambassador, Edward and Catherine obtained permission to reside with their ten children in Flanders where, in 1606, King Philip III of Spain – in consideration of their descent from Sir Thomas More – granted a monthly pension of seventy-five Escudos to Edward and twenty-five Escudos to Francis who had now reached his majority. Unfortunately reforms at the Court of King Philip in 1610 led to a reduction in the number of pensions being awarded – including that made to the Bentleys. Now with thirteen children, and facing poverty, Catherine returned to England while Edward remained in Flanders seeking employment. Back in England, Catherine lived somewhere in the area of the Barbican, close to the residence of the Spanish Ambassador, in whose chapel she attended Mass every day. In 1614 the Ambassador asked his government for permission to make an allowance out of embassy funds to help support the family, but this was turned down. A further appeal by the Ambassador in 1616 – accompanied by a petition drawn up by Edward and his son Francis – was more successful, and an allowance of 1,100 Reales as year was granted to Catherine as 'the niece' of Thomas More. This allowance seems to have continued until diplomatic relations between Spain and England broke down in 1625. It is around this time that Catherine is believed to have died. We do not know when, or where, Edward died.[75]

William Roper (jnr), born in 1555, became Sir William Roper. He married Katherine, the daughter and coheir of Sir Anthony Browne of Ridley Hall in Essex, Chief Justice of the Court of Common Pleas. *The Visitations of Kent, 1619*, record three children, Anthony, Thomas, and Mary (which should read Anne), but there would also appear to have been a John – the great-great-grandchildren of Sir Thomas More.

Surviving documents are sparse, but Sir William is recorded as having been a convicted recusant, a 'crime' for which he paid recusancy fines from before 1600. At the beginning of the reign of King James (1603) the archpriest George Blackwell, the Pope's representative, and the head of the secular clergy in England, advised Catholics that it was allowable for them to take the Oath of Allegiance and, as a person of some note, William took the Oath in front of Archbishop Richard Bancroft on 17 November 1606 and was granted a certificate of conformity which, without actually attending his parish church, he could present whenever the authorities demanded it.

Sir William was a strong supporter of the English clergy who felt threatened by the Jesuit presence in England. With Lady Roper he travelled frequently to the Continent between 1610 and 1616, most probably in support of this cause, and in support of the Convents of English nuns at Cambrai and Louvain – among whom were numbered some of their relatives. Sir William died on 2 August 1628 and was buried the following day in St Dunstan's church, Canterbury.

Anthony Roper, Sir William and Lady Katherine's eldest son, born in 1583, inherited his father's estates at Well Hall and Canterbury and later purchased Aston Hall in Derbyshire. He married three times. His first wife was Mary, the daughter of William Gerard of Trent. They married in 1612 and had an only daughter Mary. Anthony's second wife was Dorothy, the daughter of Sir Thomas Holte of Ashton in Warwickshire. No children appear to have been born of this union. His third wife was a daughter of Sir Henry Compton of Brambletye House, near East Grinstead in Sussex (c.1584–1649) and his wife Cecily Sackville the daughter of Robert Sackville 2nd Earl of Dorset. They had two children: Anne, born 1640, who never married, and Edward, born in 1641, who succeeded to the family estates at Eltham and Canterbury when his father died in 1643. He married Katherine the daughter of James Butler Esq. of Amberley Castle, Sussex, on 8 February 1666. Edward and Katherine had five children. Katherine, Margaret and Leonard are recorded as dying young. Edward, the 4 times great-grandson of Sir Thomas More was the last male of this line of descent. Born in 1672, he never married. He died as a result of wounds received during the Battle of Almansa (25 April 1707) in the Spanish War of Succession. Elizabeth, his sister, inherited the family estates at Eltham and Canterbury, taking them into her marriage to Edward Henshaw of Canterbury.

Elizabeth and Edward Henshaw had three daughters: Catherine, Elizabeth and Susanna who, after the death of their mother in 1722 and their father in 1726, inherited the family estates.As coheirs they sold the estate at Well Hall in 1733 to Sir Gregory Page of Wricklemarsh for £19,000 (approx. £2,000,000 today). He demolished the old house, by then known as 'Roper House' and built 'Page House' outside the moat. All that remains of the original buildings is a 'Tudor Barn', now a public house. The moat and some garden walls also survive, located in Well Hall Pleasance, an area of gardens on the edge of the University of Greenwich Sports Ground. Page House has disappeared without trace.[76]

As for the three sisters: Catherine Henshaw married Sir William Strickland (d.1788), and Elizabeth Henshaw married Sir Edward Dering of Surrenden, Kent, the founder of the regiment that became known as the 24th Regiment of Foot. In 1729 Susanna Henshaw married Sir Rowland Winn 4th Baronet of Nostell (1706–1765) from whom the present 6th Baron St Oswald of Nostell is descended.[77] Sir Rowland Winn bought out the shares of his sisters-in-law in the Roper's copy of the famous Holbein painting of Sir Thomas More and his family and brought it to his home at Nostell Priory. Visitors to Nostell Priory, near Wakefield – now in the ownership of the National Trust – can see it hanging in the lower hall.

Sir William and Katherine Roper's second son, Thomas, was born on 17 November 1585. On the death of his father he inherited his manors at Oakley and Croxall in Staffordshire, but he was a convicted recusant and these were later sequestered. On 24 April 1621 Thomas married Susan Winchcombe, the daughter of John Winchcombe of Henwick Manor near Thatcham in Berkshire (b.1578) and his wife Mary Verrey. Thomas and Susan had seven children: William, Mary, Francis, Thomas, Margaret, George, and Frances. Thomas made his will in 1630 leaving £50 a year (approx. £5,200 today) for the 'better maintenance' of his eldest son William, and £500 each to his daughters Mary and Margaret. Thomas died on 15 October 1647 and, because two-thirds of his lands were sequestered for recusancy, it seems the bequests were not paid to Mary and Margaret. On 23 March 1653 they petitioned the 'Committee for Compounding' (of recusancy fines) for the payment of this money.[77]

Anne, the only daughter of Sir William and Katherine Roper, born 1587, married Sir Philip Constable of Everingham in Yorkshire. Sir Philip, born probably in 1597, succeeded his father Sir Marmaduke Constable in 1632, inheriting a house in York, large estates at Everingham and Drax in West Yorkshire and at Middle Rasen in Lincolnshire. Sir Philip had been a convicted recusant since the 1620s, but he managed to avoid paying the fine of £20 per month for not attending Church of England worship. However, the 'Yorkshire Commissioners for Compounding with Recusants' – whose job it was to extract arrears – caught up with him in September 1632 when, having inherited the family estates, a full assessment of his goods and lands was made in preparation for the sequestration of two-thirds of them. The Commissioners found that

> Phillip Constable of Everingham Esqr. and Anne his wife Compoundeth for the Manor of Everingham, the Mannor of Drax; Camisleforth and other places there, Lands in Holdernes with Severall Leases, Lands and Manors in the County of Lincoln and York for the Rent of 250 li.

He was ordered henceforth to pay this sum annually in two equal installments at Martinmas and Pentecost. The first payment to begin at Martinmas in 1632. In 1636, however, by special grace of the King (Charles I), Philip was pardoned for his non-payment of fines and the two-thirds of his land which belonged to the King were leased back to him at a rent of £250 a year (approx. £26,000 today) for a period of forty-one years – 'if the recusancy of Philip so long endure'. The commencement of the lease was backdated to 1632. The King also ordered that, provided Philip paid his rent in due time, neither he nor his wife should be further 'molested' because of their recusancy.[78]

As might be expected, Sir Philip supported the Royalist Cause during the Civil War in which two of his brothers, Michael and Marmaduke, were killed fighting for the King. The family home at Everingham was plundered and ruined by the soldiery and Anne died as a result of the hardships they suffered during their flight to York. After the war most of the family estates were sequestered again as a punishment for supporting the 'wrong' side.

Sir Philip, clearly greatly impoverished by his recusancy fines, made his will on 20 February 1664 appointing his son Marmaduke his executor, and leaving him £30 out of the total of £240 (approx. £23,000 today) which he held for his father. In addition he left 'such monyes as shall appeare to bee due to my sonn for my board since wee made even last' – an indication that since the destruction of Everingham and the death of his wife he may have been living with his son, possibly in their house at York. He also made bequests to the English monks at Douai, to the English nuns at Cambrai, Louvain and Brussels, to the poor of Everingham and West Rasen and to a number of his servants. Interestingly, he left £5 to Edward Lusher, a Jesuit priest, who was the 3 times great-grandson of Sir Thomas More through his son John. He left his daughter Catherine £30 and £8 'towards my funeral' to her husband Edward Sheldon. Sir Philip died five days later, on 25

February 1664. He was buried in the parish church at Steeple Barton.[79]

Sir Philip and Anne had a number of children. Their eldest son, Sir Marmaduke, was baptized at Everingham on 22 April 1619. A daughter Barbara was professed as a Benedictine nun, and two younger sons, Philip and Thomas became Benedictine monks. Another daughter, Catharine married Edward Sheldon (b.1624) of Steeple Barton, in Oxfordshire, and they had three sons and four daughters. One of the sons, Henry, became a Jesuit, and two of the daughters, Mary and Elizabeth, became Augustinian nuns at St Monica's, Louvain. Their eldest son, Ralph, inherited the Sheldon family estates at Weston and Beoley in Worcestershire. Edward died on 30 May 1676 and was buried in the Church of St Martin-in-the-Fields, London. Catherine died 30 April 1681.

Sir Philip Constable was succeeded by his eldest son, Sir Marmaduke. He married Anne Sherburn/Sherbourne, the daughter of Richard Sherburn of Stonyhurst. Sir Marmaduke died at Antwerp in 1680 and was taken for burial to the Monastery of St Monica's in Louvain where some of his Roper and Constable relatives were nuns. He was succeeded by his eldest son, Sir Philip, who was baptized at Everingham on 25 April 1651. He married Margaret Radcliffe the daughter of Sir Francis Radcliffe, first Earl of Derwentwater. Margaret died in 1688 and Sir Philip in 1706. Their son, Sir Marmaduke, born 1682, has been called 'the last of his race'. He succeeded in building up the family estates again but unfortunately he died unmarried in 1746.[80] His elder sister, Anne, born around 1676, inherited the family estates. She married William Haggerston who came from an old Catholic Northumbrian family, and they adopted the name Haggerston-Constable of Everingham. Through marriage the name later became Constable-Maxwell.

Giles Heron and his Family

As we have seen, Giles was born in 1504 and educated at Cambridge. After his father died in 1523 he became a ward of Sir Thomas More. In his will his father left him the fortified manor house at Shacklewell, in Hackney, and an estate at Aldersbrook (also called Nakedhall Hawe or Nakedhall Grove) in the parishes of Little Ilford and Wanstead, in Essex, as well as Rycote Manor, sometimes called Rycote Palace, in Oxfordshire – a property he had bought from Sir Richard Fowler the younger in 1521 – and a 'capital messuage' called Rysingprice at Fishtoft, near Boston in Lincolnshire.[81] This inheritance was administered for him by Thomas More until the period of his wardship ended when he became twenty-one in 1525. In that year he also married Cecily More. For their home Giles chose the manor house of Shacklewell – though we do not know exactly when they moved out of the Great House at Chelsea to live there.

Giles became an 'Esquire of the Body' to Henry VIII and, initially, seems to have done well for himself. He was a member for Thetford in Norfolk in the Parliament that began in 1529 and, by 1530, he had obtained the lease of the manors of Cutlers and Canonbury from the Priory of St Bartholomew. Within a couple of years, however, he began to sell his properties – not only the properties he had obtained himself, but also some of those that he had inherited from his father and might have been expected to pass on to his own children. In 1532 he sold Aldersbrook to the Crown and also assigned most of the estates of Cutlers and Canonbury to Thomas Cromwell who drew up new leases for himself. Then, in November 1533 he sold his Lincolnshire properties to Thomas Robertson of Boston. It may not be a coincidence that his father-in-law's fall from grace began around this time and Giles, perhaps foreseeing (and fearing?) what might happen to him if the worst came to the worst, felt it prudent to reduce some of the more visible signs of his wealth.

Sir Thomas's execution in 1535 does not appear to have had any immediate effect on Giles though, like other male members of the family, he spent a brief time in the Tower being questioned. He sat again for Thetford in Henry's Parliament of 1536, and in the same year he was also foreman of the jury which decided in favour of there being enough evidence to convict Anne Boleyn of adultery. How he voted on that jury we do not know, but he was no doubt keen to maintain the favour of the King.

Giles seems to have been a somewhat difficult man to deal with and was once described as being 'wise in words, but foolish in deeds'. He took a number of people to court (including his brother Christopher) in disputes over land. One of these cases (in December 1531) was heard in Chancery before his father-in-law from whom Giles obviously expected a decision in his favour. When he didn't get what he wanted and became awkward Sir Thomas refused to deal with him any further and offered him the alternative of either going to the Tower or being bound over for the sum of 1,000 marks to appear in the Star Chamber and to abide by their decision.[82]

It was a dispute with one of his tenants that eventually led to Giles's downfall. The case in question involved a man known to us only as 'Lyons', whom Giles had expelled from his farm on the Shacklewell estate. By way of revenge Lyons reported him to Cromwell for having 'mumbled' certain treasonable words against the King in his parlour at Shacklewell. These 'mumblings' were said to have been with Sir Thomas More – so obviously some years previously – but Lyons must have known the 'added value' that this would give to his accusation. Lyons stated aim was to 'displease' Giles and to 'be quytte w^t hym', and he must have been well pleased when Thomas Cromwell introduced into Parliament an Act of Attainder against him, for high treason. This was passed on 12 April 1540. The indictment reads:

> That where Gyles Heron, late of Hackney in your Countie of Midd., Esquier, by the instigation of the devil, putting apart the dreade of god and the excellent benefites receyued of your highness, hath not only moste traitorously refused his duetie and allegeaunce whiche he ought to beare unto your highness, but also hath committed and perpetrated diuers and sondrye detestable and habomynable treasons, to the moste fearefull and extreme perrill and daungier of the destruction of your moste roiall persone, and to thutter losse, disherison and desolation of this your Realme, if god of his goodness hath not in due tyme brought his said treasons to knowledge. For the whiche, being plainely and manifestly proued, that it may be enacted by auctoritie of this present parlament that the said Gyles Heron, for his abhominable and detestable treasons by him mooste abhomynably committed and doon againste your maiestie and this Realme, shalbe by auctoritie of this present parlament conuicted and attainted of high treason.

The immediate result of Giles's attainder was the forfeiture of his lands, and this was ordered to be backdated to 28 January 1539.[83] It must have been around this time that he was forced by a private Act to sell his Rycote estate, including the Manor or Palace, to Sir John Williams.[84]

Exactly how or why the case proceeded in the way it did has never been established. The evidence was shaky and, in spite of attempts by Lyons to bribe some of his friends to support him, there were no other witnesses to his 'crime'. What we do know is that after appearing before the Council on three occasions early in 1539 he was committed to the Fleet prison.

Giles was convicted and sent to the Tower in June 1539. By a strange twist of fate, Cromwell's own downfall delayed the carrying out of the sentence on Giles until 4 August 1540 when he was hanged, drawn and quartered at Tyburn. The event is recorded in *Wriothesley's Chronicle* as follows:

> A.D. 1549. This year the fowerth of Awgust were drawen from the Tower of London to Tiburne, Giles Heron, gentleman, Clement Philpott, gentleman, late of Callis, and servant to the Lord Lile, Darbie Gynning, Edmonde Bryndholme, priest, William Horn, late a lay brother of the Charter Howse of London, and another, with six persons more, were there hanged, drawen and quartered ... all of which persons were attaynted by the whole Parliament for treason.[85]

After Giles's execution his estate at Shacklewell and lands in Hackney were confiscated and granted to Sir Ralph Sadler of Sutton Place, the King's Secretary. The Heron estate lay between Sutton Place and the parish church in Hackney, so the two families were friends and neighbours. Sir Ralph employed Giles's brothers Christopher and John as servants, and it might have been expected that he would dismiss them after their brush with the law. The King however – who must have taken a special interest in the case – commanded him to keep them in his service on the grounds that their examination should be seen 'rather a tryall of theire trueth and a purgacion of theim from all suspicion thenne any ignomynie or shame'.[86]

Giles and Cecily Heron had three children: Thomas, John, and Anne.[87] We know that Thomas and John, who were probably young teenagers at the time, appealed for help to Sir Ralph Sadler while their father was in prison, and it has been suggested that he may have acquired Shacklewell to protect their interests. The family estate at Wanstead and Ilford in Essex was returned to Thomas Heron, Giles's older son, by order of Queen Mary on 23 July 1554, but he sold it in 1566 to Alderman Thomas Rowe, a Lord Mayor of London.[88] The pedigrees of 'Heron of Cressey Hall' and of 'Jekyll' record the marriage of Thomas to Cecily, the daughter of Bartholomew Jekyll of Newington, Middlesex. She later married James Prior of Colchester, Essex. No children are recorded from either marriage. I have not been able to discover anything about John, but as Thomas died without children, and

Anne is designated 'heir' in the pedigree of Heron of Cressey Hall I can only assume that he died young and without issue. Anne married twice, but only the surnames of her husbands – Horsley and Osborne – are recorded.[89]

The Family of William Daunce

William Daunce, the son of Sir John Daunce, followed in his father's footsteps at the exchequer where he soon came to the notice of the King. Even before his marriage to Elizabeth More, the Crown had granted him (April 1522) a sixty-year lease on 'the manor of Whytechurche, Oxford, parcel of the Duchy of Cornwall, in the honor of Wallyngford'. He must have continued to serve the King well for, in June 1527, he was granted another lease on a property belonging to the Duchy of Cornwall in Kennington, Surrey. In October 1528 he was promoted 'to be one of the Tellers of the Exchequer, with the usual fees'.[90] In addition to these grants he also obtained the lease of some tenements known as the 'Exeter Rents' (because they belonged to the Bishop of Exeter) in the area between St Clement Danes and the Thames, and he had the use of a house belonging to Cardinal Wolsey in Battersea that his father-in-law had obtained for him.[91] In 1529, no doubt on his father-in-law's recommendation, he was returned by the Duchy of Lancaster to represent Thetford in Norfolk in the Parliament that began on 3 November. His brothers-in-law Giles Heron and William Roper, and John Rastell, also sat in the same Parliament. William clearly continued to prosper. In 1532 he obtained a lease for thirty-one years of the manor of Cassiobury in Hertfordshire, and in 1535 he was granted a lease on the nearby manor of Canons in Middlesex.

William has been described as 'an unpleasant and grasping man'. According to William Roper, he hoped to be able to make some money out of his connections with Sir Thomas who, when he found out, put him firmly in his place telling him that if he was dealing with a case in which his father was on one side and the devil on the other, then if the devil had the best case, 'the devil should have the right'. William also seems to have been someone whose word could not be relied on. When, for example, he took over the house belonging to Cardinal Wolsey in Battersea he apparently agreed to let Wolsey's servant and his wife and children stay on in the house, but in June 1530 Wolsey wrote to

Cromwell complaining that William had turned them out of the house and that they now had nowhere to live.[92]

Following his father-in-law's attainder William was imprisoned for a while in the Tower, but soon released. In 1543 he was implicated with other members of the More family in the Plot of the Prebendaries against Cranmer but after investigation he was pardoned 'of all treasonable words against the King's supremacy' on 24 April 1544 and does not appear to have had any of his lands sequestered.

Sir John Daunce made his will on 24 September 1545 and the provisions he made in it would indicate that William had fallen out with his father, perhaps because of his involvement with other members of the More circle in the Plot of the Prebendaries. The main beneficiary of the will was Sir John's illegitimate son Edward Maryott. When his father died on 7 December 1545 William succeeded only to his ex-monastic lands. Sir John's will was proved the following year when a warrant of Henry VIII dated 23 May 1546 states: 'William Daunce: Warrant for livery of the lands to him as s. and h. of Sir John Daunce who ... died seised of the later priory of Murseley, Bucks leaving the said William aged 45 years and more.'[93]

William and Elizabeth had five sons, John, Thomas, Bartholomew, William and Germain, and two daughters, Alice and Elizabeth – grandchildren of Sir Thomas.[94] We know that John was born in 1526, but the birth dates of his brothers and sisters are not known.

William died on 28 May 1548 and an entry in the Calendar of the Patent Roles for Edward VI, dated 20 February 1549, indicates that John was his heir:

> General livery to John Daunce, aged 23, as son and heir of William Daunce, gentleman, who died 28 May 2 Edward VI, seised of the house and site of the late priory of Muresley *alias* St. Margaret's, Bucks, and its lands in Muresley, Ivinghoo, Wynleshorn, Eddesborough *alias* Edelborough, Northyll, Northetehyll, Pyghthethorne, Pytleshorne, Fresden and Drayton, Bucks, held of the king in chief by the tenth part of one knight's fee and a rent of 32s. by the name of tenth ...[95]

Elizabeth died in 1564 after a long illness caused by a disease the name of which has not come down to us.

The Clement Family

The story of the immediate family of Sir Thomas wouldn't be complete without mention of the family of Margaret Clement (née Giggs), the adopted daughter who, he said, he loved as if she were his own.

The date of John Clement's birth is not known. Based on a letter that Sir Thomas wrote to Peter Gilles, a friend of Erasmus, he has been called his 'boy' or his 'young assistant' and is said to have been educated at St Paul's School in London before becoming a tutor in the More household around 1514.[96] There is, however, some evidence that he might have been considerably older than previously thought, of 'noble' birth, and educated at Louvain.[97]

As we have already seen, Margaret Giggs married John Clement in 1526, and the couple made their home at the Old Barge in Bucklersbury when Sir Thomas and his family moved to the Great House in Chelsea. John was admitted to membership of the Royal College of Physicians in 1528, and went on to become its president in 1544.

Margaret was renowned for her piety and devotion to the Catholic Church, and one of the few stories that has come down to us her tells of the way that she gave succour to a group of ten Carthusian monks from the Charterhouse in London who had been committed to Newgate prison in May 1532 'for traitorous behaviour against the King's grace' – that is, for refusing to take the Oath of Supremacy. The story is told in the Chronicle of the nuns of St Monica's, and I quote it here verbatim:

> Moved with great compassion of these holy fathers, (Margaret) dealt with the gaoler that she might secretly have access unto them (the Carthusians), and withal did win him with money, that he was content to let her come into the prison unto them, attiring and disguising herself as a milkmaid, with a great pail upon her head, full of meat, wherewith she fed the blessed company, putting meat into their mouths, they being tied and not able to stir, nor to help themselves; which being done she afterwards with her own hands made them clean. This pious work did she continue for divers days, until at last the King inquiring of them if they were not yet dead, and understanding they were yet alive, to his great admiration, commanded a stricter watch to be kept over them, so as the keeper durst not let in this good woman no more, fearing it might cost him his head if it should be discovered. Nevertheless with her importunity and by force of money, she obtained of him that he let

her go up to the tiles, right above the close prison, where the Blessed Fathers were. And so she discovering (uncovering) the ceiling or tiles over their heads, by a string let them down meat in a basket, approaching the same as she could to their mouths, as they did stand chained against the posts; but they not being able to feed themselves out of the basket, or very little, and the gaoler fearing very much that it should be perceived in the end, wholly refused to let her come any more. And so, soon after they languished and pined away, one after another, what with the stench and want of food and other miseries which they there endured.

A letter from Thomas Bedyll, Governor of the prison, written to Cromwell in June 1537 refers to the monks who had died as being 'despatched by the hand of God' – a convenient way of referring to death by starvation![98]

John and Margaret Clement had six children – an only son, Thomas, and five daughters, Bridget, Helen, Winifred, Dorothy, and Margaret. Of these we know only that Winifred, probably their eldest child, was born in 1527. After the suppression of Burnham Abbey by Henry VIII John and Margaret Clement gave refuge to Elizabeth Woodford, one of the Augustinian nuns from the Abbey, and she became responsible for the education of their children.

In 1545 the Clements were granted a thirty-year lease of a large country house 'Friar's Mede', Marshfoot in Hornchurch, Essex.[99] Unfortunately they were not able to enjoy country living for long as they went into exile in 1549 when they felt it had become impossible to continue to practise their Catholic faith in England under Edward VI. John went first, in July, and Margaret joined him in October. They stayed for a short time in Bruges before finally settling at Louvain, in Brabant, which was then part of the Spanish Netherlands. They were accompanied by their children and, as we saw in chapter one, by William Rastell who had married their eldest daughter, Winifred. Elizabeth Woodford also went with them. She joined the Augustinian nuns at St Ursula's, Louvain in 1549 where young Margaret Clement and her sister Helen were sent to continue their education. Their older sister, Dorothy became a Poor Clare nun.[100]

The Clements returned to England on 19 March 1554, after Mary's accession to the throne, and their lands were restored to them. Young Margaret Clement, however, refused to return with her parents and stayed on at St Ursula's where she was eventually professed as a nun on 11 October 1557 and became Prioress in 1559. When the English nuns at St Ursula's made their own foundation of St Monica's in Louvain, Mother Margaret Clement (by then blind, and referred to as 'the old Mother') went with them. She died there on 8 May 1612.

Back in England John Clement engaged in two court battles to recover some of his personal possessions – especially his precious collections of books – that had been confiscated when he fled, but he was not entirely successful in this. It seems likely that, on his return, John was again engaged as one of the royal physicians, and his son, John Clement, MA was also granted a royal annuity of £20 (approx. £3,560 today) by Queen Mary in 1554.[101]

The Clements fled to Louvain again on 3 January 1562, after five years of living under Elizabeth I convinced them that the religious situation in England would not improve. They appear to have stayed in Louvain until 1568 when they moved to Malines where they set up home at 1 Blockstraat, near the church of Saint Peter and Paul.[102]

Margaret Clement died on 5 July 1570. She was known for her piety and it is said that as she died she saw the Carthusian monks that she had helped in Newgate Prison standing around her bed and calling her to come away to them. She was buried behind the altar in the Cathedral Church of St Rombold. John Clement died two years later on 1 July 1572 and was buried next to his wife.[103] He was succeeded by his son Thomas.

Genealogical Summary

Sir Thomas More and his Children

Thomas More (1478–1535) m. (1) Jane Colt (1488–1511)
                              (2) Alice Middleton (1475–1551)
Children: (all by Jane Colt)
1. **Margaret (1505–1544): m. (1521) William Roper (1498–1578)**
   Children:
   1. Elizabeth (1523–1560): m. (1) John Stephenson – no issue;
      m. (2) Sir Edward Bray of Shere (his 2nd wife). Son: Reginald.
   2. Margaret (c.1526–c.1578): m. William Dawtrey Esq. (d.1591)
      Children: William (b. c.1547), John, Anthony, Jane.
   3. Mary (d.1572): m. (1) Stephen Clarke (no children);
      m. (2) James Bassett (1526–1558)
      Children: Philip: m. ... Verney; Charles (a Jesuit)
   4. Thomas (1533–1598): m. Lucy Browne (d.1607)
      Children: William, Henry, Francis, Charles, Thomas, Phillip, Mary, Frances, Elizabeth, Martha, Catherine, Mabel.
      Eldest son, William (1555–1628) became Sir William Roper m. Katherine Browne (d.1616).
      Children:
      1. Anthony (1583–1643):
         m. (1) Mary Gerard (d.1622), daughter of William Gerard of Trent, Somerset. Child: Mary.
         m. (2) Dorothy Holte. No children recorded.
         m. (3) Margaret, daughter of Sir Henry Compton.
         Children:
         i. Anne (born c.1640)
         ii. Edward (b.1641) m. Katherine Butler (b.1648)
             Children:
             Katherine, Margaret, Leonard (all died young)
             Edward (1672–1707), last male of this Roper line,
             Elizabeth m. Edward Henshaw
             Children: Catherine m. William Strickland (no issue), Elizabeth (m. Sir Edward Dering), Susanna (m. Sir Rowland Winn 4th Baronet of Nostell (1706–1765); line continues).
      2. Thomas (1585–1647) m. Susan Winchcombe
         Children: Mary, Francis, Thomas, Margaret, George,

Frances, William.
   3. Anne (1587–1648) m. Sir Philip Constable of Everingham (1595–1664)
      Children include: Barbara, Philip, Thomas (all OSB); Catherine (m. Edward Sheldon of Steeple Barton); Elizabeth (m. William Langdale). Son and heir, Sir Marmaduke Constable (b.1619) m. Ann Sherburn (family name later became Haggerston-Constable and then Constable-Maxwell).
   5. Anthony (1544–1597): m. Anne Cotton
      Children: Anthony (became Sir Anthony); John, Henry, Isabel (d.1622: m. Sir Thomas Wiseman); Jane.

2. **Elizabeth (1506–1564) m. (1525) William Daunce (1500–1548)**
   Children: John (b.1526, eldest son and heir. Had a son, John); Thomas, Bartholomew, William, Gerome, Alice, Elizabeth.

3. **Cecily (1507–?) m. (1525) Giles Heron (1504–1540)**
   Children:
   1. Thomas: m. Cecily Jekyll. No children
   2. John: ? died without issue
   3. Anne (recorded as 'heir'): m. (1) ... Horsley; (2) ... Osborne.

4. **John (1509–1547) m. (1529) Anne Cresacre (1511–1577)**
   See next chapter.

5. **Margaret Giggs (adopted daughter) (c.1508–1570): m. (1526) John Clement (d.1572)**
   Children:
   1. Thomas: m. (name of wife not known).
      Children: Caesar (priest) d.1626
   2. Bridget: m. Robert Redman.
      Children: Thomas (priest) d.1617
   3. Helen: m. Thomas Prideaux
      Children: Magdalen m. William Copley (1564–1643)
         Children: i. Helen (1582–1666): Augustinian nun
                   ii. Mary (1683–1669): Augustinian nun
                  iii. Thomas (c.1594–1652): Jesuit priest
                   iv. William: m. Anne Shelton
                        Children: i. Mary: m. John Weston (d.1690)
                                 ii. Anne: m. Sir Nathaniel Minshull
   4. Winifred (1526–1553) m. William Rastell (d.1565)
   5. Dorothy: A Poor Clare nun.
   6. Margaret (b. 1540): An Augustinian nun. Died 1612.

Chapter Three

The Family of John More II

The exact date of John's birth is not known, but the year in which it took place was 1509. As the family were living at the 'Old Barge' in Bucklersbury at the time it is likely that, like his sisters before him, he was baptized in the Church of St Stephen Walbrook.

John, the youngest child in the family of Sir Thomas, and the only son, has sometimes been made out to have been lacking in intelligence, and even 'simple'. In reality, however, while he may not have been able to compete with his eldest sister, Margaret, he was certainly no dunce, and his father's friends Erasmus, and Symon Grynaeus (professor of Greek and Latin at the University of Heidelberg), both spoke highly of his learning. He became a Latin scholar in his own right and his translation of a work called *The Legacy of Prester John* – an account of the first Ethiopian Embassy to Portugal – was published in 1533 when he was twenty-four years old. At around the same time he followed his father's example by publishing a translation of two works defending the teachings of the Catholic Church.

While recognizing the quality of the education that young John received with his sisters in the family homes I still think it surprising that his father did not send him to Oxford or Cambridge, or to Lincoln's Inn, where he could have met and mixed with other young men of a similar age and standing. As it was he remained cocooned and protected within his own family environment. Why his father treated him in this way remains a mystery. Basing themselves on the story of Lady Alice More chiding her husband for his unwillingness to put himself forward 'as other folke doo'[1] most of Thomas's biographers say that, while he responded to the calls made on him to accept positions of authority, he never actively sought them himself. This, surprisingly, implies that Thomas lacked ambition and, if this is true, then maybe some of this 'spilled over' into a lack of ambition for his son. My personal view is that Thomas not only liked, but psychologically also needed, to keep his children close around him. They provided him with an anchor and a sense of security that he could not find outside the home, and by keeping them close to him he felt he could protect them from the sin and evil he undoubtedly saw in the world around him.

Brought up with few outside contacts it is not perhaps surprising that John should find his bride within the family home – and, indeed, that may have been his father's intention when he bought the wardship of Anne Cresacre. The story that there was a mix-up in the deal, and that he got Anne (and the lands that went with her) by mistake seems rather far-fetched given his lawyers background.

By piecing various bits of evidence together we can say that Anne was born between 2 December 1511 and 21 April 1512.[2] As we saw in the last chapter, there is no truth in the statement that she was taken into the More household when only about three years old, and we know nothing about her early life except for the little we can glean from the proceedings of the Yorkshire Star Chamber in 1524. What these show is that her father, Edward Cresacre, held his lands *in capite*, or directly from the King. As Anne was his only child and heiress and, at the time of his death at the age of twenty-seven in 1512, only about six months old, she automatically became a ward of the Crown. This meant that any decisions about her custody and eventual marriage were to be made by the Crown.

The record of the case in Yorkshire Star Chamber is written in Tudor English and is not easy to follow. However, it appears that, after the death of her father, Anne was taken under the wing of the Cardinal Archbishop of York, Primate and Chancellor of England, and placed under the protection of a gentleman called Ralph Rokeby, an Attorney to the Duchy of Lancaster. Ralph rented his manor at Bishop Burton near Beverley in Yorkshire from the Archbishop, and it was there that Christiana Jackson 'an aged gentilwoman' was given responsibility for Anne's 'ordryng, rewle and guydyng'.

According to the evidence given to the Star Chamber the arrangements made for Anne seem to have gone unchallenged for twelve years. Then, according to the evidence of Ralph Rokeby, on 15 April 1524, Sir Robert Constable, in the company of four other gentlemen and 'many other riotous and evyll disposed persones to the noumbre of 100 or mo' arrived at the manor on horseback where, 'with bowes bent and arowes sette in their bowes ready to shote', they 'riotously besette, besieged and environed the maner place on every side'. Sir Robert, accompanied by a servant with sword at the ready, then entered the manor, passing through the hall and into the parlour where he found Anne in the company of Christiana Jackson. When Sir Robert forcibly took hold of Anne, saying that he had come to take her away she struggled and cried out for help. She told him that he had no right to take her away as she was married to John Rokeby (Ralph Rokeby's son). Christiana confirmed that Anne was married and warned Sir Robert 'I trist ye take no mannes wif away, and in especiall out of my Lord Cardinalles lordship, onles ye have good autorite lawful.' Hearing the noise, Thomas Morley, priest and chaplain to the household, came to find out what it was all about. The scene in the parlour filled him with fear and, to stop anyone else entering, he shut the door. At this, Sir Robert's servant repeatedly thrust his sword towards him, threatening him: 'Horemaister Prest, open the dore or I shall strike thy nek from thy body'. When the priest drew his own sword in self-defence Sir Robert warned him rather more politely: 'Prest, thou art a foole to resist me, for I assure you I have an hundredth persones abowt this house, and therefore it is best to yeld the, and make no more besynes.' The scene then grew more ugly as some of the mob burst into the house from the front and used a bench from the hall to break down the parlour door. Others 'brak open a bak dore of the manor place', breaking five panes of glass and injuring one of the men servants in the process. They were all shouting 'Kill the horeson Prest, kyll him'. Having gained the upper hand Sir Robert Constable grabbed Anne and forcefully carried her out shouting and screaming and proclaiming that she would rather die than forsake her husband. Ralph Rokeby concluded his evidence:

> That notwithstondyng they did carie her away on horsebak, and ordered her ferther at their pleasure, and, so yit do, and reteyn her against her will from her said husbond, contrarie to the lawes of God and your lawes, moost gracious sovereign lord, and against all good order ... Wherefore my it pleas your gracious highness to grant a writ *sub pena* to the said Sir Robert ...

Sir Robert Constable's account of what happened was rather different. He pointed out that Anne was a ward of the King and that Ralph Rokeby had not only 'untruely and unjustly' taken her into his keeping but he had also taken the profits from the lands that had been left to her by her father, profits which rightly belonged to the King. Having found out about this the King had sent letters to Sir Robert 'under the seal of his signet' commanding him to take Anne away from Ralf Rokeby with the assistance of the Sheriff of Yorkshire 'and such other of the King's subjects as he should deem necessary'. He had therefore, on 14 (not 15) April, gone to Bishop Burton with only ten people, nine of whom were his household servants. The door of the house was open, and he entered peaceably with only one servant, his 'horsekeeper'. He went into the parlour where he found Anne and the aged gentilwoman who told him that she and Thomas Morley (the chaplain) had the rule and oversight of the house. He asked her to call Morley and when he arrived he told them both the King's orders. The priest had replied that the only way he could take Anne away was to take her away in pieces! At this Sir Robert had asked his horsekeeper to go to the gate of the house to get the King's letter, but the priest had drawn his knife and moved quickly to shut the hall doors to prevent him leaving, calling on two other servants 'the one having a pitchfork, the other a great plain staff' to assist him. Sir Robert's horsekeeper had drawn his sword to defend them both, but had been told not to strike Morley because he was a priest. However, when Morley 'foyned' at him with his knife, he had only struck back with the 'flatlings' (broadside) of his sword which had caused little or no harm. Sir Robert had then disarmed Morley. Meanwhile, hearing the noise, and fearing that their master was going to be murdered, Sir Robert's servants had forced open the door and broken the panes of glass in its window. Sir Robert then took Anne out of the house and only one strike with 'flatlings' was made against a servant who refused to open the doors.

Ralph Rokeby himself was obviously not at home when these events took place. In his own defence he denied that Anne was a ward of the King and that he had taken rents from her lands that should have gone to the King. He also denied that Sir Robert had any authority from the King to take Anne away and that he had never called on the Sheriff or any other of the King's officers to assist him. He attributed the false accusations to the malicious mind and personal animosity that Sir Robert bore towards him. He accused Sir Robert of taking Anne away 'to the intent that by his extort power he might obtain unlawfully the marriage of the said Anne to one of his younger sons'. To prove his point he said that Sir Robert had already 'handfest' (promised or betrothed) her to his son Thomas.

Further details of the case come from the examination of witnesses on both sides. It transpires that Ralph Rokeby had married his son John to Anne when they were both five or six years old and that, after taking her away from Bishop Burton, Sir Robert had 'handfest' her to his eleven- or twelve-year-old son Thomas, apparently without the authority of the King. For his part, Ralph Rokeby seems to have been in league with Edward Beresford, a lawyer of Gray's Inn, who had married Anne's mother after her father's death. The reason for this 'cooperation' would seem to be the fact that Anne's mother (now Jane Beresford) had a lifetime's interest in some of lands that had been left to Anne by her father. Sir Robert Constable, on the other hand, had the support of Brian Hastings (later Sir Brian Hastings, High Sheriff of Yorkshire in 1536–7). Hastings was related to Anne, his sister Margaret having being married to John Cresacre, Anne's grandfather. Hastings said that after being removed from Ralf Rokeby's house at Bishop Burton Anne had been taken first to his house – although he was away at the time. When he returned home he had 'counselled her rather to take the son of Sir Robert than to do the contrary, or to take any other'. Later, he said that Sir Marmaduke Constable, Sir Robert's son and heir, had taken Anne to the house of John Nowell (who had married Brian Hastings's niece) with the intention of having her 'affyed' (affianced/betrothed) to young Thomas Constable.

In his evidence Brian Hastings added some clarity to Anne's status. He said that various attempts had been made to establish her wardship, but every attempt had been thwarted by the 'sinister and crafty labour' of Beresford and Rokeby. He said he was in London when Sir Richard Weston, Master of the Wards, had delivered the King's letter to Sir Richard Constable's servant – the letter ordering him to bring Anne to the King's Council 'unaffyed, contracted, or handfest'. He said that Anne had told him that she had been married to John Rokeby but that she was 'so young at the time that she knew not, nor could not remember it'. In other words, she only knew of the marriage because she had been told about it. Hastings said that he had never seen any gold ring on Anne's finger but had heard that she had given one away when she had refused to have anything to do with John Rokeby. John was, in any case, the bastard son of Ralph Rokeby. As for the supposed marriage of Anne to Thomas Constable, he said he knew well 'that a marriage was not consummated between them'.

Given the nature of the acrimonious relationship that seems to have existed between Ralph Rokeby and Sir Robert Constable (who was Lord of Flamborough in Yorkshire), it would not be surprising if the truth about what happened on the day Anne was taken away from the manor at Bishop Burton fell somewhere between the two accounts given of it. However that may be, it seems that Sir Robert *was* acting on the King's orders when he removed her from the custody of Ralph Rokeby and returned her to the jurisdiction of the Crown.

The matter was finally drawn to a close on 22 February 1525 when, in spite of having being found guilty of 'affiancing' Anne to his son Thomas 'and sufferinge hym before marriage to know her carnally', Sir Robert was pardoned of all the offences he may have committed. By that time the question of Anne's wardship had already been settled through its purchase by Sir Thomas More.[3]

John More and Anne Cresacre were married in December 1529. He was twenty and she just eighteen years old. As John was the only son and heir of Sir Thomas, and Anne his ward, their marriage and its accompanying celebrations must have been a grand affair, but unfortunately no record of the day or the place where the marriage was solemnized has come down to us. The period of Anne's wardship ceased with her marriage, and she came into possession of extensive lands in West Yorkshire, including the manor of Barnburgh, near Doncaster, and the manors of Mosseley-in-the-Moss and Tylts, all in Yorkshire.

Barnburgh, the principal seat of the Cresacre family, derives its name from the Saxon borough of Beorn, and has been known by various names down the ages, from Baronburgh, through Barmburgh and Barnborough, down to the present Barnburgh.

During the reign of Edward the Confessor (King of England 1042–1066) the lands in the area were divided into two, one part (or 'moiety') being held by William de Warren of Consiburgh (now Conisbrough) and the other by Roger de Busli, Baron of Tichell (now Tickhill). The Lordship of the part of the Manor that belonged to the honour of Tickhill then passed through the hands of a number of families, including the Fitzwilliam family of Sprotborough Manor, until the Cresacres first became Lords of Barnburgh in 1284.[4] After the marriage of Anne Cresacre to John More, the senior male heirs of the family became Lords of the

Manor of Barnburgh, a title they held until the 1800s.

Being the youngest members of the family, John and Anne may have continued to live in the Great House at Chelsea for a while after their marriage. The suggestion that they did not move to their own home until some time after Sir Thomas's death seems to be based on the fact that all their children are said to have been born in Chelsea – though I haven't seen any evidence for this.[5] Even if it were true, I do not think that the one fact necessarily flows from the other. The common custom of the time for newly married couples of sufficient means was to move into their own property, the ownership of which was often established in the marriage settlement. At the time the Barnburgh estate was inherited by Anne there was a small Tudor mansion there, called Barnburgh Hall. Nearby was the church of St Peter where some of her ancestors had been buried. The church, originally smaller than it is now, was of Norman origin being built sometime around AD 1150. The north aisle was added around 1200 and most of the church rebuilt in the 1330s. On the west face of the tower above the rounded arch of the window there can still be seen a small shield with the now barely visible three lions of the Cresacre Arms on it. Inside the church there is the Cresacre chapel, once a chantry chapel, in which there is the tomb of Sir Percival Cresacre, Anne's great-great grandfather, who died in 1477. His wife Alice, the daughter of Thomas Mounteney, died in 1450. Sir Percival is reputed to have been chased by a 'big cat' which attacked and killed him in the porch of the church. This may account for the big cat of the family crest that sits above the shield with the arms of 'three lions rampant'.

Whenever it might have been that John and Anne moved to Barnburgh I cannot help but feel that when they did Anne, at least, would have felt very much at home near the resting place of her ancestors. A local tradition says that Sir Thomas renovated and extended the Hall for the young couple as part of the marriage settlement, and that he visited them there on more than one occasion. Given the relative isolation of Barnburgh it would have been natural for Anne to travel to Chelsea before her confinements. There she could receive care and support from her family and also be near to the best possible medical care available, should it be needed.

When the net began to tighten around his father, John, as son and heir, must have had some fear for his own life, and Barnburgh would have provided him with an ideal retreat. It was far enough from London for him to be out of sight for most of the time but near enough for him to visit his family and to deal with business matters.

The story that young John was reduced to poverty after his father's death is not, I think, true. Most of Sir Thomas's properties were sequestered, so he was unable to inherit these, but the Barnburgh estate and other lands in Yorkshire belonged to Anne and these were not touched. Although not providing the couple with an income that would have enabled them to live like a lord and lady, it would certainly have been sufficient to enable them to live comfortably, and there is no evidence that they had to sell off any lands in order to make ends meet.

One of the few things we know about John was his suspected involvement in what has become known as the 'Plot of the Prebendaries' in 1543, when some of the canons of Canterbury Cathedral, inspired by Bishop Gardiner, reported Archbishop Cranmer to the King for misappropriating funds belonging to the Fraternity of Christ Church, Canterbury, and using them to spread heresy in Kent. It seems that some of the funds in question had been contributed by members of the 'More Circle' – friends and relatives of the More family – who thereby became implicated in the plot. Among the other so-called 'conspirators' were John Larke, Thomas More's former parish priest (now Blessed John Larke), John Ireland, Thomas More's former chaplain (now the Venerable John Ireland), William Roper, William Daunce, John Elrington (Lady Alice More's grandson) and, as already mentioned in chapter one, John Heywood. The King set up a commission to examine the case, and Cranmer was imprisoned for a while after having been assured by the King that he had more regard for him than to permit him to be overthrown by his enemies. The King gave Cranmer his ring to present to the commission as a sign that he had the right to have an appeal heard by him. In due course both the accused and the accusers were called to appear before the King who rebuked them all for their conduct. Cranmer, however, held on to his position – ever more keen to go along with the King's reforms – while the conspirators were, in March 1544, convicted of treason and sentenced to death and the forfeiture of their property. The conspirators were all presented with the Act of Supremacy and asked to sign. John Larke, John Ireland, Bishop Gardiner, and probably John Elrington, refused and were executed.[6] William Daunce and John More signed, and were pardoned on 24 April. John's pardon reads:

John More of Chelsith, Midd. *alias* of Bamburgh, Yorks. *alias* of London. Pardon of all treasonable words with the detestable traitors, John Eldryngton, Germain Gardyner, John Bekynsale, John Heywood, Wm. Daunce, John Larke, clk., John Irelande, clk., and any others, in wishing ill to the King and arguing against the King's supremacy, and all concealments of treasons, of which he has been accused; with restoration of goods. Greenwich, 24 April, 36 Henry VIII. *Del.* Westm. 26 April.[7]

As we saw in chapter one, John Heywood held out for a while longer. He was pardoned at the end of June and, being a more public figure, had to make a grovelling recantation at St Paul's Cross on 6 July 1544.

Although John, like all the other members of his family, signed the Act of Supremacy when it was first introduced, and signed it again after the Prebendaries affair, there is no sign that he abandoned his Catholic faith. As we have seen, Catholic doctrines and the celebration Mass remained largely untouched during the reign of Henry VIII. John died at the age of thirty-eight in 1547 – the same year that Henry VIII died. Unfortunately we do not know the exact date, the cause of his death, or the place where he was buried. It is likely to have been at Barnburgh, but the Register of Burials at the church did not start until 1558.

John and Anne had eight children: Thomas, Augustine, Edward, Gerome, another Thomas, Bartholomew, Anne and Francis. It seems likely that the first three of these, at least, were born in the Great House at Chelsea where, if Anne had not been living there at the time, it would have been natural for her to go there when the time for her confinement arrived. Later references to the children as being 'of Chelsea' does not necessarily mean that they were born there, or that they lived there; the use of locations was a common way of indicating lines of descent from particular families.

The births of seven and the death of one of John and Anne's children are recorded at the end of a family Book of Hours, as follows:

Thomas, the eldest son and heir, usually referred to as Thomas More II, 'was born at 12 o'clock on Tuesday the 8th of August, in the 23rd year of the reign of King Henry VIII, the year of our Lord 1531'. Reference to the saints days involved – St Cyriacus (8th August) and St Lawrence (9th August) – indicate that the birth took place at midnight between the two days. Thomas's godparents were Sir Thomas More, Margaret More, Lord Darcy and Thomas Hungerford.

Augustine 'was born between 12 midnight and 1 a.m. on Tuesday the 5th of August, in the 25th year of the reign of King Henry VIII, the year of our Lord 1533'. This day was noted to be dedicated to St Oswald and also to be the eve of the Feast of the Transfiguration of our Lord. Augustine's godparents were Sir Thomas Arundel, Anthony Bonvisi, Lady More, and John Staverton. The only thing we know about Augustine is that he is recorded as having died while he was still young.

Edward 'was born between 7 and 8 o'clock in the morning of Saturday the 13th August in the 27th year of the reign of Henry VIII, the year of our Lord 1535'. This day was noted as being dedicated to St Brictius, bishop and confessor. No godparents are named – it is likely that few would have wanted to be openly associated with the family so soon after Sir Thomas's execution.

Gerome More's entry in the Book of Hours is unclear, a sign perhaps that it was written at a moment of great sadness. Only his death is noted – 'Gerome my 4th son died' – and no date is given. However, he is believed to have been born after Edward and before Thomas III (see below) so it was probably in 1537. A Sir Edward, a Mr Radforth and Mrs Clement (Margaret Clement, née Giggs) are indicated as being present, presumably at his baptism.

Thomas More the younger (in pedigrees usually listed as Thomas More III) 'was born between 1 and 2 a.m. on Tuesday the 2nd of July, in the 30th year of the reign of Henry VIII, 1538'. Thomas Cromwell, Earl of Essex, Sir Richard Weston, Lady Knevet and the Lord Bishop of Durham (Cuthbert Tunstall) are listed as being present at his confirmation.

Bartholomew More, Thomas III's younger brother, 'was born at 11 p.m. on Tuesday the 10th of February in the 31st year of the reign of Henry VIII, 1540'. The day was noted as being dedicated to St Scholastica the virgin, and William Roper, John Stephenson (the first husband of his aunt, Elizabeth Roper), a Mrs Ledar and a Mr Germayn were godparents.

Anne, the only daughter of John More II, 'was born at 2 o'clock in the morning of Tuesday in Palm Sunday Week in the 32nd year of the reign of Henry VIII'. A look at the ecclesiastical calendar indicates that this was Tuesday 12 April 1541. Thomas Roper, Elizabeth Roper and Mary Roper (her uncle and aunts) were godparents.

Francis More, the youngest of the seven brothers, and the

youngest child in the family, 'was born on the 29th day of December between three and four o'clock in the afternoon in the year of our Lord 1546'. A look at the calendar for that year indicates that this was a Wednesday.

After John More's death in 1547, Anne devoted herself to bringing up her young family. She remained a widow until 1559 when, on 25 June, she married George West of Aughton and Aston, Yorkshire, becoming his second wife. They did not have any children.

Aughton and Aston, were two villages in the parish of Aston to the South of Rotherham, and East of Sheffield, in Yorkshire. While each retains its separate name they have now merged to form a small town. The Wests were Lords of the Manor of Aughton, a small estate with a Hall and around fifteen acres of land. They also owned a house and thirty acres of land in Aston as well as three houses at Canonthorpe (later known as Fawkeners), a hamlet on the edge of Aughton that has now disappeared.

George West was the son of John West of Aughton (d.1541) and, Anne, the daughter of Ralph Eyre of Offerton in the peak, Derbyshire. George's first wife was Jane the daughter of Thomas Trygot of Kirkby, Yorkshire, and by her he had had son John, and a daughter Elizabeth.[8]

After their marriage George and Anne lived at Barnburgh Hall. George was a Protestant and, during his lifetime, Ann and her teenage children appear to have accompanied him to church on Sundays. There was no chapel at Barnburgh Hall as there was at the larger houses of the more important gentry. However, a 'priest hole' discovered about eight feet up between the chimney and the exterior wall of the dining room during alterations in 1880 was found to contain around 200 silver coins from the reigns of Elizabeth I and James I. This indicates that priests are likely to have visited the family on their travels around Yorkshire during these times. The secular clergy were desperately short of money to support their dangerous missionary activity, and maybe the money was saved to help them on their way, or for use in an emergency, should a priest need to buy a safe passage out of the country.

Anne's external conformity was not uncommon, and history has given the name 'church papists' to those who did so. Those who had conformed in this way were not generally regarded as apostates and, even as late as 1592, Cardinal Allen was writing from Rome to the English secular priests, telling them that they should 'use great compassion and mercifulness towards such of the Layty especially as for mere fear or saving of their family, wife and children from ruins are so far only fallen as to come sometimes to their Churches or be present at the time of their service'.[9]

George West died in 1572 and was buried at St Peter's on 12 June. In his will he left his estates at Aughton, Aston and Canonthorpe to Thomas More II and to his nephew, Mr John Wombwell. He also left £20 to Edward More.

George West's Protestantism and her own external appearance of conformity appear to have offered Anne protection from recusancy fines during the thirteen years of their marriage. After George's death, however, she could no longer expect further toleration and, in a book of 'Yorkshire Fines' for Michaelmas Term (September) 1573, I discovered a record in which she, together with Thomas II and III and with Edward, passes her estates in Yorkshire to Thomas Jackson and John Burnsall alias Clerk/Clark. This was not a sale of the estates but a legal agreement, and I can only think that, having become a recusant, Anne feared that her estates would be sequestered, and so transferred them, as it were for safekeeping, to two friends of the family. This was not an uncommon practice. John Burnsall was certainly local to Barnburgh as his marriage to Johanna Reynolds is recorded as having taken place in the church on 14 November 1563.

The document just mentioned shows the extent of Anne's estates, and I quote it in full:

> Manors of Baronburg *als.* Bamburgh *als.* Barnebrough *als.* Barnburgh *als.* Barneburgh, near Doncaster, Mosseley in the Mosse, and Tylts, and 140 messuages, 60 cottages, and 2 watermills with lands in the same and in Baronthorpe, Harlyngton, Bylham, Meixburgh, Bolton upon Derne, Goldthorpe, Wombwell, Little Haughton, Derfeild, Langthwayte cum Tylts, Doncaster, Thorp, Marnby upon Donne, Austen, Burghwallys, Campsall, Kyrkhousegreen, Btaithwayte, Kyrk Bramwith, Trumfleete, Kyrk Sandall, Balne, Wylmersley, Egburgh, Kellyngton, and Snayth, and free fishing in the waters of the Derne, Donne and Eyre.[10]

Anne's final presentment for recusancy came in 1577 when her name was included in a list of Yorkshire recusants sent to Westminster by the Archbishop of York.[11] Her death later that year at the age of sixty-seven brought an end to her sufferings.

Anne was buried at St Peter's church on 2 December. A memorial plaque, once over her grave, and later taken into safe custody at Barnburgh Hall, is now on the wall of the Cresacre Chapel in the church. Translated from the Latin it reads:

> Anne only daughter and heir of Edward Cresacre Esq.,
> of Baronburgh near Doncaster in the County of York
> married John More only son and heir of Sir Thomas More
> at one time Lord Chancellor of England
> which Anne passed out of this life
> the second day of December in the 67th year of her life
> the year of our Lord 1577.[12]

Of the eight children born to John and Anne two died young Gerome, probably stillborn, and Francis as an infant. It is not known how long Augustine lived but he is said to have died unmarried. Their oldest son, Thomas II and his family will be the subject of the next chapter.

Edward More, four years younger that his brother Thomas, presents as an enigmatic character who led a rather colourful life well into his forties. From what we know about him he seems to have been easily bored and unable to settle at anything for long. Writing of him in his later years, Cresacre More, his nephew, said of him:

> As for mine uncle Edward, who is yet alive, although he were endowed with excellent gifts of nature, as a ready wit, tongue at will, and his pen glib; yet, God knows, he hath drowned all his talents in self-conceit in no worthy qualities, and besides burieth himself alive in obscurity, in forsaking God, and his mean and base behaviour ...

Cresacre attributes his behaviour to the fact that, unlike his older brothers Thomas and Augustine, he was born after Sir Thomas's death, and he had not therefore received the last blessing he sent to them 'so directly' as they had.[13]

Edward's 'glib pen' had, it seems, produced a number of short works including one called *A lytle and Bryefe Treatyse called the Defence of Women & Especially of English Women*, made against 'The Schole House of Women*, that was licensed for publication in 1557 and again in 1563. It is perhaps typical of what Cresacre calls his 'ready wit' that Edward should admit in the dedication of his treatise that his chosen subject would be 'a matter more mete and decent for a marryed man to entreate and wryte of than for a bachyler or prynkokes but of twenty yeares of age or lytle more'.

The use of the word 'prynkokes' is interesting as it shows us that he saw himself as a rather forward young man, and a bit of a joker with a liking, perhaps, for the saucier type of humour.

Edward wrote the *Breyfe Treatyse* at Hambledon, Buckinghamshire, and dedicated it to his friend 'Mayster Wyllyam Page, Secretary to Syr Phillip Hobdy' on 20 July 1557. The dedication gives us the only clues we have as to Edward's activities around that time – that he had been busy studying in London and that he was taking 'a lytle vacant time from studye'.[14] As we will see, Hambledon was where his older brother Thomas, now married, was living with his in-laws. There were a number of relations in or near London with whom Edward could have stayed at other times, but what the nature of his studies were remains a mystery. It has been suggested that he may have been studying at Lincoln's Inn but there is no mention of him in the records there.[15]

Whatever studies Edward may have been engaged in he doesn't seem to have returned to them, as the next place we find him is at Barnburgh where his mother was still living and where his older brother Thomas and his wife would shortly also take up residence.

If Edward's *Breyfe Treatyse* had caused his family some embarrassment, then more was to follow. In October 1559 he was arrested with three others for burgling the house of Alexander Levesey at Arksey, not far from Barnburgh. In addition to stealing plate and other valuables worth over £66 they were also accused of assaulting the householder. Edward, and presumably his accomplices, spent some time in prison, before being allowed out on bail. Edward was officially granted a pardon on 30 October 1562, probably on the grounds that the offence was the result of a drunken frolic.[16]

By 1564 Edward's behaviour had become even more bizarre. He openly boasted that he had committed fornication in the church porch with a young girl, Jane Wyn, before chasing her and her friends out of the village with a pack of dogs. He seems to have taken a positive dislike to Robert Salvin the rector of the village church of St Peter, and reported him to the Court of the York High Commission for being absent from his parish, for mumbling services, for fornication with Katherine the wife of his cousin Edward Salvin, and for assaulting him – the latter not perhaps surprising in the circumstances! For his part Robert Salvin accused Edward of regularly leaving the church after Matins and before the Communion, of disturbing the services in church by blowing a horn in the churchyard and by noisily practising archery at the village butts near the church. He also accused Edward, and his brother Bartholomew, of horseplay inside the church by 'exercising and practising indecent and ungodly manners ... specially in laughing, mocking, jesting, talking and toying with uncivil and lascivious words ... ' Finally, he said that Edward had also 'sewed with needle and thread' during divine service, and 'in the manner of wanton boys ... thrown or pricked the straws and rushes at Bartholomew his brother and others in the said church sitting nigh unto him, shewing thereby how little he regardeth and esteemeth the book of common prayer'.

The testimony of the rector's cousin tells us something about Edward's relationship with his mother and stepfather. Apparently, Edward had threatened his step-father with 'bow bent and arrow' (that is, with the bow string pulled back and arrow in place ready to shoot) in the churchyard and had pursued him and continued to threaten him when he retreated into the church – the latter act being 'in contempt of the statute in that behalf provided against chiders and brawlers in church'. He had on another occasion physically thrown George West out of the family pew in the church. He had often called his mother a whore, and his stepfather a knave and a villain, and told him that he would never accept him as his mother's husband. Edward was accused before the court of having 'grown into such an obstinacy in wickedness that divers and sundry times he has called his mother a whore openly in the said church using such scoldings and chidings with his said mother in the said church ... so that the parishioners ... have been disgusted'.

Edward was summoned to appear before the York Commissioners in September 1565. He confessed to going into the church at Barnburgh during divine service with his bow bent and was committed to York Castle in April 1566 for punishment while the court decided what to do with him. On 10 April 1557 the Commission ordered him to do public penance at communion time the following Sunday in the church at Barnburgh. He was to kneel before his mother and to say out loud 'Whereas I have called yow beinge my naturall mother hoore, I am sory for yt and therefore desire God and yow all others whom my so savenges have offended to forgive me.' He also had to ask forgiveness of all those he had offended by carrying a bent bow in the churchyard and in the church. Finally, he had to tell the congregation that his boast about having 'carnally misused' the body of Jane Wyn was not true, and that he was sorry for having said it.

As for the rector of St Peter's: he was rebuked for mumbling services, but it was accepted that he was entitled to be absent from the parish when performing his duties as chaplain to the Earl of Derby. The story of his fornication seems to have been another of Edward's inventions.

In February 1570 Edward was in more trouble with the High Commission at York. He (and his older brother Thomas) had been reported for not having received Holy Communion as often as he was required by law to do, and of not having done this for 'divers years'. Edward was also said to be the author of various rhymes, ballads and prophecies of an infamous sort and, in particular, was accused of having contributed to, or himself written a tract referred to as 'the infamous Libell & figure astronomical'. This time Edward seems to have compounded his offence by the way he 'lewdly and indiscreetly and unreverently behaved himself' towards the court. Again he was committed to York Castle while the authorities decided what to do with him. On 11 March he appeared before the court for sentence. He was made to promise 'not to make, write, compile, publish or set forth any infamous letters, writings, rhymes ballards or prognostications'. Edward and Thomas were both fined twenty shillings for not communicating and ordered to distribute it among the poor of Barnburgh parish and other local parishes or to pay it towards the repair of 'some decayed bridge thereabouts'.

The last recorded examples of Edward's brushes with the law were in 1580. On 27 August he was accused of 'disobedience in religion' – the phrase used to indicate refusal to receive Holy Communion at divine service as the law required. This time he declared that he would conform and paid a bond of £100 (approx. £16,000 today), that he would go to Communion and produce a document by October declaring that he had done so. A few days later, on 2 September he was again before the court – this time in Wakefield – accused of having spoken 'certain wordes' against the State. This was a serious charge and in spite of denying it, he was, yet again, committed to York Castle. His case was heard in York Minster five days later and he was released after paying a bond of £40 and ordered to appear before the court again on 3 October. At that hearing his bond was cancelled after he presented a certificate testifying to his having communicated at St Mary's, Castlegate, the parish in which York Castle was situated.

It was not until 14 November that Edward's case was finally dealt with. At that hearing his 'words against the State' turned out to be saying something against the Book of Common Prayer and a book of Latimer's sermons. Once again he was ordered to do public penance on the following Sunday during divine service in the church at Barnburgh. He was to declare 'that the said booke is goode and godly and that the said sermons of D. Latimer are godly and agreeing with the word of God'. This time he was required to produce a certificate for the court testifying that he had satisfied the conditions of the court.

Over the next couple of months – and with the knowledge that the Yorkshire Commissioners were showing themselves increasingly determined to weed out 'undutiful and disobedient subjects in matters of religion now established' – Edward, now forty-five years of age, appears to have come to the realization that he could, only at his peril, continue to oppose the established order, and he finally conformed to the Anglican Church. By the beginning of 1581, as if to underline his conformity, he had become one of the churchwardens at Barnburgh and, when required by the Commissioners to send them a list of those 'not comminge to churche nor receyvinge the communion', he 'presented' his brother Thomas, his family, and three of their servants, along with some other parishioners.

So far, no one has come up with a satisfactory explanation of Edward's behaviour. I suppose today psychologists might put it down to the stress of the traumatic events involving the family during his mother's pregnancy but, of course, there is no way of proving that. Had he been an adolescent his behaviour would, at least in my younger days, have been described as 'maladjusted' – and probably today he would be diagnosed with Attention Deficit Syndrome or some other syndrome used to explain unacceptable behaviour. As we have seen, he was accused with his younger brother of behaving 'in the manner of wanton boys', but Edward was not a wanton boy, he was twenty-nine, and his 'bad' behaviour continued well into his forties.

The church authorities in Yorkshire who had to deal with Edward's behaviour saw it as an obstinate refusal to conform to the law requiring attendance at the local parish church on Sunday for divine service and the receipt of Communion according to the rite in the Book of Common Prayer – both performed with due respect and decorum. In the circumstances is not hard to see how this is the only way they could see it.

From a Catholic perspective it would be easy to attribute Edward's behaviour to his adherence to the faith of his grandfather, and as a rebellion against the new religion, but there is no evidence that Edward was ever a religious man – either Catholic or Protestant – and his convictions for theft and violence, his boasts of immoral behaviour (whether true or not) and his dabbling in sorcery hardly fit either image.

On a personal level, Edward's behaviour shows that he certainly disliked his stepfather and, for all we know, he might have had reason to do so – but that hardly justifies him calling his mother a whore in public. If a final judgement is needed then, for myself, I cannot help but feel that of all the people in and around Barnburgh at that time, Edward was perhaps the most unpleasant of them all.

Where Edward managed to find the money to pay his court and prison costs, and the other bonds and fines he had to pay, has not previously been researched. It seems to have been assumed that they were paid by his elder brother Thomas II. Recently, however, I discovered an entry in the 'Feet of Fines' for Yorkshire that records a transfer of property from Edward to his brother during the summer of 1565. The transfer involved the 'Manor of Tylthall alias Great Tylse, 3 messuages with land in Tylse, Balne, Barnby-upon-Donne and Doncaster'.[17] It is quite possible that the income from this property was granted to Edward as his share of the family inheritance when he reached adulthood. However, the later recovery of the property may indicate that the family judged him incapable of managing it properly, or that they used it as a way of keeping the property within the family while providing Edward with the funds he needed to pay off his debts. Perhaps they hoped that reducing his 'pocket money' in this way might help to bring him to heel!

As we saw above we have no evidence that Edward had any further brushes with the law after the beginning of the 1580s. By this time his mother and stepfather were dead and his older brother (Thomas II) and his family were about to leave Yorkshire to take up residence in Essex. It seems likely that Edward remained at Barnburgh, but we have no idea what he did or how he lived between this time and his burial in St Peter's, Barnburgh on 2 May 1620.

Some family researchers, and one pedigree of the family published in 1874, have suggested that Edward had a daughter, Anne.[18] Unfortunately, some confusion has been caused by the fact that, as we will see in the next chapter, Edward's niece, Mary (the daughter of his older brother Thomas II), married an (unrelated) Edward More of Bampton in Oxfordshire and had a daughter Anne. Further confusion has been caused by the fact that in his will Thomas II refers to Anne More as 'daughter of the said Edward More', without making it clear to which Edward he is referring. Yet more confusion has been caused by the copyist of the will who, in different places used both 'More' and 'Moore' to spell the surname of the two families.

Having definitely conformed to the Church of England by or before 1580, Edward had, in Catholic eyes, 'become a Protestant' or, as his nephew Cresacre More later said, he had 'degenerated both from that religion and those manners, which Sir Thomas More left as it were a happy depositum unto his children and family'.[19] If he did marry and have a child before that year, then we would expect the events to have been recorded in the Barnburgh Registers for baptisms and marriages that began in 1557 and 1559 respectively – but there is no such record. There is, however, a reference to the burial of an Elizabeth More, widow, in the Barnburgh Register for 10 June 1628. If Edward did marry, this could be his wife.

In addition to Anne, who it says, became a Benedictine nun, another pedigree of the family also attributes two sons, Thomas and Henry (both of whom became Jesuit priests), and four other daughters to Edward of Barnburgh.[20] It seems that most, if not all of these were born in the years 1586 to 1600 when Edward would have been aged between fifty-one and sixty-five.

As we have seen, Edward does seem to have settled down in his fifties, and he could then have married and had a family of seven children. However, there is also no record of these children in the Barnburgh register and no mention is made of them in the will of Thomas II. Furthermore, given Edward's behaviour over many years it seems unlikely that he would have been the father of a Catholic nun and two priests. Having looked at all the available evidence my own feeling is that these children were the children of Edward's niece and her husband Edward More of Haddon. We will meet these in the next chapter.

It was, apparently, not uncommon in the days we are speaking of, for two children in a family to have the same first name, and Edward's younger brother was also given the name Thomas. As we saw above he is usually referred to in family pedigrees as Thomas III. According to his nephew Cresacre More, Thomas also 'degenerated' from the religion of his grandfather' but, worse still, he became a Protestant minister – an act for which he could find no excuse. In his will of 1606, his older brother (Thomas II) refers to the younger Thomas as 'deceased' and he left £10 each (approx. £1,500 today) to his three children, Cyprian, Thomas and Constantine. No mention is made of Thomas III's wife and her name has never been discovered. Cresacre's tells us that the family were very poor and that the children had been brought up 'in no commendable profession'. Cresacre also tells us that only the eldest of the children – who would have been Cyprian – was still alive in his time (he was writing around 1616).[21]

A list of the clergy of the Church of England is in the process of being drawn up, but inevitably, because of lost documents, it will never be complete. I have, so far, not seen a 'Thomas More' that would fit 'our' Thomas's profile.[22]

Bartholomew More was the youngest surviving son of the family. Apart from his involvement in some horseplay with his older brother Edward in and around the church at Barnburgh early in 1564 (when he was twenty-four) we know little about him. However, I have discovered that William Rastell (his cousin), in his will of 8 August 1564 – registered with the authorities in Antwerp – makes provision for an annuity of 150 florins to be paid to Bartholomew and his heirs. Interestingly, the will stipulates that the annuity will be withdrawn if Bartholomew returns to England before it is reconciled to the Catholic faith, if he fails to live an upright and moral life, or if he embraces heretical opinions.[23] In the circumstances it may be that, to avoid further embarrassment, and to get him away from his brother Edward's bad influence, Bartholomew was sent to stay with family relations who had sought exile on the Continent. In the event, however, his stay seems to have been short-lived for, when proving William Rastell's will in 1568, his executor and nephew, Ellis Heywood, SJ, said that the provision made for Bartholomew had been revoked in a codicil to the will.[24] Since Cresacre More tells us that Bartholomew had abandoned his Catholic faith, and that he died young of the plague in London he must have returned to England and died sometime between 8 August 1564 and 27 August 1565 when William Rastell died in Louvain. He would then have been twenty-five years old.

Anne More (jnr.), was the only daughter in the family of John and Anne More, and the only thing we know about her early life is that, at the age of eighteen, on 6 September 1559, she married

John West in the parish church at Barnburgh. John was her stepfather's son by his first wife, Jane Trygot.

John and Anne West appear to have been conforming Anglicans and to have lived at Aughton, though two of their children, Jane and Anne, are recorded in the family's Book of Hours as having been baptized in St Peter's, Barnburgh. Jane was born 'on saterday after our lady day [As'ucion] at the xij of the cloke in the night ... in the second yere of the reig'e of owre sovereinge lady Quene Elyzbeth And in the yere of oure lorde God 1560. Mr. Styme Trigott godfather my lady Haystynges And Mystris Mary Coplay Godmothers'. Anne 'was baptised the xxviij day of awgut and in the yere of our lorde god 1561. Mestres Anne West and mestres Lucie Trigot godmothers. Mr Edward Hawlye godfather'.

In addition to Jane and Anne, the couple had another daughter, Barbara, and a son and heir, Godfrey, who married Catherine Revel at Hansworth (a few miles to the East of Aughton) on 25 May 1579. Catherine was the daughter of Thomas Revel, the grandson of Sir John Revel of Stannington, whose estates lay a few miles to the West of Sheffield.

Godfrey and Catherine West had a daughter, Anne, who was baptized at Hansworth on 10 July 1580, and who married Godfrey Bradshaw on 20 February 1597. This line had died out by 1666.

Genealogical Summary

John More II and his Family

John More (1509–1547) m. (1530) Anne Cresacre (1511–1577)
Children:
1. Thomas II (1531–1606): eldest son and heir (see next chapter).
2. Augustine (b.1533): said to have died young.
3. Edward (1535–1620): may have married. ? daughter, Anne.
4. Gerome (b.1537): probably stillborn or died soon after birth.
5. Thomas III (b.1538; died before 1606): became a Church of England minister. Married, but name of wife not known.
   Children: Cyprian (alive in 1616), Thomas (died before 1616); Constantine (died before 1616).
6. Bartholomew (1540– c.1565): unmarried.
7. Anne (1541–1572): m. (1) John West, son of George West of Aughton/Aston.
   Children: i. Jane: born Barnburgh on 17 August 1660.
   ii. Anne: baptized at Barnburgh on 28 August 1661.
   iii. Godfrey: m. (1579) Catherine Revel, daughter of Thomas Revel of Hansworth by his first wife.
   Only daughter, Anne, baptized 10 July 1580.
   iv. Barbara
   m. (2) Thomas Revel at Hansworth on 7 June 1580. His 2nd wife.
   Children: i. Catherine (who married Godfrey West, above).
   ii. Anne
8. Francis (b.1546): said to have died when still a child.

After John More's death, Anne More (Senior) married (1559) George West of Aughton. They had no children.

Chapter Four

Thomas More II and his Family

Born in the Great House at Chelsea on Tuesday 8 August 1531, Thomas II was, as we have seen, the eldest son of John and Anne More (née Cresacre). Only just four when his grandfather was executed, he must have been aware of the stress and anxiety suffered by his parents and close relations as they struggled to survive in its aftermath. Not surprisingly, no record of his early education has come down to us, but there is no doubt that he was intelligent and that, with his Catholic faith, he inherited some of his grandfather's uncompromising principles. He was the first member of the family to feel the full brunt of the anti-Catholic legislation that began to be introduced during the reign of Elizabeth I and, although he did not 'lose' his head, his sufferings were, proportionally, greater and endured for longer than those of his grandfather. Writing of him after his death, his son Cresacre refers to his constant faith, his honesty and his true Catholic simplicity. Of all the descendants of Sir Thomas he could, I believe, be regarded as the greatest of that line of true 'Confessors' of the faith.

It was probably because of their Yorkshire connections that the More and Scrope families came into contact with each other and arrangements were made for Thomas II's marriage to Mary Scrope early in 1553. Mary was born in 1534, the third and youngest daughter of John Scrope of Spenithorne, Yorkshire, and Hambleden, Buckinghamshire, and his second wife Phillis, the daughter of Ralph Rokeby of Mortham, Yorkshire. Mary's grandparents were Henry 6th Lord Scrope of Bolton and Elizabeth, the daughter of Henry Percy, 4th Earl of Northumberland and his wife Maud Herbert. It is through this line that subsequent descendants of the More family can trace their ancestry back to Alfred the Great.

The manor of Hambleden came to the Scrope family when Sir Richard Scrope, first Lord Scrope of Bolton, took possession of it in the 1370s. The last member of the family to hold the manor was Emmanuel Scrope, first and only Lord Sunderland, who died in 1631.[1]

John and Phillis Scrope lived at Hambleden, and it was here that Thomas and Mary made their home for a few years after their marriage. Here also, their first two children, Mary and Anne, were born.

The year 1553 must have been full of hope for the young couple. Thomas was twenty-two, and Mary's accession to the throne in July gave him the promise of a relief from persecution, the return of England to its ancient faith and, for landed families, the restitution of sequestered property. For Thomas this restitution meant the return of the manor of Gobions at North Mimms to his widowed mother though, because of existing leases by the Crown to Princess Elizabeth in 1550, and by Princess Elizabeth to Sir Ambrose Cave in 1566, the family were not able to enter into actual possession until much later.

In November 1554 Thomas was elected as a Member of Parliament for Ripon in Yorkshire, a constituency that came under the patronage of the Duchy of Lancaster. His recommendation for this position may have come from Marmaduke Wyvill of Constable Burton, Yorkshire, also a Member of Parliament for Ripon, whose son Christopher had married Mary's younger sister Margaret.[2]

Unfortunately Thomas's position was short-lived due to him absenting himself 'without leave' from Parliament before it was dissolved. The reason for his absence is not certain but all the indications are that it was because he was one of a group of thirty-eight Members of Parliament who, led by Edmund Plowden, absented themselves because they were opposed to the reintroduction by Parliament of ancient heresy laws. Whatever the reason, his absence was taken to have been deliberate and, as a result he found himself in court and with a fine of 53s. 4d. to pay (approx. £500 today). This was a considerable sum of money to find and his relations came to the rescue; Ralph Scrope (his brother-in-law) and Richard Heywood (the brother of John Heywood who had married Sir Thomas More's niece Joan Rastell) offered themselves as sureties for the payment of the fine.

Thomas's unauthorized absence from Parliament seems to have blotted his copybook and no further opportunities for advancement were offered to him. This may have been one of the reasons why he decided to make his home at Barnburgh in Yorkshire where his widowed mother was already in residence with his younger brothers Edward and Bartholomew and his sister Anne.

We know very little about Thomas and Mary's life at Barnburgh. No doubt they were involved in the celebrations surrounding Anne More senior's marriage to George West in June 1959 and to the marriage of Thomas's youngest sister Anne to John West the following September.

There is no evidence that Thomas and Mary ever conformed, even externally, to the Church of England. The fact that the baptisms of eight of their children are recorded in the parish register does not necessarily mean that they were baptized in the church – the entry of all baptisms was required by law. However, when there were no Catholic priests available, it was common practice for Catholics to have their children baptized in the local parish church.

In September 1538 Cromwell had ordered the keeping of registers in parish churches where entries were to be made by the minister, in the presence of the churchwarden, after divine service each Sunday. However, no order was made as to how the records were to be kept and, as a result, many were lost. It was not until 1598 that, by a decree of Elizabeth I, they were ordered to be backdated to 1538 or, if that was not possible, to at least the beginning of her reign (1558). This time, they were required to be recorded in books made of parchment. The first entry in the Barnburgh register is for the baptism in 1557 of Thomas and Mary's eldest son, John. The Catholic Church ordered the keeping of registers for baptisms and marriages in 1563, but in England the few wandering missionary priests who had survived were not able to carry registers around with them as they moved secretly from one place to another.

At the beginning of Elizabeth's reign there was still a lot of confusion among Catholics about their religious position. Elizabeth said she wanted everyone to worship, and to worship in the same way, and to achieve this the Act of Uniformity passed in 1559 required the Book of Common Prayer to be used in all churches and imposed a fine of one shilling a time (approx. £9.00 today) on those who failed to attend church on Sundays and 'Holy Days'. At this time there were still a few openly Catholic bishops in post, with Archbishop Nicholas Heath acting as their head. Those who refused to accept the new legislation were imprisoned or placed under house arrest; some took refuge on the Continent. Archbishop Heath, who had announced Elizabeth's accession in the House of Lords, was deprived of his living in 1559 and sent to the Tower. Shortly after, however, he was allowed to retire to his house at Chobham Park in Surrey on condition that he did not interrupt the laws of the Church or State or meddle with the affairs of the realm. For their part, the clergy who refused to conform were, in the first instance, punished by the loss of a year's income and by six months' imprisonment. Second and third offences made them liable to the loss of their living and a year in prison and then to life imprisonment. There were around 8,000 parish clergy at this time and only about 300 of them are known to have lost their livings for refusing to conform. Many of the others continued to say the Latin Mass as they had always done, some before conducting the Prayer Book service in the parish church, others in private houses.

When the number of Anglican Holy Days was finalized in 1561 it required everyone to attend church on seventy-seven days of the year – and when there to behave 'in an orderly and sober manner'. In some places, those who went to church but who 'walked and talked' during the service, or who behaved contemptuously or left early were also fined the same amount as if they had absented themselves from church.[3] The money raised by these fines was used for the support of the poor in the parish, and the responsibility for collecting them was given to churchwardens. In practice, these were sometimes negligent and sometimes plainly unwilling to take money from those who, if not their friends and neighbours, might well have been their landlords.

Queen Elizabeth is reputed as having said that she wanted uniformity of worship but not a window into people's souls. In other words, as long as people went to church and didn't cause trouble she was not really interested in what they believed 'inwardly'. It is not surprising therefore that the Book of Common Prayer imposed by Elizabeth (a modified version the two earlier prayer books of 1549 and 1552) was, on important issues such as the real presence of Christ at Communion, worded in such a way as to be capable of being understood in both a 'Catholic' and a 'Protestant' sense.

The way in which services were conducted in a particular parish at this time very much depended on the 'leaning' of the rector or parson and, as we saw in the last chapter, the proceedings of the courts dealing with Edward More in 1564, tell us that the Rector of Barnburgh was often absent from his parish, thereby leaving it without any Sunday services. It was also these same proceedings that tell us that Thomas (and Edward) were, in 1570, both fined twenty shillings (approx. £175 today) for not having received Communion as frequently as the law required, and for not having done this for 'divers' years.

Having no professional qualification, or position in national or local government that we know of, we can only assume that, while his mother was alive, Thomas shared in the management of, and the profits from, the estates inherited by her. Few documents have survived, but I have discovered one, dated 9 May 1577, that records Thomas leasing out an acre and a half of meadow in Bolton Inge and a number of plots of arable land totalling ten acres in Ingfield, Eastfield and Darfield in Bolton upon Derne to a Thomas Sykes, a husbandman of Hickleton on the Hill, a village near Barnburgh. The lease is for twenty-one years and is particularly interesting because it is an example of a transaction in which the rent is to be paid in kind rather than in ready money – 'four quarters of good and clean white Bolton wheat weighed out with the measure and mett of the towne of Barnsley, and the provision of a good mower for one day a year in harvest'. Also included in the lease is the provision that if Thomas should be required at any time to provide 'for the fyndyng or setting out of any light horseman or of any horseman' for use against the enemies of the Queen or the Realm of England then an additional payment in the form of 'good barley malt' (probably for the horse's feed) will have to be made. During the term of the lease the rent is to be paid 'on feast day of St. michael tharchangel' (Michaelmas, 29 September) or, if that is not possible, on the seventh day following. The wheat is to be 'carried and brought yearly by the said Edward ... to the now dwelling house of the said Thomas More in Baronburgh, or to any place or places within four miles distant from the same at the assignment or direction of the said Thomas More his heirs and assignees'.[4]

The year 1577 is significant in that it was the first year in which we find Thomas and Mary, and Anne West (Thomas's mother), included in a list of recusants at Barnburgh sent by the Archbishop of York to the Queen's Council in London. At that time the lands belonging to Thomas and his mother were assessed – no doubt with an eye to future fines – as being worth £20 a year each (approx £2,900 each today).[5] Had it not been for the frequent absence from the parish of its rector it is quite possible that

Thomas and his family would been have been presented for recusancy more often while they remained at Barnburgh.

In December 1577 Thomas's mother died and he inherited the family's estates. Over the next few years his bachelor brother Edward calmed down and, as we have seen, by 1580 had finally conformed to Anglicanism and become a churchwarden. Life at Barnburgh may have been relatively peaceful for Thomas and Mary, and a lesser man than Thomas might have been tempted to settle for the status quo. Thomas, however, was the grandson of Sir Thomas and made of sterner stuff! With his religious position now on record, and clearly aware of the possible consequences, he decided to throw himself into the promotion of the Catholic cause, and to do that more effectively he would have to live nearer to London.

In 1581 an Act of Elizabeth made it treason to convert others, or to be converted, to Catholicism. The Act also increased the fine for recusancy – 'those convicted of forbearing to repair to some church, chapel or usual place of common prayer to hear Divine Service there' – to £20 per lunar month (approx £3,000 today). Also, Catholic recusants could now be 'presented' to the courts not just by churchwardens and constables, but also by anyone who wanted to 'inform' against them. Informers were rewarded by the receipt of one-third of the fine – the other two-thirds going first to the Crown and then, as before, to the relief of the poor in the parish. A number of individuals began to make their living by seeking out and reporting Catholics to the authorities, and these became known as 'Pursuivants'. The fine for recusancy was to be paid by every person above the age of sixteen, and anyone who remained convicted for a year was to be bound over for the sum of £200 as a guarantee of their good behaviour and until they conformed and started to attend church.

The last presentment of Thomas More at Barnburgh for 'not comminge to the churche nor receyvinge the communion' occurred on 9 January 1581 and it was certified by, among others, his own brother Edward. Included in the list were 'Mary, his wife, Henry and Grizacar (Cresacre), his sons, Marye, Katheren, Grace & Jane, his daughters'. Also included were 'Christofer Cam, An Tourner & Willm. Helaye, his servants'.[6] The omission of his other children indicates, as we will see, that they had already moved out of the family home. The fact that no further action was taken against Thomas by the authorities in Yorkshire is probably because the family had moved away from Barnburgh – leaving

Edward in residence at the Hall – before they got round to it.

We know from a Residents Registration Certificate of 1593 that Thomas first took up residence in Low Leyton, Essex (now Leyton, Greater London) on 20 March 1582. The Certificate reads:

> Notification reciting that Thomas More of Low Leyton, gentleman, ever since the eighth and twentieth day of March, 24 Elizabeth, 1582, having had and yet having a certain place of dwelling and abode in Low Leyton aforesaid, and there usually heretofore having made and yet making his common abode ...[7]

In Low Leyton Thomas became a copyhold tenant of a small estate known as the Brewhouse Estate that formed part of the larger manor of Leyton Grange. The Brewhouse Estate comprised a couple of larger houses, some cottages, and around seventeen acres of land. Thomas's house, known as 'Minims', would have been the 'capital messuage' (the main house with surrounding land) of the estate and is believed to have stood at the junction of Hainault Road and Leyton High Road (now in E 11), opposite the present sports ground.[8] A share in the estate may have come into the possession of the More family at the time of Sir Thomas's marriage to Jane Colt, or Thomas II may have obtained it from the Kemp family who were, at one time, Lords of the Manor of Leyton. His great-aunt (sister of his grandmother Jane More, née Colt) had married William Kemp of Essex.

On arrival at Low Leyton Thomas wasted no time in promoting the Catholic cause by getting involved in the work of the secret printing press which had first been set up by his cousin Charles Bassett and Fr Persons, SJ at the house of a Mr Wayfarer in Green Street, in the neighbouring parish of East Ham.[9] One of the first books off the press had been Fr Persons' own *Reasons why Catholics refuse to go to Heretical Churches*, written to refute the arguments of a manuscript book circulating in some prisons which claimed that it was not a sin to go to Protestant churches in order to avoid persecution, providing this was done with a protest that it was only being done in obedience to the King.[10] Unfortunately for Thomas, government spies were everywhere on the lookout for Catholics and the notorious Richard Topclyff, a professional pursuivant in the employ of William Cecil, Lord Burghley, must have been given a tip-off about the press. A raid was arranged, the premises searched and, after fleeing from the scene Thomas was arrested nearby. There is a manuscript of Harpsfield's *Life of Sir Thomas More* at Emmanuel College,

Cambridge, and inside the cover there is a note which says

> This book was found by Rich: Topclyff in Mr. Thomas Moares Styddye emongs other bookes at Greenstreet Mr. Wayferers house when Mr. Moare was apprehended the xiijth of April 1582.[11]

The fact that Thomas had a 'study' in the house indicates that he was more than a fleeting visitor to the house and that he was actively involved in the work of keeping the Catholic faith alive in England. It may well be that consideration was being given to publishing Harpsfield's manuscript with a view to its being distributed more widely, within the Catholic community.

Thomas was presented to the Essex Quarter Sessions held at Chelmsford on 26 June 1582 'for not coming to church since 6 March last past contrary to the Act of 13 January, I Elizabeth, 1558'. He must have been convicted in his absence because the authorities who were looking for him in the various London prisons reported that he had not been found in the Bailwick. The reason for this was because, shortly after his capture by Topclyff in Green Street he had been committed to the Marshalsea. A note in the Cecil Manuscripts records 'Thomas Moore of Chelsey in the Countie of Midd. Gent., being committed (to the Marshalsea) the XXVII of Aprill 1582'.[12]

Conditions in prisons in those days varied, and we do not know what they were like in the Marshalsea. Unlike the free board and lodging offered to prisoners today, prisoners in those days (at least those who could afford it) had to pay for their 'diett and lodging', for 'fuell', for 'candells', and for 'wasshinge'. The standard of the accommodation and services provided in prisons varied, but from bills presented by the Keeper of the Gatehouse Prison in Westminster the cost of diet and lodging in the early 1590s began at around 10 shillings a week (approx. £60 today), fuel at 4 shillings, candles at 6 pence and washing at 4 pence. Costs at the Marshalsea must have been similar.[13]

The new recusancy laws 'flooded' the prisons with Catholics and gave rise to severe overcrowding in many of them. Perhaps in order to reduce problems caused by overcrowding – and with the exception of 'close' prisoners (those ordered to be kept in close confinement) – many prisoners were granted what today we would call 'day release'. In March 1583 a visitor to the Marshalsea reported that among the Catholics inmates there were twenty-four priests who were, 'with the consent or at least the connivance of the gaolers who are either bribed or favourable to religion', able to say daily Mass. Visitors, he said, were admitted 'either for conversation or for Confession or Communion' and, even more surprisingly, they were 'allowed daily to go out of the prison to various places in the city to minister to the spiritual necessities of the Catholics, provided they return into custody at nightfall'.[14]

Conditions in the Tower remained harsh, but the relative freedom enjoyed by some inmates in other London prisons was certainly not the norm, and there were increasing reports from counties all over England of both priests and laymen being examined, imprisoned, tortured, and put to death.

We do not know what freedom, if any, Thomas was granted during his time in the Marshalsea, but we do know that he was in prison for four years – until June 1586. Thomas was a marked man, and records show that the authorities continued to investigate his case. During the questioning of a priest in an unrelated case they found out that Thomas had four sons being educated abroad: 'Mr. More, now a prisoner in the Marshalsea, hath four sons in Rheims, whereof one he sent within these eight weeks'.[15] The authorities also discovered two of his daughters, Mary and Grace (about whom more later) in the house of Elizabeth Bosaunt during a search of houses in St Mary Overies Close, Southwark, on 17 August 1584.[16] This was not far from the old Marshalsea Prison that was located somewhere near the present day Mermaid Court to the South of Guy's Hospital.[17] The most likely explanation for the presence of Thomas's daughters at the house of Elizabeth Bosaunt's was so that they could be near their father, and their placement there may well have been arranged by their cousin, Francis Browne, whose father Sir Anthony Browne had been granted some of the property of the Priory of St Mary Overie after its dissolution by Henry VIII in 1539.

While Thomas was in the Marshalsea in 1585 authorities spent some time investigating how much his assets were worth so that they could come to some agreement with him about payments before releasing him. One of their statements reads, 'Thomas More of Lowleighton in the County of Essex gent decl. his whole revenue above all charges to be but XX£ yearly ...' Out of this Thomas agreed to pay £5 yearly (approx. £650 today).[18]

Like other recusants in similar circumstance Thomas did not offer any information that might help the authorities to find out what his assets were and, naturally, he sought to minimize their value! Clearly the authorities were not impressed by his account, especially after they received a report sent to the Privy Council saying, 'We were informed by Richard Ede, porter of the Marshalsea, that Robert Beckett, Thomas More and John Grey be of greater living and hability than they declared themselves to be...'[19] Thomas and his fellow prisoners must have been engaged in some 'careless talk' about their property which was overheard by the prison porter. No doubt spying on prisoners and reporting their conversations was one way in which prison workers could ingratiate themselves with the authorities and earn a bit of extra money. Thomas's attempted deception only meant further examination of his case and further commitment to the Marshalsea. It was not until July 1586 that the name 'Thomas More theleder' appears in a list of prisoners 'to be disposed of' from the Marshalsea.[20]

Thomas's release from prison was conditional, and he had to agree to a bond of 200 marks (approx. £13,000 today) for good behaviour. He also had to agree to make himself available to return to court whenever the authorities required him to do so. This, however, did not mean freedom from further prosecution for recusancy, and the imposition of the fines that went with it.

In spite of all the attacks on him Thomas's faith never wavered. Exchequer documents show that he and Mary, and various other relations who lived with them in Leyton, continued to be called to appear regularly before one court or another – the Sessions in Chelmsford, the Essex Assizes, the Court of the Archdeacon of Essex, the Consistory Court of the Bishop of London.[21] An Act of the Privy Council, dated 20 February 1589, gives an indication of the sort of process that was involved:

> Thomas More of Low Leighton in the Countie of Essex gent. being set at libertie appon bondes for his retourne and appearance before their Lordships at a certain tyme, this date made his said appearance, which is for his indemnities entred in this Register of Counsell and thereupon by commaundement from Mr. Vicechamberlain to Mr. Ashley one of the Clarkes of the Counsell, new bondes were taken for his further libertie, which is remaining in the Counsell Chest.[22]

Overall, Thomas's response to summonses and the payment of fines for his recusancy seems to have been to treat them with the contempt he thought they were worth, so he ignored them whenever he could! The authorities, however, kept a careful record of what he owed them. A tightening of the recusancy laws in 1586 had provided for cases like this by authorizing the seizure of all the personal goods of recusants as well as two-thirds of their lands.[23] The leaving of the last third to the recusant was not an act of kindness of the part of the authorities but rather to enable him to support himself and his family and so avoid becoming a total burden on the State. In Thomas's case the authorities could not seize Gobions (the manor at North Mymms) because, although Queen Mary had restored it to his mother in 1553, it was still subject to previously existing leases and so had not come back into the actual possession of the family. Also, as a copyhold tenant of his estate in Low Leyton Thomas did not own the full freehold and so it remained in his possession. In the circumstances the only estates the authorities could seize in order to get their money were his Yorkshire estates.

After Thomas failed to pay fines for a further two years after a conviction for recusancy on 13 March 1589 his arrears had risen to £500 (approx. £67,000 today) and, on 9 December 1591, the Exchequer began the process of identifying and assessing his estates in Yorkshire and bringing in the bailiffs to farm them. A rather cursory enquiry at Barnburgh soon valued his property around there at £32 (approx £4,350 today), but a mistake was made in the calculations and the two-thirds to be seized were only valued at £10 0s. 4d. It took the authorities another eight years to discover the full extent of Thomas's lands in Yorkshire! The thoroughness of this later search is illustrated by the results of an enquiry at Pontefract on 26 April 1599 which showed that Thomas owned the manor of Barnburgh, a property called the Netherhall in Barnburgh, and the following: in Barnburgh and Harlaxton, 194 acres of land, 37 acres of pasture and 18 acres of woodland and common rented out for £30 a year. In the manor of Tylts various enclosures rented out for £30 a year. In the manor of Moseley and in Whitley, 30 acres of land, 16 acres of pasture and 10 acres of meadow rented out for £13 a year. A messuage in Little Houghton with 50 acres of land, 10 acres of meadow and 10 acres of pasture rented out for £6 a year. In Bolton-upon-Derne land rented out for £3 per year. The total rental value of all these lands was £82 (equivalent to around £9,400 today) and, for sequestration purposes, two-thirds of this was assessed at £54 0s. 4d. Six months later, on 9 October 1599, an enquiry at Wakefield brought to light further lands in the area: this showed he owned three messuages and a cottage in Womersley together with 100 acres of land, 30 acres of pasture and 12 acres of meadow rented out for £5 per year, a messuage and 23 acres of pasture in Ardwick-le-Street rented out for £1 a year, 2 messuages, 40 acres of land, 20 acres of pasture and 15 acres of meadow in Brasswith and Pigburne (now Brodsworth and Pickburn) rented out for £2 a year, as well as various closes, estimated at $24\frac{1}{2}$ acres in the hamlet of Moss rented out for £5 per year. The total value of these was £13 per year – equivalent to around £1,500 today.[24] Even though these are more complete lists of Thomas's Yorkshire properties than the earlier one, a comparison with the list given in the 'Feet of Fines' for Yorkshire in 1577 shows that they had by no means discovered all his properties – including land in various parts and another 132 messuages, 59 cottages, a stone quarry, and two watermills!

Although the recusancy laws provided a good opportunity to swell the Queen's coffers their primary aim was to bring about conformity. Lands that were seized, or 'sequestered', were intended to be returned to their rightful owner once conformity had been established. The sequestered lands were put in the hands of bailiffs who could collect rents from existing tenants and farm other lands profitably so that they could pay the required two-thirds of their yearly value to the Crown. Details of these were recorded (in Latin) in the Lord Treasurer's Remembrancer's Rolls from which the above details have been transcribed. In practice, lands were often passed to friends or agents of the family and, in Thomas's case, his wife's nephew Robert Wyvill of Masham in Yorkshire was granted some of his lands in Yorkshire and Hertfordshire.[25]

In 1593 another Act of Elizabeth imposed further restrictions on recusants. This ordered them to live in their own homes or that of their parents, and to register their names with the minister at their local parish church. It also forbade them to travel more than five miles from their place of abode. Thomas's Registration Certificate for 1 May 1593 reads:

> Certificate, directed to Mr. Bernard Whetston and Mr. Lee, Justices, that Mr. Thomas More, gentleman, recusant, has notified his coming to the parish of Leyton, and presented himself and delivered his name, and thereupon the minister has entered his name into a book which is kept in the parish for that purpose. Signed by Robert Godfrey, vicar there, and the mark of William Sanders, constable.[26]

In spite of all his difficulties at this time, Thomas managed, with the assistance of his cousin Thomas Roper, to find the money to buy back Holbein's painting of the More family that had been sequestered at the time of his grandfather's execution, and to commission a new 'composite' painting which became known as 'Sir Thomas More, his family and descendants'. Basing his painting on Holbein's original the artist, Rowland Lockey, omitted Lady More, Margaret Giggs and John Harris and demoted Henry Patenson (now almost a midget) to a place behind a curtain at the back of the group. To the right of the group he then brought in Thomas II, his wife Mary, and the eldest and youngest of their children – John and Cresacre. The picture is unusual, and to those with knowledge of the people involved it can appear quite eerie at first because, apart from Thomas II, Mary and their two sons, all the other people portrayed were dead when it was painted. For myself, I like to think that it was Thomas's way of looking back and linking his own sufferings to those of his grandfather while looking forward in the uncertain hope of better future for his own children. The painting now hangs in the National Portrait Gallery, and a slightly different miniature can be seen in the Victoria and Albert Museum.

Whatever hopes Thomas may have had for the future, they were not to be realized in his own lifetime. Strictly speaking, once his lands had been sequestered he should no longer have been liable to pay the £20 monthly fine for not attending his local church but, in spite of this, he continued to be pursued by the courts in Essex for the payment of these fines. By March 1603 he had got so fed up with this that he sent his attorney, Edward Makyn, to the Essex Quarter Sessions to point out to the Justices that he had already forfeited to the Crown all his goods and two-thirds of his lands to the annual value of £200 (approx. £25,000 today) and that they therefore had no authority or jurisdiction to proceed against him for not resorting to his parish church at Leyton or to any other place of common prayer during the time of common prayer.[27] Unfortunately, the message doesn't seem to have filtered down to the vicar and churchwardens of Layton who continued to do what they saw as their duty, and in April 1605 they sent a certificate to the Bishop of London saying that they 'do presente Thomas More and Mary More his weif, Grizatie More and his weife, Anne More, Laurence Povie, Jane his weif, and Robert Tyas whiche forbeare to come to their church and have refused att the leaste these viii or x yeres'.[28]

The accession of James I to the throne in 1603, his early announcement that he intended to remit the fines imposed on Catholics, and his desire to open up negotiations with Rome about the excommunication of trouble-making Catholics must have brought Thomas some initial hope of relief from the financial burdens imposed on him. Unfortunately, what hopes he had were dashed when the Pope, Clement VIII, declared that he would not allow Catholics to be excommunicated at the behest of a heretic King. James's response to this snub was predictable. In February 1604 he passed an Act that ordered the strict enforcement of all the Acts previously made by Elizabeth I, and added additional clauses to make anyone who went 'beyond the seas' to a Jesuit seminary incapable of retaining or purchasing any property in England, and imposing a fine of £100 (approx. £12,000 today) on anyone who sent a child out of the country to be educated. James's Act did allow convicted recusants to retain one-third of their estates, but the other two-thirds were now to be retained after their death until all arrears had been paid off in full.

When the existing leases on them ran out, the More family estates in Hertfordshire, originally sequestered by Henry VIII, finally came into Thomas's possession early in 1605. In the circumstances he could hardly hide this from the authorities, and they were soon on to him. An enquiry at Hatfield Bishop on 4 June 1605 showed that he owned a capital messuage called Gibbines, Gibbeanes, or Gobions, and 160 acres of land, pastures and woods etc. in the parish of North Mymms. These were held directly by Thomas and were valued at £80. Various other small 'holdings' and two 'groves' in the parishes of North Mymms and Hatfield, let out to various tenants, were valued at £94 13s. 4d. The total annual value of all this was estimated at £174 13s. 4d. (approx. £22,000 today), and two-thirds for sequestration came to £116 8s. 10d.[29]

While these properties had been rented out by the authorities, they had previously been valued at only £50, and the injustice Thomas felt at his treatment boiled over. Now nearly seventy-four years old, he poured out his feelings in a letter to Sir Michael Hicks on 20 June 1605. Sir Michael had become a neighbour and a friend of his in 1598 when he bought the nearby manor of Ruckholts in Leyton. As secretary of Lord Burghley, Sir Michael was a man of influence in the government, and Thomas's moving letter to him is worth quoting in full. It is addressed 'To the right worshipful Sr. Michael Hicks, knight. At his home in London.' It continues:

> Right worshipfull, my afflicted state still maketh me to have recourse unto you to entreate you to be a meane to bryng me now

in myne olde latter yeares unto soome peace and quiett. I have made it knowen unto you heretofore how in her late Majesties tyme two partes of my smale lyving in Yorksheere were seized and leased to men of smale conscience and religion: and my goodds divers tymes taken from me by Felton and his fellowes, leaving me neither horse to ryde on nor cow to give milk, besyde long and often Imprisonment and many other vexations don unto me. I and others of my religion hoped that after so long pressure and the cause of jelosie and suspicion which was supposed agaynst us heretofore, being now taken away by the Kings Majesties most peaceable and joyfull succession in this Kyngdome, and the amitie he holdeth with all christian Prynces, his Majesty out of his gracious clemencie would have had some compassion over our miseries and long sufferance. But I fynde my Estate worse now then it was before for the penall lawes being now severely executed, soome land lying in Hertfordsheere being now come unto me by her Majesties deathe which was my grannfathers, and which her Majesty leased out for fiftie pounds yearely rent or thereaboutes is now lately thrugh soome ill will which Sir Rauf Conyngesbie knight beareth unto me fownde by Commission out of th'escheker to be worth £160 by the yeare so that I daily feare the takynge of two parts of that land also from me besydes my goodes and chattels which I occupie on the same hand. I have before tyme tried you to be my verie good friend and no man better than you knoweth my qualitie and conversation. I would therefore be right gladde if it would please you to move some of your honourable friendes on my behalf that if Recusants be thought worthie of no better favour, yet that I may be tenant of my owne lands at soome reasonable rate better than my Adversarie hath procured it to be extended or, if that can not be, that his Majesty will be pleased to accept of me £20 the moneth in satisfaction of my Recusancie which I had leaver do though with much difficultie, than continually to lyve in this fearefull condicion as I now doe to have my houses ruynated, my woods cutt down and spoiled, my goods twice everie yeare taken awaie, and still lye open for every unconscionable man to practise how to praie upon me. Thus trusting in your accustomed freendship I take my leave. From Leaton this XXth of June 1605. By your poer neighbour. Thomas More.[30]

We do not know whether Sir Michael Hicks replied to Thomas's letter and therefore whether he might have been willing to use his good offices to try to improve his lot. What we do know is that the sort of sentiments expressed in his letter were shared by other Catholics in similar situations, and that the frustration they felt must have been one of the factors that led to the hatching of the Gunpowder Plot to blow up the Houses of Parliament on 5 November 1605. As might be expected, the discovery of the plot did nothing to improve the position of Catholics as it only led to further Acts against recusants and, in particular, to a new 'Act of Supremacy'. These Acts put an end to Catholic hopes of any relief from their harassment in the foreseeable future.

For Thomas, however, time was already running out. Although describing himself as 'beinge whole of mynde and of good and perfecte memorye' he may have been physically unwell when he drew up his will on Tuesday 22 July 1606, making Robert Wyvell of Great Burton in the parish of Masham, North Yorkshire (his wife's nephew) his sole executor. In the preamble he mentions his age 'Threescore and fifteen yeares' and refers to 'havinge a vigilant eye and singuler respecte unto my end and passage oute of this mortall and transitorye worlde'. After making a bequest of twenty shillings for repairs to the parish churches of Chelsea, Barnburgh, North Mymms and Leyton, with an additional ten shillings for the one in which he is to be buried, he bequeaths all his lands and property in Hertfordshire, Yorkshire and at Leyton to his son Cresacre, and after him to his (Cresacre's) eldest son and heir, while reserving the profits from one-third of them 'to the use of Marye, wife of me the said Thomas More, for and duringe all her naturall life for and in the name of part of her dower and Joyncture'. Finally, for up to ten years following his death he sets aside the rents and profits from his manor at Moseley in the Moss in Balne and his lands and tenements in Braithwaite, Pigburne and Little Houghton in the parish of Darfield (all in Yorkshire) to pay his funeral charges, debts and legacies. He stipulates that his legacies – what he calls 'parcells of money' – are to be paid as soon as the capital from the above becomes available, and in the order he sets down. He leaves £10 each (approx. £1,100 today) to his daughters in order of seniority, to his brother Edward, and to his grandchildren, and then £3 each to his niece Barbara West and his nephews Thomas, Cyprian and Constantine More (the sons, as we have seen, of his younger brother Thomas).[31]

Throughout his life Thomas had been a shining example of unshakable faith – the Catholic faith he passed on, as we will see below, to all his children. Faithful to the end, he died at Leyton on

19 August 1606, just eleven days after his seventy-fifth birthday. Although he wished to be buried in one of the four churches mentioned in his will we do not know in which one it actually took place. It seems most likely that it would have been at Leyton but, as a Catholic and a persistently convicted recusant, the burial was unlikely to have been a public event, and his name may well have been omitted from the register.

Although Mary More appears regularly with Thomas in lists of convicted recusants in Essex, I have not been able to discover any record of her making payments into court. There is no evidence of her having inherited any of the Scrope estates and so she probably had no separate income of her own. Having pursued Thomas for all they could, the authorities would have known that they would be unable to get any more money out of the family. We know that Mary was not seen as any threat by the authorities because a statement in the Act Book of the Archdeacon of Essex for 11 May 1605 says

> She hath byn a Recusant before his majesties cominge into England, she is noe seducer of others, she bringeth up hir children and servants in recusancie, she is of peacable and quiet carriage, contented to lyve to herselfe – she refuseth conference and she hathe stoode long excommunicate.[32]

Mary survived Thomas by less than six months, dying at the age of seventy-nine on 12 January 1607. Like Thomas, we do not know where she was buried.

Thomas and Mary had thirteen children – five sons and eight daughters. We know the names of eleven of these, and that of the other two one was a boy and the other a girl. Given the information we have and chronology of the births of the other children it seems likely that the two children whose names we do not know were born at Barnburgh before the church register that has come down to us began to be kept. It is assumed that they died young, probably as infants.

Thomas and Mary's first child, Mary, was born at Hambleden at 7 a.m. on Monday 25th December 1553. At her baptism her grandmother, Anne More, her uncle, John Scrope, and her aunt, Anne More, acted as godparents. Sometime after the family moved from Barnburgh to Low Leyton Mary married Edward More (sometimes spelt 'Moore') of Haddon in the parish of Bampton, Oxfordshire – as far as we know, a previously unrelated family.[33] The Mores, who farmed their lands in and around

Lower Haddon, could trace their history back to the beginning of the twelfth century when John of Haddon granted the estate to John de la More who bequeathed it to his son Thomas (later Sir Thomas) de la More, Knight of the Shire of Oxford in 1340, 1343 and 1351. The Mores of Haddon were related to the Mores of Beswick, near Holderness, Yorkshire, and the pedigree of 'More of Beswick' records Edward's father as Thomas More, son Roger More of Bicester 'a servant of King Henry VIII'.[34] However, the *Visitation of the County of Oxford, 1566 & 1574* – a much earlier source – names Edward's father as Thomas, son of John More of Haddon, Oxfordshire. Both pedigrees record Edward's mother as Dorothy, the daughter of John Lord Mordaunt of Turvey, Bedfordshire, and his wife Elizabeth de Vere. Accounts of Edward's brothers and sisters differ slightly in the two pedigrees, but in his will, dated 10 April 1561, his father refers to his eldest son and heir William, to his second son Thomas, and to his youngest sons Henry and Edward. Thomas, Henry and Edward were all under twenty-one when he died. Edward's sisters are named as Frances (married to Ferdinand Paris), Mary and Margaret (both at the time unmarried), Beatrix and Katherine (the two youngest), also unmarried.[35] Edward's eldest brother, William More of Haddon and Beswick (d.1608) inherited the Haddon Estate after the death of his mother. His cousin, John More, sold the estate to Sir Edward Yate of Buckland in 1625, apparently to pay off his debts.

We do not know how the two More families came into contact, but we do know that the Mores of Haddon were also a recusant family who gave refuge to priests in their house in Oxfordshire, and that Edward spent some time in the Clink and other London prisons between 1582 and 1586 while Thomas II was also in prison. It might well be that they met sometime during this period. We also know from recusant lists that Edward began to live at Low Leyton with Thomas II and his family sometime during this period and it seems likely that his marriage to Mary took place between these years. After their marriage they lived in Leyton, probably in one of the other houses or cottages on the small estate. They both continued to be included periodically in lists of convicted recusants at Leyton, and the report in the Act Book of the Archdeacon of Essex indicates that Thomas II acted both for himself and for Edward when trying to get this stopped in 1603. Edward died intestate in 1605 and the Latin text of the Letters of Administration granted to Mary can be translated:

On the fifteenth day letters were issued by Master Edwardes, Surrogate, to Mary More, relict of Edward More, late of the parish of Leyton in the county of Essex, who died intestate, empowering her to administer his goods and chattels, etc.[36]

In the circumstances there was probably not much to administer. After Edward's death Mary continued to live at Leyton until around 1610 when she went to live with her married sister Kathryn Byrd (about whom see below) at Stondon Massey, Essex. She is believed to have died in 1630.

Edward and Mary More had five daughters, Isabel, Joan, Grace, Anne and France, and two sons, Henry and Thomas – great-great grandchildren of Sir Thomas. Apart from her name, we know nothing else about Isabel except that she was still living, unmarried, in 1648 when her cousin Cresacre More left her some money in his will. Three of the daughters – Joan, Grace and Anne – became Benedictine nuns at convents on the Continent.

We do not know the date of Joan More's birth, but a letter written in November 1613 to her uncle Thomas More IV, a secular priest and Clergy Agent in Rome (about whom see below), reveals that she was a lay sister at the English Benedictine Convent in Brussels. Apparently she was a lay sister (a more menial status than a choir sister) because no one had found the 'portion' (the equivalent of a dowry) required for her to be professed as a choir sister, and the writer of the letter expresses amazement that no one in the family had offered to help out with this. It seems that, maybe as a result of this letter, the required 'portion' was eventually found, as she wrote to her uncle in February 1616 telling him, among other things, 'I have lived professed now a yeare and somewhat more'.[37] Joan's sisters Grace and Anne were born in 1591 and 1600 respectively. They were both founder members of the Benedictine Monastery of Our Lady of Consolation at Cambrai, in Flanders, when it was established in 1623. Grace took the religious name Agnes, becoming Dame Agnes, but Anne appears to have kept her own first name, becoming Dame Anne. They were both professed on 1 January 1625. The nuns at Our Lady of Consolation formed an 'enclosed' community and, apart from her death at the age of sixty-four on 4 March 1655, the only thing we know about Dame Agnes is that she translated into English a French spiritual work entitled *A Treatise of the Ruin of Proper Love, and of the Building of Divine Love*. Her sister Anne survived her by seven years, dying at the age of sixty-two on 9 November 1662.[38]

Frances More, the last of the sisters, married Henry Lusher, an apothecary in London. Henry was the son of Richard Lusher of North Elmham, Norfolk and his wife Anne, the daughter of Thomas Whale of Norwich, Norfolk.[39] The Lushers and the Whales were also, like the Mores of Haddon, recusant families. Henry and Frances Lusher lived in the parish of St Dunstan in the East, London – probably in Fetter Lane (now EC4) – and they had two sons and four daughters. We do not know anything about their eldest son Thomas, but it is likely that he married, as a member of the family from Fetter Lane was presented for recusancy in 1692.[40] Of their four daughters nothing is known about Anne and Elizabeth, but Mary (1624–1687) and Bridget (1633–1690) both became Benedictine nuns.

Edward Lusher, Henry and Frances' second son, was baptized in St Dunstan's in 1625. He lived with his parents until he was fifteen when he was sent to live with a merchant in the City for four years, probably with the intention of learning the trade. However, when he was nineteen, he went to Ghent to study 'Letters', and then to St Omers, a college and seminary run by the Jesuits about twenty-four miles from Calais that was, at that time, under the jurisdiction of the King of Spain. At St Omers Edward is reported to have achieved 'some success' – an indication, perhaps, that he was not very bright! After finishing his course there he decided to become a Franciscan and went to Douai where he spent some months in the novitiate of the Friars Minor before being declared 'unsuitable'.

After returning to his parents in London for a while Edward went back to St Omers for 'higher studies' and then on to the English College, Rome, where he was admitted on 28 September 1655 and ordained on 12 April 1659.[41] After ordination he stayed on at the English College to complete his studies, but was expelled on 28 January *'propter insolentias'* (on account of insolence). From an account of the incident recorded by Francis Gage, the Clergy Agent in Rome, it seems that Edward was one of the anti-Jesuit faction among the students at the College, and that he had 'violently' tried to stop two Italian Jesuits, who had been invited by the Rector to assist at a solemn Mass before the Cardinal Protector, from entering the sacristy of the church. What seems to have incensed Edward and the other English scholars was that the Rector, himself a Jesuit, had invited his Italian colleagues 'upon pretence that they (the students) were not able to perform the ceremonies with decency' and they saw this as a snub. The Clergy Agent approached the Cardinal Protector, and the Pope, to get the expulsion order reversed, on the grounds that they would be 'turned out of Rome' and that he did not then know what would become of them. He even went on to suggest that this is what the Jesuits wanted. The Cardinal consulted the Rector of the College who called Edward (and a another co-conspirator) 'blockheads', saying that 'though they had not finished their studies they were not like to be much wiser; and that others had been sent away with as little learning, and consequently these might do as well as the rest'. With these attitudes being shown by the Jesuits who ran the English College it is not surprising that the appeal failed. Edward left Rome and was in Paris in March 1561. He returned to England in July but after that nothing more is known about him.[42]

The last two of Edward and Mary More's children were Henry and Thomas, both of whom became Jesuit priests. Henry, the eldest, was born in 1586 and at the age of eleven was sent to begin his studies at St Omers. While at the College the fact that he was the great-great-grandson of Sir Thomas More – already regarded as a saint in Catholic Europe – came to the attention of 'the most illustrious Countess de Zueda, of the Court of her Serene Highness the Infanta of Spain' who, during a visit in 1601, 'immediately embraced him with maternal affection, adopted him for her own son both as to maintenance and education'.[43] Towards the end of 1602 Henry transferred to the English College in Valladolid, Spain, which had been founded by King Philip II of Spain in 1589 to train priests for the English and Welsh Mission. In the statement he made on entry to the College on 28 January 1603 he declared that he was born in a town called Leyton, near London, and that his parents and ancestors had always been Catholic.[44]

While at Valladolid Henry assumed the aliases of Talman and Parr. Here he was, once again fortunate to obtain further patronage, this time when he came to the attention of the Countess of Medinaceli. Henry seems to have suffered from bouts of poor health in Spain and, because of this, he returned to Douai in June 1607. A few months later, on 19 November 1607 he joined the Society of Jesus, entering their newly built novitiate in Louvain. I have not been able to discover the date of Henry's ordination but he was certainly a priest in 1614 when he was appointed assistant to John Gerard, the Master of Novices at the novitiate that had just transferred from Louvain to Liège. Fr Gerard did not get on very well with Henry, describing him as not being very friendly and being 'of a close and hidden disposition' to the extent that if he was upset it was difficult to find out who or what had offended him'.[45]

Henry took his final vows on 12 May 1622 and was sent to England to work on the Mission based in Clerkenwell, London. He was arrested here with seven other Jesuits on 15 March 1628 and was imprisoned until 1633. On his release he became chaplain to Robert Lord Petre at Ingatestone Hall and Thorndon Hall in Essex.

After being for some time an advisor to Richard Blount, the English Provincial of the Jesuits, Henry was appointed to succeed him in 1635 and, before the end of that year he was sent by Fr Vitelleschi, the General of the Order, to restore harmony between warring English and Waloon Jesuit professors at their house in Liège. An interesting and possibly rather tactful letter from the Father General to Henry in August 1636 gives us a rare insight into his habits. The General wrote:

> The use of tobacco, especially smoking, is said to be so much on the increase that, apart from the great waste of time involved, which they lose in taking the smoke, they take too little heed of the small edification they give. Your Reverence should do away with this abuse.

By 1642 Henry's period as English Provincial had come to an end and he was sent to the Jesuit house in Ghent where, in 1643, he became 'Master of the Tertians' (Jesuits in their last year of ascetical training) before returning to England in 1644 as Rector of the London District. Back in London, Henry became involved with representatives of other religious orders and influential laymen in trying to negotiate a way to achieve toleration from the civil authorities. Unfortunately, differing stories of what they were prepared to agree to were sent to Rome – some mysteriously tampered with on the way – and on 15 November 1647 the Pope decreed that it was unlawful for English Catholics to 'bargain with heretics'. While the Jesuit General (now Fr Caraffa) accepted that Henry had acted in good faith he felt it tactful to remove him from England and, in 1649 he was appointed Rector of St Omers. He returned to England in 1652, probably staying again at Thorndon Hall, until his appointment as Spiritual Father at the Jesuit house in Liège in 1655. By this time Henry had already translated a number of books and written some of his own. He now settled down to write his 'magnum opus', the *Historia Missionis Anglicanae, ab anno MDLXXX ad MDCXXXV* (*The History of the English Mission from 1580–1585*).[46] He continued writing this during another period as Rector of St Omers from 1657, the book being published at St Omer in 1660. In 1661 Henry, now seventy-five years old, and frail, was sent to the nearby Jesuit House at Watten as Spiritual Director and Confessor to the novices there. He died there from a stroke on 8 December 1661.

Henry's younger brother Thomas was born at Cambridge in 1587. Although his father was out of prison, the courts were still pursuing him, and his mother may well have felt it safer to go and stay for a while with her sister-in-law Frances and her husband Ferdinand Paris, whose estate at Little Linton was near Cambridge. Links between the two families would appear to have gone back some time as Sir John More left Ferdinand's grandfather and grandmother a bequest in his will, and Edward's youngest sister Katherine had, under the terms of their father's will, been brought up by Ferdinand and Frances.

Like his older brother, Thomas was sent at an early age to study at St Omers before being sent to the English College in Rome where he was admitted as one of the Pope's scholars on 15 October 1601. On his entry to the College he answered the standard set of questions put to all students at the time, these tell us (in Latin) that his name was Thomas More, that his father's name was Edward and his mother's Mary (*Respondeo, nomen meum verum esse Thomas Morus, patris Edwardus, matris Maria*). He went on to say that he had one brother and five sisters, that he had been brought up partly in Essex and partly at St Omers where he had studied and become proficient in humanities, grammar and rhetoric. In his answers he describes himself as physically strong and of a quiet rather than excitable disposition.[47] Thomas was ordained deacon and subdeacon on 14 and 23 March respectively, and priest on 1 November 1609. He stayed on at the College for a further six months, returning to England in May 1610 and joining the Jesuits in 1611. A summary of his activities tells us that during his time on the English Mission he was 'chiefly employed in assisting the poorer class of Catholics; never using a horse, but making his circuits on foot, until being seized by heretics, he was cast into prison and condemned to exile for life'. At this time, King James I preferred to exile Catholic priests when they were caught rather than make martyrs of them, and Thomas was probably one of sixty priests banished in 1618.

We do not know exactly what Thomas did over the next few years, but he spent the last year of his life undergoing the final year of his spiritual training at the house of the Jesuit Tertians in Ghent. After accompanying some of his colleagues on a brief mission to English Catholic soldiers he returned to Ghent where, the summary of his life says, 'he was seized with excruciating pains in the stomach, which caused his death in a few days. He died on 2 January 1623, probably of Cholera'.[48]

Returning now to the family of Thomas II and his wife Mary (née Scrope). Their second daughter Anne was, like her older sister, also born at Hambleden. The event is recorded as having taken place at about 3 p.m. on Wednesday 10 April 1555, and at her baptism her godparents were her grandmother, Anne More, her uncle Ralph Scrope, and Margaret Stonor, presumably a relation or friend of the family. Anne lived for some time with her brother at Leyton but later went to live with her sister Katherine Byrd at Stondon Massey. She never married and died sometime around 1630.

Margaret More was born at Barnburgh, probably in 1556. No record of her baptism has come down to us, as the records for St Peter's do not start until the following year. Margaret married John Garford of Heck by Snaith, Yorkshire, before the family moved down to Essex. John and Margaret lived on a small estate owned by Thomas II at Whitley, a few miles east of Pontefract, Yorkshire. We know from his will that this was given to Margaret for the duration of her natural life, and it seems likely that it formed part of her marriage settlement. We also know from the will that John and Margaret had one daughter, Anne, and this is likely to be the 'Ann Garfoode' recorded as a recusant in October 1629 with the Byrd family at Stondon Massey. If it is, then she would have been seventy-three years of age and unmarried.[49]

John More – commonly referred to as John More III – the eldest son of Thomas II and Mary, was born in 1557. His is the first entry in the baptismal register of St Peter's church, Barnburgh, and it reads:

> John More, the sonne and heire of Thomas More Esquire, baptised Sept 6 had for his godfathers John Rokebie, doctor of law, Francis Frobisher, esquire, and .... [unreadable] Rokebie, gentlewoman for his godmother.[50]

It has been said that John was sent to Trinity College, Oxford, in 1574, and there is an entry for a John More of Yorkshire at that

College in *Alumni Oxoniensis*, the record of the students admitted to the University. However, the John More mentioned there is said to have matriculated in 1574 at the age of fourteen, whereas 'our' John would have been seventeen in that year.[51] What we do know is that John was sent to study at Rheims where the English College at Douai, founded in 1569, had to relocate after the English were expelled from Douai in 1578, and where it remained until it was able to return in 1593. John obviously did not want to progress to studies for the priesthood and returned to England in 1581, only to find himself arrested on landing at Dover, and sent to the gatehouse prison of Westminster Abbey. By this time the Queen's Commissioners had spies on board ships and in every port, as well as in coves and small harbours around the country, all on the lookout for priests and known Catholics leaving and re-entering England. In the circumstances it is not surprising that John did not manage to evade the net.

An entry in the Prison Lists of the Gatehouse sent to the Privy Council in March 1583 indicates that John was still in prison. It reads, 'John More, a gentleman's son and a Yorkshire man born, taken at Dover coming over from beyond the seas, and sent in by your honours a two years since.'[52] We do not know when exactly John was released from the Gatehouse, but in November 1585 his name is recorded as being 'bound in 100 marks to return himself prisoner in the Gatehouse by the last of February, except further leave obtained from their lordships'.[53]

In June 1587 John's name appears for the first time alongside that of his father in the Essex Quarter Sessions Records, and he continues to be presented for recusancy with other members of the family in Low Leyton at various courts until 1599.[54] Since he is not mentioned in his father's will, and since the estate was inherited by his younger brother Cresacre it is assumed that John must have died sometime around 1600.

John's younger sister Joan (or Jane) was born at Barnburgh in 1562 and her baptism entered in the register of St Peter's on 9 August – the day after her father's thirty-first birthday. Her godparents were Richard, Beatrice and Clarissa Browne. Joan married Lawrence Povey, probably the son of John Povey/Povye of Newgate, London (now EC1). If this John was his father then it is likely that he is the Lawrence who was, according to the parish registers, baptized at Christchurch Greyfriars, Newgate Street on 17 October 1556.[55] We do not know when Joan and Lawrence were married, but they appear regularly with Thomas II as convicted recusants at Low Leyton from 1596 to 1607 so it appears that for some time they lived with him, or in one of the other smaller properties belonging to him on the same estate. Lawrence made his will on 24 August 1614, describing himself as 'of North Mymmes in the County of Hertford'. He appointed his brother Justinian Povey and his brother-in-Law John Halsey (a London fishmonger), as his executors. Lawrence died sometime between the day he made his will and 17 December 1614 when his will was proved in the Prerogative Court of Canterbury.[56] In his will he refers only to his goods, chattels, lands and tenements at North Mymms which he orders to be sold to pay his debts and to provide for his two sons, Lawrence and John, and his three daughters Mary, Grace and Prudence. The most likely explanation is that these properties were given to him by Thomas II as part of the marriage settlement. Jane received a bequest of £10 (approx. £1,100 today) in her father's will of July 1606 but she is not mentioned in Lawrence's will so it seems certain that she had pre-deceased him.

The baptism of Jane's younger sister, Magdalen More, was entered in the register of St Peter's, Barnburgh on 25 July 1563 with William Hawley, Gent., Elizabeth Hammonde and Frances Holmes, gentilwomen, as her godparents. Magdalen's life was short; she was buried at St Peter's on 7 January 1567.

Next in line is Katherine More. Her baptism was entered in the Barnburgh register on 10 December 1564, her godfather being James Washington and her godmothers Katherine Vicars and Ursula Wraye. Katherine married Christopher Byrd, the son of William Byrd (1543–1623). The earliest information we have about the Byrd family comes from a pedigree recorded during the Visitations of London in April 1571. No dates are given but the pedigree goes back to 'Richarde Birde', Christopher's 5 times great-grandfather living at 'yenge at stone' (now Ingatestone – between Chelmsford and Brentwood, in Essex). The family appear to have moved to London during the life of Richard's grandson, Thomas Birde.

William Byrd (Christopher's father) was born in London, and as a young man, studied music under Thomas Tallis. He was appointed Master of Choristers and organist at Lincoln Cathedral in 1563 and he married Juliana (also known as Ellen) Burley, who came from a Lincolnshire family, at St Margaret's in the Close, next to the Cathedral, on 14 September 1568. The family lived in a house at the back of the Cathedral where no. 6 Minster Yard now stands. A blue heritage plaque on the house records the fact. Christopher was baptized at St Margaret's in the Close on 18 November 1569 and his sister Elizabeth was baptized there on 20 January 1571. The *Visitations of Essex, 1634*, indicate that Christopher had a brother, Thomas (described as 'of Drury Lane'), and two other sisters, Rachel and Mary.[57]

Information about William's skills as a musician eventually reached the Queen and, although a practicing Catholic, he was appointed a Gentleman of the Chapel Royal in 1569 where, after moving to London in 1572, he also became an organist. The patronage of the Queen protected him from persecution at Court, and the music he composed for the Chapel made him famous. On taking up the appointment he moved the family to Westminster where his son Thomas was baptized at St Margaret's Church on 30 March 1576. His godfather was Thomas Tallis. William's position clearly brought him rich rewards as he was able to buy or lease Harlington Manor in Middlesex, taking his family there in 1577 and remaining there until 1593 when he was granted a lease on Stondon Place, a property of some 200 acres with a house, a farm and some additional land at Stondon Massey, North of Brentwood, in Essex. William appears to have spent his last couple of years in retirement at Stondon Massey where he was listed with Katherine and her son Thomas as a recusant. He died on 4 July 1623 and is believed to have been buried next to his wife's grave outside the church.[58] A slate plaque on the north wall of the choir of Lincoln Cathedral says:

> To the memory of William Byrd, the most distinguished English musician of his day. Organist of this Cathedral from 1563 to 1572. Appointed Gentleman of the Chapel Royal in 1569. Born about 1543, died 1623. Justorum animae in manu Dei sunt.

We do not know when Katherine More married Christopher Byrd but it was probably around 1589 as their son Thomas begins to appear with them in recusant lists at Stondon Massey in Essex from October 1605 and so must have reached the age of sixteen.[59] An example of how they were presented appears in a certificate sent to the Bishop of London by the parson, churchwardens and sidemen of Stondon on 6 April 1605 in which they 'doe presente that they have papisticall recusants which utterly refuse to come to the church, viz. William Bird gent. and his weif, Christopher Bird and his weif.'[60] Katherine and Christopher continued to be convicted of recusancy at Stondon Massey twice-yearly until 1615 after which Katherine is referred to as a widow. Fines for each of them ranged from £20 a time to £160 and this suggests that they were sometimes in arrears. In 1606 Mary Byrd, a spinster, begins to appear with them for a few years. This was Christopher's unmarried sister.

When William Byrd died on 4 July 1623 he left the estate at Stondon Massey to Katherine and her son Thomas. They continue to appear together in lists of recusants at Stondon Massey until October 1637. Katherine is believed to have died sometime in 1640. Thomas never married and all we know about him is that he was still alive 1651.

After Katherine, Thomas More II and Mary had two sons, Thomas and Henry. The baptism of Thomas – usually referred to as Thomas More IV – was entered in the Barnburgh Register on 13 January 1565, and he had Thomas Reresby Esquire, Thomas Wombwell, Gent., and Dorothy Killam, gentilwoman as his godparents. Henry was born just over a year later on 15 March 1567. For his godparents he had Henry Maleverer, Thomas Normanville, Gent., and Benedicta Mounteford, gentilwoman.

Thomas and Henry were both admitted to the English College at Rheims on 1 February 1583. Translated from the original Latin into English the entry in the College diary reads, '... from England came the brothers Thomas and Henry More great-grand-children of the most holy martyr Thomas More'.[61] While Henry remained at Rheims, Thomas was sent to the English school at Verdun on 15 April to continue his studies there. The College diary tells us that Henry was confirmed during the Octave of Pentecost in May, and that he received Minor Orders on 23 September. In the normal course of events he would have stayed at Rheims to continue his studies for the priesthood but, during the course of the next year, he decided to join the Minims, a strict religious order of Friars founded by St Francis of Paula. He left the College with John Wadam, a fellow scholar, in September 1584 to join the Novitiate of the Order at Nigeon, near Paris where he was professed on 28 October 1585. We know nothing about his life from that time until his death at Nigeon during Whitsuntide in 1597.[62]

After studying at Verdun for a couple of years Henry's brother, Thomas, returned to Rheims on 25 June 1585 before going on to the English College in Rome to complete his studies for the priesthood. The *Liber Ruber* (Red Book) of the College notes his admission as an alumnus of the Holy Father on 17 November

1587. He received the Tonsure and other Minor Orders between November and December 1588 and was ordained to the priesthood sometime in 1591. After ordination he went to the English College at Valladolid arriving on 1 September 1591 and remaining until 12 November 1592 when he went to Seville before returning to England in 1593.[63]

Thomas' presence in England soon came to the attention of the authorities when it was revealed during the interrogation of a priest in the Tower, but they were unable to find out where he was. He had, in fact, gone to Battle Abbey, the home of Lady Magdalen, Viscountess Montague, to whom he was related through the marriage of his cousin Thomas Roper to Lucy Browne, sister of the First Viscount Montague. Lady Magdalen kept a number of priests in her house and Thomas became her chaplain until 1609, during which time he also ministered to Catholics in the surrounding area – an area that became known as 'Little Rome'.[64]

In early 1609 Thomas was sent to Rome by the archpriest George Birkhead who was responsible for the affairs of the secular clergy in England, becoming his official 'Agent' in October. There were no Catholic bishops left in England and the appointment of the first archpriest, George Blackwell, had been made following concern among the secular clergy that the well-organized and better-trained Jesuits were taking over the English Mission. The animosity between the two factions appears to have come to a head in 1595 during what became known as the 'Wisbech Stirs' when a group of Jesuit priests in Wisbech Castle prison accused some of the secular priests and Catholic laymen of indiscipline and immorality. From the one-sided account of the breakdown of relations made later by Thomas's Jesuit cousin Henry More (mentioned above) it seems that some eighteen Jesuits in the prison had organized daily life along the lines of a religious house where they 'imitated paradise, arranging all their daytime – and indeed night-time activities – with admirable order', where 'there was frequent prayer, systematic reading, and commentary on the Scriptures at stated hours', and where there were 'debates on dogma and apologetics' and 'discourse on the rules of upright living'. The secular priests and laymen (the ringleaders of whom were described by Henry More as 'of a bitter and quarrelsome mind' and as 'untameable by nature and impatient of any discipline') revolted against this regime and what they saw as the Jesuits' domination of their lives. They began to heckle the speaker at meetings or to absent themselves from them altogether. They formed what the Jesuits called a 'separate clique' which 'took to an undisciplined and haphazard mode of existence' that led to 'drinking bouts, quarrels, noisy scenes and wordy exchanges ... and, not infrequently, to blows', all of which showed no regard for 'clerical decorum'.[65]

Unfortunately the secular clergy in England saw the first archpriest, George Blackwell, and some of the priests appointed to assist him, as being decidedly pro-Jesuit, so his appointment did nothing to quell their fears. His arrest in June 1607 and his taking, under pressure, of the new Oath of Allegiance led to his deposition by Rome and the appointment of George Birkhead to replace him in February 1608.

As Clergy Agent in Rome Thomas's job was to represent the views of the secular clergy and, in particular, to try to obtain the appointment of a bishop with full authority to rule over them. In Rome Thomas lived in a first floor apartment in the Campo di Marzo district, the area around the Pantheon. As readers who have been to Rome will know, this is only a short walk from the Vatican and so would have been a convenient base from which to conduct his business. Some of the letters from priests in England to Thomas have survived.[66] For fear of letters falling into the wrong hands, or being lost or stolen on the way, most of the letters are addressed to him under the alias of George West (the name of his grandmother's second husband), and it is interesting to see that letters from England to Rome took around three months to arrive. In addition to showing something of the trials and tribulations faced by priests in England the letters show just how much the secular clergy felt discriminated against and even abandoned by the authorities in Rome and by the Pope in particular. They complained that young priests being educated at Seminaries like Douai – 'now termed a place for fooles' – were not being properly trained for the difficult work they would have to do. They complained that they were not allowed to go abroad to study for higher degrees and also that they had no college where students could study to combat the arguments of the Protestants. Most important of all, they complained that they had no bishop with full authority to regulate their work and keep the English Mission running efficiently.[67]

In Rome in May 1609, Thomas soon found that the Jesuits, who were opposed to the appointment of a bishop, controlled most of the information going into the Curia from their base at the English

College and that they had already obtained from Pope Paul V an order forbidding any petition for a bishop that did not have the unanimous approval of all the secular clergy. In pursuit of this Thomas was sent back to England with instructions to canvas all the secular priests about their views on the need for a bishop. In the event, the task proved impossible to complete because the persecutions at the time made it too dangerous to arrange meetings with many priests, and he returned to Rome in September 1610. In Rome Thomas kept up the pressure to obtain the appointment of a bishop but it soon became clear that the matter was not going to be resolved as other political and religious issues came to the fore – whether, for example, the Princes Henry and Charles would take Catholic brides and, after the Oath of Allegiance was re-enforced in 1611, whether Catholics could find any way in which they could take it. The archpriest George Birkhead died in April 1614 and it was not until September that his replacement, Dr William Harrison, was appointed.

Thomas continued as Clergy Agent in Rome until 1617 when he was appointed Agent of the College at Douai, charged with obtaining arrears of payments due from the Spanish Court at Madrid. He stayed on in Madrid until early 1621 to help promote the plan of James I to marry Prince Charles to the Spanish Infanta, the daughter of King Philip III of Spain. Although the plan never came to fruition, the hope of English Catholics that Charles would marry a Catholic, and that this would lead to a relaxing of the penal laws, was not disappointed, as one of the conditions of Charles's marriage in 1624 to Henrietta Maria, the daughter of Henry IV, King of France, was that the recusancy laws in England should be suspended.

Pope Paul V died in January 1621 and the new Pope, Gregory XV established a commission to look into the matter of creating a bishop for England. There were still fierce arguments for and against, but the 'fors' won this time, and the death of the archpriest William Harrison in May 1621 provided the opportunity. Thomas, now back in Rome, was put forward as one of the candidates but his work in Rome was felt to be too important for him to be free to return to England and the Pope's choice fell on William Bishop who was consecrated as Titular Bishop of Chalcedon. Thomas, however, was not left without his reward as he was appointed a member of the Bishop's Chapter when it was instituted on 10 September 1623 and given the title Archdeacon of Hertfordshire and Northamptonshire.

Thomas returned to England early in 1624 but had to go back to Rome in August for consultations about the appointment of a new bishop for England after the sudden death of William Bishop after only two years in office. Seven months later, on 20 March 1625, Thomas was taken ill and an English Benedictine monk was called to his apartment to give him the last rites. On the following day he added some codicils to the will he had previously made on 26 December 1616 (and registered with a notary on 5 January 1617). In his up-dated will he resigned any claim which, as eldest surviving son, he might have on the family estates in England, leaving them to his younger brother Cresacre. After making a number of bequests up to the total value of £100 (approx. £11,600 today) to personal friends in England he ordered that the residue should be given to the Superior of the Secular Clergy in England. He left his personal effects and the profits from three mortgages to the Agent of the Secular Clergy in Rome, and his goods in Douai and in Flanders to Dr Matthew Kellison, the President of the English College in Douai.

Thomas IV died on 11 April 1625 and, 'because of the high regard in which, after his own nation, he always held the French nation and Crown', he was buried in the Church of San Luigi dei Francesi, the French church, the following day. The entry in the Burial Register reads:

Anno 1625: Anno quo supra die vero 12 Aprilis D. THOMAS MORUS presbyter nobilis Anglus aetatis suae 60 annorum mortuus est in parochial S. Augustini, et corpus eius in nostrum Ecclesiam delatum in propria sepultura iuxta sepulchrum sacerdotum conditum est.

A memorial written in Latin, and originally placed above his tomb in the middle of the church, has now been lost. Translated into English it read:

> To the memory of Thomas More, an Englishman of the diocese of York, great grandson and heir to the great Thomas More, Chancellor of England and Martyr: a man remarkable for probity and piety; who, by a sacrifice, rare indeed in England, transferred his ample patrimony to a younger brother, and became a priest at Rome. From whence he was sent for some years by order of the Apostolic see into his own country, where he laboured strenuously in propogating the faith. Afterwards he was the agent for the English clergy seven years at Rome and five in Spain, while Paul V and Gregory XV were Popes. This office he filled with great integrity and industry, and supported it at his own expense. At

length having been sent to Pope Urban VIII on a mission respecting the appointment of a bishop for England, and having happily accomplished the business, he went to receive the reward of his labours on 11th of April, 1625, in the 59th year of his age. The English clergy, lamenting his death, placed this to his memory.[68]

Because San Luigi was not a parish church an entry was also made in the register of San Agostino, his local parish church. This reads, *Die 11 Aprilis 1625. Thomas Sacerdos ex natione Hinclesi MORI abiit die anno ut supra et sepultus fuit in Ecclesia Sancti Louisii.* Thomas's funeral Mass was attended by twenty religious and secular priests and by a number of lay mourners including Lord Windsor and his family (relations of his mother), Anthony Maria Browne (2nd Viscount Montague) and his family, and Philip Roper (son of Thomas Roper and Lucy Browne).[69] His will was proved in Rome on 19 April 1625 and in Antwerp on 30 October 1625.

Consideration now only remains to be given to the last two of Thomas II and Mary's thirteen children – Grace and Cresacre. Cresacre, their youngest son, born in 1572, will be the subject of the next chapter, so that only leaves Grace, their youngest daughter.

Grace More was born at Barnburgh and her baptism entered in the parish register on 16 September 1568. Her godparents were Nicholas Denman, Gent., Grace Rokeby and Margaret Jackson, gentilwomen. Grace moved down from Barnburgh to Low Leyton with her parents in 1582 and later married Thomas Greenwood, gentleman, of Brize Norton, Oxfordshire. Because of the repetition of the name Thomas in the family I will call him Thomas Greenwood III. How the two families came into contact we do not know, but it may have been through the Mores at Haddon who were near neighbours.

The Greenwood ancestry can be traced back to Wyomarus de Greenwode-Leghe (Lee) who was caterer to the Empress Matilda, the mother of King Henry II (1154–1189). Thomas's grandfather, Thomas Greenwood I, appears to have come down from Learings (or Levings) or from Greenwood Lee in the parish of Heptonstall, Yorkshire, and to have settled in Oxford after gaining a Bachelor of Arts degree at the University. His son and heir, Thomas Greenwood II, Esquire, became a Chancellor at Law at Oxford where he lived in the parish of St Giles; his wife was Joan, the daughter of Edward Napper of Holywell (or Holwell), and the sister of George Napper the English martyr. Thomas Greenwood II and Joan were both recusants, and Thomas, a prominent figure in the town, was recorded in 1669 as having 'seldome gon to the church by reason of multitude of Causes sins he was a practitioner' and for 'only having received the Protestant Communion once since the Queen's Accession, and that seven or eight years before'.[70]

Thomas Greenwood III – referred to by his contemporaries as Thomas Greenwood the elder – was born in 1576 and attended Magdalen Hall at the University of Oxford where he matriculated on 23 October 1590. His father had bought a share in the Manor of Steeple Aston, and he inherited this when his father died in 1596. At some time around 1606 he bought the Manor (and the Lordship of the Manor) of Brize Norton from John Yate of Buckland. He later bought another Manor called Rathbones. The date and place of his marriage to Grace More is not known, but there are indications that their first child, Thomas Greenwood IV (known in the family as Thomas Greenwood the younger), was born in 1604, so it is likely to have been around that time. After their marriage they seem to have lived for a while with the other members of the More family at Low Leyton before moving to the Manor House at Brize Norton.

In addition to Thomas the younger, Thomas and Grace are recorded as having had two daughters, Cleve (or possibly Clare), and Bridget. I have not been able to discover anything about Cleve, but Bridget married William Whitbred (b.1594), the third son of Henry Whitbred (b.1556) of White Notley, Essex and his wife Ellen, the daughter of William Keyes of Essex. Like the Mores and the Greenwoods, the Whitbreds had remained Catholic and were regularly presented for recusancy in Essex. William and Bridget settled first at Writtle and later at West Thorndon in Essex. William owned lands in both Essex and Hertfordshire and in his will of 1661 he left legacies totaling £1,500 (approx. £135,000 today) to his relatives, friends and servants.[71] William and Bridget had no children and they are both buried in the Church of All Saints, Writtle, where an inscription reads, 'To the memory of Mr. William Whitbred here inhumed October 24th 1661 aetatis suae 65 years. Suscitatur cum Gloria.' This is followed by some quaint verse:

> Stay passenger and now th'hast read his name
> Know that his worth had more than common fame
> The noble actions that adorn the Just
> Sprung in this life and flourish in his dust
> To tell survivors that he cannot be
> Lost in oblivion who liv'd honestly
> His morals were exemplar and when fate
> Clipt him it left his Friends unfortunate
> So dy'd he and thus much beinge knowne tis best
> To part and leave him in his hopefull rest.

In his will William expressed the wish to be buried next to his wife, so it would appear that she pre-deceased him. Under the inscription to William it says, 'Here also lieth interred BRIDGET wife of Mr. William Whitbred. Daughter of Thomas Greenwood of Brisnorton in ye County of Oxford Esq.' No date is given.[72]

As we saw above Thomas Greenwood IV (the younger) was probably born in 1604. An indenture, dated 20 November 1615, between his father, his uncle Cresacre More (the subject of the next chapter) and some associates, gives details of the purchase of the rectory and parsonage of Easby, North Yorkshire and various tithes and lands associated with it in Skeeby, Aske, and Brompton on Swale. The Manor of Easby had been granted to Henry Lord Scrope of Bolton by Edward III and when the nearby Abbey of Premonstratensian Canons was dissolved by Henry VIII its lands were leased to John Lord Scrope. However, the Church of St Agatha, with its rectory and parsonage remained in the hands of the Crown. The parsonage had been leased by Elizabeth I to Thomas Lord Scrope and his wife Philadelphia, and later passed to the descendants of their son Emmanuel. The rectory had been granted to Francis Morris and Francis Phillipps by James I in 1612. The indenture gives details of purchase of both the rectory and parsonage from Morris and Phillipps and its re-assignment from Thomas Greenwood the elder to Thomas Greenwood the younger 'in consideration of the natural love and affection in which he beareth unto the said Thomas Greenwood his said son and heir apparent'. The income from the property is to be used 'for the necessary maintenance and education of the said Thomas Greenwood the younger' and is to pass 'to him, the said Thomas Greenwood the younger and his heirs and assigns for ever, to his and their only use'.[73] From the wording of the indenture it is clear that Thomas Greenwood the elder had bought the Yorkshire property in the name of his friends in order to avoid sequestration. Since he had used 'his own proper money and other moneys disbursed by the family of Grace his now wife' – possibly part of the marriage settlement – Cresacre More was making sure that it would continue to benefit his sister's heirs, which it did until 1773 when, for some reason, the right to ownership lapsed.

In 1634 Thomas the elder's estates at Steeple Aston and Brize Norton were sequestered because of his recusancy. They were then leased by the Crown to George Greenwood. This was probably his brother who may have become a 'church papist', outwardly conforming in order to keep the estates in the control of the family. Thomas the elder and the younger were both listed at Brize Norton in the Protestation Returns for 1642. Thomas the elder died sometime around 1646, but we do not know when Grace died, or where they are buried.[74]

Thomas Greenwood the younger was admitted to Gray's Inn on 3 February 1625. He is recorded as having married Mary, the daughter of Edward Wybarne of Haukwell in Cambridgeshire. As their first child, John, was born in 1630 the marriage probably took place in 1628 or 1629. In the 1660s they were living at Rathbones Manor or another house belonging to the estate, and this may well have formed part of their marriage settlement. In addition to John, Thomas and Mary had two daughters, Anne and Mary. Anne married Charles Trinder who was Lord of the Manor of Bourton-on-the-Water, Gloucestershire. The Trinders were also a recusant family who gave refuge to priests in their house. Mary married Charles Wareing of Buryhall in Warwickshire. John married Elizabeth, the daughter of Francis Fettiplace of Swincombe in Oxfordshire and his wife Frances Yate. John inherited the manors of Brize Norton and Rathbones when his father died. After his marriage he also came into possession of a manor belonging to his wife's family. He provided details of his family to the Heralds during their visitation of Oxfordshire in 1668. At that time he had four children, John (born 1664), George, Mary and Elizabeth.[75] The register of St Britius at Brize Norton records John's death on 21 December 1676. A monumental tablet in the chancel floor of St Britius records John junior's death at the age of forty-seven on 31 January 1711, and tells us that his wife's name was Margaret. She died 20 January 1730, aged sixty-seven years.

Thomas Greenwood the younger died on 27 February 1678 and was buried in the Church of St Britius with his daughter Anne Trinder who died on 26 October 1706. There is a memorial to them both in the floor of the chancel. Translated into English, the inscription reads:

> To God. The Best. The Greatest.
> Thomas Greenwood
> Descended from Thomas More at one time Chancellor of England
> Outstanding not only in very many virtues but also in piety
> Departed this life 26 February
> In the year of our salvation 1678.
> Anna
> Daughter of the above Thomas Greenwood
> Wife of Charles Trinder
> Most like her father in virtue on the 25 October
> In the year of our salvation 1706.
> They bore their cross with outstanding humility
> For their wisdom came from heaven. Hereafter
> May they rest in peace.[76]

Why Anne should be remembered with her father rather than Mary (his wife) remains a mystery, as does that place and date of Mary's death or burial.

The last member of the line from Thomas Greenwood and Grace More is said to have been buried in the Church of St Nicholas, Ghent, but I have no name or date for this.[77]

Genealogical Summary

Thomas More II and his Family

Thomas More (1531–1606) m. (1553) Mary Scrope (1534–1607):
Children:
1. Mary (1553–1630) m. Edward More of Haddon (d.1605)
   Children:
   i. Isabel
   ii. Joan: Benedictine nun
   iii. Frances: m. Henry Lusher
      Children: Thomas; Mary (1624–1687): Benedictine nun; Edward (bpt.1625): priest; Anne; Elizabeth; Bridget (1633–1690): Benedictine nun.
   iv. Grace (1591–1655): Benedictine nun – 'Dame Agnes'
   v. Anne (1600–1662): Benedictine nun – 'Dame Anne'
   vi. Henry (1586–1661): Jesuit priest
   vii. Thomas (1587–1623): Jesuit priest
2. Anne (1554–1630): unmarried
3. Margaret (b.1556): m. John Garford. One daughter, Anne.
4. John III (1557–1599): unmarried
5. Joan/Jane (1562–1604): m. Laurence Povey (1556–1614)
6. Magdalen (1563–1567)
7. Katherine (1564–c.1630): m. Christopher Byrd (1569–1615)
   Children: Thomas (b.1595): unmarried
8. Thomas IV (1565–1625): secular priest
9. Henry (1566–1597): Order of St Francis de Paul
10. Grace (b.1568): m. Thomas Greenwood III (1576–1678)
    Children:
    1. Thomas Greenwood IV (1604–1678) m. Mary Wybarne
       Children:
       i. Anne (d.1706): m. Charles Trinder
       ii. Mary: m. Charles Wareing
       iii. John (1630–1676): m. Elizabeth Fettiplace
          Children: i. John (1664–1683): m. Margaret ...
                        Children: John (d.1711)
                    ii. George
                    iii. Mary
                    iv. Elizabeth

    2. Cleve
    3. Bridget: m. William Whitbred. No children.
11. A daughter: name and date of birth unknown. Died in infancy.
12. A son: name and date of birth unknown. Died in infancy.
13. Cresacre (1572–1606): youngest son and heir.

Chapter Five

Cresacre More and his Family

Cresacre, the youngest of the five sons of Thomas More II and his wife Mary (née Scrope) was, after his father, perhaps the greatest of the remaining direct descendants of Sir Thomas More. He regarded himself as immensely privileged, but also heavily burdened, by the example of the great-grandfather in whose steps he trod, and who he regarded as a 'bright star' whose prayers would help guide him through the 'tempestuous storms of persecution'.

Born at Barnburgh Hall on 3 July, Cresacre's baptism was entered in the parish register for 6 July 1572 – the anniversary of Sir Thomas More's execution. However, unlike his brothers and sisters, his godparents were, for some reason, not recorded in the register.

The choice of 'Cresacre' (his grandmother's maiden name) as a first name was the cause of some confusion as he grew up. When spoken it sounds not unlike a rather slurred form of Christopher, and this seems to have been used in some circumstances from quite an early age, so that he became known sometimes as Cresacre, sometime as Christopher, and sometimes as Christopher Cresacre More. The name Cresacre was probably used within the family, and he used it himself in his will, but in some documents and letters he refers to himself, and signs himself, Christopher Cresacre. As we have seen in previous chapters, only the educated classes could write, and even they were not as particular as we are today about spelling names 'correctly'. Most official documents were written out by scribes who, it seems, often spelt names phonetically, or as they heard them. In Cresacre's case we find his name spelt in a variety of different ways – Chrisaker, Cresacre, Crissacre, Grasacre, Gressaker, Grezacre, Grisacre, Grisacres, Grizacar, Grizaker, Grizsaker, Grozacre, and even Grizatie!

Cresacre moved with his parents and his brothers and sisters from Barnburgh to Low Leyton in 1582, when he was only ten years old. However, around the time of his father's arrest and committal to the Marshalsea in 1584 he was sent to the Elementary School run by the Jesuits at Eu in the North of France. Fr Persons had founded this school in 1581 for the education of young English Catholic boys between the ages of ten and fifteen in preparation for higher studies at Douai, Rheims and Rome. Cresacre was twelve years old when he was admitted.

Following in the footsteps of older brother Thomas, Cresacre soon set his sights on the priesthood. He completed his studies at Eu and was sent to the English College at Rheims to start his study of philosophy and theology. He was admitted to the College on 30 September 1586 where the diary records his name as 'Christopherus Morus'.[1] After four years of further studies he achieved the first step on the way to the priesthood on 18 August 1590 when he received the tonsure and the four minor orders – Porter, Lector, Exorcist, and Acolyte.[2]

Cresacre was among the students at Rheims who were able to return to Douai to continue his studies when the College was re-established there in 1593. His admission as a student of theology at Douai on 22 July 1593 is recorded in the College Diary.[3] In the last two years of his studies Cresacre would have been looking forward to his ordination as Subdeacon and Deacon before ordination to the priesthood, probably in late 1598 or early 1599 when he would have been twenty-six years of age. In the event this was not to be.

As we saw in the last chapter, of Cresacre's three brothers, Henry had joined the Order of St Francis de Paul, and Thomas was already a secular priest so, following the death of his unmarried brother John, probably in 1598, Cresacre became heir apparent to his father. The unexpected death of his brother must have been shock enough for Cresacre, but this shock was followed by another when his father called on him to give up his studies for the priesthood in order to return home to take up the family inheritance and carry on the family name through marriage. If Cresacre needed any reminder of the material and spiritual inheritance that he was taking on, he could see it in Lockey's composite portrait that his father had commissioned, and that was hanging in the family home.

The secular 'chalice' offered to Cresacre was, given the religious situation at the time, a somewhat poisoned one, and for someone so far advanced in his studies for the priesthood it was a great sacrifice to be asked to make. In the circumstances it would have been difficult for Cresacre to hide his feelings and it became common knowledge – within the family at least – that he had been 'verie unwilling to enter into coniugall estate; but yet suffered himself to be over-ruled in it by the counsel of others.'[4] Among those offering his counsel there would, surely, have been his brother Thomas who was at that time chaplain to Lady Magdalene, Viscountess Montague at Battle Abbey.

Before returning to England Cresacre had gone to Rome where the *Pilgrim Book* of the English College records that he stayed for ten days in October 1599.[5] It seems likely that he went there to obtain a dispensation from the orders he had received. He was back in London in 1600, staying somewhere in the parish of St Bride where he was soon discovered, presented for recusancy, and fined £18 (equivalent to around £2,000 today).[6] Cresacre did not have to be in court for the fine to be imposed, and it seems unlikely that he would have been able to pay it as he had, at this time, no source of income that he could call his own. As later events will show, Cresacre's attitude to such fines was to ignore them, as his father often did. Perhaps in this case he thought (or hoped) that the authorities would lose track of him when he moved out of the parish.

The years 1600–04 were the years of a great plague that raged not just in London but also in many rural districts and small towns right across the country. The aristocracy and landed gentry retired to their country properties whenever they could and, for fear of infection, local courts were often not able to meet. In some areas this meant a temporary relief from presentment for recusancy. Initially, courts in Essex do not seem to have been affected, as Cresacre faced further presentments in the Court of the Archdeacon of Essex on 24 April and on 16 May 1601, and at the Essex Assizes on 23 July 1601. In the latter case he was presented with other members of the family: 'Thomas More and Mary his wife, Grisacres More yeoman, Mary, Grace and Anne More spinster, Edward Povey yeoman and Jane his wife, all of Leyton.'[7] Over the next couple of years, presentments of members of the family living at Leyton were relatively few. However, following his snub by Pope Clement VIII on the question of excommunicating Catholics, James tightened up the recusancy laws and presentments started in earnest again in the second half of 1605.

Having given up ordination to the priesthood in order to carry on the family name, Cresacre could hardly be regarded as an 'eligible bachelor' in the eyes of a Catholic girl from a similar background until he came into the possession of some property in his own right. With two-thirds of his Hertfordshire and Yorkshire estates sequestered, his father's options were limited. The most secure property he owned was the estate at Leyton where the family lived, and he passed two of his 'tenements' (houses with surrounding land) into Cresacre's ownership on 5 August 1601. As the original copyhold of the estate had been taken out in his own name, Thomas II had to follow the manorial custom of passing it back to the Lord of the Manor – at that time Edward Ryder, Gent. – before taking it out again in Cresacre's name.

As marriages at this time were generally arranged, the next problem faced by Thomas II was to find a suitable wife for Cresacre, and the person chosen was Elizabeth Gage. The Gage and More families had know each other since the time of Sir Thomas More when Sir John Gage of Firle (Thomas Gage's grandfather) had held a number of high-ranking offices during the reign of Henry VIII. The Gage family had an ancient lineage, and the Firle line had retained their Catholic faith after the Reformation.

Elizabeth Gage, born 24 August 1585, was the daughter of Thomas Gage (b. 27 January 1541), the third of the nine sons of Sir Edward Gage of Firle Place, near Lewes in Sussex. Elizabeth was named after her mother, Elizabeth Guldeford, the daughter of Sir Thomas Guldeford of Hemsted House, in the village of Benenden, Kent, and his wife Elizabeth, the daughter of Sir John Shelley of Michelgrove, near Angmering, West Sussex.[8] Elizabeth had a sister, Mary, who married Sir Thomas Pordage, and a brother, John, born 1589, who inherited the Firle estates from his uncle. In spite of being a convicted recusant John purchased a baronetcy from James I in 1622, becoming the first Baronet Gage of Firle.[9]

Previous researchers of the family have said little about Elizabeth's early life, but I have been able to discover a number of interesting facts some of which help to answer the often asked question as to where, with most of his lands sequestered, Cresacre got his money.

Elizabeth's father died at the age of fifty and was buried in the Church of St Peter at Firle. A brass plaque was set into the gravestone depicting Thomas dressed in armour, with his wife next to him and, the effigies of a son and two daughters, infants, kneeling in a prayer posture underneath them. Translated from the original Latin into English, the memorial to them reads: 'Here lies Thomas Gage, Esquire, and his wife Elizabeth, who died in the year of Our Lord one thousand five hundred and ninety, who had one son and two daughters'. According to the modern calendar, the actual date of Thomas's death was 1 August 1591.

Being only five at the time of her father's death Elizabeth was brought up with her brother and sister (both also 'infants' – that is, under the age of eight) in the house of their uncle, John Gage, at Firle. As eldest son and heir, uncle John had inherited the Gage estates at Firle and elsewhere when his father Sir Edward Gage died in 1567. He was obviously very fond of his nieces and nephew and, in Elizabeth's case, he made arrangements on 20 September 1595 for an annual grant of £26 13. 4d. (equivalent to nearly £3,000 today) to be paid out of the rents from his manors and lands in Firle towards her maintenance from his death until she attained the age of twenty-two.[10] Although he married twice, Uncle John died without issue in October 1598 when, under the terms of his will (dated 2 January 1595), the custody of Elizabeth and her sister and brother to passed to his executors who were required to find them 'meat, drink and lodging' in his house at Firle until they attained the age of twenty-two. In his will he also bequeathed £1,500 each to Elizabeth and her sister, a sum of money that was to be kept for them until they reached the age of twenty-two.[11]

In practice, the day-to-day care of the children had been taken on by a cousin, Elizabeth, the daughter of Robert Gage of Haling in the Parish of Croydon (now South Croydon) and, on 20 April 1598, an indenture, or agreement, was drawn up between Uncle John and Elizabeth granting her 'one annuitie or yearlie rente of tenne poundes ... for and duringe her naturall liefe'. This annuity, equivalent to about £1,500 today, was granted in recognition of the fact that she 'hath heretofore taken greate care and paynes in and about the Education, Instruction, Easemente and bringinge upp of John Gage, Elizabeth Gage and Mary Gage, Children of Thomas Gage Esquire Deceased and hath undertaken to continue in the same Course with them and doe the like as longe as shee maye conventyly'. In fact, Cousin Elizabeth agreed to remain with the children 'or anye of them ... until theye shall bee severallye marryed or otherwise disposed of'.[12]

We do not know exactly when Cresacre married Elizabeth, but an agreement regarding the proposed marriage was drawn up on 30 June 1603, so it was probably later that year. Although she would only have been eighteen at the time Elizabeth may well have been able to bring £1,500 left to her by her Uncle John into the marriage. If that was the case then it would have been equivalent to an inheritance today of around £176,000.

After their marriage Cresacre and Elizabeth lived on the estate at Leyton where they first appear as man and wife in a presentment for recusancy at the Essex Quarter Sessions on 6 April 1605. The discovery of the Gunpowder Plot later that year led to two more statutes against Catholics – 'An Act for the better discovering and repressing of popish recusants', and 'An Act to prevent and avoid dangers which may grow by popish recusants'.[13] The First Act required all convicted recusants to communicate once a year in their local Anglican parish church or to face a fine of £20 for the first offence (equivalent to around £2,500 today), £40 for the second and £60 for the third. As an alternative to this the King was empowered to seize all the personal property and, as in previous legislation, two-thirds of the rest of the property of the offender. The second Act forbade convicted recusants to remain within ten miles of London – a statute that, in practice, proved impossible to implement – and required them to obtain a licence from magistrates if they wanted to go more than five miles from their place of residence. These Acts were aimed particularly at Catholics who might pose a threat to the safety of King and country and, apart from their religious requirements and restrictions on movement, they also barred Catholics from holding public office and commissions in the army or navy, and from a number of professions – lawyers, physicians, and apothecaries.

Under the terms of the new legislation Cresacre and Elizabeth (and the other members of the family living at Leyton) continued to be presented and fined for recusancy at the Essex Quarter Sessions, at the Archdeacon's Court in Romford, and at the Consistory Court of the Bishop of London in West Ham throughout 1606 and, intermittently, in the following years, when the harassment of Catholics eased a little as the anti-Catholic hysteria caused by the Gunpowder Plot died down, and James I sought a more conciliatory approach to those Catholics who were not seen as a threat to King and country.[14] Again, we have no evidence that Cresacre paid all the fines imposed on him – the courts at this time being seemingly more interested in the monies owed by his father. As far as the church courts were concerned, the only thing they could do with people who refused to pay the fines they imposed was to excommunicate them and, although excommunications were quite common at that time, we have no evidence that Cresacre and Elizabeth were excommunicated. They did not, in any case, 'communicate' in their local parish church.

As we saw in the last chapter, Cresacre's father died on 19 August 1606 when his older brother, Thomas IV, officially became his son and heir. However, having become a priest, he renounced his inheritance in favour of Cresacre who now became the actual heir to the family estates. In his will, made a month earlier, Thomas II referred to the fact that he had already transferred two tenements on the Leyton Estate to Cresacre and he now added to them the rest of his 'messuages, cottages, lands, tenements and all their appurtenances within the Manor of Leyton'. In addition to this Cresacre now came into possession of the rest of his father's estates in Yorkshire and Hertfordshire – with the proviso that his mother was to enjoy the profits from one-third of them during her widowhood. Since two-thirds of the estates were sequestered for recusancy this meant that, in effect, Cresacre inherited the sequestered estates – and any debts that might go with them! The extent of the estates in Yorkshire have already been described at the end of chapter three so here we only need to recall that, in addition to land, there were 140 messuages, 60 cottages, two watermills and at least one stone quarry. The Hertfordshire estates are described in his father's will as 'my Lordshippe and manor of More and my capitytall and chief messuage and tenemente there called More Place alias Gobions with the appurtenances in the parish of Northemymes'.[15] This included 160 acres of land, pastures, lakes and woods around the manor house as well as holdings and two groves in the nearby parish of Hatfield.

As soon as the Barons of the Exchequer received notice of Thomas II's death, they ordered an *Inquisitio post Mortem* or 'Escheator's Inquisition', in order to discover the extent of his estates, to assess their value and, more importantly, to find out how much might be owed to them. Much of the 'spade work' for the enquiry had already been done before the sequestration of the Yorkshire estates in 1591 and the sequestration of the Hertfordshire estates after they came back into the possession of the family in 1605. Even so, the various authorities involved – the Sheriff of Hertfordshire among them – were given until the beginning of February 1607 to get their evidence together and present it to the Court of the Barons of the Exchequer. Among other things the court required confirmation of Thomas II's recusancy and this was provided quite soon by the Justices of the Essex Quarter Sessions when they met on 20 October 1606. Based on the evidence they had they were able to state: 'More, Thomas, of Layton, Gent. Certified by William Heigham, Esq. on 20 June last, a convicted recusant dwelling within ten miles of the City of London, and that his wife Mary was also a convicted recusant'.[16]

When the Barons of the Exchequer met at Whitehall on 10 February 1607 they went through all the evidence and came to the conclusion that, on the day he died, Thomas still owed them £500 (equivalent to about £60,000 today) assessed at the time of the sequestration of his estates in 1591 and that therefore two-thirds of his lands should remain in the hands of the King.

If the barons thought that Cresacre would bow humbly to their findings they were wrong. Like his father before him, he seems to have inherited some of his great-grandfather's legal genes and, with them, a similar dislike of injustice. On 12 February, accompanied by his attorney, he presented himself before the court and asked for a hearing – which was granted. He pointed out to the court that the £500 they claimed was still owed by his father when he died had already been paid out of the rents and profits from the sequestered lands in Yorkshire and Hertfordshire. He went on to produce a certificate signed by the Clerk of the Pipe to show that, in fact, a total of £703 3s. 4d. (equivalent to around £85,500 today) had been paid – over £200 pounds more than they were asking for! As if this wasn't enough he then pointed out to the court that, according to an Act of Parliament of 1586, when an offender had died and all 'arrearages' had been paid, then all forfeiture and any seizure of land should be discontinued. He went on to say that he could not understand why the King should continue to oppress him and he asked for a judgment to be made declaring that his father, 'recusant deceased' and all his properties, and his heirs, should be 'discharged and quit' of the debt of £500, and that the lands and properties should be taken out of the King's hands and restored to him. After due consideration of the evidence presented by Cresacre – including an examination of the Act of 1586 – Sir Henry Hobart, representing the King's interests, accepted Cresacre's plea and gave judgment that he was to be 'exonerated from all debt and restored to the possession of his lands and properties'.[17]

Any rejoicing by Cresacre was short lived for he was, of course, a convicted recusant himself. He obviously hadn't been paying his fines, and it didn't take long for the authorities to catch up with him. By this time King James had decided that he would keep the £20 pound fines imposed on those who refused to attend their parish church but that he would still take two-thirds of the lands of recusants and bestow these on the increasing number of people who were seeking some form of reward for services rendered to him. In Cresacre's case, on 20 May 1607, just three months after he got his inheritance back, it was taken away from him again and granted to a gentleman called John Grove who, at the same time, received two-thirds of the lands of Humphrey Pakington at Chaddesley Corbett near Kidderminster, Worcestershire.[18] Translated into English, the grant, signed by the King reads 'The King, on the 20th day of May, grants to John Grove two parts of the lands of Christopher Cresacre More and Humphrey Packington, recusants'.[19]

The grant to John Grove was made following a Letter Patent from the King:

> To Our right trustie and right wel-beloved Cousin and Counsellor, Thomas Earl of Dorset, our highe Tresorer of Englande, and to our trustie and welbeloved Sir Julius Caesar knight, Chancellor and undertreasorer of our Exchequer, Sir Thomas Fleming knight, chiefe Baron of our Courte of Exchequer, and the rest of the Barons there, and to all the other our officers and ministers whatsoever to whome theise presents shall come, greeting.

The letter is long, but it is worth quoting some of it to get an idea of the legal jargon and the formalities involved. After the initial greeting, it sets out the reasons for taking the lands:

> Whereas wee are informed that Christopher Cresacre More of Layton in our countie of Essex gentleman, and Humfrie Pakington late of Chadslye Corbett in our Countie of Worcester gentleman, have of late tyme forborne to come to theire parishe Churche or to anie other Church or Chapell to hearr dyvyne service contrarie to the forme of divers good lawes and statutes in that behalf made and provided, for which recusancie and contempt they the said Christopher Cresacre More and Humfreye Pakington stande thereupon severallie and lawfullie convicted according to the forme of the said statutes, as by divers severall Inquisitions thereof taken and other recordes remayneing in our said Courte of Exchequer more fullie and at large doth and may appear.

The reasons for the grant are then stated as being made:

> In Consideration of some good and acceptable service to us latelie

done by John Grove Gentleman, of our Speciall grace, certayne knowledge and mere motion, Wee have given graunted and confirmed by theise presents, for us, our heires and successors, do fully, freely and absolutely give, graunte and confirme unto the said John Grove, his Executors, administrators and assignes, during the natural lives of the saide Christopher Cresacre More and Humfrey Packington and everie of them and of the longest liver of them, contynueing in his or theire recusancie, and every of them, all and all manner of such forfeitures, sommes and sommes of money, penalties, damages and losses whatsoever, which by force or vertue of anie lawes or statutes of our Realme are due, forfeited and incurred, or in any wise shall become due, incurred or forfeited or shall happen to fall or accrue to us, our heires or successors at anie tyme or tymes hereafter by the saide Christopher Cresacre More and Humphrey Pakington or either of them for his and theire Recusancie and forbearing to come to their parish churche or to anie other church or chapel to heare dyvyne service onelie and for none other Offence or offences, matter or thinges whatsoever.

The rest of the Patent is rather repetitive but, among other details, the King orders that 'no other person or persons shall take anie benefit, profit or commoditie' from Christopher Cresacre and Humphrey Pakington and instructs the Exchequer to pass on to John Grove, 'his executors, administrators and assignes' any other money or benefit that may become due from Cresacre More and John Pakington following further convictions for recusancy. Again he stresses that this should be taken 'as of our free Gifte and favour, without anie further consideration to be given us for the same, and without anie accompte or other charge to be laid upon them'.[20]

We do not really know anything about John Grove except that he had clearly earned the favour of the King. It has been suggested that he was a lawyer who tried to deal fairly with those whose lands he had been granted.[21] If this is the case, then he may have adopted a system of 'compounding', effectively allowing his clients – in our case, Cresacre – to retain control over their estates after the payment of a suitable annual fee to himself.

In October 1607 Cresacre did something, or failed to do something, that upset the authorities and his friend and neighbour at Leyton, Sir Michael Hicks. We saw in the last chapter how Thomas II had appealed to Sir Michael about the valuation of his estate at North Mymms and perhaps Cresacre had sought his assistance following the decision of the Barons of the Exchequer. Whatever happened, it caused Sir Michael severe embarrassment, and Cresacre was made aware of it. Cresacre must have tried to explain himself either in person or via a third party, and followed it up a short while later in a letter. He wrote:

> I hope you have more favourably conceaved of my just excuse in the matter wherein you seemed to take offence. I have ever esteemed your friendship and countenance very available and necessary unto me, and therefore cannot be conceaved so much myne enemy as purposely to runne a course which might be both to you distasteful and to myself an hindrance.

What exactly Cresacre had done remains a mystery but it had something to do with his recusancy, and the possible consequences certainly frightened him for he tells Sir Michael 'Through some late notice I feare that My Lord of London, incensed by my delay, intendeth to send for me a pursuivant, which causeth me that I scarce dare either go home or be seene here in towne.' He concludes his letter, 'Thus hoping that the business which I expected above all would have procured me more and more friends, shall not endanger me to loose their favour whom I esteemed always before well-wishing unto me'. The letter, dated 23 October 1607, was sent by Cresacre from an unknown address in Fleet Street.[22]

The birth of Cresacre and Elizabeth's three children during this period must have brought some joy and light into their world – a world which, so often, threatened not just their peace and happiness but their security and freedom as well. Their first child, Helen, was born at Leyton on Lady Day, 25 March 1606. She was followed by their only son, Thomas, probably born in 1607, and by Bridget, born in 1609. Unfortunately, the joy which the children must have brought into the family home was cut short by Elizabeth's untimely death on 15 July 1610 less than a month before her twenty-fifth birthday.

After Elizabeth's death Cresacre chose not to marry again, and devoted himself to the upbringing and education of his three young children. Given the presence of a number of close female relatives living in the same house, or in properties nearby, it seems reasonable to assume that they assisted him with the personal day-to-day care of the children and that they were able to look after them when he was away from home.

At some time between July 1610 and July 1611 Cresacre commissioned an artist to paint a three-quarter-length portrait of himself. It shows him dressed rather sombrely in black and grey – perhaps a sign of mourning – with his right hand on his lower chest and his left hand holding the hilt of a sword. An inscription at the top left-hand corner tells us that Cresacre was in his thirty-eighth year and on the right there is a shield with the arms of More and Gage on it. At a time when Cresacre was under so much stress he must have felt very alone, and perhaps the picture acted as a statement of self-esteem, a reminder of the proud man that he was, a man who wouldn't be crushed and who wouldn't sell his soul for the sake of his estates.

Exactly what Cresacre did on a daily basis we will never know, and we only have a few glimpses of his movements over the next few years. What we do know is that the authorities would have carefully watched whatever he did outside the immediate environs of his home.

With the law so often set against him it is interesting to see a case at Chelmsford Assizes on 15 March 1613 when the law was, indirectly at least, acting on his side. The case involved two burglaries at the family home. The first took place on 20 September 1612 when William Wade, a labourer of Stratford (a village a few miles away) broke into the house at night while Cresacre and his family were at home and 'stole three pieces of pewter worth 3s., four pounds of butter worth 16d., and six cheeses worth 6s'. The second took place on 1 November 1612 when Wade 'stole 4 capons worth 12s'. Although Wade pleaded not guilty, two witnesses were presented to the court and he was found guilty and sentenced to hang.[23] Although the value of the items stolen does not seem much to us today, they were, in those days, items of some luxury, and their equivalent value today would be in the region of £122. Even so, the sentence appears harsh to us in an age that has, perhaps, gone too 'soft on crime', but in those days such sentences were seen as the most effective way of deterring such crimes. Had Wade stolen even less he might still have suffered the same fate, thus the old saying 'you might as well be hung for a sheep as for a lamb'!

As we saw in the last chapter Cresacre's brother (Thomas More IV, secular priest) had been sent to Rome in 1609 to promote the cause of the secular clergy, and from letters written by secular priests in England to his brother we know that Cresacre was somehow involved in this as well – as were some of his Roper cousins. It may be this sort of business that took Cresacre down to London towards the end of 1613 when John Jackson, a secular priest, wrote that he was 'in town' on 24 November 1613 and again on 26 December 1613. On the first occasion the writer reported that Cresacre and his 'little ones' were well, and on the second that 'he was with me this day & is to come againe in the morning for he lyeth in towne thease holidays'.[24]

Although the question of the appointment of a bishop for the secular clergy was important, of much more importance to lay Catholics like Cresacre was whether there was any way in which they could, with a clear conscience, take the Jacobean Oath of Allegiance. Few Catholics had any problem with the part of the Oath that declared that the Pope had no political authority in England, but the rest of the Oath could be read as implying a denial of the Pope's spiritual authority as well – and that was why the Pope had condemned it. The King's declaration that the Oath was not meant to encroach upon anyone's conscientious convictions was meant to be helpful, but the wording remained the same and still caused unease, and opinion remained divided. As one writer put it, Catholics were looking to find out 'how they might both satisfie the king in taking an oath of temporall alegeance, & not offend God by any unlawful oath'.[25] One way out that was suggested by a Jesuit priest (Fr Thomas Stephenson) was, before taking the Oath to 'protest' that they were taking it only in so far as it concerned their temporal duty or obedience to the King. Another similar suggestion was that they could get the Oath read to them, or read it silently to themselves and then to say 'This oath contayneth many difficult points which we do not understand but so much of it onely as doth truly concerne our temporall allegeance to the King we will & doe sweare sincerely and willingly.' After this, they could 'kneele downe & lay their hand upon the booke'.[26]

In 1613 Cresacre could no longer avoid taking the Oath of Allegiance that was presented to him and five other recusants on 1 June 1613. The document recording the event says, 'We whose names are hereunder written doe willingly subscribe our names unto the oath of allegiance which we have willingly taken this first day of June 1613'. It was signed by John Suffoulde, Isabel Fortesce, Edmond Twynyho, Anthony Skarpe and, Dorithy Skarpe (her mark) – all of Barking – and, lastly, by Cresacre More of Leyton.[27] We do not know with what reservations or with what sort of protest Cresacre may have taken the Oath, but compared to his clear bold signature on other documents the one on this one is small and indistinct, and this has led one writer to suggest that, maybe, he was ashamed of what he had done.[28]

During the first fifteen years of his reign James I was constantly in debt to the point where he even had to borrow money from some of his courtiers. As we saw above in the case of John Grove, the King generously rewarded those who served him well, but though it may have 'bought' him support it did nothing to swell the royal coffers. James's creation of the hereditary Baronetage in 1611 was meant to provide another layer of 'dignity' within society, but in the event it turned into another way of increasing his income when he allowed the title to be bestowed on more or less anyone who could pay £1,095 (equivalent to around £148, 000 today) for the privilege – as Elizabeth's brother John Gage did in 1622.

As concern about the increasingly desperate state of the royal finances increased various commissions were set up to look into ways of raising money. One of the easier ways was to make sure that convicted recusants paid all their fines and it was probably this that caused the Exchequer – over-zealously as it turned out – to hold an Inquisition into Cresacre's case during the Spring of 1615. The proceedings show that the Exchequer had a long memory. It brought to light unpaid debts of £180 for not going to church when he was staying in St Bride's parish, London, and £260 for similar offences at Leyton between 1599 and the end of Elizabeth's reign in 1603. Added to these sums was another £280 for offences against the Acts introduced by James.[29] A further Inquisition held at Stratford Longthorne on 14 October of the same year assessed the value of Cresacre's 'divers goods and chattels' at his 'messuage or tenement with its appurtenances in Leyton' at £100. In total, therefore, the Exchequer claimed that he owed the King £820 (equivalent to around £91,000 today) and, as a consequence it ordered that 'two-thirds of the said messuage and other premises in Leyton should remain in the hands of the King'.[30]

What the Exchequer seems to have overlooked was the fact that, because of his continued recusancy, the King had granted two-thirds of Cresacre's estates to John Grove in 1607 and that he therefore owed nothing – and even if he had owed something the money would have gone to Grove and not to the King.

When news reached Grove that the Exchequer was claiming that the sequestered part of the Leyton Estate belonged to the

King he presented himself in person to Sir Francis Bacon, the Attorney General, to show him the Letters Patent granted to him by the King in 1607. He protested against the injustice of his treatment and asked judgment:

> That the said Christopher Cresacre Moore, as concerns the aforesaid various debts and sums of money demanded from him in the Recusant Rolls and Inquisition aforesaid, and any part of parcel of them, by the said King, his heirs, successors or any of them, shall now and in future be exonerated and acquitted ... the hands of the King should be removed from his possession of the said two thirds of the messuage, land, tenements and other premises with their appurtenances mentioned in the Inquisition, and that the said John Grove shall be restored to his possession of them ...

For his part Sir Francis Bacon could not but agree with John Grove and when the whole case was put before the Barons of the Exchequer they restored John Grove to his rightful possession of the sequestered part of Cresacre's estate at Leyton. More importantly for Cresacre they also considered that 'now and for the future [he] is exonerated and stands acquitted of the various debts and sums of money owed by him in various Recusant Rolls and in the Inquisition, and of every part and parcel of them.'[31]

While the Exchequer was sorting out his case Cresacre applied to the Privy Council for permission to travel outside the five-mile limit from his home first imposed on recusants by Queen Elizabeth in 1593 and reinforced by James I in 1606. Permission was granted on 7 May 1615:

> License for Christopher Cresacre More of Low Leyton, in the County of Essex, Gent. a recusant convict, to travel out of his confinement to the Counties of Hertford and Oxford for the disposal of some affairs which require his personal attention.[32]

The seems little doubt that the visit to Hertfordshire would have had something to do with Gobions, his manor house at North Mymms, perhaps to visit tenants or to check on its condition and to begin getting it ready for his eventual move there. The visit to Oxfordshire would almost certainly have been to visit his sister and brother-in-law (the Greenwoods) at Brize Norton and, while there, to draw up the document (mentioned in the last chapter) transferring the Rectory and Parsonage in Easby, North Yorkshire, to Thomas Greenwood the younger.

Cresacre was granted further licences to travel outside the five-mile limit from Leyton on 12 May 1616 and again on 16 March 1617. Shortly after this he moved to live with his young family at Gobions in North Mymms. We don't know what prompted the move and, initially, he seems to have kept his options open by still referring to himself as 'of Low Leyton' when applying for further travel licences. It may be that he had not, at that stage, decided to remain at Gobions. However, that he did make it his permanent home we know from a Certificate of Residence granted to him on 30 April 1621 which says: 'Cressacar Moore hath been resident att Mymmes aforesaid by the space of these fower yeres last past.'[33]

On 1 April 1619 Cresacre again requested permission to leave his home area, this time to travel further afield:

> Petition of Christopher Cresacre More of Low Leyton, co. Essex, to the Council, for a licence to go to places more remote from London than the place to which he is confined as a recusant.[34]

Later that year he travelled up to Barnburgh, probably to visit his great-uncle Edward who was still living at the Hall.

From the little evidence we have, we know that Cresacre was actively involved in supporting the cause of secular priests working on the English mission – as was his cousin Sir William Roper. This was a cause his brother, Fr Thomas More had, as we have seen, championed as Clergy Agent in Rome. At the same time, he was devoting his time to educating his young children at home. In addition to this, it was around this time (1616–1620) that he began to write the life of his great-grandfather, and this no doubt involved him in travel to consult historical documents, manuscripts of the other *Lives*, and to meet with his Roper relatives.

As already mentioned in the introduction, Cresacre's *Life* was the last life of Sir Thomas More written by a direct descendant. Usually just called *The Lyfe of Sir Thomas More, Knight*, its full title is, *The Lyfe of Sir Thomas More Knight, Lord High Chancellor of England under King Henry VIII and His Majesty's Ambassador to the Courts of France and Germany*. In spite of its rather grand title the book is very much the life of his hero, Thomas More the martyr and saint. The title was probably chosen with an eye to its being published in England if the political situation in England changed. However, there was always the danger that his manuscript might be discovered and, at this time, it was not even safe for him to put his own name to it, so he assumed an alias 'M. T. M.' – believed to be 'Magister Thomas More'.

The next decade at Gobions must have been some of the least stressful years of Cresacre's life. In spite of occasional outbreaks of anti-Catholic feeling, pressure on recusants lessened as James sought a Catholic bride – first a Spanish one and then a French one – for Prince Charles. The alliance of November 1624 that provided for his marriage to Princess Henrietta Maria (the daughter of Henry IV of France) contained a clause that required the suspension of the laws against recusants and, although the relevant documents have not been traced, there is every indication that, for Cresacre, this meant the restoration of his estates. We know that it was around this time that Cresacre finished the life of his great-grandfather as he dedicated it to Princess Henrietta Maria. However, in spite of the changing religious scene he was still not able to print it in England and it was eventually printed in Douai sometime between 1624 and 1631. Cresacre obviously felt it safer to keep the alias 'T. M. T.' – an attribution that caused some confusion and led to the work being, for many years, attributed to his brother Fr Thomas More who died at Rome in 1625.

By the mid-1620s Cresacre's three children, Helen, Thomas and Bridget were all in their teens. Cresacre was very devout and tried to bring his children up in the same way. The family had a confessor, Dom Benet Jones, a Benedictine monk. Thomas will be the subject of the next chapter, so I will say no more about him here. Of his two sisters we know most about Helen whose biographer (Dom Augustine Baker, OSB), referring to her when she was fifteen years old, said 'she was of a verie good nature, gentle, affable, kinde, tractable, meerrie and pleasant, verie forwarde in naturall witte and judgment for her yeares'. As for Cresacre, he said that he 'was so delighted in her compagnie and conversation, that his life, that otherwise was solitarie, was the more tolerable and pleasing to him'. Helen was an extrovert and, like most young people of her age today, she was not particularly religious. As her biographer said 'there was not then much supernaturall in her, nor anie thing verie notable, as in regard of Religion'.[35] It is therefore surprising that, at a time when her father was said to have already determined to provide her with a 'liberal portion' for her eventual marriage, the family's confessor should suggest to her that she might like to consider becoming a nun. Dom Benet Jones, however, had his own agenda! As we will see, he was hatching a plan that involved putting the same idea into the minds of a number of other young Catholic women!

Cresacre's younger daughter Bridget, seems to have been of a similar disposition to her sister, being described at this time as 'endowed with great advantages, both of grace, and of nature which made her much esteemed by all' and, like her sister, as being very dear to her father.[36]

At the age of seventeen Helen had still not shown any real interest in marriage and Cresacre agreed to go along with Dom Benet's idea and give her an opportunity to try the religious life of a nun. As we have just seen, Helen was not particularly religious, indeed, she was later to say of this period in her life that she had 'scarce thought whether there were anie God or no'.[37] In addition, Helen could have had no idea about what the life of a nun might be like, as there had been no convents or nunneries in England since the suppression of the monasteries by Henry VIII. What seems to have happened is that Cresacre gave in to a good deal of pressure from Dom Benet Jones. He was rather a Moses-figure who had made it his mission to lead a small group of his chosen people away from slavery under the Anglican Church in England into a promised land – a monastery of English Benedictine nuns – on the Continent! It was unthinkable in those days that the monastery should be anything other than 'enclosed'. Dom Benet had been given the go-ahead by his Superior in 1621 and, after that, had sought a bishop who would allow a monastery to be established in his diocese and also allow it to be directed by the English Benedictines rather than by himself. His search was successful and, on 6 June 1622, the Archbishop of Cambrai (in Spanish Flanders) gave permission for a monastery to be established in the town. The approval of the Spanish authorities was also required and this was granted by the Infanta Isabella on 30 May 1623. Finally, the town's magistrates gave their consent on 17 May 1623.[38] In the meantime, Dom Benet had been carefully 'selecting' the young Catholic women he though would be most suitable to enable him, finally, to bring his plan to fruition.

Dom Benet initially chose eight women to start his foundation; among them were Helen and two of her cousins Grace and Anne More.[39] Although each of the women would have been provided with a small annuity by way of a 'dowry', it was Cresacre's contribution of £500 (equivalent to around £53,000 today) that enabled the project to get off the ground, and when the party set off with Dom Benet from England in the summer of 1523 he accompanied them. They went first to Douai where they stayed for some weeks in a house provided by the Abbot of St Vaast. While there, Helen fell seriously ill, but she had recovered sufficiently to move south to Cambrai with the others in the last week of September. In Cambrai they had to stay for a while at the local hospital of St James while their house in Rue St Vaast was made ready for them. The house, an old refuge originally belonging to the Benedictine Abbey of Femey, was in a very poor state of repair. Initially lent to them 'for a time' it became their own property in 1638 and remained in their possession until 1793 when the nuns, then numbering twenty-two, were ejected during the French Revolution.[40]

The small group of young women moved into their new home on Sunday 24 December 1623 and it was named the Monastery of Our Lady of Comfort (or Consolation). The following Sunday they were given the Benedictine Habit by the Archbishop of Cambrai and Fr Rudesind Barlow the President of the English Benedictine Congregation based at the Abbey of St Gregory in Douai. The average age of the postulants was twenty-two, and three experienced nuns were transferred from the Benedictine convent at Brussels to lead the new community and teach the postulants the Benedictine way of life.[41]

In religion Helen took the name Sister Gertrude (becoming Dame Gertrude after her profession). The story of her life under the title *The Life and Death of D. Gertrude More, a Religious Virgin of the English Cloister of Benedictin Nunnes in the Cittie of Cambraie* was told by Dom Augustine Baker, the Benedictine monk and priest who was an unofficial spiritual adviser to the nuns between the years 1624 and 1633. His manuscript edition, never intended for publication, was probably finished in 1635 or 1636.[42] Two main editions of this work have come down to us. The first was produced by Dom Benedict Weld-Blundell and published in 1910 as Volume I of his *Inner Life and Writings of Dame Gertrude More*. The second, a much more accurate and scholarly work (from which I have quoted), produced from all the available manuscripts by Ben Wekking was published in 2002.

The story of Dame Gertrude is, to my mind, the fascinating story of a young woman who, at the outset, clearly had no vocation to the religious life. Even Fr Baker admitted 'I cannot saie, nor well thinke, that she had anie Call from God to Religion, that she could perceave'.[43] In today's world I am sure she would probably not have got much beyond the front door of a convent or, if she had, she would soon have been ushered out again! She had in fact only agreed to go to Cambrai to please her father and, when she got there she hated it! Although she could mouth the words she found vocal prayer meaningless and meditation impossible; she 'went through the motions' regarding the daily routine of the convent, and sought as many distractions as she could. She disliked her superiors and became crafty, wilful and facetious. She suffered from bouts of serious ill-health and, not surprisingly, she became depressed. Whenever she could, she retired to her cell where 'she reflected on herself, saw the miserie of her owne case, and bitterly bemoaned it to herself'.[44]

Cresacre obviously received word of his daughter's ill-health and wrote to her telling her that if she thought she should return home because of her health he 'would not love her one whitte less but farre the more for so heroical resolutions'. She, however, wrote back telling him that she was going to stay.[45] The first profession of the nine novices was set to take place on 1 January 1625, but as the day grew nearer Sr Gertrude became more and more distressed. How could she make her profession in good conscience when she had made little or no progress and was so unhappy with herself and with the way of life she was leading? On reflection she felt that Dom Benet Jones had exercised too much power over her, and she wished that she had never heard of him! On the other hand, how could she leave? The convent depended greatly on the financial support provided by her father, and if she left what would happen to the rest? Would she be able to live with herself if her leaving was to result in its closure? If she did leave, what would she do with herself, as she had no interest in marriage? Even if she had, no respectable man would want to marry a former nun. In such a state she found herself trapped between the devil and the deep blue sea. Having forsaken the world herself, she now felt as though the world had forsaken her. She could neither go forward, nor back. As her first biographer said, 'These considerations volved to and fro in her minde (and) made her, even in the eve of her profession daie, to be unresolved what she were best to do in it'.[46] She desperately wanted (and needed) to talk to someone, but just couldn't bring herself to do it. In the end, numbed no doubt by her inner conflict, and not seeing any alternative, she decided to make her profession in which she vowed stability, conversion of life, and obedience to the rule of St Benedict.

Unfortunately her profession only made things worse, and when her father came to Cambrai shortly after – he spent three months there in 1625, staying in the guest house – she was determined to ask him to help her to get a transfer to some other convent where the Mother Superior might understand her better, and where she might be more contented. In the event, she didn't say anything to him, and pretended that she was happy. As she said herself:

> I was indeed very loath and unwilling to speake anie thing that might be a greefe to my father; and therefore I did allwaies sette the best face I could upon it, and said as much as I could that might be a confort to him; and what I could not well speake of I did forbeare, and would saie nothing at all of it.[47]

At the beginning of November 1525, on the suggestion of the Novice Mistress, Dame Gertrude approached Fr Baker for spiritual advice. She had approached him once before, but she was in such a bad state that she had not really taken any notice of what he had said and had even mocked the other sisters who tried to follow his advice and who showed obvious benefit from it. This time, in sheer desperation, she was ready to listen and learn.

The story of the rest of Dame Gertrude's life is the story of her response to the spiritual direction of Fr Baker. That story can be read in either of the two books mentioned above, and it is not my intention to repeat it here. Suffice it to say that he proved to be the means of her mental and spiritual salvation. Under his direction she was freed from the spiritual straightjacket that others had tried to impose on her and encouraged to follow what he called 'divine inspirations' – 'the secret workinge of God in the soule' – which, he said, would reveal to her the form of spirituality that was best suited to her own special needs.[48] He saw nothing wrong in her enjoyment of talking to people at 'the grate' (the barred window which was the only place of contact between the nuns and people outside the enclosure), nor did he find anything wrong in her talking about 'news, curiosities or other things', or in her reading books that were not specifically about religious topics. In her particular case he regarded these as legitimate forms of recreation or diversion that put her in a better frame of mind when the time came for quiet recollection. Since she found ordinary vocal prayer and traditional forms of meditation of little use he encouraged her to develop a form of prayer that he called 'the prayer of sensible affections' consisting of the regular verbal expression of acts of love, gratitude, etc. towards God.

The change that Fr Baker's direction gradually brought about in Dame Gertrude soon became obvious to all. Even her father noticed it when he visited Cambrai on his way to Antwerp around Easter time in 1626 and also in September 1626 on his way back from Paris to Antwerp where he was going to spend the winter. In Father Baker's own words, his teaching had 'transformed her from an obstinate, self-willed person into an amiable personality, a change which affected the whole house and eased the bad relationship between herself and the abbess.' Rather than criticizing her, constructive use began to be made of her enjoyment of practical activities by making her 'chief cellarer' (responsible for ordering and storing the food and drink of the convent) and by giving her responsibility for the oversight of the lay sisters.[49]

Dame Gertrude's transformation was so great that when the position of Abbess became vacant in 1629 her name was put forward as one of the two candidates – the other being Dame Catherine Gascoigne. Both were in fact too young for the position and a special dispensation from Rome had to be sought to enable the appointment to go through. In the event Dame Gascoigne was chosen because she was the older of the two by six years.[50]

Throughout her life Dame Gertrude remained subject to bouts of scruples – wondering, for example, whether her past confessions were valid – and to periods of deep spiritual aridity and desolation – what St John of the Cross calls 'The Dark Night of the Soul' – as well as to bouts of depression and of serious physical ill-health. Fr Baker did not see the need for any other forms of mortification over and above what these provided for her, and he encouraged her to accept and bear them patiently as being the will of God for her.

Dame Gertrude began to feel ill at the end of July 1633 and soon became bedridden as the illness showed itself to be a particularly virulent form of smallpox. One of the nuns appointed to care for her (and who was with her when she died) was her cousin Dame Anne More. The terrible effects of the disease on her were vividly described by the Dame Catherine Gascoigne, the Lady Abbess who said: 'It was the most loathsome, the most odious, and very neare the plague, and in very deede her flesh both inwardly and outwardly did rotte away, in so much that we had very much adoe to keepe the flies from makinge them selves nests in her face, and eatinge it she being alive.' The Abbess asked Dame Gertrude if she felt them (the flies) and she relied 'yes', but she made no complaint about them.[51]

On 15 August the doctor visited Dame Gertrude and, believing she was close to death, recommended that she should receive the last rites. These were administered to her by a visiting Benedictine priest in the evening, after Vespers. She finally died in the early hours of the morning of 17 August as the other nuns were singing Matins. She was only twenty-seven years old. She was buried in the cemetery of the Augustinian Canons Regular at Cambrai.[52]

Throughout her life Dame Gertrude wrote down many of her thoughts and experiences and these were first published in 1658 under the title *The Spiritual Writings of Dame Gertrude More*. They were edited and republished in 1911 as Volume II of Dom Weld-Blundell's work mentioned above. They are regarded today as the writings of a true mystic.

Bridget More, Dame Gertrude's younger sister, was born at Low Leyton in 1609 and, like her sister, was also educated at home by her father. However, unlike her sister, when she reached her teens she desperately wanted to become a nun and had to work hard to persuade her father to allow her to do so. The way she went about this is recorded as follows:

> Her father did fully deign she should marry and settle in the world to the end that he might live and die with her, she being the greatest comfort he had, and on the other side she earnestly desired to espouse herself entirely to God. And that which increased her trouble was how to propose it to her Father. Therefore she made use of her Confessor and other powerful friends to prepare and move him to it, and he being a virtuous person, was in conclusion resigned to give her to God and deprive himself of that consolation, on condition she should stay till her brother was married which he procured with all speed for her content and satisfaction.[53]

Bridget joined her sister at the Monastery of Our Lady of Consolation on 28 June 1629 where she took the name Sister Bridget More of St Peter and Paul. She was nineteen years of age.[54] Although there is no written evidence that Cresacre visited the Continent after his return from Antwerp in 1627 I would be surprised if he did not accompany Helen to Cambrai in 1629. He certainly had permission to travel abroad during that year and it would have provided him with an opportunity to see Dame Gertrude again, probably for the last time.

Unlike her sister, Bridget was a model novice and she made her profession without any qualms on 24 September 1630, becoming Dame Bridget More. A copy that Bridget made of the original schedule of her vows is preserved by the nuns of Stanbrook

Abbey. Translated from the Latin it reads:

> I Sister Bridget More of St. Peter and Paul, of the County of Hertford, Promise Stability and Conversion of my Manners and Obedience before God and His Saints, according to the Rule of the Most Holy Father Saint Benedict, and Perpetual Enclosure in this Monastery of St Mary the Virgin, of the Order of the same Saint. In the Presence of Reverend Mother Dame Catherine Gascoigne, Abbess of the same Monastery, and under Obedience to the Reverend Father Sigisbert Bagshawe, President of the whole English Congregation of the same order. 24 September in the Year of Our Lord 1630.

Dame Bridget made such progress in the religious life that, within a year of her profession she was chosen to assist the Abbess with the reformation and enclosing of another monastery in Cambrai belonging to the Religious Dames of St Lazarus – a task given to them by the Archbishop.

By the late 1640s the number of nuns at Cambrai had increased to over fifty. The building was never intended to house so many, and the lack of funds meant that the community had been reduced to a state of great poverty. The suggestion that some members of the community should disperse to other French monasteries was not acceptable to the nuns who preferred to live in poverty than be separated from each other. However, the suggestion that some of the nuns should be sent to found a daughter house was accepted, and in 1652 Dame Bridget and three other nuns (two choir nuns and a lay sister) were chosen by the President of the English Benedictine Congregation to assist in the establishment of a new foundation at Paris – the Monastery of Our Lady of Good Hope. The foundation was thought by many to be very unwise given the state of civil war that existed in France at the time but it still went ahead and, in October 1651 the small party, dressed in secular clothes and chaperoned by Fr Serenus Cressy, a Benedictine Monk, set out to make the one-hundred-mile journey south to Paris which they reached on 1 November to a welcome by Queen Henrietta Maria (the exiled widow of Charles I) and some other benefactors. In Paris they stayed with a community of English Augustinian nuns before renting a house in the Rue St Dominique in the area we now know as the Left Bank of the River Seine. In the New Year four more choir nuns and another lay sister were sent from Cambrai, and when they arrived the new community was formally established on 6

February 1652. Two weeks later, on 20 February, Dame Bridget was chosen by her fellow nuns to be the Prioress of the new community. The new foundation struggled at first, but the prudent management of Dame Bridget, and a legacy of £200 left by Dame Bridget's two nephews Cresacre and William More (about whom more in the next chapter) enabled it to survive.

Dame Bridget is described as having been 'a perfect practiser of regular observances' and as having 'a particular zeal' for the office of the choir and for silence, prayer and recollection. Her humility is said to have been remarkable for 'although she was Prioress she did not disdain to draw water, dig and weed in the garden and (do) other inferior works'.

During her period as Prioress Dame Bridget moved with the small community into a number of rented houses until, in 1664, they were finally able to purchase a secluded house with a walled garden in the Champ de l'Alouette. The following year, at her own request, Dame Bridget was relieved of some of the responsibility she shouldered and Mother Justine Gascoigne was elected to replace her on 6 August 1665. Dame Bridget became sub-prioress and Mistress of Novices and Juniors.

In 1686 the community were in a position to be able to purchase the property next door, and in 1693 they began to convert the buildings into a true monastery by adding a cloister and proper dormitory cells above. Unfortunately Dame Bridget was not to see this later development. She fell ill during Vespers on 15 August 1692, struck down by what was described as 'an unusual illness' which caused her to be confined to the infirmary. None of the remedies offered to her by the doctor were of any use and her condition deteriorated over the next two months, 'her sickness increasing with a fever and a flux, which was extremely painful'. In spite of this she remained cheerful and lucid until her death on 12 October 1692. She was eighty-three years old.

The Monastery of Our Lady of Good Hope in the Champ de l'Alouette (the Lark's field) remained the home of the community until, after a period of imprisonment, they had to flee France and return to England in 1794. After spending some years in temporary houses at Marnhull in Dorset and Cannington in Somerset the community eventually found a permanent home in 1836 at Colwich in Staffordshire. At first known as St Benedict's Priory it was granted the status of an abbey in 1928 when it was renamed St Mary's Abbey. Today, the old monastery in Paris has been converted into a block of flats – 28 Rue des Tanneries, Paris 13.

To return now to the father of our two good nuns: We have seen that Cresacre spent a good deal of time on the Continent between 1625 and 1627, staying at Antwerp, Paris, Cambrai, and at Douai – in this latter town probably making arrangements for the publication of the life of his great-grandfather. He was one of the executors of the will his brother (Thomas More IV) had made in Rome and, following his death in April 1525, he obtained probate for it at Antwerp on 30 October 1625 and must have spent some time dealing with the provisions it made regarding property in Douai and elsewhere in Flanders.

King James had died in 1625 and with Charles I on the throne Cresacre must have hoped, yet again, that he would be granted further relief from persecution. Although officially a Protestant, Charles had a Catholic Queen. There were therefore two chaplains at Court who had to work peacefully together – Bishop Taylor, the King's Chaplain, and Fr Davenport, the Queen's Chaplain. Relations between the Crown and the Vatican also improved, and in 1634 a papal representative took up official residence in London. The King had what were later to be called 'High Church' leanings, and this caused many at Court and in the country to fear that Popery was slowly returning by the back door. The appointment of William Laud as Archbishop of Canterbury in 1633 and his (Laud's) promotion of a Catholic-style liturgy performed no longer at a communion table in the body of the church, but at a raised altar back in its old railed-off position at the east end of a church, did nothing to quell the fears not just of the Puritans but of a great majority of ordinary Anglicans as well. Not that this worried Charles unduly. He was an aloof and autocratic figure who, since the end of 1629, had decided to rule England without the assistance of a Parliament and who, in the mid-1630s, was at the height of his power.

Given the divisions at Court and in the country at large it is not surprising that, in practice, the treatment of Catholics varied from county to county, often depending on the political and religious persuasion of the people who wielded authority there. While the number of Catholic priests in England grew steadily, recusancy still remained a crime and, overall, fines for recusancy increased during the 1630s. However, as we have seen, some Catholics – Cresacre included – had their lands restored to them or were able to 'compound' for them by paying an annual fee to the Exchequer. The Oath of Allegiance remained in force, and when Cresacre returned to England from the Continent in November 1627 it was tendered to him when he landed at Dover. Cresacre, ever defiant, refused to sign it – probably because, as we have seen, he had already signed it at Leyton in 1613 and did not want to go through the rather dubious process once again. As a consequence of his refusal, he was arrested and sent to London where he appeared before the Privy Council on 15 November. After the examination of his case he was remanded in custody but then released a week later after promising to appear again should he be required to do so.[55]

With his two daughters now settled away from home Cresacre's thoughts turned to the marriage of his only son who had now reached his majority. As we will see in the next chapter, the person chosen was Mary, the daughter of Sir Basil Brooke of Madeley in Shropshire, a young lady of about the same age. The marriage settlement was drawn up by Cresacre and Sir Basil in April 1629.

Relatively little is known about the last twenty years of Cresacre's life. He seems to have lived free of any great aggravation until the early 1640s when, following Charles I's disastrous attempt to reform religion in Scotland and the abandonment of his invasion of Scotland he chose, once again, to rule with the assistance of Parliament.

Sometime during the 1630s Cresacre had purchased the lease of a farm estate at Chilston in the parish of Madley a few miles west of Hereford. He had also bought land and a number of properties at Tillington, at Burghill, and at Horton in the parish of Kingsland, all to the north-west of Hereford. Apart from his farm, he leased out the other properties, in most cases, to the people from whom he had purchased them. One of the houses he bought, called 'Highland', was of substantial dimensions, with a west wing and a cross wing. In his will Cresacre refers to this property as having been 'purchased for my own use of one James Rodde', so it seems as though he may have lived or stayed there himself, though it was later let out again to its original owner.[56] Interestingly, James Rodde was also a recusant.

The estate at Chilston was the most important estate in the parish, and it appears to have been divided into two, one part, with a substantial farmhouse, in Upper Chilston, the other, probably with a smaller house, in Lower Chilston. Both properties remained in the possession of the family until the 1670s when Upper Chilston is noted as being in the possession of 'the Carpenters' and Lower Chilston in the possession of 'the

Westons'.⁵⁷ Documents held by Herefordshire Records Office show that a William Carpenter already lived in the village in 1653 and that in 1676 a John Weston was living at Upper Chilston. As the original lease was purchased from John Weston it would appear that Lower Chilston was returning to the family that had originally owned it.⁵⁸

Cresacre's reasons for purchasing the farm at Chillington, and for moving there, are not known. However, having promised (as part of the marriage agreement) to settle his main estates in Hertfordshire and Yorkshire on his son it may have been to give him and his growing family full possession of Gobions at North Mymms. As we will see later, Cresacre did not get on very well with his son and, now in his sixties, he may have been looking for a retreat in a part of the country where he was not well known, and where he could live out his days in peace. Unfortunately, however, the re-establishment of Parliament in 1640 led to greater religious intolerance, and even hatred, and there was a renewed determination among Members to root out 'the designs of priests and Jesuits, and other adherents of the see of Rome' and the 'divers innovations that have been brought into the church'.⁵⁹ In the ensuing battle Puritans were pitted against both 'High' and more traditional Anglicans, and all pitted against popery. Rumours about Charles's negotiations with Irish Catholics, with Spain, and with the Pope, convinced many that he was unfit to rule and this, coupled with other factors, led to the eventual outbreak of the Civil War in 1642.

In 1643 the recusancy laws were, once again, tightened up. This time they were to be applied to 'delinquents' – those who were seen as posing a threat to the State (mainly those who supported the Royalist cause) – and to the traditional recusants who failed to attend their local parish church. Although there is no evidence that Cresacre was an active supporter of the Royalist causes he was treated as both a delinquent and a recusant, and his estates at Barnburgh, at North Mymms, at Low Leyton and at Tillington were all, yet again, sequestered and let out to tenants. This time he was not left the usual one-third to support himself. However, the lease of his farm at Chilston does not seem to have been affected so he was able to survive there.

Even after the sequestration of his estates the authorities did not leave Cresacre alone. In 1545 the 'Committee for Advance of Money', ever on the look out for additional funds, discovered that Cresacre still had 'several sums of money and goods ... remaining about his house near Gubbins North Mymms' and they were ordered to be sought out and seized.⁶⁰ Although I have not seen any records relating to it, Cresacre must have fought the sequestration order because, in April 1646, he was declared not to be a delinquent, but only a Papist and, as a result, one-third of his lands were restored to him.⁶¹

Cresacre drew up his will on 7 March 1648, describing himself as 'in full and perfect memory but infirme and weake of bodie'.⁶² As executors he appointed his brother-in-Law Thomas Greenwood, his Cousin William Roper (presumably the son of Thomas Roper and Susan Winchcombe), his 'trustie and loveinge friende George Vaughan of Nanthelinge in the County of Monmouth', and his 'olde servant' Christopher Lewis. The will shows us that, in addition to the estates he had bought in Herefordshire, Cresacre had also purchased leases 'in divers counties', some in his own name and some 'in other men's names for my use'. Among these we can identify a 'messuage, tenement, lands and other appurtenances' near the property he already owned at Tilts, near Doncaster, a 'messuage and tenement at Swanley Bar' (between Potters Bar and his Gobions estate at North Mymms), and some 'lands' at Priesthawes in Sussex originally belonging to John Thatcher, a cousin through his marriage to Elizabeth Gage. He also mentions having 'Extents and Statutes', 'Bonds and Statutes', 'Rents and Rent Charges' which belonged to him or were for his use. All this indicates that Cresacre had become a master at spreading his assets widely and finding means of hiding them from the authorities.

In the main part of the will Cresacre makes no mention of his son Thomas, presumably because he had already agreed to settle his main properties on him after his death. The first-named beneficiary is his eldest grandson William More (see the next chapter). He then names his two eldest granddaughters, Frances and Mary More, leaving them two-thirds and one-third respectively of all the ready money he will leave behind when he dies – this money to be kept for them by his executors until they reach the age of twenty-one or until 'there shall be opportunities to prefer eyther of them in marriage'. After these he makes generous provision for his two servants Christopher Lewis (already an executor) and Thomas Lockier. To the first, he leaves the house named Highland (mentioned above), and the tenements and lands belonging to it in Herefordshire, as well as two Annuities of £20 per year for life (together equalling around £3,200 today) to be paid twice-yearly in May and September out of the Gobions estate, and his lands in Sussex. To the second, he leaves the choice of having either the messuage and tenement at Swanley Bar, or an annuity for life of £10 payable twice-yearly out of the Gobions estate.

We have already seen how Cresacre purchased property at Easby in North Yorkshire for his nephew Thomas Greenwood the younger in 1615, and in his will he also makes small bequests to his sister Grace Greenwood, to his three great-nephews (children of Thomas Greenwood the Younger) and to various other nieces, cousins and family friends.

Cresacre's will gives us the only indication we have that his relationship with his son (now thirty-eight years old) had broken down. He speaks of Thomas's many acts of disobedience and ingratitude and of all his other faults. Feelings were obviously mutual for he refers to the 'many misconceits and misapprehensions' that Thomas has of him, for reasons, he says, that he does not understand. The only 'fault' actually specified by Cresacre was that Thomas had not been 'so carefull as he ought in makinge provision for his younger children'. In itself this might not sound too bad, but it is followed by provisions which Cresacre makes for them because he 'would not have them be left without all care to be provided for' – which sounds more like a case of neglect. The children he mentions are his younger grandchildren, Cresacre More (usually called Cresacre More II), Basil More, Thomas More, John More, Margaret More and Bridget More and, in order to provide for them, he leaves his executors his 'Messuages, Lands, Rents and Tenements in Haughton Parva, Womersley, Whitley, Bolton upon Dearne, Brothwaite, Aldwick, Pigbourne under Wombwell', all in Yorkshire, and also his 'Messuages and lands' in Burghill, Tillington and Horton in Herefordshire. He specifies that the money raised from the sale of these properties – which, when the time came, must have been considerable – is given to his executors 'in trust and confidence' to be divided equally among the six children and to be paid to them as they reach the age of twenty-one, or sooner if they (the executors) 'shall see cause so to doe'.

In a moving statement added after the main will was signed and sealed, Cresacre heartily forgives Thomas for all his wrong-doings and, as a token of their reconciliation, leaves him 'the Messuage and Tenement and the Landes and other Appurtenances to the same belonging' that he had purchased near his other lands at Tilts near Doncaster in Yorkshire.

Cresacre died on his farm at Chilston on 26 March 1649 and was buried the following day in the cemetery surrounding the Anglican Church of the Nativity of the Blessed Virgin Mary in Madley. Translated from the Latin in which it is written, the entry in the parish register reads: 'Thomas More Esquire was buried 27 March 1649'. Calling him Thomas instead of Cresacre has been called a 'slip', easily made given the trouble he had with his forename, but I find this difficult to believe as the rector or vicar of the church would have known him well. Given the fact that Catholic burials at Anglican churches were actually illegal at that time and, when they took place, often had to be conducted clandestinely, I think it more likely that the entry in the register is a thinly-veiled attempt by the rector or vicar to cover up the event.

Genealogical Summary

Cresacre More and his Family

Cresacre More (1572–1649) m. Elizabeth Gage (1576–1610)
Children:
1. Helen (1606–1633): Benedictine nun at Cambrai.
2. Thomas V (1607–1660): only son and heir (see next chapter).
3. Bridget (1609–1692): Prioress of Benedictine nuns at Paris.

Chapter Six

The Family of Thomas More V

Thomas More V, the only son and heir of Cresacre More and his wife Elizabeth (née Gage), is believed to have been the second of their three children, and to have been born in 1607 or 1608. Of all the sons and heirs of the family that we have met so far, Thomas V is one of the most elusive, and the one about whom we know the least. The first time we come across him in official records is in 1627 when he was sent with his father to appear before the Privy Council in London after they refused to sign the Oath of Allegiance when they landed at Dover following Cresacre's visit to the Continent in that year. At that time Thomas would have been around nineteen or twenty years old and, as no mention is made of him in the Douai Diaries, it has been suggested that he was returning to England after leaving St Omers. Unfortunately we cannot confirm this as the records of the College were destroyed when the Jesuits were suppressed in 1778.[1]

The next time we hear of Thomas is on the day of his wedding. This took place, most probably, at the beginning of June 1629.[2] As we saw in the last chapter Thomas's sister, Bridget, had promised her father that she would not leave him to become a nun until after her brother was married. She was obviously so keen on this that arrangements had been made for her to leave for Cambrai the day after the wedding, but on the day itself she received quite a fright when she thought all her plans were going to be frustrated. The story, obviously told by Bridget herself, is recorded in her obituary:

> For on her Brothers wedding day all things being prepared & Just in the chapple to be Married, he slipped away to this his D^r sister (who was retired in the towne not to appear at the wedding) & tould her that he would goe & be a Monke which put her into such a fright that she thought she was then wholly undone, But most

seriously recommended herself, & him to Almighty God sheeding many tears Beged & prayed him to returne to his Bride. At last wth much difficulty prevailed. & they Married, she the next Morning took her Journy ...[3]

The story is fascinating for a number of reasons. Bridget, it seems, was already behaving like an enclosed nun to the extent that, although she was staying somewhere nearby 'in the town', she had decided not to attend her brother's wedding 'in the chapel'. What that town was we don't know; it could have been North Mymms, or Madeley in Shropshire where, as we will see, her brother's bride came from. The chapel could also have been in the Manor House at Gobions or in Madeley Court manor house.

Looking below the surface, I think the event may tell us more about Thomas and his relationship with his father than appears at first sight. Firstly, from the little we know about Cresacre and his children it is obvious that, after the death of Elizabeth in 1610, he doted on his daughters. We know how intelligent they were, what sort of personalities they had, and how he played games with them and delighted in educating them into their teens. In contrast we know nothing about Thomas except that he would appear to have been educated with them at home until being sent to St Omers around the age of twelve. In the circumstances I cannot help but wonder what effect this might have had on Thomas in terms of jealousy of his sisters and resentment of his father for his favouritism. Secondly, the fact that Thomas stayed on at St Omers until he was nineteen or twenty years old would indicate that he had started to study for the priesthood. The wedding day flight to his sister (who else could he turn to?) seems to me to be more an 'explosion' of suppressed feelings about what he really wanted to do in life – to become a monk – than a not uncommon attack of wedding day panic.

As we have seen, Cresacre had, much against his will, been required to abandon his studies for the priesthood in order to carry on the family name. Then, thirty years later, he found himself in a similar position to the one his father had faced. As a widower with no intention of marrying again, and with his only son Thomas studying for the priesthood and intent on becoming a monk, he was faced with the prospect of the family name dying out and the family inheritance being dispersed among minor relatives. In this situation I believe Cresacre may have 'demanded' that Thomas should make the same sacrifice as he had made, and that the resulting resentment this caused, coupled with earlier feelings about his father, led to the breakdown of their relationship and to their actual estrangement from each other.

The young lady chosen by Cresacre to be Thomas's wife was Mary Brooke, born 1608, one of the six children of Sir Basil Brooke of Madeley Court (a few miles South of Telford in Shropshire) and his first wife Etheldreda the only child and sole heir of Sir Edmund Brudenell of Deene Park, Northamptonshire.[4]

Sir Basil Brooke was the eldest of the two sons of John Brooke of Madeley (1538–1598) and his wife Anne (1538–1608), the daughter of Francis Shirley of Staunton Harold, Leicestershire.[5] John and Anne Brooke were both buried in the old church of St Mary at Madeley, which was replaced in 1794 by the present church of St Michael when the inscription from their tomb was placed on the outside wall of the church.[6] Basil's grandfather, Sir Robert Brooke of Claverley, Shropshire, bought the manor house at Madeley and its surrounding estate, including lands at nearby Coalbrookdale, from Henry VIII in 1544. Sir Robert was a Member of Parliament during the reign of Henry VIII and Edward VI and having supported Queen Mary's claim to the throne he was appointed Speaker of the House of Commons and Chief Justice of the Common Pleas in 1554. He was a notable barrister and wrote a commentary on English Law. He was knighted by King Philip of Spain (Queen Mary's husband) on 27 January 1555. He died three years later and was buried on 3 September 1558 in All Saints church, Claverley.

Basil Brooke was baptized in the parish church at Madeley on 12 June 1576. He was sent to Exeter College, Oxford, where he matriculated at the age of fourteen in 1590. After taking his degree he was admitted to the Middle Temple in 1594 where he practised as an attorney.[7] When his father died in 1598 he inherited the Madeley estate. He married Etheldreda in late 1605 or early 1606, the year in which he was knighted at Highgate by King James I. Etheldreda brought into the marriage a dowry of £3,000 (equivalent to around £350,000 today) left to her by her father, but Basil was by this time already a wealthy man, able to purchase two manors in Warwickshire from the Brudenell family for £5,350 (equivalent to around £624,000 today) as part of the marriage settlement. Basil's lands at Madeley and nearby Coalbrookdale consisted mainly of iron, coal and lime workings. He also leased charcoal-fired iron furnaces from the Royal Ironworks and Woods in the Forest of Dean. Iron-making in England had changed little since the Middle Ages, but Basil – who today we might call an iron entrepreneur – modernized it by the use of blast furnaces. In 1536 he obtained a warrant to dig for iron ore in the counties of Cumberland, Westmorland, Yorkshire and Lancashire.[8] He invented a new method of making pig iron into wrought iron and built a furnace and foundry 'in the Dale' (Coalbrookdale). He also started to manufacture steel, but unfortunately this proved to be less than successful and, in 1636, a group of cutlers, gunmakers, blacksmiths and locksmiths petitioned the Crown to be allowed to use foreign steel as they had previously done on the grounds that 'steel made by Sir Basil Brooke under patent of Elliot and Smith is worthless'.[9] In 1708 the Quaker Abraham Darby I started to smelt iron with coke at Coalbrookdale using a process invented by John Thomas thus helping to pave the way for the Industrial Revolution. The site now forms part of the Coalbrookdale Museum of Iron and Darby Homes at Ironbridge.[10]

Sir Basil was a fervent Catholic. He was a speaker of fluent French and translated *Entertainments for Lent* written by the French Jesuit Fr Causin. He had a house in Bishop's Court, London, and was a friend of both James I and Charles I at whose Courts he was well known. He was made treasurer for the contributions made by English Catholics to help to defray the cost of Charles I's expenses during the war against Scotland. In January 1641 he was one of a group of Royalists ordered to attend the House of Commons, but he absented himself and withdrew to York where he was taken into custody in January 1642. He was accused of involvement in a plot to create unrest between the City of London and Parliament; his estates were sequestered and he was committed to Newgate Prison, London, before being sent as a close prisoner to the Tower by the House of Commons on 6 May 1644. On the order of the Commons he was released into the custody of the King's Bench on 6 May 1645 to await a decision about his fate.[11] He died on 31 December 1646 impoverished by unpaid recusancy fines. His son and heir Thomas Brooke (1614–1674) inherited the Madeley estate (sequestered at the time) from his father. He was convicted for treason against Parliament in 1652 and the estate was sold to Thomas Wildman, a speculator in sequestered estates, who promptly sold it back to him – making a worthwhile profit in the process. The Court Manor House at Madeley was sold in 1705, but the estate remained in the possession of the Brooke family until the death of another Basil Brooke while still a minor in 1727. Although Madeley Court Manor

House fell into disrepair it has more recently been restored to reflect something of its former glory and it is now a hotel.

After Etheldreda's death in 1624 Sir Basil married Frances Mordaunt (see below) and had two more children, John (d.1645) and Frances. There are inscriptions to Sir Basil and his two wives on the outer wall of Madeley parish church (now badly worn). Translated from the Latin, Sir Basil's inscription reads:

> Sacred to the memory of Basil Brooke, Knight, the son of John Brooke, Esquire, and Anne, his wife, who was the daughter of Francis Shirley of Staunton Harold, in the County of Leicester, Esquire, and the grandson of Robert Brooke, Knight, Lord Chief Justice of the Common Pleas. He had two wives. Etheldreda, the daughter and sole heiress of Edmund Brudenell of Deene in the County of Northampton, Knight, and Frances, daughter of Henry, Baron Mordaunt, and the sister of John, Earl of Peterborough. He departed this life the 31st December, in the year of our Lord 1646.[12]

Etheldreda's inscription reads:

> Here lies Etheldreda, the wife of Basil Brooke, Knight. She was the daughter and sole heiress of Edmund Brudenell, Knight. A woman not only well versed in the Latin, Italian, French and Spanish languages, and in the science of music, but also an example of piety, faith, prudence, courage, chastity and gentle manners. She left to lament her loss a husband with an only son Thomas, and five daughters – namely Anne, the wife of William Fitzherbert, Esq., the grandson of Anthony Fitzherbert, Knight, Lord Chief Justice of the Common Pleas, eminent for his commentary on the Laws. Mary, the wife of Thomas More Esquire, a descendant of that renowned and upright character, Thomas More, formerly the Lord High Chancellor of England, a man in his life and death universally esteemed. Also Dorothy, Agatha, and Catharine. Of disposition the most motherly, the best of all. She died in the year of our Lord ... (the date is illegible).

Interestingly, the parish register of Deene records her burial on 26 August 1624. It was probably entered in the register there even though she was buried at Madeley.

After their marriage Thomas V and Mary could reasonably look forward to a secure future. The marriage settlement drawn up on 20 April 1629 provided for Thomas to inherit the family estates at North Mymms and elsewhere in Hertfordshire and at Barnburgh in Yorkshire after the death of his father, and for Sir Basil Brooke to provide Mary with a marriage portion, or dowry, of £2,000 (equivalent to about £246,000 today). The marriage settlement itself took the form of a three-part agreement between Cresacre More 'of the first part', Sir Basil Brooke, Thomas Roper Esq., and Thomas Greenwood, Gent. 'of the second part', and Thomas More, son and heir apparent of Cresacre More, and Mary daughter of Sir Basil 'of the third part'. This paved the way for documents to be drawn up setting out how the 'Manor of More Place, alias Gubbins' and the other family lands in Hertfordshire were to be passed down from father to son. The way in which the document was drawn up is a good example of how ownership of the estate had been divided up between family and relatives, most probably to make it more difficult for sequestrators to complete their work.[13]

We do not know where Thomas and Mary lived after their marriage. Initially it was probably at Gobions where Cresacre was living, or at one of the other properties nearby. However, in a document dated 1 July 1536 Thomas describes himself as 'of Chilstone [Herefordshire]'.[14] The document gives details of Thomas leasing some land at Bawne in the parish of Campsall, Yorkshire, for twenty-one years at a rent of £5 a year, and I cannot help but wonder if this sort of action was one of the 'disobediences' referred to by Cresacre in his will.

I suspect that Thomas and Mary moved to one of the properties that Cresacre had bought at Chilston sooner rather than later, as it is almost certain that an entry in the Madley parish register for 21 April 1635 records the baptism of their son Thomas. I also suspect that they moved to Gobions when it was restored to the family in 1646.

After his father's death in 1649 Thomas had to go through the same process as his father had done in order to obtain the restoration of all his property. As Cresacre had died without owing any monies to the Exchequer his estates should have been restored automatically to Thomas as his only son and heir. However, like his father before him, he had to fight to obtain his rights, a task made more difficult by the very different politics of the day. The King (Charles I) had been executed in January 1649, and in May 1649 England had been declared a republic, known as 'The Commonwealth' ruled by Cromwell and Parliament. In January 1650 Parliament, ever fearful of Royalist opposition, ordered all men over the age twenty-one to take a new Oath, or 'Engagement' of allegiance to the republic.

It was in this climate that Thomas petitioned the Committee for

Compounding at Goldsmiths Hall on 19 July 1650, reminding them in the first instance that the Committee of Lords and Commons for Sequestrations in 1646 had restored one-third of his estates to his father and ordered that he should receive all his rents from Lady Day (25 March) 1648 until Lady Day 1650 in lieu of arrears. He went on to inform them that, following his father's death on 26 March 1649, his estates had descended to him, his only son and heir who, he pointed out, was 'neither sequestered nor sequesterable'. He told the committee that he had already approached the Barons of the Exchequer about the matter but, due to the neglect of those acting for him and a reduction of the power of the barons to deal with such cases, he had still not been able to obtain redress. His petition went on to ask that, in view of his 'sad and deplorable condicion', the committee should be ordered to restore his property to him or, 'by a speedy day', explain why they don't pay the rents to him and why they hadn't cancelled the sequestration.[15]

Following this petition the case was referred to a Mr Peter Brereton who, after due consideration replied

> According to your order of the 19th July 1650 I have examined the Case of Thomas More of Gobions in the Countie of Hartford Esquire, thereby referred unto me, and find that ye Commissioners for Sequestration in the said Countie of Hartford in obedience to your said Order of the 19th of July 1650, doe certify that Cresacre More beinge in his life tyme sequestered for Recusancy, is dead, and that Thomas More Esqr is his eldest sonn and heire to the said Estate concerninge whome, and his condition, they have made diligent enquiry, and have received Testimony from the old Commissioners for sequestrations that he hath taken the Judament, and from divers others, of his constant goinge to Church, And that they can find noe Act done by the said Thomas More for which he is sequestrable. As by the said certificate dated 31st July 1650 and hereunto annexed, doth appeare. And the said Thomas More deposeth that Cresacre More dyed seized of the mannor of Gobions, in the Countie of Hartford, and of certaine Lands in Barnborough in the Countie of Yorke, and of certaine Lands in Low Leyton in the Countie of Essex and about 26th Aprill 1649 at which tyme the said Cresacre Mores Estate was sequestered for Recusancy only – And further deposeth that the Deponent hath taken the Oath of abjuration and had a certificate from the Officers of Lincolnes Inn of his Conformity, which Certificates are violently

deteyned from him And further deposeth that when this business was moved by his Counsell to the honourable Barons of the Exchequer, the Lord Cheife Baron himself hearinge the Cause and readinge the Certificate, commanded, that the deponent should have an order for his discharge presently out of the Court, which he trustinge his Counsell to procure, could never to this day obteine the same as by his Affidavit annexed dot appear. It is now therefore submitted to Judgement whether the said Mannor of Gobions and the rest of the premises ought not to be discharged from sequestration and the said Thomas Moore bee permitted quietly to enjoy the same according to his right and tytle. 8° August 1650. Pet. Brereton.[16]

After due consideration of the case, the Committee ordered Thomas's estates in Hertfordshire, Essex and Yorkshire to be discharged from sequestration on 15 August 1650 and it was probably around this time that he sold what remained to him of the estate at Low Leyton. It seems he had to make a separate petition for discharge of his estate at Tillington in Herefordshire and this was eventually granted by the Committee on 16 March 1653.[17]

Unlike the Oath of Allegiance taken by his father in 1613 the Oath of Abjuration that Thomas took in 1650 involved a rejection of some of the main teachings of the Catholic Church. It required the taker to declare: 'I, [name of person], do abjure, and renounce the Pope's authority over the Catholick Church in General, and over myself in Particular; And I do believe that there is not any Transubstantiation in the Sacrament of the Lord's Supper, or in the Elements of Bread and Wine after Consecration thereof, by anie Person whatsoever; And I do also believe that there is not anie Purgatory, Or that the consecrated Hoast, Crucifixes, or Images, ought to be worshipped, or that anie worship is due unto anie of them; And I also believe that Salvation cannot be Merited by Works, and all Doctrines in affirmation of the said Points, I do abjure and renounce, without anie Equivocation, Mental Reservation, or secret Evasion whatsoever, taking the words by me spoken, according to the common and usual meanings of them. So help me God.'[18]

The authorities had clearly learnt from their past experience of Catholics finding way around oaths, and the wording of this one clearly left absolutely no room for manoeuvre. There was no way in which Thomas could have taken it in good faith. He had, in addition, backed it up by a certificate attesting to his constant 'going to Church'. Of course, we do not know anything about Thomas's state of mind at the time. With the country now under the rule of the Commonwealth maybe he despaired of it ever returning to the Catholic faith – the faith he had himself retained up to now. Whatever the reason, he must have been under a great deal of pressure – desperate perhaps, like his father before him, to have some of the 'More' inheritance to pass on to his own children. We do know, however, that by taking the Oath he effectively apostatized, putting himself outside the communion of the Catholic Church and, in doing this, he was – apart from his great-uncle Thomas (b.1538) – the only member of the family to have done so since the time of Sir Thomas. Whether his taking of the Oath became public knowledge, whether he repented and sought reconciliation with the Church is something that we also do not know. What we do know, however, is that all his children, some of whom were not yet in their teens, were brought up, and remained Catholic. If that was not due to the example of their father then it must have been due to that of their mother. Perhaps she, like her mother, could also be described as having been 'an example of piety, faith, prudence, courage, chastity and gentle manners'.

As we have already seen, Thomas did not get on with his father and it is obvious from Cresacre's will that he feared that, after his death, he would try to upset some of the provisions he had made for his grandchildren. In the event his fears were realized, as Thomas did take action to recover some of the property that his father had left to the executors of his will specifically for the support of his younger grandchildren. Maybe Thomas was greedy or grasping; maybe he thought that he was the person best placed to provide for the needs of his own children; maybe he just wanted to show that he could have the last word. We will never know!

From this time until May 1659, when he sold a house and some land in North Mymms, we have no information at all about Thomas. In the sale document he describes himself as 'of Gobions', but he may not have actually been living there at the time as, in January 1660, he was at Goodman's Fields in the parish of St Mary Matfellon, Whitechapel.[19]

The 'acrid alleyways of Goodmans Fields' were to become famous, or infamous, as the stalking ground of Jack the Ripper in the 1880s, but in Thomas's time it was a pleasant, healthy place to live. Like so much else about Thomas, what he was doing there remains a mystery. I do, however, have a sneaking suspicion that Thomas may have been estranged from Mary – perhaps as a result of his apostasy. The Middlesex Session Rolls for February 1658 give details of a burglary which took place at the house of Thomas Moore Esq. at Whitechapel on the night of 25 December 1657 for which five culprits were found guilty and sentenced to hang, but we have no means of knowing whether this was 'our' Thomas's house. The extent of the haul would indicate that the owner of the house was not at home at the time, but judging by the amount of gold coins, jewellery, clothes and other goods and chattels stolen – valued at a total of £119 (equivalent to over £12,000 today) – the house belonged to a rich man.

Thomas died at Goodman's Fields on 12 January 1660. He was fifty-two or fifty-three years old. The lack of a will would indicate that his death was unexpected, and we do not know where he was buried. Had he lived another four months he might have witnessed King Charles II returning from exile in Holland and riding into London to reclaim his throne. In that case things might have turned out very differently – we will never know!

Mary survived Thomas by twenty-three years. After his death (if not before) she seems to have lived for some years with their eldest son William at Chilston in Herefordshire. We know from small bequests that William made in his will that he had two servants, and that his mother had a main manservant and maid-servant as well as some other lesser servants. It seems likely that Mary remained at Madley until around the early 1670s when she sold the estate and moved to live somewhere in London. After her death, her body was taken back to North Mymms for burial where the register of St Mary's Church records the event as follows: 'M[s] Mary More of London, was buried in North Mims church, June 18: 1683.'[20]

Thomas V and Mary had five sons – William, Thomas (known as Thomas VI), Cresacre (known as Cresacre II), Basil and John – and four daughters – Frances, Mary, Margaret and Bridget. Thomas VI is the only one for whom we have a baptismal record. However, an educated guess can be made about a probable year of birth of his brothers and sisters using family pedigrees, references to them in Cresacre's will, and other documents. For convenience I will deal with the daughters first.

From Cresacre's will it is clear that Frances and Mary were the two oldest daughters of Thomas and Mary. Frances was, I suspect, not just the oldest daughter, but also the oldest of all the children, born shortly after their marriage, probably in 1630. Frances became the first wife of George Sheldon of Canterbury, the third son of William Sheldon of Beoley, Worcestershire (1589-1659) and his wife Elizabeth, the daughter of William second Lord Petre.[21]

The Sheldons of Beoley were an ancient Catholic family who could trace their ancestry back to the time of Edward III and who, over the years, amassed lands in Worcestershire, Warwickshire, Gloucestershire, Shropshire and Herefordshire. In spite of persecution and fines for recusancy they maintained Benedictine priests as their chaplains at Beoley, and remained true to their faith. Among his four siblings George had a brother, Edward, who became a Benedictine monk, and a sister, Catherine (b.1618), who became a Benedictine nun at Cambrai in 1640. George (born 1638) and Frances had no children and when she died on 12 May 1666 she was buried at Beoley. After her death George married Elizabeth, the daughter of Sir James Hales but again he had no children. Elizabeth died on 4 October 1678, and George seven months later 8 May 1679.

Given the birth of a child almost every year in the first few years after marriage (a common practice in those days), and fitting this in with my estimate of the birth years of Thomas and Mary's sons, I believe that Mary was probably born in 1638. She became a nun in the Institute of the Blessed Virgin Mary first founded by Mary Ward at St Omer. Mary Ward took her inspiration from the Society of Jesus, and the Institute was an independent self-governing congregation of women living without enclosure. Some of the sisters lived together in houses, but others worked independently in the community, responding to need wherever they found it. Although some of the sisters were working in England before that time, the first official foundation in this country was made in 1631 at Heworth Manor, the home of Sir George Thwing a few miles outside York. The new community consisted of 'three coachfulls of nuns', headed by Mary Ward herself, and accompanied by a number of children entrusted to their care.[22]

Existing records do not say when or where Mary joined the Institute of the Blessed Virgin Mary, but since the members of the Institute withdrew to Paris in 1650 during the period of the Commonwealth and did not return to England until 1667, it may well have been there. The Institute returned to England in 1667 and in 1677 made a foundation in a property owned by Sir Thomas Gascoigne at Dolebank a few miles from Fountains Abbey, near Ripon, Yorkshire. The members of the community were rounded up after the so-called 'Popish Plot' to assassinate the King was revealed to the authorities by Titus Oates and his accomplice Israel Tonge in August 1678.[23] Mary may have been an outreach worker from the Dolebank community, living on a farm belonging to her mother. As she was listed as a recusant at Doncaster General Sessions on 21 January 1678 the farm was probably one of the many properties belonging to the family which were scattered around the Barnburgh area. Mary was arrested later in 1678 and, after refusing to take the Oath of Allegiance and Supremacy she was convicted under the Statute of Praemunire and committed to York Prison. She survived the harsh conditions of the prison for ten years and was released in 1685 during the brief reign of James II. She was probably a founder member of the Michelgate Bar Convent in York when it was established in November 1685. She is believed to have gone to one of the Institute's houses in Bavaria with Mother Frances Bedingfield in 1699. If, as I suggest, she had been born in 1638 she would, at that time have been around sixty-one years old. The record of when and where she died has not come down to us.[24]

Margaret More, Mary's younger sister, was probably born sometime between 1641 and 1647. Like her sister she also joined the Institute of the Blessed Virgin Mary, probably soon after its members were able to return to England in 1667. She was living with her sister on the farm belonging to their mother and was listed with her as a recusant at the same Doncaster Sessions in January 1678. She was arrested with her sister later in the year and sent with her to York Prison. Unlike her sister, however, she survived the conditions there for only a year, during which time she was described as 'a great sufferer'. The prison was in the parish of St Mary, Castlegate and Mary was buried there on 10 September 1679.[25]

Bridget More, the youngest of Thomas and Mary's children, was born in 1648. Apart from a reference to her marriage and the date of her death I have not been able to discover anything else about her. The Marriage Allegations in the Registry of the Vicar General of the Archbishop of Canterbury, 1669–1679, contain the following entry for 3 February 1669:

Thomas Gifford, of St. Giles, Cripplegate, London, Merch^t Bach^r , abt 35, & Mrs Bridgett Moore, of St. Giles in the Fields, Midd., sp^r, ab^t 21, with consent of her mother Mrs Mary Moore, of Madley, Co. Hereford, at St Giles in the Fields.[26]

Pedigrees of the More family notes that Thomas Gifford was the second son of Sir ... Gifford, Baronet, and that Bridget died on 10 June 1673 when she would have only been about twenty-five years old.

Turning now to Thomas and Mary's sons: William More, the eldest, was born in 1632 or 1633. He appears to have been staying with his grandfather Cresacre in Chilston in early 1649 when, although only about fifteen or sixteen years old he was one of the witnesses to the codicil of his will. The following year he was sent to study at Douai where the entry in the College Diary (translated from the Latin original) reads:

> 9th day of September (1650) came William More, age 17, known here as Brooke, of Chilston in the parish of Madley in the County and Diocese of Hereford ...[27]

The 'known here as Brooke' indicates the common practice of giving students from well-known families an alias to avoid them being identified by spies who might want to report back to the authorities in England about their presence on the Continent at a time when it was illegal for Catholic children to be sent abroad to be educated.

William's stay at Douai was short-lived as the diary records that he left for Paris on 7 September 1651. It seems likely that, having no desire to go on to study for the priesthood, his brief period of formal education had come to an end and that, although we have no record of it, he returned to England to take up residence on the farm at Chilston that he had inherited from his grandfather Cresacre. Although he inherited Gobions and the other family property in Hertfordshire and Yorkshire when his father died in 1660, he seems to have lived for the rest of his life at Chilston. He never married.

William made his will on 5 June 1664 at which time he described himself as 'weake in body but in perfect memory'.[28] He made his sister Mary and two good friends, Bodenham Gunter, Lord of the Manor of Thruxton, to the South of Chilston and Madley (a fellow Catholic of Welsh origin) and Thomas Lockier, his executors. It is clear from his will that his mother was living with him at the time, and he left her all his 'goods, chests and chattels', as well as the goods and chattels that had been given to him by her when she administered his father's estate. He also left her £100 (equivalent to around £9,500 today), and his coach and horses! He left £200 pounds to his Aunt Bridget (Dame Bridget) – money that, as we saw in the last chapter, helped to set up the Monastery of Our Lady of Good Hope in Paris. He left £100 to his sister Frances – by then married, as he calls her 'my sister Sheldon' – and £500 to his sister Mary. He also left £100 each to his sisters Margaret and Bridget – money that would have probably provided a dowry for them when they joined the Institute of the Blessed Virgin Mary – and to his brother John.

It is obvious from his will that William was very conscious that he had inherited from his father the lands that his grandfather had bequeathed to his younger brothers and sisters, but that his father had recovered for himself. In order to right this injustice, and after noting that he has already given to his brother Basil 'his full portion of the said lands in full satisfaction of his right therein', he goes on to bequeath an additional £100 each to his sisters Margaret and Bridget and his brother John 'in satisfaction and recompense of the rents and profits I have received of the aforesaid devised lands'. In all, William ordered his executors to raise a total of £2,000 (equivalent to around £190,000 today) out of his 'Messuages, Lands, Tenements and hereditaments' in Hertfordshire, Yorkshire and 'wheresoever in the Kingdom of England' to cover their own expenses, to pay these and other minor legacies, to pay the wages of his servants, and to cover the cost of his funeral.

William died six days after making his will. Like his grandfather, he was probably buried in the churchyard of Madley parish church, but records for that time are incomplete and no trace of the grave remains.

Other than noting his name, pedigrees of the family provide no information about William's younger brother, Thomas VI. However, as I have briefly mentioned above, he was, I believe, born at Madley in 1635. The entry in the baptismal register for 21 April of that year reads: *Thomas filius Thomas More esq et Maria uxor eius bapt. fuit* – in English 'Thomas More son of Thomas More Esq and Maria his wife was baptized'.[29] We don't know where Thomas VI was educated; unlike his older and younger brother, there is no record of him in the Douai Diaries. Although named in Cresacre More's will as one of his younger grandchildren he is not mentioned in William's will where he makes provision for his younger brothers. Because of this, and because their younger brother Basil took over the family estates when William died, researchers of the family have assumed that Thomas must have died before 1664 – and this may be the case. However, when I came across an out-of-print book on the Moore family of Moore Hall in County Mayo, Ireland, I discovered a claim that they were descended from this Thomas. For convenience, I will return to this in a separate section at the end of this chapter.

Thomas's younger brother, Cresacre II, was born in 1636. He is mentioned in the same entry as his older brother William when they were admitted to Douai College on 9 September 1650 at which time he was stated to be fourteen years old. Like his brother he took their mother's maiden name as an alias. He was not, however, known as Cresacre Brooke – that might have given the family connection away – but as Thomas Brooke. He is also listed with William as leaving the College on 7 September 1651 to go *versus Parisios* – towards Paris.[30] After that, we know nothing more about him. Like his older brother Thomas VI, Cresacre II was named in his grandfather's will as one of his younger grandchildren, but he is also not mentioned in William's will. From this we can assume either that the family had lost contact with him, or that he had died before 1664.

Basil More, the fourth son of Thomas V and Mary was probably born in 1639 or 1640. He and his family will be the subject of the next chapter so I will say no more about him now.

John More IV, the youngest son in the family, was, I believe, born sometime between 1641 and 1647. Pedigrees of the family record that he married, but the name of his wife is not given. They also record his death on 27 April 1697. He is said to have had a son, also named John (who would be John More V), who died on 17 February 1702 (see lineage below).

The Lineage of the Rev Edward Moore

The Pedigree of 'More of Barnborough Hall' compiled by Joseph Foster in 1874 contains an additional section on the lineage of the Rev Edward Moore or More, one time vicar of St Chad's church at Over, in Cheshire. This 'Protestant' lineage is also found in old editions of Burke's *Landed Gentry* under 'Moore of Frampton Hall', but it is not mentioned in the main Catholic pedigree of the family preserved in Foley's *Records of the Jesuits* or in Robert

Clutterbuck's or Joseph Hunter's pedigrees of 1815 and 1829 respectively.[31]

Foster states that his pedigree is authenticated by members of each family; I suspect that in the case of the Rev Edward Moore's lineage he is referring to Colonel Charles Thomas John Moore (1827–1900) of Frampton Hall, FSA, JP and DL who spent many years collecting documents on the Moore/More family. Colonel Moore was a well-known antiquarian and may well have been responsible for the lineage being included in Burke's *Landed Gentry*.

The entry describes the lineage as follows:

> Rev. Edward Moore, LL.B., Vicar of Over, co. Chester, son of John Moore was, it is stated, of a Lancashire branch of the Barnborough family, and in descent, by a junior branch, from the Lord Chancellor More, whose arms he bore. He was b. 1696, and died 1755, leaving issue seven sons ... and a daughter ...[32]

It is interesting to see that in his pedigree Foster offers two spellings 'Moore' and 'More' for Edward's surname, though his father was a 'More' – like all the mainline descendants of Sir Thomas. This was presumably a transitional device to enable him to make the transfer to 'Moore' for the rest of the line. Burke, on the other hand, calls both Edward and his father by the name 'Moore'.

The Rev Edward Moore's descent from Sir Thomas More via John Moore/More was said by Colonel Moore to be a 'tradition'. In some private notes in my possession he also said that the Rev Edward Moore was ordained and held his first curacy in Norfolk, but this is clearly not true. I have discovered that Edward was admitted to Merchant Taylor's School on 12 September 1712 and that he later went to Trinity Hall, Cambridge, where he matriculated in December 1724 and obtained the degree of Bachelor of Law in 1728. His status at Trinity was that of 'Sizar' which means that his tuition fees and most of the charges for his board and lodging were met by an allowance paid to him by the college in return for acting as a servant to other students. This status was usually – but not always – granted to some less well-off students. Whereas Burke's *Landed Gentry* and the Foster *Pedigree* give 1696 as the year of Edward's birth, the Register of Scholars admitted to Merchant Taylors' School and the list of Students at Cambridge in *Alumni Cantabrigiensis* record his birth date as 6 October 1702.[33] Further confusion about the year of Edward's birth is caused by an inscription on a piscina in St Chad's church that, like the pedigrees, gives the years of his birth as 1696 – see below. Regarding the place of Ordination, the *Alumni Cantabrigiensis* also states quite clearly that Edward was ordained at Chester on 22 December 1728, that he became vicar of Over in Cheshire, and that he died in 1755. I see no reason to doubt this statement, but when trying to check it with the Cheshire Records Office I was informed that the Diocesan Records of ordinations for this period have not survived.

I do not know the origins of the claim (in Burke's *Landed Gentry*) that Edward was of a Lancashire branch of the Barnborough family, and in my research I have not come across any such branch. There was a Moore family of More Hall and Bank Hall in Lancashire who traced their ancestry back to a time long before Sir Thomas More, but I do not know of any connection between the two families. The *Alumni Cantabrigiensis* records that Edward was 'of Retford, Notts'. and that he was 'son of John'. Unfortunately a search of the church register at Retford did not turn up any John or Edward Moore or More during the period in question. If Edward was descended from Sir Thomas More, and if he was born in 1702 – 6 October 1702 to be precise – then his father must have been the son of John More IV, as John More IV had died in 1697.

The pedigree in Burke's *Landed Gentry* attributes seven sons, but only one daughter (Esther) to Edward, and it does not name his wife. However, Foster's *Pedigree* records seven sons and three daughters. This seems to indicate that Foster's *Pedigree* was produced after Burke's *Landed Gentry* and is therefore more up-to-date. Foster's *Pedigree* records 'Mary' as the name of Edward's wife, and a document in my possession indicates that her name may have been Mary Keene, and that she was related to Dr Edmund Keene who became Bishop of Chester in 1752. Further research shows this to be unlikely.

While researching Edward Moore's lineage I discovered that, before he became vicar of Over, he was curate at St Andrew's Church in Sedbergh, Cumbria. The 'advowson' (or right of appointing ministers to a vacant benefice) of St Andrew's belonged to Trinity College, Cambridge, and it seems likely that a connection with this neighbouring College led to his appointment as curate. The baptisms of six of his children are recorded in the parish register. Interestingly, there was another Edward and Mary Moore living in the parish at the same time but in the register 'our' Edward is referred to as 'Revd Mr Moore' or as 'Revd Mr Moore Curate'. I have not been able to discover when Edward took up his position as curate at Sedbergh but he had previously been minister at Bidston, Cheshire (now Merseyside).

Edward was appointed to the post of vicar at St Chad's on 14 July 1753. His name appears on a list of the succession of vicars of the parish displayed inside the church. Unfortunately, after officiating at a wedding sometime in 1755 he was standing under the bell tower when the church bell fell from its mounting above and killed him. A plaque in the church records the event as follows: 'In Memoriam. Rev^d. Edward Moore, sometime Vicar of this Parish, accidentally killed in the old Tower Vestry of this Church. A.D. 1755.' After his death his eldest son is said to have presented the piscina in the church which, underneath the bowl, has a small shield with the Arms of More quartered with those of Cresacre on it (now badly eroded). Above the bowl there is an inscription that reads: 'To the glory of God and in pious memory of Edward Moore, LLB., Vicar of Over, born 1696, died 1755; and Mary his wife, born 1703, died 1772, whose bodies are buried near this spot. The piscina has been relocated from its original position on the wall of the church at the side of the altar to its present place in the vestry.

The Rev Edward and Mary had ten children who, by all accounts, did very well for themselves. Edward, the eldest, was born in 1735, but the actual date and place of his birth and baptism are not recorded in pedigrees of the family. Edward attended Sedbergh School and later became a Barrister at Law. He is described as having been 'of Stockwell House, Surrey'. He was also Lord of the Manor of Leigh Priors, one of the five manors of Westbury, Wiltshire, which is where a number of his children were born. He was an active politician and was appointed secretary to Henry Fox, First Lord Holland (1705–1774), becoming a personal friend of his third son Charles James Fox (1749–1808), the Whig politician. He was also a personal friend of Richard Brinsley Sheridan, the Irish dramatist and politician. Edward married twice, and through his second wife Sarah Grey he was the grandfather of Colonel C. T. J. Moore (mentioned above). Edward became a wealthy man, and in his will of 20 July 1792 he made bequests of totalling over £69,000 (equivalent to around £5,000,000 today) to his wife and children. Edward died later in 1792. Sarah died in 1807.

George Moore, the Rev Edward and Mary's second child was

born at Bidston in 1740. Apart from that we know nothing else about him.

The baptism of Edward and Mary's next six children are recorded in the parish register of Sedbergh. Esther Moore, baptized 10 April 1743, married Arthur Windus (1738–1818), of a family which became famous for the manufacture of carriages in Hackney, London. Arthur was the son of William Windus (1710–1785), a gentleman of Hertford with a legal practice in Chancery Lane, London, and his wife Millicent Ann Hunt (d. 1799).

Thomas Moore was baptized on 19 September 1745. He became a merchant and settled in Liverpool where he married Lydia Dawson. They are said to have had a large family, but the names of their children are not recorded on the pedigree. The children took the name Dawson-Moore. Thomas was still alive in 1792 as he is mentioned in his brother Edward's will.

Nancy Moore was baptized 18 May 1748. She married Daniel Quare and they had three children: Daniel (b.1783), Nancy (b.1786) and Edward (b.1788). They appear to have lived in the St Pancras area of London where Daniel (junior) married Ann Linley at Old Church in November 1808.

Paul Moore was baptized on 11 November 1750. He is said to have died young.

Peter and Bernard Moore were twins, born and baptized on 12 February 1753. Bernard only survived for one month, his burial being recorded in the Sedbergh register on 3 March 1753. Peter joined the Civil Service and went to India where he married Sarah Webb in 1774. Sarah was the daughter and co-heir of Colonel Richmond Webb of Rodbourne Cheyney in Wiltshire. Peter later returned to England where he was elected Member of Parliament for Coventry, a position he held for twenty-five years. He had a house in Great George Street, Westminster, and with his eldest brother Edward he purchased the manor of Monken Hadley in 1791 thereby becoming the Lord of the Manor. As a result of some business deals that went wrong in 1825 he appears to have got into serious debt and, to avoid arrest he fled to France where he died at Abbeyville on 5 May 1828. Peter and Sarah had six sons (five of whom died without issue) and three daughters. Descendants of his fifth son Macartney Moore (1788–1831) and his wife Henrietta Halhead are still living today.[34]

Finally, the *Pedigree* lists a Robert Moore and Ruth Moore. Robert was baptized at St Chad's, Over, on 15 October 1755. He is said to have had an only son who perished in the ship *Kent* belonging to the East India Company. We have no date of birth or baptism for Ruth.

As this line is not my main interest, I do not intent to continue it further. Suffice it to say that many descendants in the 1800s distinguished themselves in the Army, in the Civil Service and in the Church, and various branches of the family have continued down to the present day.

The Moore Family of Moore Hall, Co. Mayo

The Moore family of Moore Hall, Co. Mayo claimed descent from a 'Thomas Moore' of Barnborough, born 1535. The main source of information on this family is a now out-of-print book, *The Moores of Moore Hall* written by Joseph Hone and published by Jonathan Cape of London in 1939. I have made use of this, and information on the family from various Internet sites for the history that follows.[35]

As we have seen above Thomas More VI was baptized at Madley, near Hereford, on 21 April 1635. Although the family was not 'of Barnborough' at that time, Barnborough/Barnburgh Hall became the final 'seat' of the family after 1693 and the name by which the main line of the family from Sir Thomas downward was often identified – as, for example in Foster's *Pedigree*.

The story of the descent of the Moores of Moore Hall from Sir Thomas More seems to have first come to light during the lifetime of George Moore who was born at Ballina, Co. Mayo in 1729 and who, after emigrating to Alicante on the South Eastern Mediterranean coast of Spain as a young man, made a fortune as a wine and brandy merchant, and from the profits in the manufacture of iodine shipped in his own fleet from Galway. The story tells that, in order to obtain access to the Spanish Royal Court at Madrid in the 1760s, George Moore had to present a reputable Catholic pedigree to the authorities, and the one he presented was that which showed his descent from Thomas Moore (b.1635) of Barnborough, a descendant of Sir Thomas More whose martyrdom was well known in Catholic Europe and especially at the Spanish Court where, as we have seen, his great-grandson Fr Thomas More had earlier been involved in the unsuccessful negotiations for the marriage of Infanta of Spain to Prince Charles.

Later, in 1773, George Moore obtained a grant of arms from the

Ulster Herald. The Arms granted depicted a chevron dividing three Moorcocks – the arms originally granted to Sir John More and later 'quartered' by Sir Thomas with the three unicorns' heads, the arms belonging to the family of his first wife Agnes Graunger. The granting of such arms is not, of course, any guarantee of descent from the original grantee, as similar arms were often granted to unrelated families with similar names, but I am not in any position to confirm or deny the claim made by George Moore. Joseph Hone, the family's biographer, was non-committal on the subject, saying only that there might be some truth in it. My own discovery that Thomas More VI (whose date of birth is not recorded on any English pedigrees of the family) was born in 1635, may add some credence to the claim.

The pedigree of the Moores of Moore Hall, Co. Mayo (dated 1770), like that of the Rev Edward Moore, makes a convenient transition from the name 'More' to 'Moore'. It starts with the claim that Thomas Moore, born 1635, married Mary ApAdam, the daughter of John ApAdam of Flint, in Wales. There are some problems with this, as the old Welsh 'Ap' means 'son of', and Mary could not be a son of anyone. The word 'Verch' was used for daughters so Mary should have been Mary VerchAdam. Also, the parish register of Flint for baptisms between 1598–1685 does not contain a reference to any Ap or Verch Adam, though there were two children (but not a Mary) born to a John Adam in 1637 and 1640. This evidence, however, is not conclusive. A walk through any old Welsh churchyard will show that many Welshmen were identified only by whose son they were, and by the town or village where the family came from. Following that tradition Mary's father John, the son of Adam (ApAdam) might have been described as 'of Flint' in the same was as Thomas More was described as being 'of Barnborough'. On the positive side as well, we do know that the family had friends with contacts in both North and South Wales.

According to the Irish pedigree, George Moore Esq. (born 1666) – from now on I'll call him George Moore I – the only recorded child of Thomas Moore and Mary – is said to have gone to live in Ireland where he settled in Ballina and married Catherine, the daughter of Robert Maxwell of Castle Feeling in Scotland. We know nothing else about him except that he was buried in the cemetery at Straide. On his tombstone he is given the title of 'Captain' and the records of the Ulster King of Arms refer to him as Vice-Admiral of Connaught. A number of modern sources suggest that he was a Protestant, but I have seen no evidence to support this.[36] As we have seen, his father was brought up a Catholic and the subsequent history of the family would seem to indicate that, perhaps with some accommodation, they remained so.

George Moore II, son of George Moore I, born 1680, settled in Lognafouca – a place I have not been able to locate on a modern map. He married Sarah, the daughter of John Price of Foxford who was Canon of St Patrick's Cathedral in Dublin. They had two children, George Moore III of Clongee (whose line became extinct in 1832) and John Moore, born 1706, of Ashbrook House, near Straide. He married Jane Lynch-Athy of Renvylee in Co. Galway. Besides a son and two daughters who are not named on the pedigree John and Jane also had Robert Moore of Ashbrook who became a Doctor in Galway and died without issue in 1783 (he was also buried in the cemetery at Straide), and George Moore IV, born 1729, who is described as 'Merchant of Ashbrook, Alicante, Spain and Moore Hall' – the man who presented his lineage at the Royal Court in Spain.

George Moore IV married Katherine de Kilkelly in Spain. She is said to have been the granddaughter of one of the 'Wild Geese' – Irishmen who left their homeland to serve in Irish Regiments in the French and Spanish armies. In 1784 he sold his property in Alicante for the sum of £250,000 equivalent to over £20,000,000 today. Penal Laws against Catholics in Ireland began to be relaxed after 1771 and the First Catholic Relief Act of 1778 allowed them to buy land again. It was probably around this time that George IV bought his estate of over twelve thousand acres in Muckloon, Ballycally and Kileen, though he does not seem to have returned to live in Ireland full-time until 1790. In 1792 work started on the magnificent Georgian house he built as the family seat on an estate of around hundred acres on the shore of Lough Carra, just over three kilometres from Carnacon and about sixteen kilometres from Castlebar in County Mayo. The house was completed in 1796 and he named it Moore Hall.

George Moore IV and his wife Katherine (née Kilkelly) were the founders of a line of Moores born at Moore Hall, whose lives were intricately bound up with the history and politics of the time. The full story of their lives has been told elsewhere so I will only give a brief summary here.

John Moore, the eldest son of George Moore IV and Katherine, was born at Moore Hall in 1767. Like a number of members of the

English More family he was sent to the English College at Douai, about twenty miles south of Lille in northern France where he adopted the alias of Bellew. Having completed his studies in Humanities, and not intending to go on for the priesthood, he then went to the University of Paris to complete his education before returning to Ireland. John's main claim to fame was his appointment as first President of the Republic of Connaught after he sided with the French forces that, under the command of General Humbert, 'invaded' Co. Mayo in 1798. Unfortunately, he only held this position for a week before he was arrested by the English, tried, and sentenced to death, a sentence shortly after commuted (it is said due to Spanish influence) to deportation. John's health was by this time in decline and his way to Duncannon fort to await transportation he died during a stop at the Royal Oak Tavern in Broad Street, Waterford. He was buried in Ballygunner cemetery from where his remains were removed and reburied with full military honours at Castlebar on 31 August 1961. An inscription on his grave includes the words: 'Ireland's first president and a descendant of Saint Thomas More, who gave his life for his country in the rising of 1798.'

In addition to John (above) George Moore IV and Katherine had three more children. We do not know anything about Thomas and Peter who both died without issue, but George Moore V was born at Moore Hall in 1770. He married Louisa, the daughter of the Honourable George Brown, granddaughter of the First Earl of Altamont and cousin of the first Marquess of Sligo. George V inherited the family estates when his brother died in 1798. He spent much of his time at Moore Hall pursuing his interest in literature and history and building up his library which is said to have become one of the best private collections of books in Ireland. He wrote a history of the French Revolution (found among his possessions after his death), and a history of the British Revolution of 1688 that was eventually published in 1817.

George Moore V and Louisa had three children, George Henry, born 1810 (see below), John who was born in 1812 and died without issue after a riding accident in 1829, and Augustus, born 1817, who went to Cambridge where he showed promise as a mathematician but who gave it up for a life of racing and hunting. He died after falling from his horse 'Mickey Free' during the Grand National at Aintree and was taken back to Ireland where he was buried in the family vault at Kiltoom, near Moore Hall.

After being educated by governesses at home until the age of nine, George Henry was sent to St Mary's Catholic School at Oscott near Birmingham until he was seventeen when he went to Cambridge. He did not seem to be able to keep his mind on his studies either at Cambridge – where he only stayed for two years – or in London where he started to study law. At some stage he married Mary, the daughter of Maurice Blake of Ballinafad, Co. Mayo.

George Henry's main interests seem to have been horse riding and racing, hunting and gambling. During the great famine in Ireland he became well known for the way he protected the tenants on his estate from starvation. In 1846 his horse 'Coranna' won the Chester Gold Cup and he used his winnings of around £17,000 (equivalent to over £1,000,000 today) to import grain to help to feed them. He also reduced their rents and gave them gifts in kind. In 1847 George Henry was elected Member of Parliament for Mayo, becoming a founder member of the Irish Party at Westminster to which he was returned a number of times. He used his position to promote the cause of Home Rule for Ireland. He died on 19 April 1870 and was buried in the family vault at Kiltoon.

George Henry and Mary had four sons: George Augustus, Maurice, Augustus, and Julian, and a daughter, Nina, some of whom have descendants living today. Of these I will mention more about only the first two. George Augustus – known generally by his first Christian name as 'George' – was born at Moore Hall in 1852. Like his father before him, he educated at home before being sent to St Mary's, Oscott. Unlike his father, however, he hated it and was expelled when he was sixteen as being idle and worthless. He later gave up Catholicism altogether. His father died when he was eighteen and he inherited the family estates. While living with his family in London he developed an interest in art and moved to Paris in 1873 to study it further. There he met most of the famous Impressionist artists of the day – Monet painted a portrait of him – but, finding himself lacking the necessary talent to make his living as an artist himself, he began to write. His writing of Naturalist-realist novels and his creation of a new literary genre, fictional autobiography, brought him great acclaim. He returned to Ireland for a few years in 1901 where, in Dublin, he played a prominent part in the Irish literary revival and the founding of the Abbey theatre. Moore Hall ceased to be used by the family after 1912 and George returned to live in London. He died at his home in Ebury Street, London, on 21

January 1933 and his ashes were taken to be interred on Castle Island, on Lough Carra.

George's younger brother Maurice was born in 1854 and, like his brother was educated at St Mary's School, Oscott. Having failed to get into the French army he joined the British Army and fought in the Zulu and Boer Wars, becoming a Colonel in the Connaught Rangers. He fell out with his brother George Augustus who had offered to pay for the education of his eldest son Rory as long as he was brought up as a Protestant – something to which Maurice would not agree. Maurice supported the Nationalist cause and was elected to the first Irish Senate in 1922. He died in 1939 and was buried at Kiltoom.

On 1 February 1923 Moore Hall was gutted by a fire started by republican forces opposed to any treaty with England. The house remains a ruin, but a Restoration Committee has been set up and the hope is that it will, in due course, be restored.

Genealogical Summary

The Family of Thomas More V

Thomas More (1607/8–1660) m. (1629) Mary Brooke (1608–1683):
Children:
1. Frances (1630/1– 1661): m. George Sheldon (1638–1679). No children.
2. William: born 1632 or 33. Unmarried. Died 1664.
3. Thomas VI: born 21 April 1635. Date of death not known. (It is claimed that he married and had a son George who went to Ireland and became the progenitor of the Moores of Moore Hall, Co. Mayo).
4. Cresacre II: born 1636. Date of death not known.
5. Mary: born 1638. Became a nun in IBVM. Alive in 1699.
6. Basil: born 1639 or 1640. Eventual heir. See next chapter.
7. Margaret: born 1641/1647. Became a nun in IBVM. Died a prisoner in York Castle, 1679.
8. John IV: born 1641/1647. Died 1697.
   Children: John: date of birth unknown. Died 1705.
   (It is claimed that John had a son Edward More/Moore who became vicar of Over, Cheshire.)
9. Bridget: born 1648. m. Thomas Gifford. No children recorded.

Chapter Seven

Basil More and his Family

Basil More was what I would call the last of the old-style Mores. Of all the descendants of Sir Thomas, the most prolific, a practical man rather than an intellectual, a country squire with business interests in London, an unwavering Catholic, proud of his line of descent, and a collector and preserver of family portraits handed down to him.

No record has been found of Basil's birth or baptism but, as we saw in the last chapter, secondary evidence strongly suggests that he was born in 1639 or 1640. Like his brothers he was probably educated at St Omers, though college records from that time have not survived. As a young man he became a servant in the household of Francis Pardeney, a Catholic merchant who lived in the parish of St Dunstan's in the East, London. An 'Act for Convicting, Discovering and Suppressing of Popish Recusants', passed on 26 June 1657, put renewed pressure on Catholics and it was no doubt due to this that Francis Pardeney and Basil were both presented for recusancy at the Quarter Sessions in January and April 1658 and then convicted in July 1658 and again in January 1659.[1]

Even though, as we saw in the last chapter, we know next to nothing about Thomas More V at this time he was obviously well-known enough, and rich enough, to be able arrange a marriage between Basil and Anne Humble on 25 February 1659. The event was recorded in the parish register of the Church of St Peter, Paul's Wharf, a church destroyed six years later in the Great Fire of London.[2]

Anne was the eldest of the seven daughters of William Humble of Stratford Langthorne, Essex, and his wife Elizabeth Allanson. Anne's baptism, like that of most of the members of her family since the time of her great-great-grandfather, was entered in the register of the Church of St Mary Woolnoth, Lombard Street, on 17 March 1641. The Humble family could trace its history back to the Humbletons who were Keepers and Governors of Beverley in the mid-1300s and who gave their name to (or took it from) the village of Humbleton in Yorkshire where they had their family seat.[3] By the 1500s, however, they had adopted the name 'Humble', and were living in the parish of St Mary Woolnoth, London, and earning their living first as goldsmiths, then as stationers, and later as leathersellers. Anne's father, William, the son of George Humble and Agnes Moody, was baptized in the Church of St Mary Woolnoth on 6 June 1611. William became a Freeman and a Citizen of London in 1636 and was Alderman of Langthorne Ward in 1651. He was a Royalist and, after the restoration of Charles II to the throne in 1660 he became Sir William Humble when he was granted a baronetcy in consideration of the £20,000 (equivalent to around £2,000,000 today) that he had given to Charles II while he was in exile. He was appointed Sheriff of Surrey in 1664–1665 and of Lincolnshire in 1672–1673. A leatherseller of Pope's Head, Lombard Street, at the southern end of Langthorne Ward, he was elected Master of the Leatherseller's Company in 1653.[4]

Although no record of it has survived, Anne would have brought a handsome 'portion' into the marriage, and this would certainly have enabled Basil to develop his own business interests in London, probably in partnership with Francis Pardeney his former 'master'. Exactly what the nature of this business was we don't know, but we do know from one of his letters that he 'banked' with a London goldsmith who at one stage caused him considerable difficulty when he went bankrupt.

It seems likely that, after their marriage, Basil and Anne lived in London, probably in one of the properties owned by Sir William. The birth of their first child, Mary, is recorded in the register of St Mary Woolnoth.

After the death of Basil's older brother William in June 1664, arrangements were made for Basil to take possession of the manor of Gobions and the other More estates in Hertfordshire and Yorkshire. The transfer of the Hertfordshire estates was brought about by an indenture enrolled in the High Court of Chancery by which they were first mortgaged to Sir William Humble and his heirs for £1,500 (equivalent to around £143,000 today) with the proviso that they could be 'redeemed' some time later on payment of £1,590. This sum must have formed the bulk of the money which, as we saw in the last chapter, William More wanted his executors to raise in order to pay the legacies he stipulated in his will.

It has been suggested that a man of Sir William Humble's standing in the City was unlikely to have been a Catholic.[5] However, there seems no reason to doubt that Anne was a Catholic. If Sir William was not a Catholic then his purchase of the Hertfordshire estates, and other estates belonging to the More family in Yorkshire, – was almost certainly a way of avoiding an official 'Inquisition post mortem' after William More's death. Given Basil's status, as a convicted recusant such an inquisition would almost certainly have led to the sequestration of the estates. In view of their size, the sum of money involved could only have been a token, and I have not been able to discover any reference to its having been repaid. It may even have formed a pre-arranged part of the marriage settlement. Later indentures show that Sir William Humble retained an interest in the estates throughout his life, indicating that he – and later his heirs – held them 'in trust' for the More family – another way of continuing to protect them from any threat of sequestration that might arise. Whatever the nature of Sir William Humble's ownership may have been, on 7 September 1664, three months after William More's death

> In consideration of five shillings [his executors] bargained and sold unto Basill More of London, Merchant (Brother of the said William More) all and singular the said Messuages, Landes, Tenements & Hereditaments to hold for and during one yeare from the last day of June then last past.

This was followed three days later by another indenture that passed all the properties into the 'actual possession' of Basil for him and his heirs to have 'for their own proper use and behoofe for ever'.[6] The transferring of a property for a limited period before passing it permanently to a new owner was a common way of transferring property by a system of what was known as 'lease and release'.

Throughout the first eighteen years or so of their married life Basil and Anne appear to have lived relatively free of harassment. Although after the restoration of Charles II to the throne in May 1660 the hopes of Catholics that he would fulfil his promise of granting liberty of conscience for those whose views did not disturb the peace of the kingdom were not realized, they nevertheless benefited from the constant 'jousting' that went on between the King and Whig and Tory factions in Parliament on matters of religion – the King trying to promote his policy of toleration, and Parliament (and the Anglican bishops) trying to oppose it. In 1661 Parliament gained the upper hand and passed the Corporation Act that, among other things, required everyone who held official positions in towns to take Communion in an Anglican church at least once a year. This was followed in 1662 by a new Act of Uniformity that effectively re-established the Church of England as the State Church – a position it had lost during the period of the Commonwealth when Puritans and Presbyterians ruled supreme. The provisions of the Conventicle Act of 1664 that forbade more than four people to assemble for any form of worship other than Church of England worship and restricted the movement of other clergy to within five miles of their place of residence was reasonably easy to get around. It would perhaps have been rather difficult to police given the fact that Catholics, when they were able, had continued to attended Mass in the houses of the gentry, and priests had continued to move around the country secretly or in disguise.

The outbreak of the Great Plague in 1665 may have played a part in Basil's decision to give up, or at least scale down his business interests in London and to move to North Mymms with Anne and their three young children. We know they were living there in April 1666 because the birth of their fourth child is recorded in the register of St Mary's, the parish church of North Mymms, on 7 April of that year.[7]

Although the old Penal Laws were never repealed they remained in abeyance and, apart from banning Catholics from any form of public office – which we have no evidence Basil ever sought – the new measures seem to have had little effect on the family.

In 1672 the situation began to change for the worse after the King took it upon himself to issue a 'Declaration of Indulgence'. This suspended all the old penal laws 'in matters ecclesiastical', for not attending the established Church in England, and not receiving Communion according to its rites. It also permitted people to worship in their own way in private houses and in chapels. The declaration applied not just to Catholics, but also to people of any other Christian church or sect, and to people of any faith. It also ended the requirement that they should be required to take religious oaths before taking up civil or military office. Unfortunately, the reprieve was short lived as, the following year,

Parliament got its own back by passing the Test Act that not only compelled the King to withdraw the Declaration of Indulgence – on the grounds that only Parliament could suspend the penal laws – but also extended the exclusion of Catholics from office in their local towns to cover everyone who held public office or positions of trust. These were now required to receive Communion publicly in the Church of England once a year, to take the Oaths of Allegiance and Supremacy, and to subscribe to a declaration against transubstantiation.

One of the first casualties of these new Acts was the King's brother, James, Duke of York, the heir to the throne, who had to resign his position as Lord High Admiral. James had secretly become a Catholic a few years previously and his refusal to receive Anglican Communion at Easter in 1673 brought his Catholicism into the open.

The Declaration of Indulgence, the conversion of the heir to the throne to Catholicism, and his marriage in September 1673 to Mary of Modena, daughter of Alfonso III, Duke of Modena (his first wife, Anne Hyde, having died in 1671) began to cause panic in Parliament and renewed anti-Catholic feeling in the country at large.

It may have been Basil's reaction to the increased uncertainty of the times that caused him to enter into a number of property transfers – mainly leases, and mortgages – between the years 1673 and 1676 that, once again, appear to be designed to protect the estates from sequestration should the need arise. The indentures setting out these transactions show that, in addition to manor of Gobions and the lands and woods immediately surrounding it, Basil owned land and houses in the surrounding area, including Osborne's Farm, Waltrotts Farm, Rohite Farm, Sleap Farm, and other lands in North and South Mymms, Hatfield, Essendon, and St Albans.[8] As no mention has been made of these before, they may have come to Basil as part of the marriage settlement.

In 1678 the burning embers of discontent against Catholics were fanned into flame by the revelations of Titus Oates about an alleged 'Popish Plot' to assassinate the King to make way for a Catholic heir and to bring about the destruction of the Protestant religion.[9] Two of Basil's sisters who, as we saw in the last chapter, were members of the Institute of the Blessed Virgin Mary in Yorkshire, were the first members of the family to feel the effects of the new wave of anti-Catholic persecution – and it would not be long before Basil would feel them as well.

In January 1679 the Hertfordshire Justices ordered all churchwardens and constables to search out and 'to take exact account of the name and surnames of all such persons as are popish recusants or reported so to be, as well as householders, lodgers and servants' and also to 'disarme all popish recusants and all others as are popish or justly suspected to be.' All those who were listed were ordered to appear before the Justices on 28 February in order to take the Oaths of Allegiance and Supremacy. The constable of North Mymms was not slow to act, but when he reached Gobions he was disappointed, and he had to report back 'I have made enquiry after Basill esquire and weare at his house but not finding him at home nor any of his family but servants I could not proceed further.[10] Basil must have heard of the imprisonment of other Catholics in a similar position – over 2,000 between 1678 and 1681 – and, fearing that he would suffer the same fate if he refused to sign the required oaths, he decided to absent himself by taking the family to Barnburgh.

Unfortunately, Basil's success in outwitting the authorities in Hertfordshire did not prevent him from coming to the attention of the constable of Barnburgh once the family had settled there and, at the Doncaster Sessions in January 1680 'Basvile Moore Esq, Mary (sic) More his wife, Frances and Bridget More his daughters, Mrs. Julian his servant, and Mrs. Alice Luland' were presented as papists.[11] We have no record of any further action being taken against Basil in Yorkshire and sometime between January and February he returned to Gobions leaving Anne and the children at Barnburgh. Anne, however, was obviously worried, and in a letter dated 23 February 1680 she wrote to Sir John Reresby asking him to put in a good word for them with the local justices.

Sir John Reresby had his family seat at Thrybergh Hall a few miles north-east of Rotherham and about ten miles south of Barnburgh. Although a Protestant, he was a staunch supporter of Charles II and spent a good deal of his time in London and was often at Court. He was High Sheriff of Yorkshire in 1667 and Appointed a Justice of the Peace for Middlesex and Westminster in 1668. He was returned as a Member of Parliament for Aldborough, Yorkshire, in November 1673 and again in February 1681. He later became Governor of Bridlington and of York.[12]

Sir John was clearly a man of great influence, sympathetic to the plight of Catholics, and on friendly terms with his near neighbours, the Mores. In her letter Anne tells him that they only came up to Barnburgh for a short visit, that Basil has since left so that she is now on her own with five of her daughters, the youngest of whom is only ten years old. She suggests that, had the Justices at the last Quarter Sessions known that they were 'strangers' in the area, they would not have dealt so harshly with them. She acknowledges the generosity and good will that Sir John has shown them in the past, and says that this gives her the confidence to ask him to write or speak to the Justices in order to get their names 'Crost out of ye Booke of ye Clark of ye Peece'. Until that is done, she says, she will not feel safe.[13]

Anne's letter was taken to Thrybergh by a servant who must have brought word back of Sir John's imminent departure for London because, the following day, Anne wrote to him again to wish him a happy and safe journey. The rest of the letter is interesting as it refers to a bill for £50 and a picture of Sir Thomas More that Sir John seems to have got for them. Perhaps the £50 was the price of the picture. Anne asks him to send the picture back with her servant, sealed up in thick paper so that no one can see it. She tells him that Basil has business which prevents him coming to Barnburgh at present and finishes by saying that she is glad to hear that he and his lady are well.[14]

Anne may have been pregnant at this time, as her letter only refers to her being accompanied by five daughters, and the burial of a son, Michael Bartholomew, is recorded in the Barnburgh parish register for 5 September 1680.

Basil was down at Barnburgh again in December, probably to spend Christmas with Anne and the children. On 22 December he wrote to Sir John Reresby expressing his disappointment at not being able to be entertained by him due to the bad weather. Sir John was well known for the parties he put on for his friends at Christmastime and in the letter Basil refers to an occasion a few nights before when it sounds as though he may have got drunk. He says:

> ... I send you my excuse if the effects of your good liquor caused any rudeness the other night ... I send you one hound and I am making enquiry where the rest of my dogges are so that if you please to lett me know whither I shall send a couple more. They shall be att your service, your obligations have ever been such to me that I want words to express how much I am yor truly obliged servant, Basil More.[15]

Back in Hertfordshire Basil's convictions for recusancy went ahead even though he did not appear in person in court. Records are incomplete but those for the Assizes at St Albans show that on 5 August 1680 he was fined the statutory £20 per month for not attending church during the previous month. Basil followed the old family tradition of not paying these fines and arrears began to mount up, reaching £120 by the following February. Whether he paid this or not we do not know, but other records show that he was still being fined, and that in September 1683 he still owed the Exchequer £220 (equivalent to around £25,000 today) for the previous eleven months.[16]

During these years Basil must have felt harassed on all sides. In Yorkshire he had to respond to a military levy that required him to provide a man (suitably armed) and a horse for the defence of the realm. As he was not a permanent resident in the county he seems to have appealed to his friend Sir John Reresby who sent out a 'Contradicting Order' but, in spite of this, he still received a bill for £10 for the levy. Basil clearly thought that the bill (equivalent to about £1,100 today) was unduly high and he wrote to Sir John complaining about it. His letter gives us the briefest glimpse of how he thought of himself, for he says: 'though I may cum behind others in prudence yet I dare rank my selfe in front for justice'. The final sentence of the letter is tinged with sadness when he tells Sir John 'my Wife lies in now, though the young one dead' – a reference to one of a number of stillbirths suffered by Anne. The letter is dated 7 September 1682.[17]

The Treasury Books for 3 March 1683 show that the Receiver General of Recusants Forfeitures was paid an allowance for an enquiry into the extent and value of Basil's estates in Hertfordshire, but there is no evidence that the estates were sequestered.[18] The lack of action by the authorities on this occasion may be because the wave of persecution caused by the Titus Oates affair had died down and the political scene was dominated by the debate about whether a Catholic should succeed to the throne or not. The two opposing parliamentary parties – the Whigs wanting a Protestant successor and the Tories recognizing the hereditary right of James (Duke of York) to the throne – fought each other for supremacy until the King, faced with the possibility of another civil war, dissolved Parliament (the last Parliament of his reign) in March 1681.

Charles II died on 6 February 1685 and was succeeded by his brother who was crowned James II of England (and VII of Scotland) at Westminster Abbey on 23 April. Once again, Catholics hoped for relief from the heavy burdens so often placed on them in the past, and James did not disappoint them. He knew he could not destroy the Church of England outright, but he hoped that, if he granted toleration to all 'dissenters', not just to Catholics – though they were in the majority – and allowed them to play a full part in the political life of the country, it would only be a matter of time before most people returned to the faith of their ancestors. In pursuit of this policy James reintroduced the position of Vicar Apostolic to govern the Catholic clergy in England and established four districts for them to oversee. He also began using his royal 'dispensing power' to appoint Catholics to serve as officers in the army as well as at local and national level in the Civil Service, the Privy Council and the universities. When this latter measure was opposed by Parliament he prorogued it in November 1685 and, undaunted, followed it up with a 'Declaration of Indulgence' on 4 April 1687 – His Majesty's gracious declaration to all his loving subjects for liberty of conscience. In the first place this offered protection to the clergy and members of the Church of England 'as by law established' but then it went on to suspend all the penal laws 'in matters ecclesiastical' for not going to church, for not receiving the Sacrament or for any other form of religious nonconformity. It also abolished the Corporation Act and Test Acts that required people in civil or military office to take the Oaths of Supremacy and Allegiance. Finally, it granted 'free and ample pardon' to all nonconformists, recusants and other subjects 'for all crimes and things by them committed or done contrary to the penal laws made relating to religion and the profession or exercise thereof', and discharging them from 'all pains, penalties, forfeitures and disabilities by any of them incurred or forfeited'.[19]

Apart from removing the threat of further prosecution and conviction for recusancy, the only other benefit that the More family gained from the policies of James II during these years was the granting of a commission to Basil and Anne's son, Basil Junior (about which see later). In the mean time, increasing opposition to the King's policies in the Church of England and among the various dissenting groups, followed by the birth on 10 June 1688 of James Francis Edward, a Catholic heir to the throne, appeared to dash any hope of a future Protestant succession. The rest, as we say, is political history. Although Parliament was not sitting, the Whig and Tory factions combined and invited William III of Orange (who had married James's Protestant daughter Mary) to raise an army and invade England from his base in Holland in order to save it for the Protestant cause. William accepted the challenge and, after landing with 15,000 troops at Torbay on 5 November 1688, made his way towards London. He met with little resistance as the major cities and towns declared in his favour. James set out to attack him but thought better of it on the way and retreated back to London from where, on 22 December 1688, he fled to France leaving Parliament with another succession crisis on their hands – a crisis they soon solved by passing a Bill of Rights which declared that only a Protestant could succeed to the throne. The problem, however, was not quite as simple as that because, even if James could be regarded as having vacated the throne or even as having abdicated, it was his sister Mary and not her husband William III of Orange who should succeed him. For his part, William refused to pay second fiddle and, in February 1689, after a lot of political wrangling, Parliament finally declared William and Mary to be joint monarchs – becoming King William III and Queen Mary II of England. What became known as the 'Glorious Revolution' had taken place.

In the mean time, Louis XIV, the King of France, had allowed James II to set up his own English Court in the Royal Palace at Saint-Germaine-en-Laye on the outskirts of Paris and, while he remained alive, Catholics – and, rather reluctantly, many members of the Church of England – still regarded him as the legitimate heir to the throne. They were prepared to accept William and Mary as Regents for a while, but they would not swear an Oath of Allegiance to them. Those who refused to take the Oath became known as Nonjurors.

Within a few months of William and Mary's accession to the throne a Toleration Act was passed that allowed dissenters a limited freedom to worship if they took the Oath of Supremacy and Allegiance and made a declaration against the Catholic doctrine of transubstantiation – something that, obviously Catholics could not do. While no major legislation was passed during the reign of William and Mary, Catholics remained subject to 'niggling' harassment such as the imposition of a double land tax in 1692 and the passing of a statute in 1696 prohibiting them from being called to the Bar and therefore from practising as barristers. They could, however, still occupy chambers in the Inns of Court and undertake work as special pleaders and conveyancers – a career taken up (as we will see) by two of Basil's sons. The 'Act for the further preventing of the growth of Popery', passed in 1699, was more serious as, among other measures it forbade any Catholic over the age of eighteen refusing to take the Oaths of Supremacy and Allegiance to inherit their family's estates which had, instead, to be passed to the nearest Protestant relative.

It seems clear that, in addition to his pension from Louis XIV, James II also relied on contributions made by his followers in England. According to Sir Henry Chauncy, a contemporary historian, Basil More suffered great losses as a result.[20] As we saw earlier, Basil described himself as lacking in prudence, and maybe he had made promises of monetary support that he could hardly fail to honour when the time came for it to be delivered. Certainly by early 1692 he seems to have been experiencing serious financial difficulties, and documents from the period show how, over the next eighteen months, he began to gather his Hertfordshire properties and lands together out of the hands of people who held them in trust for him, or to whom he had leased them, to enable him to sell them. The onset, or perhaps the realization of his difficulties, appears to have been quite sudden because, at the beginning of October 1691, he had drawn up a lengthy indenture detailing the way in which the manor of Gobions – 'also known as Gybons, Gubins and More Place' – should pass down through his six surviving sons in the (unlikely) event that the male line of each preceding son should fail. Only eight months later, however, he drew up another indenture in which he declared his previous arrangement null and void.

The indenture detailing the sale and transfer of ownership of Gobions and the other Hertfordshire estates is dated 25 August 1693. It lists Basil More and his eldest son and heir Christopher Cresacre (about whom see later) as the first parties to the sale that was made to Sir John Holman of Weston, Northamptonshire in trust for Sir Edward des Bouverie of London. The price paid was £10,300 (equivalent to around £1,000,000 today).[21]

The sale of this part of the More inheritance must have hit Basil hard. He may, however, have taken some comfort from the fact that he had done it in support of the Catholic cause and not part of a deal involving him in selling his soul to the Protestant cause.

After the sale of his Hertfordshire inheritance Basil and Anne moved to live permanently at Barnburgh Hall. It seems likely that he used some of the money from the sale of Gobions to improve the property by building the stable block that is believed to date from around this time. Sadly, Anne did not live long enough to enjoy the relative serenity offered by the move to Yorkshire.

Probably worn out by the stresses she had been under, and by the constant succession of pregnancies – somewhere between eighteen and twenty-four in thirty-five years of marriage – she made her will on 30 March 1694 and must have died soon after as she was buried at Barnburgh St Peter on 2 April 1694.

Anne appointed Edward Turner of Barnard's Inn as her executor, and the will was witnessed and signed by her daughter Bridgitt (that is how she wrote her own first name), and her daughter-in-law Katherine More (née Wharton) who were presumably visiting her at Barnburgh during her last illness. The will is interesting in that it shows that her father, Sir William Humble, had set aside several sums of money in trust for her, specifying that Basil should have no power to 'demand, receive of dispose' of them. The exact amount of money involved cannot be determined from the will as, after making bequests totalling £75 (equivalent to around £8,000 today) to pious causes, to her executor, to two aunts, to her eldest son Christopher Cresacre and his wife, and to her eldest daughter and her husband, she left the remainder of the money (an unspecified amount) to her two youngest daughters Mary and Bridgitt, and to her six surviving younger sons. An indenture drawn up by Anne's children, and her sister and brother-in-law (Katherine and John Scarlett) on 23 November 1698 refers back to the will of Sir William Humble who had died in December 1686 and shows us that the monies he set aside for Anne were to be taken out of a quarter portion of the manor of Haldanby 'and divers lands and tenements in Haldanby and elsewhere in the County of York'. The manor of Haldanby near Adingfleet in East Yorkshire, must have been one of the estates held by Sir William Humble 'in trust' for Basil's descendants in the same way, and for the same reason, that he had taken on the Hertfordshire estates.

Anne More's will was not finally proved in the Prerogative Court of Canterbury until 8 September 1705, by which time her daughter Mary, then Mary Morgan, had been granted authority to administer it.[22]

Basil survived Anne by eight years. He died intestate on 17 November, and was buried at Barnburgh St Peter's church on 20th November 1702. No traces of his or Anne's graves remain in the churchyard.

All the documents from this period that I have seen confirm my belief that Basil did not make a will because he had no time – as would have happened if he died suddenly or unexpectedly – but because he and his older children, aided and abetted by Sir William Humble, had quite deliberately set out to spread what remained of the family's estates so widely among relatives and friends as to disguise their real ownership and make it almost impossible for the authorities to discover anything worth sequestrating.

Basil and Anne had eighteen children born alive, and another six who were stillborn. As we have seen, the birth of Mary, their first child, is recorded in the register of St Mary Woolnoth for 9 December 1661. We know nothing of Mary's childhood, but from two indentures detailing property transfers drawn up on 25 September 1699 and on 25 December 1704 we know that she married James Morgan a 'Gentleman' of the parish of St Giles in the Fields, London, sometime between those two dates. Almost everything else we know about Mary and James comes from their wills and from details of his Yorkshire estates given by James in 1616 following an Act of King George I requiring all papist to register their names and estates with the Clerk of the Peace in the county where they were located.[23] Between them these documents show us that, as her marriage portion, Basil gave Mary a share – described as 'one seventh part of three fourths' – 'in the Manor of Haldanby with the lands, tenements and hereditaments thereunto belonging being in the Lordship Towns, parishes and precincts of Haldanby, Haldanby Park, Uslett, Eastoft, Swinefleet and Fockerby' (South East of Goole) as well as a half share in a 'Messuage with lands and tenements' and a cottage in Whitley (near Pontefract) and a half share in a cottage with lands in Adwick Le Street (near Doncaster). When these lands were registered with the authorities in 1716 the annual value of the rents from them would be equivalent to around £6,000 today.

I have not been able to discover anything about James's parentage, but he had a sister Sarah who had died before he made his will. I have also not been able to discover anything about James's profession although, in his will, he left a bequest to Viscount Montague who he refers to as 'my partner', and to Viscount Montague's daughter Catherine Collingwood. This last bit of information enable us to identify the Viscount Montague in question as Henry Brown, 5th Viscount Montague, whose daughter Catherine had married George Collingwood.

Whatever his profession may have been James was, by all accounts, well off. He lived with Mary in a house he leased in Southampton Street, Bloomsbury, and he also owned 'several parts and shares' in two properties in Thames Street, in the parish of St Magnus the Martyr near London Bridge. One of them was 'called or known by the name or sign of the Cross Keys' and the other 'called or known by the name or sign of the King's Arms'. The Cross Keys and King's Arms sound very much like public houses (or perhaps more fashionable coffee houses) and, although I have not come across any other reference to them, they are said to have been part of Mary's inheritance.

Mary made her will on 17 August 1721, and in it makes no monetary or property bequests. Her only concern seems to have been to make sure that 'all the Letters of Administration, and all Papers, Writings, Scripts and Muniments' that she had regarding various members of the More family – and that could be found 'in chests of drawers, and Clossetts and rooms in my now Dwelling House' – were passed to her nephew, Thomas More (the subject of the next but one chapter), whom she appointed her sole executor. She died the following day, 18 August 1721, a few months before her sixtieth birthday.

James made his will on 27 June 1716, a date which, I suspect, may have more to do with the need for Catholics to register their estates and inheritances than with any illness from which he recovered. James was obviously a generous and a compassionate man. In his will he left monetary bequests worth around £53,000 today to a number of relatives and friends, to two of his maid servants (should they be living with him when he died), and to a number of deserving causes including one, equivalent to around £3,500 today, to a Mrs Mary Rhodes, a manteau maker, 'who is burthened with many children' – maybe she had made his manteaus, or cloaks, for him.

Following Mary's death James added a codicil to his will bequeathing all the properties he had inherited from her to his nephew Thomas More. Then, in addition to the bequests he had previously made, he left an unspecified share of around £215,000 (today's value) to his 'dearly beloved niece Catherine More, Sister to my Nephew Thomas More' – monies that were due to come to him from the re-sale of a property that had been purchased 'by several persons' some years previously.

James added the codicil to his will on 9 December 1721 and he died on or shortly before 19 February 1722 when his will was proved. In his will he stipulated that his funeral expenses should not exceed £12 (equivalent to around £1,400 today), the cost of a very modest funeral – and he asked to be buried in St Pancras churchyard (the churchyard of what is now called Old St Pancras church in Pancras Road, London NW1). This is where he was laid to rest on 22 February 1722. The churchyard of Old St Pancras church is said to have been a favourite place for Catholics to be buried because of the burial there of twelve people martyred as a result of the so-called Popish Plot.[24]

The fact that neither Mary nor James make any mention of children in their wills indicates either that they did not have any or that, if they did, they had pre-deceased their parents.

Basil and Anne More's second daughter, Frances, was born on 21 March 1663. A 'Marriage Allegation', or official notification of intent to marry, dated 18 April 1689, records the following:

> Edward Goate, of Middle Temple, London, Gentleman, Bachelor, about 23 and Mrs. Frances More, of North Mimms, Herts., Spinster, about 22, with consent of her mother; alleged by Katherine Best, of St. Bride's, London, Widow, at St. Mary, Savoy, Middx ...[25]

Frances and Edward were probably introduced to each other by mutual friend or relatives, and Katherine Best who registered the Allegation with the authorities was one Frances's maternal great-aunts. She must have been quite old at that time, and this is perhaps the reason why her estimate of Frances's age was four years out. In the event, and after what appears to be rather short notice, the plan to marry at St Mary, Savoy, was cancelled and it actually took place at St James, Dukes Place, on 22 April 1689.[26]

The Church of St James escaped destruction in the Great Fire of London but it fell into decay and had to be rebuilt in 1666. Its great history came to an end when it was demolished in 1874.

Edward Goate (usually referred to as 'the younger') was the eldest son of Edward Goate ('the elder'), Gentleman, of Bottesdale in the parish of Redgrave, Suffolk. He had a sister whose name we do not know, and a younger brother, John, who pre-deceased him, and who was buried in the churchyard of St Mary's church, Redgrave, in 1736 where a tomb was erected to his memory.[27]

Most of what we know about Edward 'the elder' comes to us from the will that he made on 31 August 1707.[28] This tells us that his wife had pre-deceased him as, in it, he asks to be buried in Redgrave church – St Mary's, the parish church for Bottesdale – 'as near my dear wife as conveniently may, and with as much privacy as in prudence shall be necessary upon that occasion'. The cautious wording of this request, and the fact that most of his lands (see below) were held in trust for him and his heirs by various relatives suggests that Edward was a Catholic asking to be buried in an Anglican church.

Frances More brought to her marriage with Edward Goate the younger a share equal to that of her older sister in the manor of Haldenby as well as a share in the cottages at Whitley and Adwick. The document giving details of the agreement was drawn up between Edward Goate (senior), Edward Goate (the younger), Frances More, Sir William Humble (the younger), and Frances's brother William More, on 8 April 1689. For his part Edward (junior) brought to the marriage from his father the manor of St John's, Suffolk – a manor I have not been able to locate.

Edward would appear to have been sent to be educated in the law in London where he became a member of the Inner Temple on 6 December 1686.[29] However, in the 1690s he was party to a number of indentures relating to his father-in-law's properties in Hertfordshire where he is described as 'of Staple Inn, London'. Staple Inn was an Inn of Chancery in High Holborn and this may well be the area in which the family lived. Family pedigrees indicate that Frances died in 1712 when she would have been about forty-nine, but I have not been able to discover any will made by Edward or any reference to the date of his death.

From their grandfather's will we can identify the names of three of Edward and Frances's children – Edward, Charles and Susan who were all under twenty-one at the time. I have not been able to discover anything about Charles except that his grandfather left money to be invested for him so that he could be apprenticed to some trade that would provide him with 'a livelyhood which his Father and Mother shall best approve of'. Her grandfather also left Susan some property, the profits from which were to be used by her and her heirs 'for ever'. In his will, dated 5 September 1720, Edward, the eldest son, described himself as 'of the Parish of St. Clement Dane in the County of Middlesex, Gent'.[30] At that time – when he can only have been in his late twenties – he was 'weak in body but of perfect mind and memory', and his wife Frances (daughter of Anthony Wroth Esq., of Bury St Edmunds) was 'bigg' (pregnant) with their first child. He did not survive long as his will was proved in the Prerogative Court of Canterbury five days later, on 12 September 1720. In his will he leaves all his 'lands, tenements and hereditaments, both freehold and copyhold, leasehold and charterhold, lyeing and being in any place in that part of Great Brittain called England' to his wife, and to his yet unborn son or daughter when he or she reaches the age of twenty-one. He makes separate mention to the estate at St John's in Suffolk, to the share in the manor of Haldenby and to the properties at Whitley and Adwick, leaving these to be sold to pay off his debts, legacies and funeral expenses.

Basil and Anne More's eldest son, born 1 May 1665, was named after his father and became known as Basil Junior. He was sent abroad to be educated – probably to Douai – but when this was forbidden under a proclamation during the reign of Charles II he was brought back to England. An entry in the Calendar of State Papers for 5 June 1679 records the following: 'Pass for Matthew Askue going to Flanders to fetch over Basil Moore from a Seminary there'.[31] We do not know whether Basil actually had any aspirations to become a priest but if he did the opportunity was denied him. Back in England Basil was set to study law, gaining admission to Lincoln's Inn on 1 May 1683, when he had just turned eighteen. The Admissions Register calls him 'son and heir apparent of Basil More of Gubbins, Herts.'[32] Four years later, on 9 December 1687, when James II was looking to reward the families of Catholics who had supported his cause Basil was appointed Sheriff of Hertfordshire, an appointment that was cancelled ten days later when he was replaced by a John Lacey. There were, apparently, two or three contenders for this important post, and Basil probably lost out because of his age – he was only twenty-two at the time.[33] It was perhaps some consolation to him that less than two weeks later, on 30 December 1687, he was appointed to be one of the Deputy Lieutenants of Hertfordshire. There were eight other people approved at the same time, including six with the title 'Sir', so Basil (referred to in the list as 'Bazill More Jnr') was in good company![34] This appointment was followed in July 1688 by another one to become a member of a commission set up by James II to look into the monies that had been raised from the forfeiture of the estates of Catholics since 1677 – a commission whose work came to an abrupt end with the flight to James II to France.[35]

Basil Junior appears to have obtained a commission as a captain in the army on which James II was becoming increasingly dependant for his safety and security before his flight to France in December 1688. This would certainly have been another way in which he could have served his King. The Calendar of State Papers for this period contains the following entry:

Oct. 9 1688: Warrant to George Lord Dartmouth, Master General of the Ordinance – after reciting that by warrant dated the 3rd inst. it was directed that the Regiment of Foot now raising under command of Col. Henry Gage should be armed at Chester – to cause one Company thereof under command of Bazill More to be armed out of the stores in the Tower of London in proportion of muskets, pikes, etc. as directed in the warrant aforesaid.[36]

The existence (in a private collection) of a portrait said to be of Basil Junior in full armour provides some circumstantial evidence that this may be 'our' Basil.

Foster's *Pedigree* says that Basil Junior went into exile with James II but I have not been able to find any other evidence to substantiate this claim. However, it may well be true. Given his open support for the King, and the positions that he had held, it seems likely that he would have had to remove himself to the safety of France after James's flight. Like other supporters of James he may well have been hoping to be given some sort of position at the Court in St Germain-en-Laye but, if this was the case, he was, like many others, disappointed. That he went abroad is certain, as all the main pedigrees of the family note his death, unmarried, at Louvain on 1 June 1689. What he was doing in Louvain we do not know. It would be nice to think that perhaps he was visiting the last resting place of his distant cousins William and Winifred Rastell and John and Margaret Clement who, as we saw in chapters one and two, were buried in churches there. He may well have visited and perhaps stayed at St Monica's, the monastery of the Augustinian Canonesses Regular of the Lateran, where some of his Roper and Constable cousins were nuns. The news of Basil's death seems to have taken some time to filter back to England and it was not until 28 November 1690 that the chambers he had previously occupied at Lincoln's Inn were declared vacant.[37]

After Basil Junior's death his younger brother Christopher Cresacre More became his father's heir apparent. Christopher Cresacre was exactly eleven months younger than Basil and, as he will be the subject of the next chapter, I will not say any more about him now.

Bridgitt More was the first child of Basil and Anne More to appear in the register of St Mary's church, North Mymms. The entry reads: 'Bridgitt the daughter of Basill Esq and of Anne his wife was born and baptised May 25th 1669'.[38] In 1688 Bridgitt became the second wife of John Forcer of Harbour House and Kelloe in County Durham. The marriage was probably solemnized in the chapel at Harbour House. In the marriage settlement Bridgitt is described as having been 'of Coxhoe' a village close to Kelloe.[39] She may well have been staying at Coxhoe Hall with friends or relatives of the Forcer family. Like her older sisters, Bridgitt brought to the marriage 'one seventh part of three fourths' of the More estates at Haldenby, Whitley and Adwick.

The Forcer family can be traced back to John Fossour (died 1433) who held the manors of Harbarowes and Kelloe as well as other estates in the County Palatinate of Durham. He came into possession of the estates when he married Johanna (born 1332) the daughter of William de Kellaw, or Kelloe, whose family had probably taken its name from the manor. The manor of Harberowes took its name from the old English word 'Herberwe' which means 'lodgings', but by the 1600s it had become known as Harberhouse and later as Harbour House. Although it formed part of the parish of St Oswald in Durham, the manor was situated a few miles East of Plawsworth, between the present A167 and the A1(M) about four miles NNE of Durham. Harbour House farm, which can still be located on a Phillip's *Navigator Roadmap*, is said to have been built on the site of the original mediaeval manor house.[40] A chapel (of which little remains) was added to the manor house in 1432.

In the family pedigree the earlier Forcers are described as 'of Kelloe' only becoming 'of Harberhouse' in the time of Thomas Forcer who moved from Kelloe to Harberhouse around 1603. Thomas, a convicted recusant, was married to Margaret, the daughter of Francis Trollop of Eden and when his estates were sequestered for recusancy they were leased by the Crown to his father-in-law who must therefore have been either a church papist or a Protestant. Two of Thomas's sons became Jesuits, and Jesuits regularly stayed in the house throughout the sixteenth and seventeenth centuries.

John Forcer's parents were George Forcer of Harberhouse (1645–1687) and his wife Isabel, the daughter of John Swinburne Esq., of Capheaton in Northumberland and his second wife Isabel, the daughter of Sir Thomas Tempest, 2nd Baronet of Stella. Bridgitt was John's second wife, his first wife having been Althea, the daughter of Charles 5th Lord Viscount Fairfax of Emely in Co. Tipperary, Ireland, whose home was at Gilling Castle in Yorkshire. By Althea, John had had two sons, George (who died without issue), and Francis (who died an infant), as well as two daughters Elizabeth (1689–1728) and Mary (1694–1760).[41] Charles Lord Fairfax was a Catholic and Elizabeth and Mary were both sent to be educated by the English Benedictine nuns at Our Lady of Consolation in Cambrai which they are recorded as having left at the ages of sixteen and eleven in July 1705.[42] Elizabeth and Mary never married.

The births of John and Bridgitt's children were, as required by law, recorded in the registers of the churches of St Nicholas and St Oswald in Durham. They would, however, have been baptized in the chapel at Harbour House. Of their five daughters – Jane (born 1688), Bridget Frances (born 1699), Anne (born 1700), Catharine (born 1703), and Barbara (born 1707) – only Barbara survived into adulthood. She never married and her burial in 1776 is recorded in the register of St Margaret's church, on Crossgate in Durham. Of their six sons, four did not survive into adulthood – John (born 1695), Henry (born 1704), Peter (born 1705), and James (date of birth unknown). Thomas (born 1715) died unmarried in 1738 when his older brother Basil (born 12 May 1702) became the sole surviving son and heir (see below).

As a Catholic, John was required to register his estates with the local Justices after an Act of 1715. At that time the family were living in the Old Elvet area of the City of Durham. The annual income from John's estates in County Durham was valued at £500 17s. (equivalent to around £54,000 today), and the income from the Manor of Haldenby in Yorkshire that was being held in trust for members of the More family was estimated to be £325 9s. (equivalent to around £35,000).[43]

John Forcer made his will on 26 July 1725 bequeathing Bridgitt the annuity of £150 (equal to about £16,000 today) for life that he had promised her as part of their marriage settlement. He bequeathed £700 each (about £73,000 today) to Elizabeth and Mary (his daughters by his first marriage) – the money to come out of his lands at Kelloe – and £700 each out to his son Thomas and his daughter Barbara – to come out of his lands at Haldenby, Whitley and Adwick (which had come to him via Bridgitt). After these legacies had been paid he bequeathed the whole of his estates at Harberhouse and Kelloe and his share of the Haldenby, Whitley and Adwick estates to his son Basil with the proviso that should he not have any children the latter estates should pass to his nephew Thomas More in trust for his three sisters and for the children of Austin More (Bridgitt's younger brother) who, as we will see, had died in 1715.[44]

John died on Christmas Day 1725, the event being recorded in an old register of the Jesuit Mission of St Cuthbert in Durham. Bridgitt died on 24 November 1727. They were both buried in the chapel at Harbour House.[45]

Basil Forcer (the younger) married Anne, the daughter of John Tempest of Old Durham, on 12 March 1732. They had no children and Anne predeceased him. The 1767 Returns of Papists indicate that after Anne's death Basil went to live with his sister Barbara in Old Elvet, Durham. He died in London sometime between 4 November 1774 (when he added a codicil to his will of 8 August the same year) and 16 December 1774 when it was proved in the Prerogative Court of Canterbury.[46] The will is interesting in that it shows that, apart from his only surviving sister, Barbara – to whom he left £1,000 (equivalent to around £82,000 today) – he seems to have remained closer to his mother's family than to his wife's family. He left his aunt, Mary Waterton (née More), the equivalent of around £16,000 today and an additional £78,000 (today's value) for her to invest for her children. He also left Mrs Ullathorne, the married daughter of his aunt Anne Binks (née More) the equivalent of around £8,500 today.

Compared to the above we know relatively little about the rest of the children of Basil and Anne More. William, their third son, was born on 22 October 1670 and his baptism recorded in the register of St Mary's North Mymms on 28 November.

William was sent to London to study law at Barnard's Inn, an Inn of Chancery, where he lived in chambers. He was there in 1691 when he was assessed for the Poll Tax but not charged, probably because he was just under twenty-one. He was admitted a Member of the Inn on 27 May 1693 and in 1694 had to pay a Poll Tax of £25 (equivalent to around £2,600 today). His assessment for this included a note to the effect that he was a suspected papist and, because of this, he was probably charged double the normal rate. He was assessed again in 1696, but this time only for £10. This was noted to be double the normal rate.[47]

As we have seen before, William would not have been allowed to be called to the Bar, but he would have been able to carry out the work of a modern solicitor – representing clients at Local Assizes, drawing up legal documents relating to property, drawing up wills, etc. It is in this capacity that he seems to have become the family solicitor, as his name is included as a major player in most of the extant documents surrounding the sale of his father's Hertfordshire Estates. He also seems to have taken over responsibility for administering the estates in and around Haldenby – in which he also had a share – probably making sure that his sisters each received their share of the profits from them.

Describing himself as 'of Barnard's Inn, Holbourn' William drew up his will at Sprotborough, near Doncaster, on 27 September 1710.[48] This is in an area where the Mores had a number of properties and, maybe, he had a house there. I have not, however, seen mention of it in any documents. In his will he makes no mention of a wife or any children. He appoints John Forcer his executor, and bequeaths his share of the More estates in and around Haldenby and a lease of 'Lead Work' on John Forcer's estate at Kelloe for him to use to pay off his debts and, after that, to keep them 'in trust' to benefit his (John Forcer's) children. The rest of his real and personal estate he leaves to his brothers Christopher More and Austin More for them to divide equally among their children. William must have died shortly after making his will as it was proved at York on 12 October 1710 and John Forcer and Christopher Cresacre More were granted permission to administer it two days later, on 14 October 1710.

The birth of Thomas More is recorded in the register of St Mary's, North Mymms, on 17 December 1671. I will note him as Thomas VII. We know nothing about his childhood or education, but we do know that he was admitted to Lincoln's Inn on 11 March 1695, but here is no record of him leaving, or of him later practising as a lawyer.[49] Some pedigrees of the family say that he died unmarried in 1696, aged twenty-five. However, the register of St Peter's church Barnburgh includes the baptism of three children – Mary More (29 June 1689), Gervas More (3 November 1691), and John More (5 July 1694), the first of whom is said to be the daughter of Thomas and Sarah More and the other two as the children of Thomas More. These three children are included under members of the More family at Barnburgh in Kirk's *Biographies of English Catholics*, published in 1909 and there is, to my mind, no reason to doubt that they are the children of this Thomas.[50] According to the family tree handed down for many generations in my family line there was also a daughter Irene, from whom I am descended. She may well have been born in London while Thomas was studying at Lincoln's Inn. Irene's parentage would appear to be confirmed by a manuscript once held at St Joseph's Catholic church, Pontefract – but now sadly lost – which describes her as the daughter of Thomas More of Barnburgh. The manuscript records her marriage to Alexander Nicholson of Barkstone Hall near Sherburn in Elmet,

Yorkshire, in 1732.[51] The Nicholsons of Barkstone had a history of recusancy dating back to the time of Queen Elizabeth, and in 1680 William Nicholson and his wife Margaret, and three of their children, Anne, Mary and William (probably Alexander's father) were imprisoned in York Castle for being 'popish recusants'. I suspect that, as a young adult Thomas moved out of the family home at North Mymms and settled in one of their properties in the Barnburgh area before moving to London to start his legal studies.

The baptismal register of St Peter's Barnburgh contains an entry for the baptism of a Thomas More, son of Thomas More, on 22 February 1686. This can hardly be the son of Thomas (above) who was only fifteen at the time, and it may well be that 'Thomas' was wrongly entered as the name of the father instead of Basil – a mistake that had been made before. Basil and Anne are known to have had another son Thomas who died while still an infant, and this may well be him. If this is true, then he would have been born during one of his mother's visits to Barnburgh.

According to family pedigrees John More V was born on 30 December 1673, but his name is not recorded in the North Mymms or Barnburgh registers. He is said to have become a lawyer in one of the Inns of Chancery but the records of this, like many of the chancery records, have not survived. I have not been able to discover any record of a will or the date of his death. However, he was alive and well on 20 November 1698 when his signature appears on an indenture in which he and his older brother William – with the agreement of their sister Frances Goate and her husband Edward, as well as of Austin More and Charles More – became trustees of the estates in and around Haldenby following the death of Edward Turner, the executor of their mother's will. John is said to have died unmarried.

The birth of Anne More is recorded in the register of St Mary's, North Mymms on 5 December 1672. Anne joined the English Canonesses Regular of the Lateran at St Monica's in Louvain where she was professed on 5 May 1693, taking the name Sister Theodora. She died on 6 June 1699.

George More is recorded as having been baptized at St Mary's North Mymms on 5 February 1674. Pedigrees of the family record only that he died unmarried on 7 June 1697.

Augustine More, known in the family as 'Austin', was born on 11 August 1676, but the event is not recorded in the North Mymms or Barnburgh parish registers. Augustine is said by Foster to have been a woollen draper, but he is not recorded as a member of their guild, and I have not found any other evidence to support this. I have, however, discovered that when he was sixteen he was apprenticed to a wax chandler in London. An abstract of the entry in the Company's Register for 1693 reads: 'Moor Austin, son of Basil, 'Gubbings' Hertfordshire, Esq., to James Cook, 28 April 1693 Wax Chandlers' Company'.[52] The wills of his older brother William and his brother-in-law John Forcer both refer to him as Austin More of Whitechapel and indicate that he married and had children – said to have been a son and a daughter. While serving his apprenticeship in his late teens and early twenties he appears to have lodged in the parish of St Mary le Bow where the baptism of Elizabeth, daughter to Augustine and Elizabeth More is recorded on 13 August 1701.[53] Family pedigrees record Augustine's death at the age of forty-three on 15 August 1719 and, after his death his children are believed to have gone to live with their uncle at Barnburgh. If this is the case, then it seems likely that the Elizabeth More who is included as a member of the family in Kirk's *Biographies of English Catholics*, and who is recorded as having married Mr Hodgshon of Southwell at Barnburgh St Peter on 18 July 1721 is Austin's daughter.[54]

Basil and Anne More had two children named Charles. The first of that name was baptized at St Mary's, North Mymms, on 3 October 1678 and is said in Foster's *Pedigree* to have died when he was about three. The birth of the other Charles is recorded in the register on 15 November 1683. According to Foster's *Pedigree* he lived in London where he was a 'drugster' – what we would call a chemist. He is said to have died, unmarried, on 1 February 1716.

The lack of information about the younger sons of the family – those born after William – leads me to believe that some 'streamlining' of the family tree may have taken place – possibly to enhance the position of the members of the family who became heirs to the family estates.

Family pedigrees credit Basil and Anne with three other children. The birth of Catherine is recorded in the register of St Mary, North Mymms on 12 March 1691, but we do not have any dates for Elizabeth or for a second William. Foster's *Pedigree* says these three all 'died as soon as christened'.

Genealogical Summary

Basil More and his Family

Basil More (1639/40–1702) m. Anne Humble (1641–1694)
Children:
1. Mary (1661–1721): m. James Morgan (d.1721). No children.
2. Frances (1663–1712): m. Edward Goate the Younger
   Children: Edward, Charles and Susan.
3. Basil Junior (1665–1689): unmarried.
4. Christopher Cresacre (1666–1729): eventual heir (see next chapter).
5. Bridgitt (b.1669) m. (his second wife) John Forcer (1666–1725)
   Children: Jane, John, Bridget Frances, Anne, Basil (eventual heir; no children), Catherine, Henry, James, Peter and Barbara.
6. William (1670–1710): unmarried.
7. Thomas VII (1671–1696): m. Sarah (?) ...
   Children: Mary, Gervase (b.1691), John (b.1694), Irene, Anne (b.1697).
8. Anne (1672–1699): an Augustinian canoness at Louvain.
9. John V (1673– after 1698): unmarried.
10. George (1674–1697): unmarried.
11. Augustine/Austin (1676–1719): m. Elizabeth ...
    Children: Elizabeth (b.1701); name of second child?
12. Charles (b. 1678): died aged about three years.
13. Percival Bartholomew Michael More: born and died 1680.
14. Thomas (b.1686): died an infant.
15. Charles II (1683–1715): unmarried.
16. Catherine (b.1691): died an infant.
17. William: died an infant.
18. Elizabeth: died an infant.

Six more stillborn sons.

Chapter Eight

The Family of Christopher Cresacre More

If, as I said that the beginning of the last chapter, his father was the last of the 'old-style' Mores, then Christopher Cresacre was by the same token the first of the 'new-style' Mores. By this I mean that, in adulthood, he lived at a time of considerable political upheaval as England began the process of slowly transforming itself into a modern state with a modern monarchy. For Catholics this meant the end of any faint hopes they may have had of a Catholic king returning to the throne and the acceptance of the fact that the Established Church in England was, and would remain, Protestant. While continuing steadfastly in their Catholic faith, and fiercely proud of their descent from Sir Thomas, whose portraits they hung in their homes, and whose relics they preserved, the Mores began to look forwards rather than backwards. Christopher Cresacre's life is located at the very beginning of this period of transformation when he, and other Catholics, still had to pay a price for their adhering to the faith of their fathers, a price not perhaps as great as in the past, but a price still considerable.

Christopher Cresacre was born in the family mansion at North Mymms and his baptism entered in the parish register on 7 April 1666. The entry reads: 'Christopher Crisacre More the son of Basill More by Ann his wife baptised Aprill the 7th A⁰ Dom 1666.'[1] Throughout his life he seems to have been known by some as just Christopher, and by others as Christopher Cresacre, though in documents that have survived he always signed himself using both his first names.

I have not been able to discover where Christopher Cresacre was educated. In the normal course of events I would have expected him to have followed his older brother Basil into one of the schools on the Continent and to have been brought back to

England when the Edict of James II forbade the education of Catholic children abroad. However, as we have seen, he was not mentioned on the pass that was granted to bring his brother Basil back in 1679, and no similar pass has so far been discovered.

With his older brother busying himself in the service of King James, and his younger brothers going off to study law in London, Christopher Cresacre appears to have occupied himself by helping his father with the management of the estates in Hertfordshire and Yorkshire to which, after his older brother Basil's death in 1689, he became 'heir apparent'. In this capacity he was involved in all the property 'deals' leading up to the sale of Gobions and the other Hertfordshire estates in 1693.

In his mid-twenties Christopher Cresacre made his home in London where, as we saw in the last chapter, the family had a number of relations. There he met and married Katherine, the daughter of Humphrey Wharton of Westminster. The Wharton family was of ancient lineage, Gilbert de Querntan (the original family name) having come over from Caen in France with William the Conqueror. The family name later became 'Wharton' and gave its name to Wharton Hall, South of Kirkby Stephen in Cumbria where the family had one of its principal seats. It also had seats at Gillingwood Hall and at Aske Hall, a few miles north of Richmond in North Yorkshire.

I have not been able to discover the date or place of Christopher Cresacre and Katherine's marriage, but it was most probably in 1688 as their first child was born in June 1689. I have also not been able to discover what money or property Katherine brought to the marriage, but in 1691 Basil transferred the ownership of Gobions and other properties in North Mymms to Christopher Cresacre and Katherine in an agreement which is described as 'being a settlement on the marriage of Christopher Crisacre More and Katherine his wife'.[2]

Throughout most of the years 1689–1713 England was at war in Europe, principally against France. Queen Mary died in 1694 and William ruled alone until his death in March 1702. For both of these, and for Queen Anne who followed them, one of the main problems was finding the money to finance the wars. In a pre-industrial society this inevitably led to an increase of taxation especially on the landowning classes who, in 1692, had been subjected to a land tax of four shillings in the pound – a tax that had been doubled for Catholic landowners. At home, the war years were also years of increasing Protestant dissent that the

High Church party in the Church of England tried, unsuccessfully, to stem. Catholic dissent, however, was still not tolerated.

In 1699 an 'Act for further preventing the growth of Popery' declared that Catholics over the age of eighteen who refused to take the Oaths of Supremacy and Allegiance would not be able to inherit or to buy any land. Fortunately, the future of most of the More estates and the purposes for which they were to be used had by this time already been established through a series of indentures drawn up by senior members of the family. In one such transfer, dated 21 September 1699, between Basil More, Christopher Cresacre and Katherine his wife, Mary More and Edward Goate, the ownership of the Manor of Moseley in the Moss was transferred to William More for him to hold in trust with the ultimate aim of using it to pay off Basil's debts after his death, with the proviso that, in the mean time, Basil should continue to take the rents and yearly profits for his own use.

The manor of Moseley appears to have been quite substantial, comprising a manor house known as Jett Hall with outhouses, stables, barns and surrounding pasture land, meadows and woodlands as well as a number of other houses. When William More leased this estate to a fellow lawyer at Barnard's Inn for a term of ninety-nine years from Christmas Day 1703 the annual rent was set at £300 – equivalent to around £34,700 today. This money was put in a trust fund to provide for the various members of the family who had an interest in it.

After Queen Anne came to the throne in 1702 anti-Catholic legislation continued to be enforced and, to get an idea of the size of her 'problem', she ordered a special 'Return of Papists' to be drawn up in 1706 – a census of Catholics that could be used, if necessary, to raise money from the sequestration of their estates and/or for the collection of the land tax. With the war, however, and with political squabbling between Whigs and Tories in Parliament, and religious squabbling between various factions in the Church of England, the Queen had bigger problems on her hands and, during this period, apart from continuing to pay the double land tax, and occasional presentations for recusancy, most Catholics remained relatively free of active persecution.

Christopher Cresacre, Katherine and their three young children took up permanent residence at Barnburgh around the time of Basil More's death at the beginning of November 1702. It seems to have taken Christopher some time to sort out his father's affairs and, in December 1704, he used the 'Moseley' agreement of 1699 (mentioned above) to raise £210 (around £25,000 today) to pay off his funeral expenses and remaining debts. It seems likely that the debts were due to the rather causal attitude that we know his father took towards the payment of his fines of £20 per month for not attending worship at the local parish church or for other recusancy fines.

In 1706 Christopher Cresacre and Katherine were both 'presented' for recusancy.[3] Whether this was because they had not been paying their fines, or because a local Justice wanted to make a show of his authority we do not know, but, given the lack of any evidence to the contrary, we can only assume that they paid the necessary fines after their presentment.

The failing health of the Queen in 1713 once again raised the question of the succession. Although the Act of Settlement of 1701 had established that any future succession would be a protestant one, there was still considerable support for Prince James Francis Edward, son of the late James II. While he remained the 'Pretender' to the English throne, the possibility of a Jacobite rebellion, and the return of a Catholic to the throne, could not be completely ruled out.

Queen Anne died on 1 August 1715 and was succeeded by George I – the 'Hanoverian' grandson of Elizabeth, the Protestant daughter of King James I – who was crowned on 20 October. Around this time, fears of a Jacobite rebellion were realized when, in September 1715, a group of Scottish Jacobites raised an army in the Highlands and a group of Lowland Jacobites marched down into England, passing through Lancaster and reaching Preston at the beginning of November before finally being stopped and forced to surrender. By the time the Pretender had landed in Scotland just before Christmas 1715 the Rebellion was more or less over and he was forced to flee back to France.

Once again the Jacobite Rebellion did no favours for Catholics in England and, in 1716, Parliament passed 'An Act to Oblige Papists to Register their Names and Real Estates'.[4] The Act applied to all Catholic Nonjurors (those who refused to sign the Oaths of Loyalty and Supremacy), no matter how much or how little money they had. Details of the property they owned or leased, as well as the names of their tenants with details of their tenure and the rents they paid had to be given either in person or via an Attorney to the Clerk of the Peace in every county where the property was situated. Christopher Cresacre duly complied with the law and registered his ownership of Barnburgh Hall, and the manor of Haldenby and its associated properties, the annual income from which was declared to be £357 2s. 1½d. (equivalent to around £39,000 today). While this may seem quite a reasonable income to us, we must not forget that, as a Catholic, in addition to any recusancy fines he might have had to pay, Christopher Cresacre also had to pay double the ordinary Land tax on these properties, which would have been equivalent to around £12,000 a year today.

Like the male heirs to the family estates before him, Christopher Cresacre was Lord of the Manor of Barnburgh, a position that meant that he played a major part in local affairs. From 1702 his name replaces that of his father in the Barnburgh Township Account Book that shows him paying regular sums of 18s. 2d. Poll Tax for the support of the poor, and being party to discussion about things like the fines to be paid by people who did not ring the noses of their pigs in order for them to be tethered and so prevented from grazing on common land. In 1717 – a year in which he and Katherine were again presented for recusancy – he was involved in discussions about the provision of a building for a school in the village.[5]

Christopher Cresacre died at the age of sixty-three and was buried at St Peter's church on 25 April 1729. After his death Katherine went to live with her daughter Mary Waterton (about whom see below). Katherine died in 1744 and her body was taken back to Barnburgh for burial at St Peter's on 16 October.

Christopher Cresacre and Katherine had three daughters and one son. The birth of their first child, Anne, is recorded in the register of St Mary's church, North Mymms. The entry reads: 'Anne the Daughter of Mr. Christopher More by Catherine his wife was born the nineth day of June 1689, about fowr of the clock in the forenoon.'[6] Anne married William Binks, Gentleman, of Richmond and Easingwold in North Yorkshire. The Bynks family came originally from Stony Keld, north of Bowes, where in 1590 they were well-established as 'Yeomen' owning considerable estates in Stony Keld and around the Bowes and Barnard Castle area. From here branches of the family spread north to Newcastle and south to Richmond, Easingwold, Pocklington and Hull. The family name, originally 'Bynks', seems to have suffered a gradual transformation through 'Byncks' to Binckes' and, finally, to 'Binks'.

William was born in 1685. I have not been able to discover the date or place of his marriage to Anne, but it probably took place in the early 1720s when William was prosperous enough to be able to keep a Jesuit chaplain at his house in Richmond. The marriage has been described as 'unhappy', but two children, William (said to have been killed in the Indies) and Mary, were born from the union.[7] The line from Mary leads down to William Bernard Ullathorne, the first Bishop of Birmingham, and to Mgr Canon John Leonard Longstaff; I will deal with these in a separate section at the end of this chapter.

The birth of Catherine More, Christopher Cresacre and Katherine's second child, was entered in register of St Mary's, North Mymms, on 12 March 1691. As we saw in the last chapter her uncle, James Morgan, left her a considerable sum of money when he died in 1722 but, apart from this, the only other thing family pedigrees record is that she never married, and that she died at Brussels.

Thomas More, Christopher and Katherine's only son, was born in February 1691. As he and his family will be the subject of the next chapter I will not say anything else about him here.

The baptism of Mary More, the youngest child in the family, is recorded in the register of St Peter's, Barnburgh on 8 September 1703. This was only a short time after the family moved to live permanently at Barnburgh. Mary married Charles Waterton of Walton Hall.

The *Pedigree of Waterton of Walton* traces the Waterton family back to Norman de Andreci (d'Areci) who was granted thirty-three Manors in Lincolnshire by William the Conqueror. Sometime around 1177 his grandson, Reiner de Normanby, was granted an estate at Waterton, in the Isle of Axeholme, Lincolnshire, by Gilbert de Vete, the Abbot of Selby and, having become Lord of Waterton he adopted the name for himself. In 1435 John Waterton married Constance Assenhull and through her came into possession of the estates at Walton and Cawthorne Park (West of Barnsley).[8]

Mary and Charles married in 1733. Born on 20 March 1704, Charles was the eldest son and heir of Charles Waterton Esq., of Walton, and his first wife Anne, the daughter of Sir William Gerard of Bryn in Cheshire. Like the Watertons, the Gerards had held on to their Catholic faith in spite of constant persecution and the resulting reduction in their estates.

After their marriage Charles and Mary lived at Walton Hall. In 1745 Charles was imprisoned for a while in York Castle because the authorities thought that he might support the Jacobite invasion of England under Prince Charles Edward Stuart (Bonnie Prince Charlie) before the Battle of Culloden. Charles died on 12 September 1767 and was buried in the Waterton chapel in the Church of St Helen at Sandal Magna.

Charles and Mary had four sons (Thomas, Charles, Christopher and Bertram), and three daughters (Mary, Anne and Catherine). Their eldest son and heir, Thomas, born 1738, married Anne, the daughter of Edward Bedingfield, Esq., of Oxburgh/Oxborough Hall in Norfolk – yet another recusant family. Thomas pulled down the Elizabethan Hall at Walton and built a new one in 1767. Thomas and Anne were the parents of Charles Waterton of Walton Hall, the famous adventurer and naturalist – and friend of Charles Darwin. Charles married Anne, the daughter of Charles Edmonstone of Cardress Park, Dumbartonshire in the chapel of the English Convent at Bruges on 11 May 1829. Their only child Edmund, born 7 April 1830, became a Privy Chamberlain to Pope Pius IX and was a Justice of the Peace for the West Riding of Yorkshire. On 20 August 1862, also in the English Convent, he married Margaret Alicia Josephine Ennis the second daughter of Sir John Ennis, Baronet, of Ballinahown in County Westmeath, Ireland. Their line continues down to the present day. Edmund, who died in 1887, sold Walton Hall. It is now a hotel called the Waterton Park Hotel.

The Ullathorne and Longstaff Connections

As we saw above, Anne More married William Binks of Richmond and Easingwold, and they had two children, William (date of birth unknown) and Mary, born 1726. I have been unable to discover when Anne Binks died, but it may have been around 1735 when Mary, at the age of only nine, was boarded out with the Anne family, a Catholic family – and friends of the Mores – who lived at Burghwallis Hall.[9] Why Mary was not taken in by her brother and his wife at Barnburgh or at York remains a mystery. In 1743 William is recorded as living alone in a house in the Bedern area of York where he owned two properties. On 3 March of that year a warrant was issued for constables to search houses of papists or reputed papists in York to look for arms, weapons, gunpowder and ammunition, as well as for horses valued over £5. William's house was duly searched and, when he refused to swear the Oaths of Allegiance and Succession, he was bound over in the sum of £50 (equivalent to over £6,000 today) to appear before the Justices.[10] What the final result of the action was, I have not been able to discover, but it may be that William decided it was safer to live in Easingwold as that is where he died in 1748.

Mary Binks appears to have come into possession of her father's properties in Easingwold and York after his death and to have brought them as her 'portion' into her marriage with John Ullathorne on 17 December 1749. John was not a Catholic, and his branch of the Ullathorne family came from Ampleforth where his grandfather had been a Church of England minister, and where he was born and baptized on 28 March 1725. At some stage John was sent to live with a doctor in York but he was, apparently, so terrified of finding a skeleton in the cupboard of his bedroom that he ran away and apprenticed himself to a shoemaker. Later, however, he became a draper in Easingwold.[11]

In 1765 the press in London and the provinces stirred up a lot of anti-Catholic feeling and, probably as a response to this, the Archbishops of Canterbury and York ordered the bishops of all the Anglican dioceses in England and Wales to compile a list of papists or suspected papists in the parishes under their jurisdiction in 1767. The results of this census were known as the 'Returns of Papists, 1767'. In most places Catholics only needed to be identified by their initials and, under Easingwold (Archdeaconry of Cleveland), we find the entry 'M wife of J.U.' (Mary, wife of John Ullathorne). As he was not a Catholic 'J.U.' was not listed separately. The census shows that there were thirteen other Catholics living in the parish – seven adults and six children. The census also tells us that Mary worked as a 'staymaker'.[12] Mary died in 1788 and John, at the age of sixty-three, married Anne Rawlins at All Saints church, Easingwold on 19 September 1789. They had one daughter, Sarah, before John died in 1794.

John and Mary Ullathorne had five sons, and two daughters born between 1751 and 1771, all of whom were brought up as Catholics. John (1752–1782), their second son, was the father of William Ullathorne who married Hannah Longstaff, the daughter of John Longstaff the Chief Constable of Spilsby and later of Halton Holgate in Lincolnshire. Hannah was born on 14 July 1781 and baptized at Halton Holgate on 25 September in the same year. The couple met while they were both working in Townshend's drapery business in Holborn, London and, through William, Hannah was converted to Catholicism. After their marriage they moved to Pocklington in Yorkshire where William set up his own business running what today we would call a general store – selling groceries, spirits, fabrics and even coals. He obviously did well for himself as it was said of him that he did 'half the business of the town', even 'discounting bills' as there was no local bank.[13] William and Hannah had ten children, six of them born at Pocklington and four at Scarborough, after the family business was moved there around 1812. I have not been able to discover when William died, but Hannah died in 1860.

The story of William and Hannah's eldest son, William, is recorded in his autobiography originally published by Burns & Oates in 1891. A new edition made from the original draft, and entitled *From Cabin Boy to Archbishop*, was published by Hollis & Carter in 1943. Sadly, this went out of print, and a new life entitled *The Devil is a Jackass* was published by Gracewing in 1995. Below, I give a brief summary of his life based on the 1943 edition.[14]

William was born at Pocklington on 7 May 1806. After the family moved to Scarborough he attended a small school there until he was twelve years old when he was put to work in his father's office to learn how to handle the accounts. William, however, had different ideas. Life in the seaside town of Scarborough, and his mother's tales of her cousin Sir John Franklin, the famous Arctic explorer, gave him a taste for the sea and, after much pleading, his father allowed him to sign on as a cabin boy on a ship sailing from Hull to the Mediterranean and Baltic seas.[15] He made several voyages, during one of which, through the influence of the ship's mate, he 'rediscovered' his faith. Having returned to dry land, and thinking that he might have a vocation to the religious life, his father sent him to the Benedictine monastery at Downside, near Bath, in February 1823. After spending a year catching up on his studies he received the habit on 12 March 1824 and was professed in 1825, taking the additional name Bernard. After six further years of study for the priesthood he was ordained at Ushaw College, Warwickshire, in September 1831.

In 1832 William Bernard volunteered to go to Australia and, having arrived there in February 1833, he took up his post as 'His Majesty's Chaplain in New South Wales' (with a small government salary), as parish priest of St Mary's in Sydney, and as Vicar General of Australia. He was shocked to see the way convicts were treated and the almost total lack of religious provision for them, and fought tirelessly to bring the system of transportation to an end. He returned to England in June 1836 to make people more aware of conditions in Australia and to recruit a number of priests and nuns to serve in the colony. During this time he also went to Rome to report to the Pope on the situation of the Church in Australia. Returning again to Australia he continued his work until December 1840 when he came back permanently to England. Having served for a while on the Catholic Mission in Coventry he was, in 1846, consecrated a bishop and made Vicar General of the Western District and then of the Central District. In 1848 he was sent to Rome to plead for the re-establishment of the Catholic Hierarchy in England. When this was finally achieved in September 1850 he was appointed the first Bishop of Birmingham. He worked tirelessly in this position until, in 1888, ill-health forced him to retire to Oscott College, Warwickshire. In recognition of his achievements and long service he was appointed to the honorary position of Archbishop of Cabasa. He died on 21 March 1889 and was buried in the chapel at St Dominic's Convent, Stone, Staffordshire – a convent he had helped to found.

The Archbishop's sister, Lucy Ullathorne, was born at Scarborough on 9 July 1812. She became the first wife of her first cousin John Charles Longstaff when they married at the Catholic chapel in Scarborough on 9 October 1844. Lucy and John seem to have lived in the town of Barnard Castle (where the Longstaff family had their roots) before moving to Stockton on Tees. Two of their children, Frederick Owen, and Eadbert John, were born at Barnard Castle in 1845 and 1847 respectively, and two more, Leonard, and Willingham Robert, were born at Stockton in 1848 and 1850. Leonard married Helena Lucy Argent at Rhyl, Flintshire (now Clwyd) on 11 July 1876, and they made their home in Liverpool where their eight children were born. Their eldest son, Leonard William Longstaff was born on 22 May 1877. As an adult he devoted much of his free time to researching his family's descent from Sir Thomas More. He made contact with a number of other descendants and, with them, attended Thomas More's canonization in Rome on 19 May 1935. His research resulted in a substantial collection of around 850 books, pamphlets, newspaper cuttings, photographs, artwork, etc., by and about Thomas More, his contemporaries and descendants, covering the years 1504–1953 – the year of his death at Harvington, near Evesham in Worcestershire. His collection, totalling about 1,900 items, was purchased in 1954 by Loyola

Marymount University, a Catholic university in Los Angeles. Known as Special Collection 047, it is now housed in the University's Charles Von der Ahe Library.

Leonard William was survived by two daughters and a son, John Leonard Longstaff (1913–1986), who became a priest and, eventually, a canon of the Diocese of Westminster. From 1956 until his retirement in 1983 he was rector of St Mary's church, Cadogan Street, London. Following in his father's footsteps, he collected a great deal of information on the descendants of Sir Thomas More, especially on those living during his lifetime. This collection is now held by the 'Moreanum' at the Université Catholique de l'Ovest, in Angers, France.

Genealogical Summary

Christopher Cresacre More and his Family

Christopher Cresacre More (1666–1729) m. Katherine Wharton (d. 1744)
Children:
1. Anne (b.1689): m. William Binks (1685–1748)
    Children:
    i. William (killed in the Indies)
    ii. Mary (1726–1788): m. (1749) John Ullathorne (1725–1794). Seven children. (Their second son, John (b.1752), was the grandfather of Archbishop William Bernard Ullathorne (1806–1889). Archbishop Ullathorne's sister, Lucy (b.1812), and her husband John Charles Longstaff, were the grandparents of Canon John Leonard Longstaff.
2. Catherine (b.1691): died unmarried in Brussels.
3. Thomas VIII (1691–1739): son and heir (see next chapter).
4. Mary (b.1703): m. (1733) Charles Waterton of Walton Hall, near Wakefield (1704–1767)
    Children:
    i. Thomas: born 1738. Married (1780) Anne Bedingfield and was the father of Charles Waterton (b.1782) the naturalist, and six other children.
    ii. Charles: became a Jesuit in 1762. Drowned 1773.
    iii. Christopher: married as his first wife Anne, daughter of Dr John Waddell, and was the father of six children.
    iv. Bertram: died unmarried and buried at Sandal Magna.
    v. Mary (unmarried).
    vii. Anne: married Charles Daly of Demerera in the West Indies.
    viii. Catherine (died unmarried).

Chapter Nine

Thomas More VIII and his Family

The End of the Barnburgh Line

Thomas's birth was entered in the parish register of St Mary's, North Mymms on 28 February 1691. Nothing is known about his early education, but he was admitted to Lincoln's Inn to begin his legal studies on 20 October 1711.[1] As a Catholic he was not allowed to be called to the Bar, but he appears to have completed a full course of study and, presumably, to have practised for a while in some form of legal capacity, probably as an attorney. Certainly, when he registered his estates with the Clerk of the Peace for the West Riding of Yorkshire in a document dated 9 December 1718 he described himself as 'Thomas More of Lincoln's Inn, in the County of Middlesex, Gent.'[2]

Thomas married Catherine Giffard. Born in 1694, she was the eldest daughter of John Giffard of 'Black Ladies' at Brewood in Staffordshire and his wife Catherine, the daughter of John Taylor of Fockbury in Worcestershire. The Giffard family (sometimes spelt 'Gifford') were Lords of Longueville in Normandy before the Norman Conquest. Three members of the family came to England with William the Conqueror and were granted estates in various parts of the country. One branch of the family became Lords of the Manor of Brewood in Staffordshire and of nearby Chillington, just over the border in Shropshire. In the Church of St Mary and St Chad in Brewood there are four large tombs to members of the Giffard family, the largest being that of Sir John Giffard (died 1556) who was Standard Bearer to King Henry VIII and who, like Sir Thomas More, attended him at the Field of the Cloth of Gold. The tomb shows him with his two wives and a total of eighteen children, thirteen of whom died in infancy. After the dissolution of the monasteries the two priories on their estates came into the possession of the family. One, the Priory of St Mary at Brewood – known as 'Black Ladies' – from the black habits of the Benedictine nuns who lived there, and the other the Priory of St Leonard – known as 'White Ladies' – from the bleached habits worn by the Augustinian nuns. The original timber-framed house built by the Giffards at White Ladies no longer exists, but the ruins of the priory can still be visited. The present Chillington Hall, built nearby in 1787 is still the seat of the Giffard family. The House at Black Ladies was sold out of the family in 1918.[3]

After the Reformation, the Giffard family suffered much for their adherence to the faith of their ancestors and during the Civil War supported the Royalist cause. In September 1651, Colonel Charles Giffard took Charles II to White Ladies and then to Boscobel House, his hunting lodge in the forest nearby, to hide him during his flight to France after his defeat by Cromwell at the Battle of Worcester.[4]

We know from the information given at the time he registered his estates in 1718, that Thomas More's marriage to Catherine took place between 3 July 1718 when she is referred to as 'Catherine Giffard, spinster', and 9 December 1718 when she is referred to by Thomas as 'now my wife'. The document also tells us that on 3 July 1718 Thomas and his father 'sold' the Yorkshire estates to Edward Wharton Esq., of Surrey Street in the parish of Saint Clement Danes and Charles Wharton Esq., of North Street in the parish of St Andrew's, Holborn. As we have seen before, an act of 1699 had forbidden Catholics to inherit land, and the sale of the estates to the Wharton relations (Thomas's uncles) was, no doubt, a device for holding them in trust for Thomas and Catherine, and for their heirs.

With his father still in possession of Barnburgh Hall, and the manors of Moseley and Haldenby there was, initially, not much left to provide for the support of Thomas and his family, and the registration document of 1718 shows that his income came from eight smallholdings, each with a house or a cottage and some land, all situated in the parish of Barnburgh and the nearby hamlet of Harlington. All of these properties were rented out, and the names of the tenants were given in the registration document. Five of the properties were obviously farmed by their tenants as they included barns, stables and outhouses and, one of them, a malt kiln. Two of the three other properties were probably let to local craftsmen as they had workshops and outhouses. The remaining property was 'A Watermill standing upon the River

Dearne, a House and Outhouses with the Land thereunto belonging'. The total annual rental value for them came to £400 7s. 6d. which, after the deduction of the double land tax of eight shillings in the pound, is equivalent to around £28,800 today. What is interesting is that, in addition to their rent, five of the eight tenants also had to provide each year 'a couple of fatt Capons and the loading of a Waine Load of Coals from Barnsley Pitts to Barnbrough Hall'. That was certainly one way of keeping the home fires burning! This payment in kind seems to have been fairly applied as the tenants of the three smallest properties only had to provide two fat capons each year.

Although the penal laws against Catholics were not repealed during the reign of George II, little action was taken against them from the 1730s onwards. They remained subject to the double land tax, but two further attempts by the authorities to draw up 'Returns of Papists' in 1736 and 1767 met with a patchy response. In terms of land ownership the Mores were by now 'small fry' and, politically, they were not seen as posing any threat to their King and country. As we will see below, when the First Catholic Relief Act of 1778 restored to Catholics the right to inherit and purchase land the only male member of the main line of the family still alive, and still in possession of what remained of the family's estates, was Fr Thomas More, SJ.

Although Catholic clergy were not officially allowed to practise their ministry until the Second Catholic Relief Act was passed in 1791 (during the reign of George III) Catholic gentry families were able to keep chaplains in their houses from where they served Catholic families in the surrounding area, and in some places – Durham and York, for example – Catholics began to build chapels where they could worship as a community.

After their marriage Thomas and Catherine are said to have gone to live in Ghent for a while. Catherine's father had died in 1709, and we know from his will made shortly before, that he left her £400 (equivalent to around £35,000 today) as a marriage portion and they may have used that to fund their stay.[5] Exactly how long they remained in Ghent is not known, but it may well have been until the death of Thomas's father in April 1729 after which, as we saw in the last chapter, Thomas's mother went to live with her Waterton relations at Walton Hall, and the hall at Barnburgh became vacant.

On their return to England Thomas and Catherine took up residence at Barnburgh Hall. A son, Basil, was born to them there in

1730 but he did not live long as his burial is recorded in the parish register for 11 January 1731.

Thomas's name appears in the Barnburgh Township Account book in 1730 when 3 shillings and 3 pence were claimed for taking him to the Justices for refusing to pay his assessment – probably a land tax assessment – and in 1731 he is described as 'Overseer of the Highways'. In 1735 a census was ordered to be made of Catholics in the Diocese of York, and Robert Ayde, Rector of Barnburgh, reported that

> In the Parish of Barnburgh there are these Popish Recusants: namely, Thomas More Esq. and Catherine his wife; Mr. Walter Giffard, Brother in Law to the said Mr. More, William Ward, John Thompson, Edward Oram, his manservants; Elizabeth Myers, Frances Pinder, Elizabeth Peacock, Anne Bayley, Frances Smallpage, his maid-servants.[6]

As there were no other Catholics in Barnburgh at this time, the family must have felt very isolated. There is no evidence that they were able to afford to maintain a private chaplain at the hall and it would have been difficult for them to attend Mass and receive the Sacraments. It may well have been considerations like these that led them to move to York – to a house in Colliergate. Among the possessions they took with them was a copy of Holbein's famous painting of Sir Thomas More and his family that had hung at Barnburgh since the time of Basil More. They perhaps feared for its safety when the hall became empty or when tenants moved in.

York was a city with a thriving Catholic community, especially in Colliergate, Micklegate and the Bedern area. A number of families maintained their own Jesuit chaplains, and a secular priest had charge of a Catholic chapel in Lop Lane. There was also a school for young Catholic girls run by the nuns of Institute of the Blessed Virgin Mary, an order to which – as we saw in chapter six – two of their distant cousins had belonged.

The house in York was owned or leased by Walter Giffard, Catherine's brother, who never married and who lived there with them. The family later moved to another larger house, as the 1767 Returns of papist records them as having lived for seventeen years in the parish of Holy Trinity, King's Court. This must have been quite a substantial residence as, in addition to Mrs M and Miss M (her daughter Catherine), and Mr G (Walter Giffard), there was also a priest as well as two male and four female servants.[7]

Thomas VIII drew up his will in January 1739 and he died seven months later, aged forty-seven. His burial is recorded in the parish register on 28 August 1739. His will, witnessed by Walter Giffard Esquire, by Peter Maire of Barnburgh, Gentleman, and by William Ward and Elizabeth Myers, two servants, was registered at Wakefield on 5 October 1739. The record in Wakefield Archives is brief, and only mentions his estates at Haldenby, Jett Hall farm and the other properties at Aldwick, Whitley and Pigbourne. As we will see, Thomas's eldest son had not, at this time, reached his majority and the administration of the estates was granted to two members of the extended family, Walter Giffard and Thomas Waterton of Walton, and to two other associates, John Graham of Woodhall (Yorkshire), Gent., and William Crowe of Pontefract. As so often in the past, it is clear that arrangements had already been made for the profits from the Manor of Haldenby to be used to provide for the upkeep of, and any eventual marriage portions for, the daughters of the family.

Catherine survived Thomas for another twenty-eight years. She died at York at the end of November and was buried on 4 December 1767.

Thomas and Catherine had three sons and two daughters. Their eldest child, Thomas IX, is recorded in family pedigrees as having been born on 19 September 1722, but it is not known whether he was born before or after the family moved to Ghent. Like many of his earlier cousins Thomas IX was sent to St Omers where he was a student from 1736 until he went on to higher studies at the Scots College, Douai, on 11 February 1741. How long he spent at Douai we do not know, but he does not appear to have regarded himself as having a vocation to the priesthood at this time and returned to England after a while – presumably to York – where the family had been based since before the death of his father. Although the family estates were held in trust for him he was to all intents and purposes now the owner of what remained of the family estates originally inherited from the Cresacre family.

By the time he was approaching thirty years of age Thomas IX had obviously come to the conclusion that married life was not for him, and he decided to join the Jesuits. The decision cannot have been an easy one to make and I cannot help but wonder whether had his father had still been alive to counsel him, his decision might have been different. On the other hand his decision may reflect a changing attitude to the priesthood and the development of the idea that a vocation to the priesthood is the result of a direct call from God which therefore overrides all other interests. Whatever Thomas's motives might have been have been for choosing the priesthood, it went against the family tradition of keeping unbroken the main line of the family, even if it meant, as in the case of his great-great-grandfather Cresacre, giving up any desire to become a priest. As we will see, Thomas's younger brother had, at this time, already joined the Jesuits so, when he made his decision, he knew that the line, unbroken for over two hundred years, would die out with him.

Thomas could not start his religious training in England so he had to travel to Bruges where he was received into the Society of Jesus on 19 July 1752. While he was absent from England the oversight of his properties was placed in the hands of Walter Giffard and the other trustees who had previously been appointed for that purpose. One of the few documents that has survived from this time tells us that the Barnburgh estate was managed by a steward, Joshua Wilson, Gentleman, and gives us an insight into the workings of the old manorial courts.[8] Though Thomas was abroad at the time life had to go on, and in June 1754, Joshua gave notice to the Bailiff of the 'Manor of Barnbrough' as follows:

> You are hereby commanded to proclaim and give Notice that the Great Court Baron of Thomas More Esquire, Lord of the said Manor will be held at the house of Joseph Johnson in Barnbrough within the said Manor on Thursday the Fourth day of July next at (unreadable) of the clock in the forenoon and you are to Summons all Freeholders and others who are part of or within the said Manor to appear at the Said Court to do their respective Suits and Services there and you are also to Summons and return a good and substantial Jury to appear and be at the said Court and you are to be there present and to make a return of this precept Given under my hand and Seal this fifteenth day of June in the Year of Our Lord 1754.

A list of twelve jurors was drawn up by the bailiff and as two of them did not turn up at the court to be 'Inpannell'd & Sworn for the Lord of the said Manor' they were, as was the custom, each fined one shilling for the offence and two others appointed in their place. The court dealt with some thirty-four issues and set fines for those named individuals who had failed to do things like mending their hedges and 'diking' their ditches, or who had 'stubbed up' brushwood, or ploughed too close to, or actually on land, that did not belong to them. The court also made sure that seasonal jobs were carried out, so that every commoner was to provide a man once a year to assist the Overseer of the Highways, and every inhabitant was to 'Dyke his Dykes before Midsummer' or face a fine of twelve pence a rood. A seasonal order was also made allowing geese to be kept till Christmas but only in one field. The penalty for not complying was set at fifteen pence a flock.

Thomas was sent to Watten for his novitiate, and his spiritual formation there was followed by two years of philosophy (1753–1755) and four years of theology (1756–1760) at Liège. After his ordination to the priesthood in 1760 he spent two years as 'Minister', or administrator, at St Omers College, followed by a year in the same position at Liège, before being sent onto the English Mission in London in 1763.[9]

By this time Thomas had shown himself to be an able administrator and, in addition to whatever priestly duties he may have carried out from his base in Gloucester Street (now Old Gloucester Street), Queen Square, and nearby Little Ormond Street (somewhere under the site of the present children's hospital), Thomas took charge of the finances of the Jesuits in England. In the past, these had depended heavily on investments made by their agents in France in the transport and sale of sugar and coffee from the Jesuit Mission in Martinique but when this ran into difficulties they (the French Jesuits) had to borrow money from other Jesuit Provinces, including England, as well as from a bank in Marseilles – which, unfortunately, collapsed. The after shock of this affair led to the closure of English Preparatory School and College at St Omers and the novitiate at Watten, and their transfer to Bruges (then in the Austrian Netherlands) and Ghent respectively. Ultimately, it led to the expulsion of the Jesuits from France in 1763 and the suppression of the Society by Pope Clement XIV in August 1773. All of this was part of an anti-Catholic religious and political movement that culminated in the French Revolution of 1789–1799.

During his years as procurator, or administrator, Thomas began the work of paying back the monies that had been lent to the English Jesuits to help them pay off their debts. He continued this work until has appointment as Provincial, or overall Superior of the Jesuits in England on 19 July 1769. He remained Provincial of the Jesuits in England until their suppression.

Unlike many of their brethren in Europe the English Jesuits now had a good relationship with the secular clergy and this helped them when, after their dissolution, they came under the jurisdiction of the Vicars Apostolic. The bond which bound the ex-Jesuits together was recognized, and Thomas was given a special responsibility for the welfare of those working in the London District, though he was generally regard as their Superior by all the Jesuits in England – there were around 140 of them at that time. As there was always hope that the Society would be restored, Thomas also oversaw their finances and worked hard to try to ensure the survival of their former colleges at Bruges and Liège on which so many English children depended for their Catholic education.

No doubt worn out by his activities Thomas retired in 1793 and went to live with Bridget Dalton, his widowed sister, in Bath. He died there on 20 May 1795 and was buried in St Joseph's Catholic chapel, Trenchard Street. Details of the location of his grave and of a memorial stone with a long inscription in Latin have been lost.[10]

Thomas's will, drawn up on 2 June 1794, and proved in London on 16 June 1795, makes no mention of the family estates in Yorkshire and it seems clear that, after the First Catholic Relief Act of 1788, when Catholics were once again allowed to own and inherit land, arrangements had been made for them to be transferred to his sister Bridget. She was the main cash beneficiary of his will, receiving £1,670 2s. 11d., (equivalent to around £116,000 today) described as 'in the 5 per cent stock' which had been held in trust for his use and profit by a banker in Henrietta Street, Covent Garden, London. The other beneficiaries of his will were his nephew and niece, William Dalton and Lady Bridget Fitzgerald, and his cousin Thomas Waterton (to each of whom he left the equivalent of about £7,500 today). He left his sister Mary, and his widowed niece Teresa Metcalfe (née Throckmorton) the equivalent of about £2,000 today.[11]

Thomas's younger brother, Christopher More, is recorded in family pedigrees as having been born on 10 May 1729, probably in York. He followed his brother to St Omers where he was admitted to the Preparatory School in 1739. Unlike his brother he seems to have been set on becoming a religious and a priest from the beginning. He completed his senior studies at St Omers in 1746 and joined the Society of Jesus on 7 November in that year. After his novitiate at Watten he studied philosophy and theology at Liège and was ordained priest in 1754. After ordination he went to teach at St Omers for a few years before being sent onto the English Mission. There is some confusion about exactly when

Christopher came to England and about his movements afterwards. What little evidence there is seems to point to him having spent most of his time as chaplain to his sister Bridget and her second husband Robert Dalton first at Thurnham Hall, Lancashire, then at their house in the parish of St Michael le Belfry, York, when they went to live there in 1764 or 1765 and, finally, at Bath after they moved there in the early 1770s. He died at Bath on 27 November 1781 and was buried at Bath Abbey.[12]

In addition to their three sons Thomas and Catherine had three daughters, Bridget, Catherine, and Mary. As Bridget survived her two younger sisters I will consider her last.

Mary More, known affectionately in the family as 'Mally' was born at York on 1 April 1732. As a child she attended the school run by the nuns of the Institute of the Blessed Virgin Mary at the Bar Convent in nearby Mickelgate but later, probably when she was eleven or twelve, she was sent to the school run by the English Augustinian Canonesses Regular of the Lateran at their convent in Camersstratt, Bruges. In the convent archives there is a letter written to her by her sister Catherine in 1748 while she was a pupil there. The English Augustinian nuns had connections with the extended More family going back to before 1606 when the English Convent of St Monica's in Louvain had been founded by Mother Margaret Clement the daughter of John Clement and Margaret Giggs (the adopted daughter of Sir Thomas More). The convent at Bruges was a foundation made from St Monica's in 1629 and, as we saw in the last chapter, Mary's great-aunt Anne (Sister Theodora) had been a nun there.[13]

In 1752, after completing her education, Mary joined the Augustinian canonesses at Bruges where, at her profession on 4 December 1753, she took the name Dame Mary Augustina. Sixteen years later, in 1766, the community elected her Prioress. During her period in office she helped a number of Jesuits who had fled to Bruges after the suppression of their order in France and later, in 1783, gave refuge for a while to a group of Carthusian monks when their monastery in Holland was suppressed. Early in 1794 it was the nuns turn to experience exile when they were expelled from France at the beginning of the French Revolution. They fled to England where they were offered a sanctuary at Hengrave Hall in Suffolk, the home of Sir Thomas Gage, where they arrived on 12 July 1794. They remained there under the leadership of Mother Mary until she was able to take them back to Bruges in 1802. She died there on 23 March 1807 and was buried in the Convent chapel. The inscription erected in her memory still remains in place between the pillars of the chapel.

Catherine More, Dame Mary Augustina's younger sister, was born at York in 1733. It seems likely that, like her older sister, she attended the school run by the nuns at the Bar Convent, but she did not follow her sister to the school at Bruges – perhaps she was not seen as having any inclination to become a nun. Catherine never married, and appears to have lived with her mother in York until she died in 1767, and then to have remained in the house until her own death in 1784. In her will, dated 1 March 1776, she appointed her brother Thomas her sole executor, and left him her portion of the family estates as well as her 'Bonds and Securities'. She left £500 (equivalent to around £39,000 today) to her brother Christopher, and £50 each to her sister Mary, her cousin Mary Ullathorne and to Thomas Nixon, the family chaplain.[14]

The birth date of Bridget More, the eldest daughter of Thomas VIII and Catherine, is not recorded in family pedigrees that say only that she was born at Ghent. If she was the eldest child in the family then her birth is likely to have been around 1720, if not, given the birth dates of her brothers and sisters, it would have been sometime between 1723 and 1728. Within the family Bridget was known affectionately as 'Biddy'.

Bridget married twice. Her first husband was Peter Metcalfe of Glandford Briggs (now known as Brigg), in Lincolnshire. Peter's immediate ancestors came from Kirton in Lindsey, and Brigg. His grandfather, also Peter Metcalfe, who died in 1692, was a linen draper in Brigg.[15] Peter's parents were Nicholas Metcalfe and his wife Anne, the daughter of Marmaduke Morley. In addition to Peter, they had two other sons, Nicholas and Marmaduke, and a daughter Jane. The family pedigree does not record their birth dates, but it does note that Nicholas was 'of weak wits', that he 'left the church for a lira', and that he 'died unmarried'. Marmaduke Metcalfe married Elizabeth Penithorne and had an only child, Jane (1735–1817), who married Robert Cliffe of Broughton Hall, near Brigg and had three daughters, Anne, Elizabeth and Harriet. Jane Metcalfe married a Mr Shuttleworth of Hodsock Park, near Blyth in Nottinghamshire.[16]

Peter Metcalfe is said to have built 'a very substantial house in Brigg', and this is, presumably, where he and Bridget lived after their marriage. The date of their marriage has not come down to us, but it was probably around 1753. Their eldest child, Thomas Peter, was born on 4 July 1756. He was followed by Catherine who, born the following year, died when she was four in 1761, and by Bridget Mary who was born on 5 February 1758, six months after the death of her father, and who died the following month on 20 March 1758.

Bridget and Peter's marriage was cut short by Peter's death in August 1757. His death was, presumably, unexpected as he died intestate, and Bridget was granted permission to administer his estate on 27 September 1757. It is said that Peter's ghost appeared in their house on the nights of 27 November and 9 December 1757.[17]

After Peter's death Bridget married again. Her second husband was Robert Dalton Esq., of Thurnham Hall, Lancashire, and they married on 30 October 1759. The Hardwick Marriage Act of 1753 had made it compulsory for all marriages, except those of Jews and Quakers, to be conducted in the local parish church. At the time Brigg was not a parish in its own right and the marriage is recorded in the parish register of St Mary, Wrawby, which included the southern part of Brigg within its boundary. The new law obviously presented a problem for Catholics but, given the circumstances, it was generally accepted that they could go through with the Anglican service providing that they did not kneel or join in the prayers, and that they followed it up with a marriage before a Catholic priest.

The Dalton family originally hailed from Bispham in the Parish of Croston, Lancashire. Robert Dalton of Bispham bought the Thurnham estate in 1556 and the family later acquired the Park Hall estate at Charnock Richard through the marriage of Elizabeth Dalton to William Hoghton of Park Hall in 1683.

Bridget was Robert Dalton's third wife. His fist wife – by whom he had three sons and four daughters – was Cecilia, the daughter of John Butler of London. They married in 1740 and before her death in 1749 they had three sons and four daughters. Two of the sons died as infants and two of the daughters became nuns, one at York and the other in Liège. Robert's second wife was Elizabeth Dempsey of York. They married in 1753 and before her death they had two sons – both of whom died without issue – and two daughters, one of whom joined her half-sister as a nun at Liège.[18]

It seems likely that Bridget and Robert became acquainted through their mutual relations in York. In the marriage settlement drawn up on 25 October 1759, Robert conveyed his Mansion House at Park Hall in Charnock Richard, Lancashire, and the estate surrounding it, to Walter Giffard and John Graham of

Woodhall, Yorkshire, for them and their heirs to hold in trust for himself and Bridget, and for the successive 'heirs male' of their line – as long as they were lawfully begotten – for a term of two thousand years. The arrangement provided for Robert to take the rents from the estate and, after his death, for Bridget to take an annuity of £130 out of it (equivalent to around £14,000 today).[19] The marriage settlement does not mention the 'portion' that Bridget received from her own family, but we know from her will (to be referenced later) that she was granted the personal use of £2,000 (equivalent to around £225,000 today) out of the profits of the Haldenby estates that had been built up in the fund managed by Walter Giffard and his fellow trustees.

At the time of his mother's re-marriage, Thomas Peter Metcalfe was only three years old and he and his two-year-old sister went to live with her in Lancashire. As it was through his line that the More estates were finally dispersed I will return to it in a separate section at the end of this chapter.

Robert and Bridget had three children: Constance, William and Bridget Ann. The only thing we know about Constance is that she died unmarried. The birth of William, on 10 September 1763 is recorded in the register of St Michael's church, Cockerham. At the request of his father he added the name Hoghton to that of Dalton. However, from his mother's will, we know that, although he signed himself William Dalton Hoghton he was usually known only as William Dalton. William married Louisa, the daughter of Frederick Smith Esq., of St Mary-le-Bone, London, and they had a son William John and other children whose names I have not been able to discover.

Bridget Ann Dalton married Sir James Trant Fitzgerald, 7th Baronet of Castle Ishen, Co. Cork, Ireland in 1789. They lived in Bath and had a daughter, Maria, and a son, James, who on the death of his father became Sir James Fitzgerald, the 8th Baronet. He married Augusta Henrietta, the second daughter of Vice Admiral Sir Thomas Freemantle, on 27 September 1826 and they had three sons and three daughters. Their eldest son, James George, succeeded his father, becoming Sir James George Fitzgerald, the 9th Baronet. When he died without issue in 1867 the title passed to his younger brother who became Sir Gerald Richard Fitzgerald, 10th Baronet.[20]

Robert Dalton made his will on 26 July 1777. As we have seen he had already made provision for Bridget in their marriage settlement and to this he added another £100 (equivalent to around £7,800 today) and the furniture from the 'Lodging Room' in his house in Brook Street Bath! He left his three daughters who had become nuns £400 each, and his house in Charles Street, Lancaster, in trust for two of his unmarried daughters. The rest of his estates he left in trust for his other surviving children, the profits to be divided equally among them.[21] Robert died in 1785.

Bridget drew up her will on 3 August 1795 and added codicils on 4 June1796 and 13 January 1797. She died at Bath on 7 May 1797 and her will was proved in the Prerogative Court of Canterbury on 17 May 1797.[22] Bridget's will shows that she had invested her monies wisely. She had used her capital to buy two estates in Yorkshire and then mortgaged them back, with interest, to their owners – probably a way of helping them out of financial difficulties. She also bought a number of annuities and bonds that paid a good rate of interest. At her death her estate was worth the equivalent of around £2,000,000 at today's value. The double land tax on Catholics had been abolished in 1794 and the benefits of this had, no doubt, begun to show itself in increased profits from her lands.

As the bulk of Bridget's fortune had come from her husband it is not surprising that the main beneficiaries of her will were her son William Dalton Hoghton and her daughter Lady Bridget Anne Fitzgerald, but she also made smaller bequests in the form of the interest from a trust fund for her grandchildren James and Bridget Maria Fitzgerald until they reached the age of eighteen.

The End of the Barnburgh Line

Although we do not have any details of it, we know that before the marriage of Thomas More and Catherine Giffard a 'Deed of Entail' had been drawn up determining the way in which the remaining More estates should be passed down in the family in the event of the failure of the male line. As we have seen, it was Bridget's brother, Thomas IX, who inherited the estates on the death of his father. However, having become a Jesuit priest – and with his only other surviving sister a nun at Bruges – he 'resigned' his claim on the estates to Bridget before his death in 1795. Thus it came to pass that, through the line from Bridget and her first husband Peter Metcalfe of Brigg the last of the More inheritance became dispersed.

As we have seen, Bridget (More) and Peter Metcalfe's only son,

Thomas Peter Metcalfe, born on 4 July 1756, was still an infant when his father died and, on his mother's re-marriage, he became part of his step-father's extended family, first at Thurnham Hall, then at York, and finally, at Bath where he continued to live as an adult. On 28 August 1789 he married Teresa Throckmorton, the only daughter of George Throckmorton of Weston Underwood, Buckinghamshire, and his wife Anna Maria Paston.

The Throckmorton family traces its history back to the 1100s when John Throckmorton took his name from or gave it to the Manor of Throckmorton in the parish of Fladbury in Worcestershire. His son Thomas Throckmorton obtained the estate at Weston Underwood by marriage and, in the early 1400s Sir John Throckmorton, Under Treasurer of England, came into possession of the Coughton Estate near Alcester in Warwickshire. George Throckmorton would have inherited the Coughton Estate but he died before his father and so never came into possession of it. The Throckmorton's of Coughton, of Weston Underwood and later of Buckland remained Catholic throughout the Reformation and suffered much for their recusancy. Coughton Court, in particular, became famous not only as a centre of Catholic activities throughout the Reformation, but also because it was one of the first places to which news of the failure of the Gunpowder Plot was taken on 6 November 1606. After the Second World War Coughton Court was given to the National Trust but, by a special arrangement, the family still live there.

Teresa, born in August 1759, had four brothers, John Courtney, George, Charles and William, the first three of whom succeeded to the family title and became successively the 5th, 6th and 7th Baronets Throckmorton.

I have not been able to discover what marriage portion Teresa brought to the marriage, but we know from her will that, on the occasion of their marriage, Peter's mother had promised him £3,000 (equivalent, at that time, to around £210,000 today) from the profits of her Barnburgh and Haldenby estates – a sum of money that was not actually paid at the time.

After their marriage Thomas Peter and Teresa lived in Bath where the baptism of their three children – Maria Teresa on 6 February 1791, Mary Anne on 4 October 1792, and Thomas Peter on 25 April 1794 were recorded in the Catholic chapel there. Of these, Mary Anne survived only three months, her burial being noted in the register of the Catholic chapel as having taken place on 16 January 1793.

For Catholics, these were the years in which, during the Reign of George III, they began to be received back into English society on an almost equal footing with their Protestant contemporaries. The First Catholic Relief Act of 1788 had allowed Catholics to inherit and own land once again, and the Second Relief Act of 1791 had granted legal existence to Catholic chapels for the first time since the Reformation, and allowed Catholics to become members of most of the professions from which they had previously been excluded. During the French Revolution some 1500 Catholic priests fled to England. Penniless and with nowhere to live, many of them were, initially, housed in hostels funded by the Government. There was, in some places, a Protestant backlash to these measures – for example, the Gordon Riots of 1780, and the burning of a number of Catholic chapels around the country – but it was short-lived. The movement towards the acceptance of Catholics back into society was now unstoppable and, in 1828, it culminated in the repeal of the old Test Acts of 1673 and 1678, and the passing of the Catholic Emancipation Act in 1829. It was Thomas Peter and Teresa Metcalfe's children and descendants who would bring the history of the descendants of Saint Thomas More full circle – from their exclusion to their re-integration into English society.

Thomas Peter Metcalfe's marriage to Teresa was cut short after four years by his death, at the age of only thirty-seven, on 21 October 1793. His will, dated 13 September 1791, was proved in the Prerogative Court of Canterbury in London on 3 November 1793.[23] It is clear from his will that he had received a share of the profits from the Barnburgh, Moseley and Haldenby estates, as well as a Metcalfe estate at North Kelsey, South of Brigg, probably as part of his marriage settlement. The income from these had obviously been well invested, and he left £7,090 in mortgages and bonds arising out of these (equivalent to around £540,000 today).

Teresa drew up her will on 27 November 1821 but survived until 24 September 1824 when she died at the home of her daughter Maria Teresa Eyston at East Hendred in Berkshire (but now in Oxfordshire). She was buried near the Throckmorton estate in the church of St Mary at Buckland, Oxfordshire, where there is a tablet to her memory.

Teresa's will was proved in the Prerogative Court of Canterbury in London on 27 October 1824. In it she calls herself 'Teresa Metcalfe widow of Thomas Peter Metcalfe of Barnborough', indicating perhaps the importance she placed on the Barnburgh connection and her descent from Sir Thomas More.[24]

In her will Teresa makes mentions of a number of paintings in her house at Bath – two of Sir Thomas More, one of Bishop Fisher and one of Cardinal Pole – which she says were kindly lent to her by her son Thomas Peter More, and which it was obviously her intention should be returned to him when the lease on her house was given up – which, she says, should be one month after her death. Four other paintings are mentioned: one of her brother Courtenay Throckmorton she leaves to Thomas Peter, and two of her other brothers George Throckmorton and Sir John Throckmorton she leaves to her married daughter Teresa Maria Eyston. She does not disclose the subject of the fourth picture, but she says it was painted in Paris and she leaves it to Charles Eyston, her daughter's husband. As Thomas Peter had already taken possession of the More and Metcalfe estates that descended to him by the Deed of Entail mentioned above, all of the other bequests were of personal and household items. In particular she left a number of maps, all her annual registers (account books?), and the books with the Arms of More on them, as well as his father's globe and gold watch, to Thomas Peter. To Teresa Maria she leaves her glass and linen as well as some plate with the Arms of More and Metcalfe on it. Attached to the will are a series of nine codicils added between November 1821 and September 1823 that give the impression that she kept going over the small items, even trinkets, that she possessed, deciding to whom she should leave them.

As we have seen, Teresa's only son, Thomas Peter Metcalfe, was born on 25 April 1794. In her will of 1795 Bridget Dalton, his grandmother, had requested that the King be approached for permission for change his surname from 'Metcalfe' to 'More' in order to continue the More family name. So it was that, just over seven weeks after her death, on 24 June 1797, he became Thomas Peter More by Royal Sign Manual. Although his mother obviously agreed to this change there is some indication that she may have resented it as, in her will, she requests that any children he had should be christened Metcalfe 'in respect of his dear Father'.

On the death of his grandmother in 1797, Thomas Peter received £1,500 from the original £3,000 that she had invested in annuities and promised, but not paid, on the occasion of his father and mother's marriage. His sister, Maria Teresa, received the other £1,500. This is equivalent, to around £105,000 each today.

Thomas Peter More does not appear to have lived at Barnburgh, his home being at Shottery near Stratford-upon-Avon, Warwickshire, from where he managed his estates through an agent. Thomas Peter drew up his will on 21 June 1832, leaving his Yorkshire estates at Barnburgh, Moseley and Haldenby in Yorkshire, and his estate known as Harrington Manor at North Kelsey in Lincolnshire to Robert George Throckmorton of Buckland and Ferdinand Eyston of Overbury, for them to hold in trust for his sister Maria Teresa Eyston and, after her death, to her husband Charles Eyston and their heirs.

On 1 July 1833 Thomas Peter added a codicil to his will in which, after making various small bequests to his servants and friends, he finally discloses that he had two 'natural' (i.e. illegitimate) daughters, Matilda and Mary Anne, by an Anne Richardson living in Highgate near London. To each of these he left £200 (equivalent to around £12,000 each today) with the instruction that the money should be used to place them in 'some reputable employment'. He died at Birmingham five years later on 20 July 1838 and his body was taken for burial in the parish church at Coughton. His will was proved in the Prerogative Court of Canterbury at London on 18 September 1838.[25] It may be around this time that the copy of the Holbein portrait of the family of Sir Thomas More was transferred to the home of the Eyston family at East Hendred where it still hangs.

Thomas Peter More was survived by his older sister Maria Teresa Metcalfe. Maria Teresa married Charles Eyston of Hendred House, East Hendred at St Mary's Catholic chapel, Queens Square, Bath, on 13 October 1814. Charles was nine months older than Maria Teresa, having been born on 17 May 1790. The Eystons were a Catholic family who had lived at Hendred House since 1453 when the estate came into their possession through marriage. Like so many of the families into which her ancestors had married the Eystons had also suffered constantly for their adherence to the Catholic faith and, after Maria Teresa's marriage into the family, were proud of their descent from Sir Thomas More.

Charles and Maria Teresa Eyston had eight children born between 1815 and 1828. Maria Teresa died at Leamington Spa in Warwickshire on 19 March 1848 and her body was taken to Kemerton, Gloucestershire, for burial. Charles died in London on 24 February 1857 and was also buried at Kemerton.

Charles Eyston was succeeded by his eldest son, Charles John

Eyston, who married Agnes Mary Blount, the daughter of Michael Henry Blount Esq. of Mapledurham House near Reading in Oxfordshire, on 10 September 1863. Descendants of this line still live at Hendred House.

Charles John Eyston was a partner in the firm of Eyston and Mills, Lawyers, of Gray's Inn Square in London and, after the death of his father, he sold the Barnburgh estate at an auction held at the Angel Inn in Doncaster on 11 October 1859 – a sale sanctioned in the will of his uncle Thomas Peter More. Thus the history of its ownership by descendants of Sir Thomas More for nearly 300 years was brought to an end – and so my story has come full circle.

In the Prologue to his life of his great-grandfather, Cresacre More said that he had 'ventured to discourse a little of the life and death of this glorious martyr, not as one that might be thought fit to set his life forth with good grace, but as one moved by a natural affection for his ancestor'. I hope it may not sound too pretentious for me to say that what Cresacre did for his great-grandfather I have, with the same motives, tried to do for his descendants – my ancestors as well. Though not martyrs, or even saints, they were, almost all of them, true 'Confessors' of their Catholic faith.

And so, to paraphrase Shakespeare in *The Tempest*, I can now say: 'These our revels are now ended, and these our actors are melted into air, into thin air', and with him we can remind ourselves that, in the end, 'all we inherit shall dissolve and leave not a rack behind'.

Postscript

At the time of its sale in 1859 Barnburgh Hall had been let to tenants for over seventy years. Henrietta Griffith, the widow of Rev John Griffith, Rector of Handsworth, near Sheffield and her three spinster daughters, Elizabeth, Henrietta and Anna Marie, are recorded as living there in 1785, and the spinster sisters appear to have continued to occupy the hall until 1841 when Henry Hartop, the manager of Elsecar Ironworks north of Rotherham, took up residence. It remained in his family until 1911, after which it passed through various hands until it was bought by the Denaby and Cadeby Colliery. After the Second World War, when the mines were nationalized, it became the property of the National Coal Board who rented it out to some of their managers. In spite of it being a Grade II Listed Building, it was demolished in 1969 due to damage caused by mining subsidence. Local residents, however, claim that the damage could have been repaired, and that the real reason for its demolition was that this was a cheaper option than restoring it. The site of the hall is now occupied by a modern housing development called Barnburgh Hall Gardens. However, some of the garden walls, and the original Dovecote, a Grade II Listed Building, still stand, and the old stable block has been converted into a row of cottages.

Genealogical Summary

Thomas More VIII

Thomas More VIII (1692–1739) m. Catherine Giffard (1694–1767)
Children:
1. Thomas IX (1772–1795): became a Jesuit priest
2. Christopher (1729–1754): became a Jesuit priest
3. Basil (1730–1731)
4. Mary (1732–1807): became 'Mary Augustina' an Augustinian nun at Bruges
5. Catherine (1733–1784): unmarried
6. Bridget (b.1720/1728 – d.1797) m. (1) Peter Metcalfe of Brigg (d.1757)
    Children:
    i. Thomas Peter (1756–1793) m. Teresa Throckmorton (1759–1824)
        Children:
        i. Maria Teresa (1791–1848) m. Charles Eyston (1790–1857)
            Children: three sons and five daughters.
            [Succeeded by eldest son Charles John (1817–1883) who married Agnes Blount and had issue.]
        ii. Mary Anne (1792–1793)
        iii. Thomas Peter Metcalfe (1794-1838): assumed the name 'More' by Royal Sign Manual. Unmarried.
            Had two illegitimate children, Matilda and Mary Anne by Anne Richardson of Highgate, London.
    ii. Catherine (1757–1761)
    iii. Bridget Mary (born and died in 1758)
    m. (2) Robert Dalton (d.1785)
    Children:
    i. William Dalton Hoghton (b.1763) m. Louisa Smith
    ii. Bridget Anne m. Sir James Trant Fitzgerald and had issue.
    iii. Constantia (died unmarried)

Notes

Introduction pp. 1–11

1. It was Thomas More's friend, Erasmus, who witnessed the scene. See Marius, p. 87.
2. For a fuller description of the lives of Thomas More see Chambers, pp. 24–42.
3. The jewels, preserved for many years at St Omers, were transferred to the Jesuit College at Stonyhurst in 1794. They are now on long-term loan to the British Museum.
4. Archives of the Venerable English College, MS. 321.
   See: www.philological.bham.ac.uk/more/ms.html

Chapter 1 pp. 12–42

1. Pedigree of More of Barnborough Hall in *Pedigrees of the County Families of Yorkshire* by Joseph Foster, London, 1874.
2. Margaret Hastings, *Sir Thomas More's Ancestry*, Guildhall Miscellany 2:1 (1961).
3. A. Colin Cole, 'St Thomas More's quartering ... and a new "old grant"', in *The Coat of Arms*. N.S. vol.1 no. 93 (Spring 1975), pp. 126–31.
4. Germain Marc'hadour, 'The Death-date of More's Mother', in *Moreana*, no. 63 (Dec. 1979): 13–16.
5. *A Survey of London* (revised edn, 1602). Edited by H. Morley, 1912.
6. Over the years the name has been spelt in various ways including Northmymes, Northmymmes, Northmymys, and North Mimms. In 1939 the Parish Council, with the approval of Hertfordshire County decreed that the place would from then on be named North Mymms.
7. *The History and Antiquities of the County of Leicester*, vol. 4, part I, p. 225.
8. Robert Clutterbuck, *The History and Antiquities of Hertford*, 1815, vol. II, p. 449.

9. National Archives, Kew. Prob. 11/23.
10. Ackroyd, p. 9.
11. The Coat of Arms, ancestry and descent of this family may be seen under 'Staverton of Warville' in the *Visitations of Berkshire, 1623*, published by the Harleian Society, London, 1907.
12. The full wording of the entry of Thomas's birth has led some to suggest that the year of his birth was 1477. However, 1478 is now generally accepted.
13. For information about these families I am very much indebted to the following works: Bolwell, Robert W., *The Life and Works of John Heywood*; Reed, A. W., *Early Tudor Drama: Medwall, the Rastells, Heywood and the More Circle*; Gosse, Edmund, *The Life and Letters of John Donne*; Jessopp, Augustus, *John Donne Sometime Dean of St. Paul's*; Bald, R. C., *John Donne: A Life*.
14. Reed, p. 2.
15. This information comes from a court case in which John Rastell sought to recover money made by a third party for the hire of his costumes. See Bolwell, pp. 21–2.
16. National Archives, Kew. Prob. 11/26.
17. *Calendar of State Papers, Domestic Series, 1547–1580*, ed. Robert Lemon, London, 1856, p. 122.
18. The will was discovered by Professor Bang among the magisterial documents at Antwerp for the year 1564 and published in *Englische Studien*, vol. 38, p. 246.
19. This was granted at a meeting of the Common Council on 22 May 1523 the record of which says 'At the contemplacion of the Kynges letter, John Heywoode ys admitted to the liberties of this citie.' Letter Book N, ff.222 and 239. Quoted in Reed, p. 45.
20. See *Dictionary of National Biography* under 'Heywood, John', and compare with Reed pp. 37–40. Reed shows that 'our' John has been confused with another John Heywood who was in the royal service as a yeoman of the Crown.
21. *The King's Book of Payments, Henry VIII*, quoted in Bolwell, p. 8.
22. Brewer, *Letters & Papers Hen. VIII*, vol. III, pp. 445, 479, quoted in Bolwell, p. 11.
23. In 1517 Pope Leo X authorized the sale of indulgences and relics as a means of raising money to rebuild St Peter's in Rome.
24. Brewer, *Letters and Papers Henry VIII*, vol. V, p. 306, quoted in Bolwell, p. 13.
25. John Foxe, *Acts and Monuments*, London 1684, vol. II, p. 479, quoted in Bolwell, pp. 160–1.
26. John Stow, *Annales, or a Generall Chronicle of England*, London, 1631, p. 617, quoted in Bolwell, p. 55.
27. *Dictionary of National Biography* under 'Heywood, John'. Also, Bindoff, S.T. vol. II, pp. 335–7.
28. At the dissolution of the Abbey in 1539 Cromwell seized Broke Hall and the other abbey lands for himself. However, after his death, and by a grant signed at Windsor Castle on 21 November 1540 the lease was returned to John Heywood for a period of 21 years, at an increased rent.

29. Brewer, *Letters & Papers Henry VIII*, quoted in Bolwell, p. 42.
30. *Calendar of State Papers*, ed. Mary & Elizabeth Domestic, vol. I, p. 112, London, 1856.
31. *The Diary of Henry Machin, from 1550–1563*, quoted in Bolwell, p. 62.
32. See Bolwell, p. 68.
33. Modernized abstract from *State Papers*, quoted in Bolwell, p. 69.
34. W. Bang in *Englische Studien*, band 38, p. 238.
35. Quoted in Bolwell, p. 74.
36. *Bibliothèque de la Compagnie de Jésus*, Nouvelle Edition, par Carlos Sommervogel, SJ, Bibliographie, Tome IV, Alphonse Picard, Paris, 1893. Jesuit Archives, Naples.
37. See Bolwell, p. 66.
38. Anthony à Wood, *Athenae Oxoniensis*, ed. Philip Bliss, vol. I., p. 663, quoted in Bolwell, p. 65.
39. *Dictionary of National Biography* under 'Heywood, Jasper'. Also Reed, p. 66.
40. *Diccionario Histórico de la Compañía de Jesús*, Biográfico-Temático. vol. II, Universidad Pontificia Comillas, Madrid, 2001. Jesuit Archives, Naples.
41. From *Documents Relating to the English Martyrs*, Catholic Record Society, vol. V, 1908, p. 60, quoted in Bald, pp. 41–2.
42. *Istoria della Compagnia di Giesu Appartenente Al Regno di Napoli*, Descritta da Francesco Schinosi. Parte Seconda. In Nap. Nella Stampa di Michele Luigi Mutio. 1711. Jesuit Archives, Naples.
43. See Bald, p. 36, note 4.
44. All the properties in Bread Street were destroyed by the Great Fire of London in 1666.
45. Bald, pp. 20–1.
46. Ibid. p. 115.
47. Ibid. p. 267.
48. Ibid. p. 231.
49. *The Records of the Honourable Society of Lincoln's Inn: Admissions 1420–1893*, compiled by R. A. Roberts, published by Lincoln's Inn, London, 1896.
These records are known as the *Black Books*. Information on John's membership of Lincoln's Inn kindly provided from the *Black Books* by the archivist at the Inn.
50. Bald, p. 72.
51. Bald, R. C., op. cit. Also Stubbs, John, *Donne The Reformed Soul*, Viking/Penguin Books, 2006.
52. Bald, pp. 128–54.

Chapter 2 pp. 43–89

1. Although a long tradition has given the name 'Jane' to Thomas's wife – and I will follow that tradition – it seems certain from the earliest literary reference to her that she was actually called Joan. See *Moreana* XXIX, 109 (March 1992), pp. 3–22.

2. Rowse, pp. 28–9.
3. The family name has been spelt variously as 'Colt', 'Colte' and 'Coult'.
4. *Roper's Life of More*, Early English Text Society, pp. 106–9. Also *Visitation of Suffolk, 1561*, Harleian Society, London, 1981.
5. *Miscellaneous Essex Pedigrees* (Harleian Soc. vol. XIV, 1879) and *Visitations of Suffolk, 1561* (op. cit.) both, wrongly, call Jane's Mother 'Jane'.
6. *Harpsfield's Life of More*.
7. The original church was destroyed in 1666 during the Great Fire of London. The present Church, built 1672–9, was designed by Sir Christopher Wren.
8. See *John Clement and His Books* by A. W. Reed: The Library, 4th Series, vol. VI (1926), pp. 329–39. See: www.tertullian.org/articles/reed_john_clement _and_his_books.htm
9. English Historical Review (1892), vii. 714. Quoted in E. M. G. Routh, *Sir Thomas More and his Friends*, p. 46n.
10. Harpsfield, pp. 93–4.
11. Ruth Norrington, *In the Shadow of a Saint*, pp. 9–19 and p. 63.
12. Quoted in Marius, p. 225.
13. Bridgett, pp.132–4. Also Routh, pp. 124–6.
14. Norrington, p. 41 and Stapleton, p. 93.
15. It was not until the Council of Trent in 1545 that the Catholic Church finally accepted that women had souls – a matter much in dispute till then!
16. Quoted in Stapleton, p.105.
17. *Yorkshire Star Chamber Proceedings, Vol. IV*, ed. John Lister, The Yorkshire Archaeological Society Record Series, vol. LXX, 1926, pp. 28–36.
18. *The Visitations of Derbyshire* record a family of Ropers/Roopers in Heanor, in the 1600s.
19. See *Roper's Life of More*, EETS, Introduction pp. xxix–xxxi.
20. John Aubrey, *Brief Lives*, unpublished at Aubrey's death in 1697. Quoted from 1950 edition by O. L. Dick. See *Utopia*, Penguin Classics, 1965. Notes, p. 133.
21. This was one of the charges later levelled at Anne Boleyn.
22. E. E. Reynolds, 'More's Manors' in *Moreana* 12 (1966), p. 81.
23. Harpsfield, Historical Notes, p. 314.
24. Armitage, p. 2.
25. Harpfield, p. 86.
26. Quoted in Ackroyd, p. 226.
27. Ford Castle remained in the Heron family until 1718. The present castle (only a part of which now remains as a ruin) was built by Cuthbert Heron in 1621.
28. Sir John had made his will three years previously at Calais. He was buried at Hackney. (See Lincolnshire Pedigrees, vol. II, Harleian Society, vol. LI., 1903.)
29. Sir John Crosby rebuilt an existing property in 1466 to create Crosby Hall. It is called 'Crosbies Place' in Shakespeare's King Richard III. (See Clapham, W. and Godfrey, Walter H., 'Some Famous Buildings and their Story'. The Hall was taken down and moved to its present location in Chelsea in 1910.

30. Armitage, *Allegations for Marriage Licences issued by the Bishop of London: 1520–1610*. The wedding is recorded as having taken place in the Allington Chapel. However, Norrington, p. 53, points out that it was in the Elrington Chapel.
31. See (1) The paper by F. Carpinelli, 'Thomas More and the Daunce Family', in: Moore, Michael J. (ed.) *Quincentennial Essays on St.Thomas More*.
32. Routh, p. 143.
33. The site of the landing stage is believed to be near the present footings at the North end of Battersea Bridge.
34. Clapham and Godfrey, pp. 77–102.
35. Quoted in Routh, p. 139 and Norrington, p. 63.
36. Guy, p. 78.
37. See *The Thomas More Family Group Portraits After Holbein*, Lesley Lewis, FSA for Thomas More Picture Trust, Gracewing, 1998.
38. Nostell Priory, the ancestral home of the Winn family, is managed by the National Trust from whom details of opening times can be obtained.
39. William Roper, *The Lyfe of Sir Thomas More*, Internet Modern History Sources, 1998, p. 13.
40. Harpsfield, p. 145.
41. Stapleton, p. 144.
42. Norrington, p. 38.
43. The 'Farm House' was rebuilt by Sir Theodore Mayerne, Physician to James I, and later again (c.1674) by the Earl of Lindsey from whom it took the name 'Lindsey House'.
44. Antonia Fraser, *The Six Wives of Henry VIII*, Weidenfeld & Nicholson, London, 1992, p. 186.
45. Roper's *Life*, in Rowse, p. 66.
46. Norrington, pp. 82–4. Ackroyd, pp. 356–7.
47. Ackroyd, p. 380.
48. Stapleton pp. 180–1.
49. Stapleton, pp. 191–2. Norrington, p. 108.
50. See Note in *Harpsfield's Life of More*, Early English Text Society, p. 278.
51. Norrington, pp. 109–19.
52. Clapham and Godfrey, pp. 79–103.
53. *Roper's Life of More*. EETS, pp. xxxiv–xxxvi. John Roper was buried in the Roper vault in the chapel of St Nicholas in the church of St Dunstan's, Canterbury on 7 April 1524.
54. Ackroyd, p. 253.
55. *Roper's Life of More*, EETS, pp. xxiv–xlii.
56. Ibid.
57. Harpsfield, pp. 89, 331.
58. *Roper's Life of More*, EETS, p. xxxi.
59. *Dictionary of National Biography*, see under 'Roper, William'.
60. *Roper's Life of More*, EETS, pp. xxxi–xxxiv.
61. National Archives, Kew. Prob. 11/60.
62. Hugh O. Albin, 'Opening the Roper Vault in St Dunstan's Canterbury and

thoughts on the burial of William and Margaret Roper', *Moreana* 63 (1979), pp. 29–35.
63. *Roper's Life of More*, EETS, pp. xxxix–xl.
64. For information about the Roper descent I have relied heavily on *The Visitations of Kent, 1619*, Harleian Society, vol. XLII, London, 1898. Also *Roper's Life of More*, EETS.
65. See Burke's *Commoners* pedigree of Bray of Shere.
66. See Burke's *Commoners*, vol. IV, pp. 10–11. Also 'Dawtrey' in Hasler, P. W., *The History of the House of Commons: 1558–1606*, vol. II. See also the History of Scardeville Family at: http://pwl.netcom.com/~gbell/scardevl.htm
67. See Bindoff, vol. I, pp. 392–4.
68. See Harpsfield, p. 334.
69. National Archives, Kew. Prob. 11/42A.
70. Ibid. Prob. 11/54.
71. Catholic Record Society: Miscellanea. vol. IV, 1969 edition, p. 71.
72. See Bindoff, vol. I, p. 393.
73. *The Venerabile*, 24 (1967–68), pp. 281–90.
74. See *The Parish Church of St. Dunstan, Canterbury, Kent* by Hugh O. Albin, 1988. Also Bindoff, vol. III, pp. 214–5.
75. See *Moreana*, vol. 8, no. 29, March, 1971, pp. 13–15 and *Moreana* vol. 11, October 1954, pp. 41–5. Also, the *Responsa Scholarum of the English College, Rome*, Part I: 1598–1621. CRS, 1962, pp. 116, 176.
76. See pedigree on inside back page of *Guide to Nostell Priory*, National Trust, 2001.
77. *Calendar of the Committee for Compounding, 1643–1660*, vol. IV, HMSO, no. 3009, 1992.
78. Catholic Record Society, *Miscellanea*, Recusant Records, vol. 53 (1961), pp. 344, 427–31.
79. Catholic Record Society, *Miscellanea IV*, 1907.
80. For details of the Constable family of Everingham I have relied heavily on *The Chronicles of the English Augustinian Canonesses Regular of the Lateran, at St. Monica's in Louvain*, pp. 229–36.
81. *Victoria County History of Middlesex*: Ossulstone Hundred. Also Powell, Victoria History of Essex, Vol. VI, pp. 166–7. Also *Lincolnshire Pedigrees*: Heron of Cressey Hall. Also *Letters and Papers of Henry VIII* (1533), vol. VI, no. 299, p. 140.
82. Harpsfield, p. 53; Guy, p. 137.
83. Private Act 32 Henry VIII, ch. 38: 'An Act for the Attainder of Giles Heron'. Also: Parl. Roll, 32 Henry VIII, c. 56. Both quoted in *Roper's Life of More*, EETS. pp. 118–19.
84. Private Act 31 Henry VIII. ch.19: 'Assurance of Rycott Manor to Sir John Williams.' For more about Rycote see: www.thamehistory.net/places/RycotePalace.htm
85. *Roper's Life of More*, EETS. p. 120.
86. Proceedings of the Privy Council. Quoted in *Roper's Life of More*, EETS. pp. 120–1.

87. Stapleton, p. 93.
88. *Victoria County History of Middlesex:* Ossulstone Hundred.
89. *Lincolnshire Pedigrees,* op. cit. Also Burke, *Family Records,* p. 347.
90. From the Letters and Papers of Henry VIII, vol. III, pt. II and vol. IV. Quoted in Moore, *Quincentennial Essays,* p. 8.
91. See: www.middlesexpast.net/exeter.html
92. See Roper's 'Life of More' in *A Man of Singular Virtue,* pp. 59–60. Also Marius, p. 374.
93. Letters and Papers, Foreign and Domestic of Henry VIII, vol. XXI, part II (1546), no. 476.
94. Stapleton, p. 93.
95. Frank Carpinelli, 'Thomas More and the Daunce Family' in Moore *Quincentennial Essays,* p. 3.
96. Thomas More, *Utopia,* Penguin Classics. Notes 8 & 10, p. 134.
97. Thomas Merriam, John Clement: his identity, and his Marshfoot House in Essex, in *Moreana* XXV (March 1988), p. 146.
98. *Chronicle of the English Canonesses Regular of the Lateran at St. Monica's in Louvain,* pp. 3–4, 9.
99. *Moreana* XXV (March 1988), p. 146.
100. *Chronicle of the English Canonesses Regular of the Lateran at St. Monica's, Louvain,* pp. 24–7.
101. *Moreana* XXV (March 1988) p. 147.
102. Ibid. p. 148.
103. *Chronicle of the English Canonesses Regular of the Lateran at St. Monica's in Louvain,* pp. 6–7.

Chapter 3 pp. 90–111

1. Harpsfied, p. 95.
2. *Roper's Life of More,* EETS, Historical Notes pp. 108–9.
3. *Yorkshire Star Chamber Proceedings,* vol. IV, ed. John Lister. Yorkshire Archaeological Society Record Series. vol. LXX, 1926, pp. 28–36.
4. Rev J. Hunter, *Classic County Histories: South Yorkshire,* J. B. Nichols, London, 1828. p. 371. See also Parker, Rev. W. J. *The Cresacre Treasure: The Church and Village of Barnburgh,* Privately printed.
5. Norrington, p. 69.
6. Norrington, p. 115 and footnote 177, p. 143.
7. Letters and Papers of Henry VIII, 1544, Part 1, 444 (6). Quoted in *Roper's Life of More,* EETS. pp. 116–17.
8. Pedigree of West of Aughton/Aston in Clay, J. W. (ed.), *Visitation of Yorkshire, 1585,'* Vol. II.
9. Quoted in Hyland: *A Century of Persecution Under Tudor and Stuart Sovereigns',* p .133.
10. 'Feet of Fines for the Tudor Period', Pt. II: 1571–1582/3. Yorkshire

Archaeological and Topographical Association Record Series, vol. V. 1888, p. 39.
11. Hugh Aveling, 'The More Family in Yorkshire', in *Essential Articles for the Study of Thomas More*, R. S. Sylvester and G. Marc'hadour (eds), Archon Books, Hamden, Connecticut, 1977, p. 35.
12. 'Monumental Brasses in the West Riding' in *Yorkshire Archaeological Journal*.
13. Cresacre More, *Life of Sir Thomas More*, pp. 291–2.
14 From a copy in the British Museum.
15. *Essex Recusant*, CRS Series, vol. 3, 1961.
16. The pardon is to be found in *Calendar of Patent Rolls, Elizabeth, vol. II 1560–1563*, p. 245. HMSO 1948. For this and all that follows on Edward I have relied heavily on the following: (1) Shanahan, D., 'The Family of St. Thomas More in Essex, 1581–1640', in *The Essex Recusant*, vol. 3, 1961, pp. 118–19. (2) Aveling, Hugh OSB, 'St. Thomas More's Family Circle and Yorkshire', in *Recusant History: Continuing Biographical Studies*, vol. 6, pp. 240–2, Arundel Press, Bognor Regis, 1961–62. (3) Aveling, J. C. H., 'The More Family and Yorkshire', in CRS, *Recusant History*, vol. VI, No. 5. pp. 26–48.
17. See Yorkshire Archaeological and Topographical Association, Record Series II, 'Feet of Fines of the Tudor Period, Pt 1', published 1887. Note: The 'Feet of Fines' were not records of fines in our sense of the word, but an amicable means of transferring property through a proper legal process. The fine itself was a tax paid to the Exchequer for the process involved.
18. 'Pedigree of More of Barnborough Hall' in Joseph Foster's *Pedigrees of the County Families of Yorkshire*.
19. Cresacre More, p. 291.
20. See 'Pedigree of More of Barnborough' in Foley's *Record of the Jesuits,'* vol. XII, facing page 702.
21. Cresacre More, p. 291.
22. See: http://eagle.cch.kcl.ac.uk:8080/cce/
23. The will (in Latin) is reproduced in an article by Prof. W. Bang entitled '*Acta Anglo-Lovaniensia*', in *Englische Studien*, Band 38, 1907, pp. 238–41.
24. Ibid. pp. 243–4.

Chapter 4 pp. 112–50

1. *Victoria County of Buckinghamshire*, vol. III, p. 48.
2. Mary Scrope is recorded as having five brothers: Ralph (eldest son and heir of his father), Adrian, Robert, Henry, and John, and one sister, Margaret. See 'Scrope of Cockerington' in *Lincolnshire Pedigrees*, vol. I.
3. CRS, *Miscellanea: Recusant Records*. vol. LIII, 1960, p. 291.
4. West Yorkshire Archive Service, Calderdale. Deeds relating to Bolton. Ref: KM/382.
5. *Essex Recusant*, vol. I, no. 2 (Aug 1959), p. 68.

6. Aveling, op. cit., p. 39.
7. Essex Record Office. Document Ref. Q/SR 125/52.
8. *Victoria County History of Essex*, vol. VI, OUP 1973, p. 223.
9. Shanalian, Mgr D., 'The Family of St. Thomas More in Essex: 1581–1640', in *Essex Recusant*, vol. 1, no. 2 (Aug. 1959). Green Street can still be seen in Greater London Street Maps running between the Romford Road to the north and Barking Road to the south.
10. 'The Memoirs of Fr. Robert Persons' in CRS, *Miscellanea*, vol. IV, 1907. pp. 3–5.
11. Quoted in Harpsfield, p. 294.
12. Quoted in Hyland, p. 390.
13. CRS, *Miscellanea: Recusant Records*, vol. LIII, 1960, pp. 245–79.
14. 'The Memoirs of Father Robert Persons', in CRS, *Miscellanea*, vol. IV, 1969, p. 79.
15. State Papers, Domestic, Elizabeth, clxviii, n. 35, quoted in *Essex Recusant*, vol. 1, no. 3 (Aug. 1959), p. 70.
16. State Papers, Domestic, Elizabeth, clxxii, n. 104. Quoted in *Essex Recusant*, vol. 1, no. 3 (Aug. 1959), p. 70.
17. The Marshalsea made famous by Charles Dickens in his *Little Dorrit* was a Victorian replacement for the Marshalsea where Thomas was a prisoner. The Victorian prison was built near to the old one.
18. Loseley Papers vol. V, no. 29, quoted in Hyland, p. 403.
19. Ibid. p. 396.
20. State Papers, Domestic. Elizabeth cxcv, n. 74, quoted in *Essex Recusant*, vol. 1, no. 2 (Aug. 1959), p. 71.
21. Ibid.
22. Quoted in *Essex Recusant*, vol. 1, no. 3 (Dec. 1959), p. 97.
23. Act of 29 Elizabeth, ch. 6.
24. 'The Family of Thomas More in Essex: 1581–1640: Thomas More II continued' in *Essex Recusant*, vol. 3, no. 2, (Aug. 1961), pp. 71–80.
25. Ibid.
26. Essex Record Office: Q/SR 125/52 (1593).
27. Essex Quarter Sessions: Session of March 1603. See Essex Record Office: Q/SR 162/72.
28. Historical MSS Commission 10th Report, Appendix IV: The Manuscripts of the Earl of Westmorland, p. 485.
29. *Essex Recusant*, vol. 3, no. 2 (Aug. 1961), p. 75.
30. British Museum, Lansdowne MSS 89, f. 60. Quoted in Essex Recusant, vol. 6, no. 3 (Dec. 1964), pp. 96, 97.
31. National Archives. Stafford Quire 51–101. Prob/11/108.
32. D/AEA 23 fol. 137a, quoted in *Essex Recusant*, vol. 1, no. 3 (Dec. 1959), p.102.
33. Spelling of family names was more fluid in those days, and some documents (invariably copied by clerks) spell the Haddon family as 'Moore'. However, Edward and Mary's daughter Joan spelt their name 'More' so I have assumed that this is the way the family wrote their own name.
34. *Yorkshire Pedigrees* transcribed and edited by J. W. Walker, John Whitehead and Son, Leeds, 1944.

35. National Archives. Cat. Ref: Prob/11/29.
36. Guildhall Library Ms. 9186/16. Fo. 8v, quoted in *Essex Recusant*, vol. 18, p. 88.
37. Questier, p. 253-4.
38. See Wekking, pp. 14-16. Also: CRS, *Records of the Abbey of Our Lady of Consolation at Cambrai, 1620-1793*, XIII (Miscell. VIII), London, 1913, p. 40.
39. *Visitations of London, 1633-35*, p. 71.
40. Godfrey Anstruther, OP, 'The Insolence of Fr. Lusher' in *London Recusant*, vol. I, p. 64-7.
41. CRS, *The Responsa Scholarum of the English College, Rome, Part II: 1622-1685*, vol. 55, 1963, p. 554.
42. 'The Insolence of Fr. Lusher'. See note 40 above.
43. 'Annual Report of St. Omers College, 1601', in Foley's *Records of the English Jesuits*, vol. II, p. 417.
44. *Essex Recusant*, vol. 23 (1981), p. 13.
45. For this and what follows on Henry I have relied heavily on the Introduction to Edwards, Francis, SJ (ed.), *The Elizabethan Jesuits*, Phillimore Co. Ltd, 1981, pp. 1-9.
46. This is now edited, translated and published with the title *The Elizabethan Jesuits*. Cf. note 45 above. His other works were *Vita et Doctrina Christi Domini in meditationes quotidianas per annum digesta* (published in Antwerp in 1649), an English version of the same called *Life and Doctrines of our Saviour Jesus Christ* (published in Ghent in 1656 and in London in 1880). His translations were *Manual of Meditations* (published in 1618 – a work originally by Jerome Platus), and *Happiness of the Religious State* (published in 1632, and originally by Thomas de Villa Castin).
47. CRS, *The Responsa Scholarum of the English College, Rome, Part I: 1598-1621*, vol. 54 (1962), p. 105.
48. For information on Thomas I have relied heavily on John Foley's *Records of the Jesuits*, vol. XII, pp. 702-3.
49. Essex Quarter Session Rolls in *Essex Recusant*, vol. 25 (1983).
50. Transcripts of parish register, courtesy of Doncaster Records Office.
51. See Foster, J., *Alumni Oxoniensis, 1500-1714*.
52. Prison Lists published in CRS, vol. II (1906), p. 224.
53. *Essex Recusant*, vol. 19, no. 1 (1977), p. 3.
54. Ibid. p. 4.
55. See under 'Lawrence Povey' on www.FamilySearch.com Other Internet genealogy sites record Lawrence's mother as either Elizabeth Hobson or Alys Hyarde but none offer any source for this information.
56. National Archives, Kew. Register: Lawe Quire, nos. 67-127. Cat. Ref: Prob. 11/24.
57. Harleian Society, vol. XIII, 1878.
58. For information about William Bird and his family I have relied on John Harley's *William Byrd: Gentleman of the Chapel Royal*, Scholar Press, Aldershot, 1977.
59. See lists of Essex Recusants in 'Exchequer Documents, 1582-1642' in *Essex*

Recusant, vol. 1, no. 2 (Aug. 1959), pp. 51–61; vol. I, no. 3 (Dec. 1959), pp. 95–103, vol. 3, no. 1 (April 1961), pp. 24–30. Also in vol. 22 (1980); vol. 23 (1981); vol. 25 (1983).
60. Historical MSS Commission 10th Report, Appendix IV: The Manuscripts of the Earl of Westmorland. p. 486.
61. Knox, p. 193.
62. Ibid. p. 202.
63. For information on Thomas IV and Henry I have relied heavily on the article by Francis G. Murray in 'The Contribution of the More Family to the Counter-Reformation' in *Venerabile*, 25 (1969), pp. 113–23. See also CRS, *Registers of the English College at Valladolid, 1589–1862*, vol. XXX, 1930, pp. 16–17.
64. Smith R., *An Elizabethan Recusant House*, ed. Southern, pp. 42–3, 80–1.
65. Edwards, pp. 185–7.
66. Questier, pp. 41–278.
67. Letter of Christopher Bagshaw to Thomas More, 4 August 1609, in *Newsletters ...*, p. 50.
68. See Introduction by Joseph Hunter to his *The Life of Thomas More* by Cresacre More, p. xxvii.
69. For details of Thomas IV's death and a summary of his will (original in Westminster Cathedral Archives) I have relied on Mgr Shanahan's article 'Thomas More IV Secular Priest 1565–1625' in *Essex Recusant*, vol. 7 (1965), pp. 105–14.
70. National Archives: Ref. SP 12/60/70. Quoted in notes to Cresacre More's will in *London Recusant*, vol. 3 (1973), pp. 91–8.
71. See Nolan, M. M., 'Two Whitbred Wills' in *Essex Recusant* vol. 7 (Dec. 1965), pp. 115–25.
72. 'Papist Tombs in Essex Churches' in *Essex Recusant*, vol. 3 (April 1961), pp. 36–7.
73. I have a copy of this indenture, the original of which belongs to another descendant of Sir Thomas More.
74. *Victoria County History of the County of Oxford*, vol. XI, p. 27.
75. *Visitations of Oxford, 1669 and 1675*, Harleian Society New Series, vol. 12, London, 1993, pp. 22, 23.
76. The Latin inscription uses the 'Kalends' of the Julian Calendar which has here been converted to give the modern equivalent.
77. CRS, *Miscellanea*, vol. XII, 1921, p. 98.

Chapter 5 pp. 151–82

1. The Fathers of the London Oratory (eds), *The First and Second Diaries of the English College, Douai*, 1878, p. 213.
2. Ibid. p. 232. The Minor Orders were abolished in the 1960s.
3. Ibid. p. 250.

Notes

4. Wekking, p. 11.
5. Foley, vol. VI, p. 570.
6. Public Records Office: Ref. E. 337/8 (London/Middlesex).
7. Essex Record Office, Assize File 35/43/T/94.
8. The Mansion of Michelgrove was eventually bought by one of the Dukes of Norfolk who demolished it in 1828. Hemsted House was rebuilt in 1860 and now houses Benenden School, one of the top public schools for girls in England.
9. See under 'Gage' in Burke's *Peerage and Baronetage*.
10. Archive of the Gage Family of Firle. East Sussex Record Office. Ref: SAS/G21/59.
11. Ibid. Ref: SAS/G7/12.
12. Ibid. Ref: SAS/G21/60.
13. Public Act, 3 James I (1605), chapters 3 and 4.
14. Mgr D. Shanahan, *The Family of St. Thomas More in Essex, 1581–1640*, Essex Recusant, vol. 4 (1962), p. 58.
15. National Archives. Stafford Quire 51–101. Prob/11/108.
16. For what follows I have relied heavily on transcribed and paraphrased extracts from the Lord Treasurer's Remembrancer's Memoranda Roll, 4 James I, Hilary Term. Quoted in *Essex Recusant*, vol. 3, no. 2 (Aug. 1961), pp. 74–8.
17. Essex Quarter Session Rolls. Quoted in *Essex Recusant*, vol. 21 (1979), p. 12.
18. In addition to his estates at Chaddesley Corbett, Humphrey Packington owned Harvington Hall, near Kidderminster which may have been the family home. The Hall, famous for its priest-holes, passed to the Throckmorton family through the marriage of his granddaughter. The Hall now belongs to the Archdiocese of Birmingham and is open to the public.
19. Calendar of Patent Rolls 5 James 1 (fol. 33v.), Quoted in *Essex Recusant*, vol. 4 (1962), p. 60.
20. Patent Roll, National Archives: C.66/1739 (item 3), Quoted in *Essex Recusant*, vol. 4 (1962), pp. 60–2.
21. Ibid. p. 63.
22. British Museum. Lansdowne MSS. 90., No. 46, fol. 91. Quoted in *Essex Recusant*, vol. 4, no. 3 (Dec. 1962), pp. 103–4.
23. Cockburn, J. S., *Calendar of Assize Records*, HMSO, London, 1982, pp. 131–2.
24. Questier, p. 161.
25. Ibid. p. 120.
26. Ibid. p. 121.
27. Essex Record Office. Ref: Q/SR 203/123.
28. Mgr D. Shanahan in *Essex Recusant*, vol. 4, no. 3, p. 106.
29. Memoranda Roll of the Lord Treasurer's Remembrancer. Hilary Term 12 James I. PRO E368/556, membrane 206. Quoted in *Essex Recusant*, vol. 5, no. 2, August 1963. pp. 51–3.
30. Quoted in *Essex Recusant*, vol. 5, no. 2, August 1963, pp. 53–6.
31. Ibid. pp. 55–6.
32. Quoted in *Essex Recusant*, vol. 8, no. 3. Dec. 1966, p. 100.

33. 34. PRO E.115/126/69, quoted in *Essex Recusant*, vol. 6, no. 1 (April 1964).
34. *Calendar of State Papers (Domestic) 1619–1623*, vol. I, p. 32. Longman, Brown, Green, Longmans & Roberts, London, 1858.
35. Wekking, pp. 12–13.
36. *The English Benedictine Nuns of Paris, now at Colwich*, Notes and Obituaries in CRS vol. IX (Miscell. vol. VII), London, 1911, p. 365.
37. Ibid. p. 23.
38. Mgr D. Shanahan, 'The English Benedictine Convent in Cambrai 1623–1793', in *Essex Recusant*, vol. 17, no. 1 (April 1975).
39. Dame Frideswide Sandeman, OSB, *Dame Gertrude More*, Gracewing Fowler Wright Books, Leominster, 1997, p. 5.
40. After a period of imprisonment in Compiegne (where four of them died) they were released in April 1795 after the fall of Robespierre and made their way to England. Here they had various homes until finally settling at Stanbrook Abbey in 1838.
41. Wekking. op. cit. pp. 13–14.
42. Ibid., p. xxii.
43. Ibid., p. 19.
44. Ibid., p. 21.
45. Dame Frideswide Sandeman. op. cit. p. 11.
46. Wekking, op. cit., p. 30.
47. Ibid., p. 33.
48. Ibid., p. xxx.
49. Ibid., p. xiii.
50. Ibid.
51. Ibid., p. xiv.
52. Ibid.
53. For this and what follows regarding Dame Bridget More I have relied on her obituary dated 1692, quoted in CRS, Vol. IX, 1911, pp. 365–8. Also on the Colwich Abbey Website at www.colwichabbey.org.uk
54. *Records of the Abbey of Our Lady of Consolation at Cambrai, 1620–1793*, CRS, vol. XIII (Miscellaneous vol. VIII), 1913, p. 43.
55. Acts of the Privy Council, quoted in *Essex Recusant*, vol. 6, no. 1, p. 5.
56. National Archives, Fairfax Quire 1–57. Prob. 11/207.
57. Robinson, Rev. Charles J., *A History of the Mansions and Manors of Herefordshire*, first published 1872, Scholar Press edition, p. 192.
58. Ref. AW28/21/10 and AW28/20/14.
59. Preamble to the Protestation Oath. See Kenyon, J. P. (ed.) *The Stuart Constitution, 1603–1688*, 2nd edition, 1986, p. 200.
60. Calendar of the Committee for Advance of Money, Pt. I, p. 7, quoted in *Essex Recusant*, vol. 1, no. 6 (April 1964), p. 7.
61. Documents of the Committee for Compounding with Delinquents. National Archives SP. 23/100,757, quoted in 'Cresacre and Thomas More during the English Revolution, 1640-1660', *Moreana* 42 (1974).
62. National Archives, Fairfax Quire 1–57. Prob. 11/207.

Chapter 6 pp. 183–208

1. *Essex Recusant*, vol. 6, no.1 (April 1964), p. 5.
2. Thomas's sister Bridget set off for Cambrai the day after the wedding and arrived there on 28 June 1629. The journey in those days seems to have taken around three weeks.
3. *The English Benedictine Nuns of Paris, now at Colwich*, Notes and Obituaries, CRS, vol. IX (Miscell. VII), London, 1911, p. 365.
4. Mary E. Finch, *Five Northamptonshire Families, 1540–1640*.
5. According to Manuscript Notes on the Brooke family in Shropshire Archives, after the death of their mother in 1606 Basil's brother Francis went to Ireland where he and his wife (née Leinster) lived at Maglerabeg and Brooke Manor in Donegal. Their son and heir, Henry Brooke, became Governor of Donegal and received grants of land in County Fermanagh for services rendered to the Crown during the rebellion of 1641. These lands became known as Brookborough. The family residence about five miles away later became known as 'Coalbrooke', a combination of the names Brooke and Cole – Henry Brooke's son Thomas having married Catherine the daughter of Sir John Cole.
6. Monumental Inscriptions. Madeley church 1815. British Museum 21, 181.
7. Foster, *Alumni Oxoniensis 1500–1714*.
8. *Calendar of State Papers James I: Domestic (1625–1649)*, Eyre and Spottiswoode (eds), Longman, Browne, Green, Longman & Robertson, London, 1858, p. 533.
9. Ibid. p. 18.
10. See www.ironbridge.org.uk/v_museums.asp
11. See *Dictionary of National Biography* under 'Brooke, Sir Basil. Also, *Victoria County History of Shropshire*, vol. XI, pp. 35–8.
12. Frances was the widow of Sir Thomas Neville, but by birth the daughter of Henry, 4th Baron of Turvey, Bedfordshire. By her Sir Basil had a son, John, who died in April 1645, and a daughter, Frances, who married Richard Fermor of Somerton, Oxfordshire.
13. Hertfordshire Archives and Local Studies. MS. 10475.
14. Sheffield Archives. Catalogue Ref. SY265/Z.
15. Documents of the Committee for Compounding. National Archives: SP. 23/100, 766.
16. Ibid. SP. 23/100, 757.
17. Ibid. SP. 23/11, 7.
18. Firth, C. H. & Rait, R. S., *Acts and Ordinances of the Interregnum, 1642–1660*, London, 1911, vol. I, p. 254.
19. Hertfordshire Archives and Local Studies. Ref: DEGA/23696-23697.
20. Courtesy of Hertfordshire Archives and Local Studies.
21. 'Sheldon Pedigree' in Foley's *Records of the Jesuits*, vol. V, facing p. 550.
22. Kirkus, pp. 1–2.
23. In *The Stuart Age: England 1603–1714* the historian Barry Coward says: 'There was no Popish Plot. Most of the details of the conspiracy master-

minded by the Jesuits to assassinate the king had their origins in the twisted minds of Titus Oates and Israel Tonge.' 3rd edition, Pearson Educational Limited, 2003, p. 325.
24. Kirkus, pp. 132–3.
25. Ibid. p. 132.
26. Armitage, George (ed.), *Marriage Allegations in the Registry of the Vicar General of the Archbishop of Canterbury 1669–1679*, Harleian Society, vol. XXXIV, London, 1892, p. 26.
27. Burton and Williams, p. 506.
28. National Archives: Prob. 11/322.
29. Courtesy of Herefordshire Record Office.
30. Burton and Williams, p. 512.
31. Joseph Foster's pedigree is in *Pedigrees of the County Families of Yorkshire*, vol. II: 'West Riding'. Robert Clutterbuck's pedigree is in *The History and Antiquities of Hertfordshire*, vol. I, p. 452. Joseph Hunter's pedigree is in *Classical County Histories*, vol. III: 'South Yorkshire', p. 376.
32. I am afraid I only have an old copy of the relevant page in Burke's *Landed Gentry*. The page number is 1184, but I have no record of the edition in which the pedigree first appeared.
33. Robinson, p. 35. Also: Venn and Venn, *Alumni Cantabrigiensis*, Part I. From the earliest times to 1751, vol. III.
34. Cass, Frederick Charles, *Monken Hadley*, J. B. Nichols and Sons, Westminster. pp. 73–6.
35. See the following:
    http://o'reillydesign.com/moorehall/fammain.html
    www.moorehall.com/historyhall.htm
    www.doon.mayo-ireland.ie/moores.html
36. E.g. Kevin Coyne in *The Moores of Moorehall* at http://doon.mayo-ireland.ie/moores.html, p. 4.

Chapter 7 pp. 209–33

1. *London Sessions Records: 1605–1685*, CRS vol. XXXIV, London, 1934, vol. XXXIV, pp. 134, 138 and 151.
2. Register of Marriages at St Benet and St Peter, Paul's Wharf, Harleian Society, Registers, vol. XL, p. 311, London, 1911.
3. *Victoria County History of Yorkshire*, vols 1, 3 and 6.
4. Rev. Alfred B. Beaven, *Aldermen of the City of London*', vol. II, p. 78, quoted in *Essex Recusant*, vol. 6, no 2 (August 1964), p. 39. Also, Burke's *Extinct and Dormant Baronetcies*, 2nd edn, 1841.
5. P. R. P. Knell, 'The Descendants of St. Thomas More in Hertfordshire 1617–1693', pt. II, in *Essex Recusant*, vol. 6, No. 2. (August 1964), p. 39.
6. *The Title of Basil More Esq to his Estate in the County of Hertford (interalia)*, Hertfordshire Archives and Local Studies. Ref: 10475.

Notes 281

7. Courtesy of Hertfordshire Archives and Local Studies Department from which copies of this and later entries were obtained.
8. Courtesy of Hertfordshire Archives and Local Studies. Document Refs: DEGA 23708, 23710, 23709, 23711, 23712, 23714, 23715,
9. Titus Oates, a former Anglican minister, had set his sights on becoming a Catholic priest but he had been expelled from the English Colleges at Valladolid and St Omers. His invention of the plot seems to have been an act of revenge.
10. *Essex Recusant*, vol. 6, no. 2 (Aug. 1964), p. 41.
11. Ibid.
12. Andrew Browning (ed.), 'Memoirs of Sir John Reresby'.
13. West Yorkshire Archive Service. Ref. WYL 156/R/15/31.
14. Ibid. Ref. WYL 156/R/15/19.
15. Ibid. Ref. WYL 156 /R/15/84.
16. P. R. P. Knell, 'The Descendants of St. Thomas More in Hertfordshire 1617–1693', p. 42.
17. West Yorkshire Archive Service. Ref. WYL 156/R/21/13.
18. Calendar of State Papers: Domestic (CSPD) Treasure Books, Vol. 7, pt. 2, p. 1062. Quoted in Knell.
19. For full text see: www.jacobite.ca/documents/16870404.htm
20. Sir Henry Chauncey, *The Historical Antiquities of Hertfordshire*, London, 1700, p. 532.
21. Courtesy of Hertfordshire Archives and Local Studies Department. Document Refs: DEGA/23767–23768; 23770; 23704; 23771; 23774–23775; 23779.
22. National Archives. Prob. 11/487.
23. National Archives. Prob. 11/581 and 11/583.
24. Rev G. Anstruther, 'Some London Burials 1707–1743', in *Essex Recusant*, vol. 12, no. 1 (April 1970), p. 29.
25. *Allegations for Marriage Licences issued by the Vicar General of the archbishop of Canterbury: July 1687–1694*, Harleian Society, vol. XXXI, 1980, p. 102.
26. Parish Registers of St James, Dukes Place, 1665–1872. Also in Boyd's Marriage Index, 1528–1840 (Courtesy of English Origins at: www.englishorigins.com
27. Samuel Tymms (ed.), *The East Anglian; or Notes & Queries*, vol. I, Samuel Tymms, Lowestoft, 1864, p. 105.
28. Courtesy of Norfolk Record Office.
29. Information kindly provided by the Archivist of the Inner Temple.
30. National Archives. Prob. 11/575.
31. F. H. Blackburne (ed.), *Calendar of State Papers, Domestic Series: Jan 1st 1679–31st August 1680*, HMSO, London, 1915, p. 253.
32. Information courtesy of the Archivist at Lincoln's Inn.
33. Privy Council Register P.C. 2/67. p.11. Quoted in *Essex Recusant*, vol. 6, no. 2 (Aug. 1964), p. 45.
34. Calendar of State Papers Domestic Series, James II, vol. III, HMSO, London, 1972. no. 647, p. 123.
35. CSPD Treasury Books, vol. 8, pt 4, p. 1981. Quoted in *Essex Recusant*. vol. 6.

no. 2. (Aug. 1964), p. 45.
36. *Calendar of State Papers Domestic Series, James II*, vol. III, HMSO, London, 1972. no. 1660, p. 306.
37. From Lincoln's Inn *Black Books* (Council Minutes and Memoranda). Courtesy of the Archivist.
38. For this and later entries in the register see Hertfordshire Archives and Local Studies. Ref: D/P 69/1/2. Basic details can also to be found on the International Genealogical Index (IGI).
39. Marriage Settlement. Durham Record Office. Reference: D/Lo/D126.
40. See: www.thisisthenortheast.co.uk/the_north_east/history/echomemories/durham/204/040604.html
41. 'Pedigree of Forcer of Kelloe and of Harberhouse' from *The History and Antiquities of the County Palatine of Durham*, Robert Surtees of Mainsforth, 1816, vol. I, p. 65.
42. *Records of the Abbey of Our Lady of Consolation at Cambrai, 1620–1797*, Catholic Record Society, vol. XIII (Miscell. VIII), London, 1913, p. 61.
43. Estcourt and Payne, pp. 48, 312.
44. Durham Record Office. Ref: D/20/Lo/D127.
45. Payne, *English Catholic Missions*, p. 4.
46. National Archives. Prob. 11/1003.
47. Brooks, p. 119.
48. Courtesy of the Borthwick Institute, York.
49. Lincoln's Inn Admission Register. Courtesy of the Archivist.
50. Kirk, p. 169.
51. Woodward Manuscript. Once held at St Joseph's Catholic Presbytery, Pontefract. Now sadly missing.
52. Guildhall Library: Document 9488. *Register of Apprentice Bindings 1666–1749*.
53. Harleian Society, vol. XLIV, London, 1914, p. 44.
54. Various attempts – some contradictory – have been made to connect Augustine More (son of Basil) with a Colonel Augustine Moore of Virginia, claiming that they are one and the same person. This claim, however, cannot be reconciled to any of the known facts about Augustine of the Barnburgh line.

Chapter 8 pp. 234–45

1. Hertfordshire Archives and Local Studies. Doc. Ref: DP 69/1/2.
2. Hertfordshire Archives and Local Studies. Doc. Ref: DEGA 23769–23799.
3. J. C. H. Aveling, 'The More Family and Yorkshire' in *Essential Articles for the Study of Thomas More*, p. 44.
4. I George I. St. 2. c. 55.
5. Courtesy of West Yorkshire Archive Service, Wakefield.
6. Hertfordshire Archives and Local Studies. Ref: D/P 69/1/2.
7. Aveling, p. 44.
8. 'Pedigree of Waterton of Walton' in *Pedigrees of the County Families of*

Yorkshire, compiled by Joseph Foster, vol. II: West Riding.
10. York Minster Archives. Liberty of St Peter. Cat. Ref. F2/3/4/7, 9, 10.
11. W. B. Ullathorne, *From Cabin Boy to Archbishop: The Autobiography of Archbishop Ullathorne*, Introduction by Shane Lesley, Hollis & Carter, London, 1943, p. 1.
12. E. S. Worrall, *Returns of Papists 1967*, vol. 2, Catholic Record Society, 1989, pp. ix, 56.
13. Ullathorne, p. 1.
14. Leo Madigan (ed.), *The Devil is a Jackass*, Gracewing, 1995.
15. Through the marriage of her grandfather, James Longstaff jnr. of Hagnaby, to Hannah Hall of Stickney, Lincolnshire, Hannah was related to Sir John Franklin (1780–1847), the famous Arctic explorer. Hannah Hall's sister, Mary Hall, had married John Franklin of Sibsey, Lincolnshire, who was the grandfather of the explorer.

Chapter 9 pp. 246–65

1. Information courtesy of the Archivist at Lincoln's Inn.
2. For this and later references see: West Yorkshire Archive Service, Ref. QE 28/64. (Registration of Papist Estates).
3. See British History Online at the following two sites: www.british-history.ac.uk/report.asp?compid=39931 and www.british-history.ac.uk/report.asp?compid=37844
4. Although White Ladies and Boscobel were owned by the Giffard family they did not live there at the time. The houses were looked after by their servants, members of the Penderel family, some of whom also fought on the Royalist side at the Battle of Worcester and were also fleeing the scene.
5. National Archives. Prob. 11/665.
6. Catholic Record Society. *Miscellanea*, London, 1932, p. 214. See also Aveling, op. cit., pp. 45–8.
7. E. S. Worrall, (ed.), *Returns of Papists 1767*, vol. 2, Catholic Record Society, 1989, p. 40.
8. West Yorkshire Archaeological Society. Ref: MD314/10/3.
9. G. Holt, SJ, *The English Jesuits 1650-1829. A Biographical Dictionary*, Catholic Record Series, vol. 70, London, 1984, p. 169.
10. For fuller information on Fr Thomas IX see Foley's *Records of the Jesuits*, vol. VII, pp. 703–4. Also Holt, Geoffrey, SJ, *Haeres ... Thomae More Cancellarii: Fr. Thomas More 1722–1795*, Catholic Record Society, Recusant History Series, no. 24 (1998), pp. 76–88.
11. National Archives, Prob: 11/1262
12. Holt, p. 169.
13. In 1551 Margaret Clement had gone to school at St Ursula's Convent of Augustinian Canonesses in Louvain. She later became a nun there and, from there, made the foundation at St Monica's for the English nuns.

14. Courtesy of the Archives of the British Province of the Society of Jesus, Mount St, London.
15. National Archives. Prob. 11/410.
16. Metcalfe Pedigree. Lincolnshire Archives, Lincoln. Ref: Dixon 15/1, vol. 29.
17. Ibid.
18. See 'Lord Burghley's Map of Lancashire' in Catholic Record Society, *Miscellanea* IV, p. 169; 'Convicted Recusants, Charles II' in Catholic Record Society, *Miscellanea*, V, pp. 211–12. Both published in 1969.
19. Lancashire Records Office. Ref. DOAL 124.
20. Metcalfe Pedigree. Lincolnshire Archives, Lincoln. Ref: Dixon 15/1, vol. 29.
21. Lancashire Records Office. Catalogue Ref: DDAL 132.
22. National Archives. Prob. 11/1290.
23. National Archives. Prob. 11/1239.
24. National Archives. Prob. 11/1691.
25. National Arcives. Prob. 11.1901

Bibliography

Books and Articles

Ackroyd, Peter, *The Life of Thomas More*, Chatto and Windus, London, 1998.
Bald, R. C., *John Donne: A Life*, Clarendon Press, Oxford, 1970.
Bindoff, S. T., *The House of Commons 1509–1558,*' 3 vols, Published for the History of Parliament Trust by Secker & Warburg, London, 1982.
Bolwell, R. W., *The Life and Works of John Heywood*, AMS Press Inc., New York, 1966.
Bridgett, Rev T. E., *The Life and Writings of Blessed Thomas More*, Burns Oates and Washbourne Ltd, 1924.
Browning, Andrew (ed.), *Memoirs of Sir John Reresby*, Jackson, Son & Co., Glasgow, 1936.
Carey, John (ed.), *John Donne: The Major Works*, Oxford University Press, 1990.
Chambers, R. W., *Thomas More*, Jonathan Cape, London, 1935.
Edwards, Francis, SJ, *The Elizabethan Jesuits*, (Historia Missionis Anglicanae Societatis Jesu (1660)), Phillimore & Co. Ltd., London, 1981.
Gosse, Edmund, *The Life and Letters of John Donne*, 2 vols, first published 1899. Reprinted by Peter Smith, Gloucester, Mass., 1959.
Guy, John, *Thomas More*, Arnold, London, 2000.
Hamilton, Dom Adam, OSB, *The Chronicle of the English Augustinian Canonesses Regular of the Lateran at St. Monica's in Louvain*, Sands & Co., London, 1904.
Harley, John, *William Byrd: Gentleman of the Chapel Royal*, Scolar Press, Aldershot, Hants., 1997.
Harpsfield, Nicholas, *Harpsfield's Life of More*, published for Early

English Texts Society by Oxford University Press, 1963.
Hasler, P. W., *History of the House of Commons, 1558–1606*, 3 vols, published for the History of Parliament Trust by Secker & Warburg, London, 1981.
Heywood, Ellis, *Il Moro* (Dialogue in Memory of Thomas More), translated and edited by Roger Lee Deakins, Harvard University Press, 1972.
Hitchcock, Elsie Vaughan (ed.), *Roper's Life of More*, Early English Text Society & Oxford University Press, 1958.
Hunter, Rev Joseph (ed.), *The Life of Sir Thomas More*, William Pickering, London, 1828.
Jessopp, Augustus, *John Donne*, Methuen & Co., London, 1897.
Kirk, J., *Biographies of English Catholics in the 18th Century*, Burns & Oates, London, 1909.
Marius, Richard, *Thomas More*, Phoenix Giant paperback, London, 1999.
More, Cresacre, *The Life and Death of Sir Thomas More, etc.*, Antwerp (?), 1631.
Norrington, Ruth, *In the Shadow of a Saint: Lady Alice More*, The Kylin Press, Waddesden, 1983.
Reed, A. W., *Early Tudor Drama: Medwall, the Rastells, Heywood and the More Circle*, Methuen & Co., London, 1926.
Reynolds, E. E., *Life of Margaret Roper*, by E. E. Burns & Oates, London, 1960.
Routh, E. M. G., *Sir Thomas More and His Friends: 1477–1535*, Oxford University Press, 1934.
Rowse, A. L., *A Man of Singular Virtue*, The Folio Society, London, 1980.
Stapleton, Thomas, *The Life and Illustrious Martyrdom of Sir Thomas More*, translated by Philip E. Hallett, The Catholic Book Club, London, 1966.
Stubbs, John, *Donne The Reformed Soul*, Viking/Penguin, 2006.
Weld-Blundell, Dom Benedict (ed.), *The Inner Life of Dame Gertrude More*, R. & T. Washbourne, Ltd, London, 1910.
Wekking, Ben (ed.), *Augustine Baker O.S.B. The Life and Death of Dame Gertrude More*, University of Salzburg, 2002.

County and Other Histories:

The Victoria County History of Middlesex.
The Victoria County History of Essex, W. R. Powell (ed.), vol. VI,

Oxford University Press, 1973–1976.
The Victoria History of the County of Hertford, 1902, reprinted 1971.
Victoria County History of Buckinghamshire, published for the University of London Institute of Historical Research by Dawsons of Pall Mall, London, 1969 edition.
Clutterbuck, Robert, *The History and Antiquities of Hertfordshire*, vol. I, 'North Mimms', 1815.
Finch, M. E., *Five Northamptonshire Families: 1540–1640*, Northamptonshire Records Society, 1956.
Hunter, J., *Classical County Histories: South Yorkshire*, 1829.
Robinson, Rev Charles J., *A History of the Mansions and Manors of Herefordshire*, first published 1872.
Robinson, Rev Charles J., *Mansions and Manors of Herefordshire*, Scholar Press Edition, 1872, p. 192.
The History and Antiquities of the County Leicester, first published by John Nichols in 1798. Republished in 1971 by S. R. Publishing, in association with Leicestershire County Council.

Visitations:

The Visitation of Berkshire, 1623, W. Harry Rylands, FSA (ed.), vol. I, London, 1907.
The Visitations of Buckinghamshire, Harleian Society, vol. LVIII, 1909.
The Visitations of Essex, 1552,1558,1570,1612 & 1634, Walter C. Metcalfe (ed.), Harleian Society, vol. XIII, London, 1878.
Visitation of London, 1633, 1634 & 1635, Howard, Joseph Jackson (ed.), vol. II, Harleian Society, vol. XVII, London, 1883.
Visitations of the North (Flower's Visitation in 1563–1564 and 1604), Surtees Society, 1921.
The Visitation of Northamptonshire, 1681, Harleian Society, vol. LXXXVII, London, 1935.
Visitations of the County of Nottingham, 1569 & 1614, Harleian Society, vol. IV, London, 1871.
The Visitation of the County of Oxford 1566, 1574, 1634, Harleian Society, vol. V, 1871.
The Visitation of Shropshire, 1623, Glazebrook, George and Rylands, John Paul (eds), Harleian Society, vol. XXVIII, London, 1889.
The Visitation of Surrey, 1662–1668, Harleian Society, vol. LX, 1910.
The Visitation of Worcestershire, 1569, Harleian Society, vol. XXVII, London, 1888.

Flower's Visitation of Yorkshire 1563–1564, Harleian Society, vol. XVI, London, 1881.
Dugdale's Visitation of Yorkshire, 1666, J. W. Clay Esq. (ed.)., vol. II, Harleian Society, 1907.

Pedigrees

Burke, John, *A Genealogical and Heraldic History of the Commoners of Great Britain and Ireland*. Also known as *Burke's Commoners*, London, 1836.
'Familiae Minorum Gentium', Harleian Society, 1894.
Lincolnshire Pedigrees, Harleian Society, vol. 3, 1903.
Miscellaneous Essex Pedigrees, Harleian Society, vol. XIV, 1879.
'The Pedigree of More of Barnborough' in Foley's *Records of the Jesuits*. See under Foley, below.
Pedigrees of the County Families of Yorkshire: Compiled by Joseph Foster and authenticated by the members of each family, 1874, vol. II (of three): West Riding.
Surtees, Robert of Mainsforth, 'Pedigree of Forcer of Kelloe and of Harberhouse' in *History and Antiquities of the County Palatine of Durham*, vol. I, 1816.
Walker, J. W. (transcribed and edited), *Yorkshire Pedigrees*, John Whitehead & Son, Leeds, 1944.

Miscellaneous

Armitage, George J. (ed.), *Allegations for Marriage Licences issued by the Bishop of London: 1520–1610*, vol. I, London, 1888.
Ashworth, P. Burke (ed. of *Landed Gentry*, etc.), *Family Records*, Heraldic Publishing Co., New York, 1965.
Aveling, Dom Hugh, *The Catholic Recusants of the West Riding of Yorkshire*, Leeds Phil and Lit., vol. X.
Boyd's *Citizens of London*.
Brookmans Park Newsletter (www.brookmans.com) with pictures of Gobions courtesy of Hertfordshire Archives and Local Studies.
Brooks, Christopher W., *The Admission Register of Barnard's Inn 1620–1869*, Selden Society, London, 1995.
Burke's *Commoners of Great Britain & Ireland*.
Burke's Peerage and Baronetage.

Burton, Edwin H. and Williams, Thomas L. (eds), *The Douai College Diaries: Third, Fourth and Fifth 1598–1654*, Catholic Record Society, London, 1911.
Catholic Record Society, *Miscellanea*, IV, William Dawson & Sons Ltd London, 1969.
Catholic Record Society, *Miscellanea*, V, William Dawson & Sons Ltd, London, 1969.
Clapham, Alfred W. and Godfrey, Walter H., *Some Famous Buildings and their Story*, Technical Journals, Ltd, London, 1931.
Edwards, Francis, SJ (ed.), *The Elizabethan Jesuits*, Phillimore & Co. Ltd, 1981.
Estcourt, Very Rev Edgar E. and Payne, John Orlebar (eds.), *The English Nonjurors of 1715: Being a Summary of the Register of their Estates, with Genealogical Notes*, 2nd edn, Gregg International Publishers Ltd, Farnborough, Hants, 1969.
Foley, Henry, *Records of the English Province of the Society of Jesus*, 7 vols, London, 1875–1883.
Foster, Joseph, *Alumni Oxoniensis 1500–1714*, Parker & Co., Oxford, 1891.
Guilday, Peter, *English Catholic Refugees on the Continent, 1558–1795*, Longmans, Green, and Co., London, 1914.
Hyland, the Rev St George Kieran, *A Century of Persecution under Tudor and Stuart Sovereigns from Contemporary Records*, Kegan Paul, Trench Trubner & Co. Ltd, London, 1920.
Inquisitions Post Mortem Relating to the City of London: Tudor Period, British Record Society, 1896.
Kenny, Anthony (ed.), *The Responsa Scholarum of the English College, Rome: Part One: 1598–1621*, Catholic Record Society, London, 1962.
Kenyon, J. P. (ed.), *The Stuart Constitution, 1603–1688*, 2nd edn, 1986.
Kirkus, Sr Gregory, IBVM (ed.), *An I.B.V.M. Biographical Dictionary of the Members and Major Benefactors*, Catholic Record Society, London, 2001.
Knox, T. F. (ed.), *The First and Second Diaries of the English College, Douai*, David Nutt, London, 1878.
London Recusants, 4 vols in Catholic Central Library, London.
Madigan, Leo (ed.), *The Devil is a Jackass*, Leominster, Gracewing, 1995.
Moore, Michael J. (ed.), *Quincentennial Essays on St. Thomas More: Selected Papers from the Thomas More College Conference*, Albion Books, Department of History, Appalacian State University,

Boone, North Carolina, 1978.
Murray, Francis G., 'The Contribution of the More Family to the Counter Reformation, Part 1: Charles Bassett. Part II: Thomas More IV, Henry More, Thomas More V, SJ', from *The Venerabile*, 25 (1970), 113–23.
Musgrave's Obituaries, Harleian Society, vol. XLVI, 1900.
Payne, John Orlebar, *English Catholic Missions*, Burns & Oates, 1889.
Questier, M. C. (ed.), *Newsletters from the Archpresbyterate of George Birkhead*, Cambridge University Press, 1998.
Registers of St Benet Paul's Wharf, Harleian Society Registers, vol. XL, 1911.
Robinson, Rev Charles J., *A Register of the Scholars Admitted to Merchant Taylors School*, vol. II, Farncombe & Co., Lewes, 1883.
Rowlands, Marie B. (ed.), *English Catholics of Parish and Town: 1558–1778*, Catholic Record Society, London, 1999.
Shanahan, Mgr D., Unpublished typed notes on the More Family Pedigree by
Essex Recusants (20-vol. collection of papers prepared in the 1960s for the Essex Recusant Society. Privately printed for circulation to members.
Dr Sykes's Notes on Yorkshire Wills. Sykes vol. XXVII. Held at Doncaster Archives.
Sylvester, R. S. and Marc'hadour, G. P., *Essential Articles for the Study of Thomas More*, Archon Books, Hamden, Connecticut, 1977.
Talbot, Clare (ed.), *Miscellanea: Recusant Records*, Catholic Record Society, London, 1960.
Taylor, John (ed.), *Northamptonshire Notes and Queries*, vol. III, Dryden Press, Northampton, 1890.
Transcripts of the Baptismal, Marriage and Burial registers of Barnburgh St Peter 1558–1900. Held at Doncaster Archives.
Unpublished information (and pedigrees) on the Brooke Family of Madeley and Claverley. Courtesy of Shropshire Records Office.
Venn, John and Venn J. A., *Alumni Cantabrigiensis*, Cambridge University Press, 1924.
Yorkshire Archaeological & Topographical Society Records Series. vol. II.

www.ingramcontent.com/pod-product-compliance
Lightning Source LLC
Chambersburg PA
CBHW070938230426
43666CB00011B/2480